THE PRACTICE OF LAW SCHOOL:

Getting in and Making the Most of Your Legal Education

Christen Civiletto Carey, Esq.
and
Professor Kristen David Adams

2003

ALM Publishing
New York, New York

Cover Design: *Michael Ng*

Interior Page Design & Production: *Amparo Graf*

Christen Civiletto Carey Photograph: *Inimage, by Royce*

Library of Congress Cataloging-in-Publication Data

Civiletto Carey, Christen, 1968-
    The practice of law school : getting in and making the most of your legal education / by Christen Civiletto Carey and Kristen David Adams.
        p. cm.
    1. Law—Vocational guidance—United States. 2. Law—Study and teaching—United States. I. Adams, Kristen David, 1971- II. Title.

KF297.C58 2003
340'.023'73—dc21   2003050022

Dedication

For our parents: Larry and Priscilla Adams and Chuck and Judy Civiletto, whose love, example, support, and encouragement have made this book—and so many of our other dreams—a reality.

Acknowledgments

We would like to acknowledge our former colleagues: Joseph D. Wargo, whose continued mentoring and training have taught us by example what it means to be a lawyer, and J. Scott Carr, Windy Hillman, Jeanine Gibbs, C. Celeste Creswell, William Weber IV, Joseph Ozmer II, Jeremy White, David Pernini, Michael French, Michael Kabat, Charles Whitney, Debbie Barrow, Julie Jared, Jack (Mike) Martin, and many other current and past professionals of the Duane Morris LLP and Kritzer & Levick firms, including and especially Agnes Bridges, Vickie Walker, Mary Fertitta, and Amy Thomas. Moreover, our former colleague David Pardue contributed in a significant way to this book, and for that we are very grateful.

We also want to thank the many lawyers, clerks, students, clients, law school deans and other professionals, some of whom are former colleagues and all of whom were willing to share their thoughts on law school and practice, including L. Elizabeth Bowles, Jean Eliason (both of whom provided wonderful insights about their past experience and gave freely of their time), Paul Nix, David Baum, Todd Bair, Don Macaulay, Richard Andrade, Stan Chess, Mike Kelly, Angela Hsu, Benjamin Bratman, David Wender, Mike Powell, Sam Tutterow, Pam Malone, LaRonica Lightfoot, Sam Arden, Dean Melinda Saran, Cynthia Coleman, Holly Pierson, Sidney Barrett, Dick Page, Allison Jackson, Leslie Jutzi, Neda Matar, Jennifer Giusto, Jacqueline Hutter, Jim Mansour, Donna Mancusi, Bob and Jennifer Smiles, Andy and Angela Galeziowski, and Richard

Galeema. We also want to extend our thanks to Lisa Gandy Wargo, whose initial thoughts have helped carry us to points we did not anticipate.

We want to thank the staff of American Lawyer Media who not only worked on the book but also listened to our ideas and worked with us to bring this project to completion, especially Caroline Sorokoff and Pat Rainsford.

Kristen's additional acknowledgments:

I would like to extend my personal thanks to Larry, Priscilla, Clay, Kyle, and Rhett Adams, and to Kate Day, Dave and Catherine Dixon, Leeanne Frazier, Mark, Teresa, and Mackenzie Neil, Monica Richman, and Stephanie Shack. Greatest personal thanks, however, are due to my co-author Christen for her vision, patience, determination and great friendship.

I would like to extend special thanks to the faculty, administration, and staff of Stetson University College of Law. Dean W. Gary Vause and Vice Dean Darby Dickerson deserve particular thanks, Dean Vause for his support, encouragement, and investment in my professional development and Dean Dickerson for her friendship and inspiration. Both are outstanding as mentors, role models, and educators. In addition, I am grateful for the friendship, wise counsel, and tremendous example of Professor Peter F. Lake, who has served as the chair of my mentoring committee at Stetson. I would also like to acknowledge Professors Robert D. Bickel, James J. Brown, John F. Cooper, Kelly M. Feeley, Roberta K. Flowers, James W. Fox Jr., Julian R. Kossow, Rebecca C. Morgan, Bradford Stone, Michael I. Swygert, and Thomas C.

Marks; these colleagues and friends each deserve special thanks for reasons too individual, and too numerous, to list here. In addition, no Stetson-based endeavor would be possible without the expertise, attention to detail, and thoughtfulness of Ms. Connie Evans and the best faculty-support-services department in legal education. Stetson student Ms. Kristy Parker gave generously of her time and effort by serving as a research assistant when this project was in its infancy.

I would also like to thank the Yale Law School, particularly Dean Anthony T. Kronman and Associate Dean Barbara J. Safriet, without whom my dream of being a law professor would remain unrealized. In addition, I would like to thank the Honorable Guido Calabresi, who will always be the finest law professor—and one of the finest people—I have ever had the privilege to know. Professors Jules L. Coleman, Robert C. Ellickson, Owen M. Fiss, and Stephen Wizner are all extraordinary legal educators who have given generously of their time and whose example continues to challenge me.

I am grateful for the support, mentoring, and encouragement of Emory Law School Dean Emeritus Howard O. Hunter, and Professors Martha G. Duncan, Richard D. Freer, Nathaniel E. Gozansky, and Charles A. Shanor. Most of all, however, I am grateful for the compelling example set by the late Professor Donald W. Fyr and humbled by the memory of his extraordinary dedication to his life's work as a law teacher.

I would also like to acknowledge the students, faculty, staff, and administration of the University of Georgia School of Law, where I have greatly enjoyed—and benefited from—my year's stay as a visiting professor. Dean David E. Shipley, Associate Dean Paul M. Kurtz, Professors Peter A. Appel, J. Randy Beck, Ann Proffitt Dupre, Thomas A.

Eaton, Alexander W. Scherr, and Erwin C. Surrency, and Ms. Nancy Watkins each have been of particular assistance and encouragement.

Finally, I would like to thank and acknowledge my students at both Stetson University College of Law and the University of Georgia School of Law. Each student in each class has contributed in some way to this effort, and watching each of them grow, learn, and succeed is a source of great inspiration, pride, and sustenance to me.

Christen's additional acknowledgments:

In addition to my parents, I would like to thank others in my family, whose lifelong guidance, support and unconditional love has blessed me beyond measure: my children—Julia Noelle, Mark Anthony Jr., and Matthew Maxson Carey, who displayed curiosity about this book and patience with their mother that belies their years. I love you. In addition, Camille Civiletto (who provided unconditional love and logistical support even before the first interview was conducted or word written), Charles Mark, Reyna, and Gianna Civiletto, Yola Civiletto, Elma Catherine, Jeanette and Tony Scibilia (and the entire Scibilia family), Elio Desiderio, Cindy and Robert Krause, Judy and Clarke Gould, Jacqueline and Thomas DiFonzo and family, Antoinette and Tony DeMiglio, Mary Jane and Lou Marcantonio, Nancy Aello, the entire Catherine family, and many, many cousins, aunts, and uncles who regularly check in and offer encouragement. My extended family has been instrumental in ways both large and small and I am very thankful to them as well: Ronald and Christine Carey, Barbara and Nick DeAngelo, Mark Carey, Amy Carey, and Rebecca, Michael, Brendan, and Madeleine Rohan. Rebecca also provided valuable writing and editing insights, and I appreciate her expertise greatly.

I would like to acknowledge the invaluable support and love of other close friends, including my dear friend and co-author Kristen (our collaborations extend far beyond this book and are incredible sources of strength and love for me), because all of you enrich my life and that of many others: Barbara Luba, Jennifer and Brian Steinberg, Nicole Oursler, Susan Steffan, Tracey Axnick, Ronnie Kihlstadius, and Carol Haines. Also, my friends Dan and Karen Leary, Chris and Chantel Morris, Andrea MacMillian, John and Susan Fanning, and several others have been wonderful sources of encouragement to me. Thank you to Ashley and Haley Schilling, and Amy and Dina Lipman, for helping me in many ways, particularly with the children.

Vanderbilt University Law School has not only launched me and many others into practice, but also offered continued support and guidance for years thereafter—I am so grateful to those incredible individuals at the school who have unreservedly given of their time and insights into legal education and practice, including Dean Kent Syverud, Assistant Dean Elizabeth Workman, and Assistant Director Dorris Smith. Also, I want to thank Angela Chapman, Lisa Doster, and Kathy Baugus for their professionalism and encouragement.

We would like to thank Café Sunflower on Roswell Road in Atlanta for the great vegetarian food that fueled the early days of this work. Above all, we thank God for bringing us together for this project, for the challenges (and surprising joys) of the past year, and for carrying us—we aren't yet sure how—to the finish line of this wonderful adventure.

Foreword

Attorneys often lament that law school teaches "nothing practical." These naysayers point to new attorneys' poor negotiation or interviewing skills, or even lack of knowledge of black letter law, as evidence that law schools serve a very limited purpose. Attorneys have widely differing views on what that purpose is, of course. Their ideas range anywhere from law school being a "ticket to punch," as one large-law-firm partner believes, to the view that law school is an early training ground for future lawyers. Some view certain law schools as a means to a particular type of practice; for example, some schools are known for turning out prosecutors, while others may provide a networking investment for those with future political aspirations.

The truth is, law school is many of these things, and all of them are important for a lawyer's development. Becoming a great lawyer is a process. That process requires a certain amount of intellectual competence, passion for the law, and ability both to learn from experience and to apply those lessons to practice. Those important life experiences are happening now, both in law school and in life outside of law school. Would-be lawyers sometimes get fixated on law school and the subsequent bar exam as a means to an end—fulfilling the prerequisites to become eligible to practice law. Law school, however, can be so much more than a thoroughfare. Each student must recognize for himself or herself the academic, career, and life lessons to be learned in law school and incorporate those lessons as an essential part of his or her legal training.

A lawyer's professional development truly starts in law school, if not before. There, students develop work habits that will remain with each of them when they begin this new career. For example, students choose whether to sleep late or to arrive on campus early and make good use of this bit of extra time. Students choose to be meticulous about proper citation procedure for every note, brief, or article, or to take shortcuts that limit the future usefulness of any of these items as writing samples or reference materials. In law school, students make friends and acquaintances who will seek counsel from one another in practice and who will eventually be in positions to refer business to one another. Law students, from the first day of law school, make impressions on those who may be their future business partners, judges, clients, and fellow committee members. At the same time, and in the same place, students are meeting professors, each with particular areas of research and expertise, who may later serve as expert witnesses for the future lawyers' clients. Furthermore, students are learning how to approach judges, become effective advocates, and handle substantive and procedural questions. In addition to learning to think and act like lawyers, law students are also developing the ability to write like lawyers. Those law school writing assignments—briefs, memoranda, and miscellaneous tasks—are jobs that lawyers do, too, albeit in far more compressed time frames than those given to law students for the same work. Many lawyers, including those who thought law school was a waste of time, prepare for their first oral argument in court the same way that they did for the final round of a moot-court competition. These lawyers once again find themselves practicing for a particularly important argument out loud, in front of a mirror, and before any willing set of ears, human or otherwise.

Why? Because, like so many other skills they developed in law school, it works. The chapters that follow explain how law school can, and in many instances does, provide an excellent foundation for the training and development of lawyers.

We wrote this book with a two-fold goal in mind. We want to provide present and future law students with the practical knowledge to choose the right law school and to excel while there. We have given you our thoughts on the "who, what, when, why, where, and how" of law school, from pre-law preparation to law school graduation and beyond. You will learn the ins and outs of the law-school application process, how to evaluate study groups, effective exam-taking strategies, how to balance family life with school, and much more. But we also want to challenge law students to take charge of their legal careers now—in law school. This book will demonstrate some of the ways in which students can begin to think like practicing lawyers and attain experience that is useful, even essential, and very, very practical. We firmly believe that law students who take charge of their professional development early will find themselves to be satisfied and fulfilled as lawyers.

Contents

CHAPTER 1

Does Law School Matter?

THE *PRACTICE* OF LAW SCHOOL

This book is about law school. It discusses how to succeed in law school in the traditional sense—getting into a top school, earning high grades, and graduating with honors. But, more important, it teaches the student how to make law school *matter* in a way that is relevant to his or her professional development as a lawyer. Throughout the application process and during every semester, students can benefit by developing lawyering skills to assist them in understanding and tackling the tasks before them. Being aware of the skills necessary for the job often goes hand in hand with being a more focused and fulfilled lawyer. This ability enables lawyers not only to meet the needs of each individual client, but also to maintain a perspective that makes them better attorneys, period. It follows, then, that putting law school academics and extracurricular activities into context, and using events going on the world and in daily life to fit the pieces together, are invaluable for the work that each law student eventually will do as a lawyer. The benefits are not all long-term. Students who develop these skills (especially during the pre-law and application processes) usually thrive in law school.

Some people call this practice-oriented approach having the "big picture." Others refer to it as context, perspective, or a "reality check." The rest do not even know that it exists. Indeed, some people look at law school as simply a way to get from point A to point B. Surviving those three years, they maintain, is no more than the dues a lawyer must pay to practice law. These people regard law school classes, and especially the legal theory used to teach them, as nothing more than ivory-tower nonsense. Moreover, many attorneys believe that law school fails to teach the practical skills of being a lawyer—including how to treat clients, hire a secretary, and negotiate a business deal—in other words, how to run a law practice. On some levels, that is true. Law school might not *overtly* teach students how to serve a particular client or how to negotiate a given settlement. Law school does, however, provide many opportunities for the student to learn these skills. In fact, every time a student interacts with a scholar about a law review article, or with a professor inside or outside the classroom, the student is learning how to treat a client and a supervisor. Every moot-court round teaches the student about courtroom decorum and the proper respect due to a judge, even to one who may not earn that respect. Where and how law students learn those skills is the substance of this book.

A student who approaches law school focused only on what she needs to do to graduate and get a job is likely to find that that is exactly what law school will be to her: a ticket to punch. She will have paid her dues and moved on to what she deems the "real" experience—the practice of law. However, if she wants a relevant experience, in which her money and time will be spent to her best advantage, and one that is economically and personally rewarding, then she should read this book. By employing the methods presented in this book, students will learn how to take a big-picture, practical approach to applying to and thriving in law school. And that, in a nutshell, is the *practice* of law school.

HOW TO USE THIS BOOK

Students should recognize that there is no single valid approach to succeeding in law school. There is no single way to practice law, either. There are, however, tried-and-true methods for bringing new concepts and experiences together in a way that is meaningful. Certain methods work better for some people than others, but all involve taking possession of the law school experience and tailoring that experience to fit each student.

This book is organized on two levels. It addresses the law school experience in what is roughly a chronological format, beginning in Chapters 2, 3, and 4 with pre-law-school preparation, including the financing and application process. Chapter 5 deals with making the transition to law school and some of the ways in which students can prepare without going overboard. Chapter 6 deals with the theories, policies, and approaches used by different schools to teach law and attempts to give the prospective student some overall direction. Chapter 7 gets down to the nuts and bolts of the law school experience—such as appropriate classroom behavior and approaches to studying. The following chapters address specific, important areas of the law school experience: preparing for and taking exams (Chapter 8), how a student can distinguish himself outside the classroom (Chapter 9), handling disappointment or discouragement (Chapter 10), legal research and writing (Chapter 11), course selection for upperclassmen (Chapter 12), and the summer experience (Chapter 13). The remaining three chapters center around the student's second and third years of law school and making the transition to practice, addressing such topics as the bar examination (Chapter 14), continued professional development and judicial clerkships (Chapter 15), and, finally, some parting words of advice (Chapter 16).

Interwoven with this chronological treatment of the law school experience is guidance on handling various tasks, including academics and other activities, by using skills and thought processes that are important to lawyering every step of the way. For example, this book examines a student's responsibility for the development of his or her own career (yes, even in law school), and demonstrates how a student can improve technical skills such as advocacy and writing, engage in active learning, and establish a personal code of ethics. Although certain portions of the book will be more relevant than others at different times in a student's legal education, the overarching themes of active learning, personal responsibility, and practical application are relevant at whatever stage a student finds himself or herself when reading this book.

WHAT LAW SCHOOL IS AND IS NOT

A prospective law student should have some understanding of what law school is and what it is not.

Law school is *not* like undergraduate school. Unlike learning undergraduate history, mathematics, science, or any other undergraduate survey course for which students have a frame of reference from previous education, learning law is singularly disorienting for most new students, at least at first. Students are not building on foundational knowledge, as they might as undergraduate English majors, taking a series of courses in pursuit of a degree and then refining their knowledge about the literature of a particular time and place. Law is different from this undergraduate model in that it is not studied in a linear, or chronological, fashion. Although law students may find that professors introduce new concepts with older cases before teaching them the current state of the law, the entire process has a different feel because law students are, in each course, learning a series of concepts and themes that do not necessarily fit together until the end of the course. In the law of torts, for example, students often find it difficult to understand cases relating to the legal concept of "negligence" until they understand all of its elements (including duty, breach, causation, and damages) and have learned how it evolved, a process that may not be completed until the end of the first semester, or even the end of the first year.

Moreover, law school differs from undergraduate school in that the *process* of learning is often even more relevant than the actual material learned. For example, the first-year curriculum for law students will almost always include at least one semester of contracts. The professor may not tell students the elements of a contract at the beginning (offer, acceptance, consideration, and so forth) but, through reading many cases, students will put the pieces together for themselves. At some point, the student will understand, from his or her own careful reading of the law, that an offer alone is not enough to create an enforceable contract; rather, some element of assent to that offer is necessary. Although subsequent cases will elucidate the concept of acceptance, again, the professor may not come out and explain the parameters for assent, but may expect students to assemble the pieces for themselves. In doing so, the student is engaging in much the same process that the early courts did to delineate the concept of proper assent in the first place. The process of learning the law therefore mirrors that of the evolution of the law. In other words, process is important. If the professor takes this approach, it is because she wants the students to experience, and thus better understand, the evolution of that law and the underlying reasons for its development. Chapter 7 discusses this approach to teaching. Some may regard this approach as "hiding the ball," and many will find the process to be difficult and frustrating, but this technique has persisted because it can be a very effective way to focus students on the *process* that is crucial to the law's development.

Law school, as the reader may have gathered already, differs from undergraduate school in the manner in which information is presented. In most undergraduate classes, information is provided in a lecture format, and students are expected to study that information and then prepare to be tested on it. In law school, information may be presented conceptually, or by first introducing the components of a legal construct (such as the "consideration" part of a contract, which describes the price of the transaction), rather than the actual legal construct (such as "contract") itself. Students are expected to put these pieces together themselves for purposes of the exam. That difference is one reason why law school can entail such an adjustment. Most new law students are not accustomed to being taught or tested in the law school manner, which requires a great deal more personal effort and responsibility than is required of most undergraduate students.

Moreover, a law student cannot necessarily rely on the skills that got him through his undergraduate studies, except perhaps a strong work ethic. For example, in mastering applied sciences, it may be important to memorize formulae, terms of measurement, or the properties of minerals, and to learn the basic scientific method. Although memorization is a component of the first-year experience in law school, it is not the sole, or even the most important, learning approach the student will use. Instead, the focus will be on applying what has been learned to new fact patterns. As discussed in Chapter 7, this process of applying "old" knowledge to "new" facts, although it may seem strange to a new law student, requires many of the same skills that a lawyer will employ when she interviews a new client or researches the law underlying a case.

To reach the stage at which she is able to function at this high level, a new law student must develop skills that go beyond her experience as an undergraduate. Developing these new skills takes time. It may require that the student try different methods of study (for example, study groups, outlining, or flash cards of the student's own design) until she finds what works best for her. This is an important process, and students should not be embarrassed if they encounter difficulty and require support. Few of us would have attempted to go our own way in learning college-level calculus.

Undergraduate classes and law school classes also differ from each other in that the former are in many ways simply a continuation of the schooling students received in primary and secondary school, while the latter are specifically focused on job preparation. As such, law school should be regarded as the student's "job." As discussed more fully in Chapters 2 and 7, law school is a professional setting, and students should expect to treat their colleagues with the consideration and respect that they would afford to their business colleagues, while approaching professors with no less respect than they would give to a supervising attorney, a client, or a judge. In both instances, students will find that their reputations—good or bad—are quickly established, as individuals and collectively as a class unit.

Law school is also not primarily about learning generally accepted legal principles, also known as "black letter law." Rather, as discussed above, the focus is on the process of learning. It would be impossible for law professors to teach students the law that is applicable to each case that each student will encounter in his or her career, both because the law is constantly changing and because every case requires its own carefully tailored arguments. Instead, legal education prepares students to discern for themselves the law that will be applicable to each case encountered. The difference between the approaches is like the difference between giving a person a fish and teaching that person to fish: law students, using the language of this metaphor, must learn to fish so they can feed themselves for a lifetime.

Finally, law school is not cheap. In fact, even taking into account the rising cost of undergraduate education, most students will find their legal education to be more expensive than their undergraduate education was. These financial differences are important because law school graduates find that the array of options available to them in making use of their law degrees varies greatly according to their income requirements. In other words, a student with little debt may be able to afford to take an interesting, attractive, even prestigious job with a comfortable lifestyle that may not be feasible for a classmate with more debt. As further explored in Chapters 3 and 4, students should bear this reality in mind when deciding where to apply to law school, how to finance it, and whether to work part-time.

Having explored, at some length, what law school is *not*, it becomes apparent that defining what law school actually *is* can be a much more difficult task. Law schools vary considerably, with regard to everything from student life to the school's theory of legal education. As a result, the educational experience is not the same from school to school. A law school in the midst of a major university in a "college town" may have a very active student culture. Another, in the middle of a major city and with a large part-time student population, may tend to attract students who are less interested in campus life because of their own outside interests and priorities.

Furthermore, students experience law school differently. Each student has his or her own motives for applying to law school, some of which are discussed in more detail later in this chapter, and students will have widely varied prior educational and work experiences. For some people, how they finance their law school education may affect the effort they put forth or the way they perceive school: those who are footing the bill personally, or who have worked before they applied to law school, may understand more fully the opportunity cost of the decision to attend law school. These students may expend more effort on their coursework than those whose education is financed by a scholarship or through the generosity of family members. Even so, independent of these educational and experiential differences, there are certain truisms that apply no matter which law school a student attends or how she applies herself.

Law school, as an educational experience, has less to do with traditional schooling and more to do with practical lawyering than the name might suggest. As discussed earlier, approaching law school as a job rather than simply as "school" is fundamental to achieving success in law school. Many of the skills that lawyers use to develop cases, create strategies, research law, work with clients and opposing counsel, and prepare for oral argument are ones that are important in law school, too. Law school can, and should, teach a student how to think like a lawyer, tackle a legal problem, research previous law on a particular issue (a concept known as precedent), write a coherent argument, act as an advocate in oral presentations, and, yes, even learn some substantive law.

Much of a law student's learning occurs on her own, outside of the lecture hall. The expectation, as the student enters a classroom each session, is that she will already have read and done her best to learn the assigned material and is now prepared to have her professor guide her in extending those concepts she learned to a new and perhaps more challenging set of facts. Taking an established rule of law and stretching it to accommodate a new factual wrinkle is, in large part, what practicing lawyers do.

The way in which law students learn the core material in school is best described by the phrase "active learning." This method of learning is characterized not only by extensive out-of-class preparation and intensive in-class drilling, but also often by the use of what is called the Socratic method of questioning. The Socratic method, which is further discussed in Chapter 7, involves a professor's eliciting the answers to a series of questions and hypothetical fact patterns from students, and directing student analysis subtly through the crafting of the questions, rather than presenting the material in the lecture format that is common in many undergraduate classes.

Law school, despite its decidedly different approach to education, uses familiar assessment mechanisms to evaluate success: namely, testing and grading. Grades do indeed matter in law school, although for reasons that may not be immediately apparent, as potential clients are unlikely to inquire about a student's grades in law school. But because grades matter to law firms in hiring new attorneys, they matter to the law students who are interested in joining those firms, and they matter to the law school, which hopes to see its students well-placed, fully employed, and, ideally, contributing generously to their alma mater. After all, what good is a law school if its graduates cannot find work when they leave?

Having said this, it remains true that grades are an imperfect tool for assessing what is most important to an attorney, post-graduation: lawyering skills. In a perfect world, i.e., one in which grades are not the major determinant of school success or failure, law schools would find a way to credit students for improvements in the practical lawyering skills and abilities they develop in law school. To do so, however, would require a major upheaval in the way schools are organized. New methods of subjective examination would be necessary, different ways to measure improvement would be needed, and class rankings would convey much different information about the students at the top and bottom of the scale. Moreover, law firms and other legal employers would have to be on board with such an effort and would have to look at new ways of evaluating potentially great lawyers. (To some extent, some law firms have tried to evaluate students on factors other than grades, but, given limited time and resources, the fact is that grades are one of the few objective and concise indicators that firms currently can use in hiring new attorneys.)

Because grades, while an imprecise measure of a student's actual potential as an attorney, are so important to traditional notions of success in law school, a student's arguably more relevant pre-professional achievement, in developing the social and technical skills that are important to being a lawyer, is probably undervalued. Thus, law school "success" and true "success" might not be one and the same. However, as discussed in Chapter 7, some aspects of traditional law-school assessment techniques—like the analysis of complex hypothetical fact patterns—are indeed relevant to the law student's practical development as an attorney.

Because of the emphasis placed upon in-class performance, out-of-class learning, and grades, many students find law school to be extremely intimidating. This is especially true during the first semester and is compounded by the fact that, in many schools, the student receives only one grade per course per semester (given on the basis of his or her performance on a single examination). Some professors foster this sense of intimidation by being particularly strict with or unavailable to first-year students. But even these techniques, while uncomfortable for many students, convey important lessons for lawyers-to-be. Some professors choose to run their classrooms in this fashion to ensure that their students will learn how to be prepared to articulate their positions persuasively as practitioners, even without positive feedback. Many believe that tactics of this sort will better prepare students to face the rigors of court or a difficult negotiation. Therefore, should students encounter such a professor, they should understand the career lessons to be learned from the experience, instead of feeling discouraged.

Law school can be the beginning of many professional relationships and personal friendships. These relationships matter, and not solely because these people can refer business to the student when she begins her professional career. Fellow students are future clients, judges, colleagues, bosses, and friends. The impression that students make on one another is important and lasting. As further discussed in Chapter 7, other students will remember, five years or ten years after law school, who was reliable in school, who regularly attended class and showed up on time, who did what he said he was going to do, and who worked hard.

Students will also remember who was arrested, who lied, and who was lazy.

Law school professors, deans, and administrative staff provide a support base for a future legal career. As students progress in their chosen fields, and especially as their careers take some twists and turns, they are likely to find themselves turning to these members of the law school community for support, assistance, or even legal advice. A constitutional-law teacher who is a nationally recognized expert on the First Amendment may be a tremendous ally to a former student who needs to rely on that expertise in guiding a client or testifying in court. Furthermore, a former student may decide to leave the practice of law to teach law school and, in doing so, is likely to turn to her school for letters of recommendation, practical advice, or even a job. Finally, many law schools actively promote or support the legal endeavors of their former students by publicizing their achievements and providing support; such support in invaluable to attorneys both personally and professionally.

IS THE LAW FOR EVERYONE?

The practice of law, like the practice of law school, is intensive and demanding. Indeed, not everyone is suited to being a lawyer. Some people lack the social skills to generate business, instill confidence, manage lower-level attorneys or staff members, or interact with judges, clients, or colleagues on a professional level. Others lack self-control, and may react inappropriately to routine, stressful situations.

Some people may be ill-equipped for a career in the law because they find it difficult to cope with the stress of a legal practice. Conflict and confrontation with other lawyers, judges, colleagues, and even clients, can be a daily part of a lawyer's life.

This kind of interpersonal dynamic affects some people in a way that is inordinately negative. Those who shy away from confrontation of any type, even healthy discussions that can be characterized as aggressive or even simply energetic, should probably steer clear of careers in the law. Having said this, however, advocacy is a learned skill, and many students who might otherwise characterize themselves as gentle or even shy may find themselves to be excellent advocates for a cause in which they firmly believe.

Other people may lack the writing skills necessary for both law school and practice. Attorneys are paid to communicate, and accuracy and precision are essential in their written and oral communications. It is very difficult to teach the fundamentals of grammar and the basics of the English language to an adult for whom English *is* her first language, especially while that same adult is seeking to master the complexities of legal analysis at the same time. There are few opportunities in law school or in practice to learn how to write, particularly at a remedial level. Some schools and law firms will provide writing coaches and remedial-writing help; this assistance is not the norm, however. Some students who face serious challenges with reading and writing have been able to meet these challenges and succeed in law school. One student, despite numerous learning disabilities, actually doubled his first-semester grade point average in his second semester and found himself well on the road to a solid performance, mostly through sheer force of will and hard work. Doing so, however, required dedication, effort, discipline, *and* resources that others would have been unable, or unwilling, to bring to bear.

Finally, some people simply lack what is sometimes called a "legal mind," which includes a combination of a love of learning, a keen analytical sense, and common sense, which is not to say that people lacking these abilities or talents do not graduate from law school every year. They do, but they do not represent law at its finest. Lawyers are entrusted with matters of great importance—the custody of a child, for example, or the liberty of a criminal defendant who is facing jail time. Given this extraordinary level of responsibility, potential law students must understand the commitment that is required to be a lawyer. Practicing the law *properly* requires tremendous energy and time. Those who are ill-suited to the law, and yet practice anyway, often do their clients more harm than good. For them and for their clients, practice can be especially frustrating, even dangerous, and sometimes can result in the lawyer's disbarment.

For other prospective students who may have the requisite ability, temperament, and interest, the timing for law school may simply not be right. They may have small children or elderly parents who need their time and attention, they may lack financial support, or they may have health problems that will be exacerbated by law school. Reduced-course-load arrangements, discussed in Chapters 3 and 10, and the Americans with Disabilities Act, which is discussed in Chapter 10, may ameliorate these concerns in some situations, but may not always suffice.

Given the myriad personal characteristics and life factors that the decision to attend law school involves, this decision must be made by the prospective student herself, not by a pre-law advisor or teacher, and certainly not by default. At the same time, however, prospective students should discuss the pros and cons of law school, including their own suitability for the practice of law, with family members as well as knowledgeable third parties such as practicing attorneys, school advisors, financial planners, and teachers. It may even be appropriate in some cases to consult with a doctor and weigh any potential negative physical or emotional issues. Those students who are unable to attend law school at any given time because of personal circumstances can always return to school once the situation becomes more favorable.

RECOGNIZING THE MANY FACETS OF LAWYERING

So, assuming that a prospective law student has already debated the merits of law school and has decided to apply, how does he or she get from being a student or an employee in a non-legal field to being a lawyer? The student must begin by educating himself or herself about what lawyers do.

Lawyers play many roles, often in the course of a single day. To get an accurate picture of what lawyers do, potential lawyers must go beyond general descriptions of lawyering tasks, like "litigation," "negotiation," or "drafting," and figure out what lawyers do from a practical standpoint.

Lawyers are teachers. They spend a great deal of time educating themselves and others. This is why communication skills—writing, advocating, speaking, explaining, and simplifying—are so fundamental to the practice of law. Every matter handled by a lawyer involves teaching. Lawyers teach themselves the law underlying the legal claims (also called "causes of action") at issue in a case and apply that law to the facts of the case. This same educational process is also an important part of a lawyer's fact-gathering for a case. Lawyers must teach themselves the ins and outs of pertinent documents, such as contracts and medical records. Sometimes, in this teaching effort, lawyers draw diagrams to assist in understanding complicated fact patterns or corporate structures. Some lawyers use mnemonic devices to remember the issues and pertinent parties in each case.

Once they have learned the pertinent law and the factual background of the case, lawyers then teach their clients—who may be sophisticated or not—the law and its application to the facts underlying the matter. The client may, for instance, be a lawyer for a major corporation (often called "in-house counsel"); in this situation, the outside lawyer's job is to educate the in-house attorney so that he or she may, in turn, teach the corporation, which is his or her own client.

Lawyers teach juries the law underlying their clients' positions as well as that of the opposing parties. Lawyers teach juries how to arrive at the desired conclusion. Lawyers teach other lawyers, either junior lawyers who are new to the area of law or senior lawyers who are extremely busy and have not had time to come up to speed on a given issue. Lawyers teach judges, who are presented with conflicting arguments and may not be as familiar with the pertinent law on point as are the two opposing attorneys.

Lawyers teach other lawyers and students, in seminars and law school courses. Many lawyers supplement their incomes or fulfill a long-held desire to teach by involving themselves with the skills courses at local law schools. Others teach what are known as continuing legal education (CLE) courses that other lawyers take to satisfy state licensing requirements and thus continue to practice law. In so doing, these teacher-lawyers are communicating what they have learned, sometimes through having handled a unique case. Some attorneys take the time to teach younger lawyers in a less formal setting, acting as mentors by instructing them in the ways of the profession. Senior lawyers show junior lawyers, through their conduct and, less often, through their words, how to market to clients, serve them properly, handle a client meeting diplomatically when something has gone wrong, and review other lawyers in a way that is both instructive and constructive.

Lawyers are also detectives: they track down people and information. Every new matter involves getting all of the pertinent documents, records, checks, letters, e-mail correspondence, and so forth from the client. Sometimes this process requires checking with the administrative staff, the managerial employees, or the records custodian of a corporate client. Some clients will produce the pertinent records immediately, while others require several reminders. Sometimes, despite these reminders, attorneys must actually go to the client's location to look through documents, because the client is either unwilling or unable to select the appropriate materials. An attorney, acting as a detective, must make sure that she has all of the facts and will not be surprised later by learning of something that was within her client's control, but was not made known to her at an earlier time.

As a detective, the lawyer's job is to run down every potential surprise, whether it might relate to a document or a witness. Lawyers must be vigilant in tracking down witnesses and people with knowledge about the matter in dispute. Often, a legal dispute does not arise for several months or years into a business relationship. During the intervening period, employees are likely to get fired, quit, or simply forget essential facts. Sometimes no one knows where these former employees are. The attorney's job is to find them and to supervise others in assisting with this process. The attorney can look online, contact her firm librarian (if she is fortunate enough to have one), use an Internet-savvy firm employee, call a private investigator, or call people believed to have been friends with these potential witnesses. It is always wise to develop a good relationship with a private investigation firm, just for these last-minute searches for witnesses.

Sometimes, a lawyer must track down his client's adversary to serve him or her with the appropriate lawsuit papers. This adversary, wanting to avoid being served, may avoid the attorney, lie to the process server (the individual delivering the lawsuit papers), pretend that he is someone else and has not seen "that person" (himself) for ten years, or make up any one of an infinite number of other stories. None of this changes the fact that it is the attorney's responsibility to find the adversary and pursue that person legally.

In acting as a detective in all of these situations, the lawyer may find herself sifting through investigative reports, or even regularly checking Peoplefinder or any number of Internet sources to track people down. Sometimes, the lawyer will subpoena information from one source hoping that it will provide information about someone else.

Corporate attorneys, too, act as detectives. Investigative skills are relevant when performing due diligence, which is the process of becoming familiar with all of the contractual and legal obligations of a business that may be sold or purchased. Among other things, due diligence requires looking through correspondence, reports, answers to specific questions that attorneys have posed, and statements made on disclosures in a contract, and ensuring that things are as the other party says they are. The attorney is looking for information that does not add up, or even things that just do not "smell right"—irregular payments made to an accountant who is not the regular accountant for the company, for instance.

Finally, all of the attorney's greatest investigative skills will be brought to bear when she actually attempts to collect on any judgment for a client. Here, again, her adversary may run, hide, or lie. She may have to hire another attorney or private investigator to assist her. She may have to subpoena information from banks. She may have to prepare carefully worded questions directed to her adversary on what money he, she, or it has and where the money is located. Sometimes, the adversary pays. Payment may be in the form of a check drawn on insufficient funds, or it may be in the form of actual cash. Dealing with all of this, however, is part of the attorney's job. These practical considerations demonstrate why good grades alone are not an accurate predictor of which attorneys will do well in practice. Sometimes, success requires street smarts, gut instincts, and strong detective work, as well as intellectual prowess.

Lawyers are storytellers. Every legal matter is a story of what happened or is happening to someone or something. Some stories are success stories. A business owner who has turned a novel idea into a thriving business may now need an attorney's help in taking it to the next level. A couple that has found a child to adopt may need an attorney's help in working through the legalities of the matter. Other legal matters are tales of business disappointments, outright fraud, or injury to a person's physical or emotional self. Legal matters involve people, together with all of the issues, problems, dreams, motives, and plots that humanity includes. It is the lawyer's job to make sense of legal matters by first asking what happened and why the situation has unfolded as it has. Lawyers discover who the principal players are, determine the motives underlying decisions or incidents, and begin to formulate a sense of where these stories are going. Lawyers make sense of a matter by weaving together a coherent story that accounts for the facts, the evidence adduced thus far, and the motives of the parties, both for past behavior and for what each party is now seeking to do. These stories may be as simple as a newspaper headline: "large, faceless organization tries to take advantage of mom-and-pop company," or "disgruntled employee seeks revenge on former employer." Sometimes the story is more complicated, as in a case in which an appliance manufacturer that had been losing its market share to a competitor is accused of illegally copying the look and feel of the competitor's products and using unfair advertising practices to market its own products as the better alternative. Understanding the story and weaving it together for the outside world (including judges, juries, and the court of public opinion) to understand and connect with, helps attorneys not only to make sense of the facts and formulate an appropriate strategy, but also to persuade others to see legal disputes in a way that favors their clients. Good storytelling brings coherence and unity to the events that have precipitated the litigation. Good storytelling provides a theme and a framework for juries and judges to understand the evidence and actions taken by people in response to those same events.

Lawyers are writers. Writing is central to virtually every lawyer's practice. For lawyers who write and argue cases at the appellate level, writing may be the primary focus of practice. Alternatively, the lawyer may have an active trial-court litigation practice that involves the regular writing of memoranda and briefs.

For other attorneys, writing may be a secondary, but still important, part of practice. Virtually every lawyer has clients with whom he or she communicates in writing. That writing likely includes an engagement (or retention) letter, which sets forth the essential nature of the dispute and the terms of the client's engagement of the attorney. The attorney's ability to articulate with specificity what the attorney is, and is not, being retained to handle is very important to setting appropriate parameters and expectations for the future working relationship. Moreover, the attorney should be able to set forth plainly who will perform the work and at what rate. In other words, the first piece of writing for a client is a contract between the attorney and the client that must be well-written and comprehensive. Having a solid engagement letter is essential should a problem develop down the road.

Lawyers also communicate in writing with others, such as judges and adversaries, on a client's behalf. The lawyer is the client's advocate and spokesperson, and the ability to write well and clearly is fundamental to that representation. Lawyers must use specific and clear language, unless they are intentionally trying to avoid such specificity, and must use legal terms of art correctly. Some say "The client will be painted with the same brush as the lawyer." Therefore, if the attorney's communications are poorly written, contain grammatical or syntactical mistakes, or do not communicate properly the issues at hand, then the judge, opponent, or other recipient of the correspondence may question not only the competence of the represented party or its lawyer, but also the merits of that party's position.

Lawyers are historians. A lawyer must understand the history of the case or business deal, including anything that happened in the matter, procedurally or legally, since its inception. Indeed, lawyers often are not involved in legal matters from the beginning. Instead, another lawyer may have started the work, or the client may not have sought legal advice until a relatively late stage in the matter that is now giving rise to the litigation or business transaction. A lawyer must understand not only this procedural history, but also the history of the relationship between the parties. Even if the client does not himself have a full picture of all that has transpired, the attorney must take it upon herself to assemble and understand this information. Frequently, lawyers piece together the background of a litigated event for the first time, by interviewing witnesses or others with some knowledge about the event or transaction involved. In other words, the lawyer acts as a historian in piecing together and understanding the history of the relationship and then using that knowledge to help the client make appropriate strategy decisions about the matter at hand.

Furthermore, lawyers sometimes outline for judges the historical or policy considerations affecting a matter, as well as the legal precedent binding the judge, which is essentially an understanding of how an issue of law has been handled by courts in that jurisdiction over time. Lawyers are often historians of the law as well as historians of the matter for which they have been retained.

Lawyers are businesspeople and advisors. Routinely, attorneys representing corporations, whether as in-house counsel employed by the company or as outside lawyers advising company managers, are called upon to give advice about a dispute that may have financial and practical implications for the client's business, as well as legal implications. Because of these business implications, attorneys cannot simply assess the legal ramifications of any given course of action. Instead, they must understand the client's business objectives and work towards resolving the legal matter so that the client can get on with its real business.

Having some business sense is also essential for lawyers who run their own practices or act as voting members of law firms. As business people in this capacity, lawyers will be called upon to make financial decisions about rent, advertising, hourly rates, staff bonuses, insurance subsidies, and fees to be paid to legal recruiters. Along the same lines, attorneys may be asked to decide which library resources will provide the best value to the firm. These are all business decisions that lawyers must make. The business aspect of practicing can be overwhelming at times, but it is certainly a daily part of the practice of law.

Lawyers are negotiators. Lawyers making legal and business decisions do not do so in a vacuum. Instead, within the lawyer's own business or client base, he or she may be called upon to persuade partners or clients to make certain decisions. Sometimes disputes develop between partners in a firm and must be worked out within the firm. Other times the identity of the attorney's client within a corporation may not be clear, and this situation may itself require negotiation; there may, for instance, be a vice-president and a general counsel to whom the attorney is reporting. These individuals may not agree on the proper course of action for a matter and it may be up to the lawyer to help broker an arrangement between them.

In addition to these internal negotiations, lawyers often negotiate with third parties on a client's behalf to settle a legal dispute or to close a business deal. Skilled negotiators are able to secure for their clients the terms about which the client is most concerned, and to "give," appropriately, on other, less material, terms. Alternatively, the lawyer may be negotiating salary and benefits with her own potential or current employees and colleagues. Depending on the size of the firm or group within which the lawyer works, this may be a frequent use of a lawyer's negotiation skills.

Lawyers are counselors. In handling a client's legal matter, lawyers deal with people and their mistakes, intentional acts, business goals, or personal family crises. Make no mistake: these matters take a tremendous toll on clients, emotionally, financially, and sometimes physically, and attorneys must be aware of this strain. The source of tension is obvious when a family business is breaking up or a deportation order has been handed down. Less obvious to many law students is the toll that legal matters may take on a corporate client. For example, a department's budget (and, therefore, the career of more than one person) may hinge upon a patent application being granted. It is up to the attorney to facilitate that process and secure the patent. Alternatively, a company and its president may have been sued for sexual harassment. In such a situation, not only will the company experience upheaval associated with the matter, but the president and his or her family will also be affected. Clients experience stress, and communicate stress to their attorneys, in myriad ways. Some days, a client might be angry; on other days, that same client may simply be afraid. In each instance, the client needs appropriate reassurance and needs the attorney to communicate competence and, sometimes, simply to confirm a belief in the client's side of the story.

A lawyer is also a listening ear for secretaries, junior attorneys, and other staff members. These individuals may need the attorney's guidance in handling problematic lawyers with whom they work, insurance problems, or personal matters that are affecting the work environment. Moreover, attorneys will be listening ears for one another: the legal profession sometimes exacts a toll that will be evident on the faces of many an attorney's colleagues. Lawyers experience disproportionately high rates of depression, divorce, and alcohol and drug abuse. Lawyers are likely to see the symptoms of these difficulties in their colleagues long before they understand the real issues underlying them; in any event, they may be called upon, either overtly or less obviously, to provide counseling. This counseling is crucial: lawyers spend a significant amount of time together and often take no time to care for themselves emotionally or physically. As a result, colleagues often rely on one another to assess difficult personal and professional situations, and also to work on solutions. At the same time, colleagues must assist one another in ensuring that all clients are receiving appropriate legal representation, even as they deal with important and difficult issues of great personal significance.

Lawyers are librarians. At a minimum, they must know their way around a law library and must be proficient in the use of online legal research tools like Westlaw and LEXIS, as well as the Internet. Furthermore, lawyers must be resourceful in the way that a librarian is, patiently examining a problem from each angle to determine all of the legal issues that may be implicated, and to analyze each such issue. More than one attorney has gotten herself in trouble by declaring that she knew the answer too early, thereby failing to uncover additional, important facts that further research would have revealed. Often lawyers, in the rush of deadlines and the pressure to move on to the next task, have difficulty in distancing themselves from the matter at hand and asking, critically, as a librarian would, whether all of the appropriate sources have been consulted before announcing that the research is complete.

Lawyers are marketers, selling their time and expertise to potential clients. Although the law can be a wonderful and exciting profession, there is no practice of law without clients. Lawyers, who are so well trained to advocate for the positions of others, often fail to advocate for themselves in making their expertise—and availability for representation—known in a way that is both effective and professional. Marketing know-how is a valuable asset, particularly since clients are not always likely to recognize lawyers by name, and loyalty to a particular firm or lawyer may, especially in difficult economic times, give way to a consideration of which lawyer provides the best value. As a result, lawyers are constantly focused on how to get more business and keep the business they already have. For these reasons, lawyers are increasingly using professional marketing firms and consultants, not only to prepare marketing materials, but also to help law firms create a recognizable brand name. For instance, many law firms are now using marketing slogans in association with their written and online materials. These industry changes reflect the extreme importance of each lawyer's ability to market himself or herself effectively.

Lawyers are scholars. Lawyers advocate positions within the law, but they also stretch existing interpretations of the law to advance a client's interest. For example, in recent years, lawyers have tried to determine how the law of defamation applies to Internet message boards and chat rooms. The context in which the defamatory statement is made and the means by which it spreads is different from how defamation occurred before the Internet existed. In such situations, the lawyer finds herself at the cutting edge of the law, proposing changes in the law or demonstrating how existing law can be used to address her client's situation. These are some of the most exciting opportunities for lawyers, because they provide a chance to influence the very direction of the law's evolution.

Lawyers are sometimes problem makers, expending time and resources in attempting to delay a deal or stall the progression of a lawsuit. In so doing, these lawyers may be acting on the wishes, stated or unstated, of a client. Indeed, it is sometimes in a party's best interest to slow down a transaction, negotiation, or litigation. The economy may be expected to make a recovery, which could drive the value of the company up. Alternatively, a company may hit a snag in the research-and-design process of a new product, which may also affect the value of an impending deal. Along the same lines, a company that is being sued may recognize that drawing out a lawsuit may make the plaintiff more anxious to settle the matter and get it over with. Other times, lawyers unnecessarily delay matters simply because they are inept. As lawyers, these individuals may be unprepared for and uneducated about a case, and may therefore make decisions that materially impair the interests of their own clients. Sometimes this ineptness is so extreme that it can be considered intentional behavior, such that these lawyers may justifiably be referred to as problem makers.

Lawyers are advocates. Lawyers are hired to speak for parties who either cannot represent themselves, or who recognize that it would be better if a third party with more specialized knowledge and ability represents them. A lawyer, acting as an advocate, helps a party advance its interests in a way that is consistent with both the law and the facts. Sometimes, a lawyer may act as the front-line advocate for those who are disenfranchised or otherwise not represented in society. For example, a volunteer lawyer may be appointed to represent the interests of children in a custody action, who may not otherwise have a voice expressing their unique interests and concerns in the legal proceedings. A lawyer acting in this capacity is referred to as a *guardian ad litem*. The lawyer as advocate, however, not only represents those who do not have a voice, but may also be the mouthpiece for a very powerful voice; for example, a lawyer may act as a lobbyist in Washington, D.C. for a well-financed national professional association.

Lawyers are actors and performers. Lawyers are, from time to time, called upon to set the appropriate tone in a legal action. A contrite criminal defendant, for instance, needs his or her lawyer to convey the appropriate message of penitence before the judge or jury. Alternatively, a party that believes itself to be morally right, or "wearing the white hat," needs its lawyer to convey a sense of uprightness. In representing the client's interests, it may be appropriate for an attorney to display righteous indignation from time to time. Sometimes, the lawyer may genuinely feel this sense of moral purpose, especially when a particularly sympathetic party is involved, and such situations make it easy for the attorney to convey those feelings. The lawyer may not always, however, feel strongly about a client's cause. For each client he represents, regardless of his personal feelings about the case, the lawyer must present the client's interests in a sympathetic and inoffensive way. This takes talent, as this effort requires acting ability or, at a minimum, good presentation and persuasion skills. For many lawyers, this is the fun part of lawyering. Anyone who asks a trial lawyer to explain how it felt to give an effective closing argument at trial will understand, by her enthusiastic response, why that lawyer chooses to make her career in litigation.

Despite the many roles a lawyer may play, potential law students should not overestimate the flexibility of a law degree, at least during the first few years after graduation from law school. There is much that someone with a law degree can do, and there are many skills that are transferable from the private practice of law to other careers. In addition, many students attend law school, but never intend to practice law: such students may look forward to working in related fields such as business or accounting, managing a family corporation or building one of their own, teaching, or even pursuing additional advanced degrees. It is important to understand, however, that a number of the options that a student may wish to pursue—such as working as in-house counsel for a corporation or working as a permanent clerk for a judge—are generally available only after three years or so of practice. For those who seek to use their law degrees in such traditional ways, these first three years will be spent learning how to be a lawyer and gaining credibility in the field as a professional. These three years might be deemed similar to the residency requirements for a doctor.

KEEPING EXPECTATIONS REASONABLE

Once a potential law student has a general understanding of what lawyers do, she may find it useful to identify why she wants to attend law school in the first place and what she expects to get out of it. Prospective law students give myriad reasons why they want to attend law school: "Law school seems like the logical thing to do after college." "I've watched fifty episodes or re-runs of *The Practice* and *Law and Order* and thought, 'I can do that!'" "I'm upset at the way my family's business was devastated by lawyers, and I want to make sure that never happens again." "I am a good reader." "I am a good debater." "I want to make money." "My aunt is a lawyer." "My current career offers little in the way of advancement potential." "Everyone has always told me, 'You should be a lawyer.'"

These reasons are as varied as the types of people who apply to law school. Many of them revolve around the speaker's *perception* of what lawyers do or even how much money the speaker believes lawyers make. Although these perceptions were shaped by all manner of people and events—a lawyer-family member; television shows; a brush with the legal system as a victim, party/participant, or juror; or a generalized understanding that lawyers argue or debate in representing clients—they all reflect only a partial understanding of what lawyers actually do. Nevertheless, many people apply to law school and spend the equivalent of a small fortune earning a J.D. degree so as to become a lawyer, without knowing what it really means to be a lawyer. For some people, this course of action works out just fine. They simply adapt to any differences between what they thought being a lawyer is like and what it actually is. Others, who are less able to accept the differences between their fantasy or perception and the realities of practicing law, are disappointed. Their disappointment is often compounded if they are tens of thousands of dollars in debt for law school loans and have little hope of making the money to re-pay those loans absent a large paycheck, a situation that may require them to practice law. Still others feel cheated by law school and do not believe that they were taught information that is relevant to the practice of law. As with any other field, having expectations that are in line with reality is half the battle in being successful.

Finally, before discussing the practice of law school in detail, beginning with the application process and the financial issues to be addressed, it is important to keep law school in perspective. Law school is *practice* for *the practice* of law. Therefore, it is best to learn, to explore, and to make mistakes in law school so that they may be avoided later in the practice of law. Unlike when practicing law, during law school, no one else's fortunes or life or liberty is in the student's hands. Therefore, law school is the time to learn the rules of the practice of law. Indeed, although many students find law school to be stressful, it is important to remember that law school is far less pressured, in many respects, than the practice of law. This may be one reason why those who have worked prior to attending law school may seem to be less anxious than others about exams, grades, and the whole law school experience. One returning student described law school as a "job with no pressure." Another, who had worked a regular, twelve-hour workday prior to law school, went so far as to describe law school as a "vacation." Of course, not all law students would agree with this characterization. Nevertheless, students should keep law school in perspective, learning how to learn the law, soaking up the experiences to be offered and the lessons to be learned, and preparing for the practice of law, but still maintaining other priorities, like family, friendships, and outside interests. In this way, the practice of law school should be a positive influence on the later practice of law.

Pre-Law
Preparation

Preparing for law school is not just about reading the right books, taking the recommended courses, or talking with enough lawyers. Instead, much of a future lawyer's preparation involves experience: experience with coursework, with people, and with life itself. Law school preparation is also about developing the maturity to assimilate life lessons and apply them to the processes of learning the law and learning how to advocate for others. Finally, becoming a lawyer includes gaining the technical competence and self-confidence necessary to succeed in this challenging and important profession. This chapter looks at pre-law preparation on several levels, not only helping the pre-law student to evaluate his undergraduate course selections, but also encouraging the student to seek practical experience that will help him to get the most out of his classes in law school. Ultimately, being both well-rounded and well-educated will give the lawyer the tools that are necessary to address his clients' needs comprehensively. Having a broad perspective from which to examine each new issue and experience each new opportunity is fundamental to the successful practice of law school and of law. This chapter is meant to assist both those who intend to begin their legal studies immediately after undergraduate school and those who have decided to leave behind another career to attend law school.

FROM LAYPERSON TO LAWYER: THE TECHNICAL REQUIREMENTS FOR BECOMING LICENSED TO PRACTICE LAW

The technical requirements for applying to law school are relatively straightforward and well defined. To matriculate in a law school that is accredited by the American Bar Association, an individual must have earned a four-year undergraduate degree, such as a Bachelor of Arts degree or a Bachelor of Science degree. Alternatively, the individual must reasonably anticipate that the degree will be awarded before he begins law school. A potential law student may have majored in any subject whatsoever as an undergraduate, may have accumulated additional degrees before law school, and may have earned each degree very recently or many years in the past. In each of these respects, law school admission committees are flexible; rather than looking for individuals who fit a certain profile, most are looking for well-rounded students of demonstrably high intellect and ambition who are committed to the study of the law for a variety of reasons. Just as there is no required pre-law undergraduate major, there are no prerequisite classes that a student must take before entering law school.

All law schools that belong to the Law School Admissions Council, a nonprofit corporation with a membership consisting of approximately 198 law schools in the United States and Canada, use the Law School Admissions Test (LSAT) as one factor in making their admission decisions. The LSAT is a half-day, multi-section, objective, standard-scored exam. The LSAT purports to measure an applicant's reading comprehension, analytical reasoning, and ability to think logically. The applicant's undergraduate grade point average (GPA) is another objective factor that law schools consider in making their admissions decisions. Each law school decides for itself what constitutes an acceptable score on the LSAT or a sufficient GPA for an applicant to merit admission. The range of acceptable scores will vary, depending on each law school's relative reputation and ability to attract qualified applicants. Often, law schools will use a formula that combines the GPA and LSAT score. Based on each applicant's score, as computed by this formula, some students may be admitted automatically, others may be excluded automatically, and still others may be the subjects of discussion among members of the admissions committee.

Thus, when the law school admissions committee examines each student's application file, the major focus, as discussed in Chapter 3, is likely to be some combination of the student's undergraduate grade point average and LSAT score. For those students whose scores are somewhere in the middle, not subject to automatic (or presumptive) admission or rejection, certain extracurricular activities, honors, and academic achievements may factor into the school's decision-making process, as well. Law schools may view an applicant who was a student advocate, an honor-court judge, a member of the debate or mock-trial team, or a leader in student government with particular favor. These activities suggest that the applicant possesses leadership skills, integrity, and the ability to communicate, all of which are characteristics of an excellent attorney.

Most students who attend law school full-time will receive their J.D. in three years, barring any leave of absence, significant overseas exchange that does not result in a full transfer of course credit, or academic difficulties such as being required to re-take a course. Part-time students, and those working toward a joint degree, such as a law degree combined with a Master of Business Administration, may require four or more years to complete the coursework for a law degree. A student who successfully completes her law-school coursework is awarded a *juris doctor* degree, also known as a J.D. Eighty-eight hours of coursework is standard for the degree. The J.D. degree is a professional master's degree, and represents the standard training required of all who wish to practice law. Lawyers who complete the requirements for a J.D. degree can also work toward a Master of Laws degree, or LL.M. The LL.M degree is not required for the practice of law, but is useful additional training for law school graduates who either wish to pursue a career in legal education or are interested in certain highly specialized areas of the law, such as taxation. This degree, and the final, dissertation-based doctoral degree in law, variously called the S.J.D. or J.S.D., are discussed more thoroughly in Chapter 15. The S.J.D. is most commonly pursued by those who are committed to a career in legal education.

Once a law school graduate is awarded a J.D., and before she may practice law, she must apply for admission to practice in the state, commonwealth, or territory of the United States (each of which is known as a "jurisdiction") in which she wishes to work. Admission will be based on the student's law school performance, demonstrated moral character, and performance on a standardized bar examination, all of which are discussed in Chapter 14. It is only when these requirements, among others, are met that the lawyer will be licensed to practice law in the applicable jurisdiction. A lawyer may not, however, practice law in a separate jurisdiction unless he or she is (1) also licensed to practice law in that second jurisdiction, or (2) provisionally admitted to practice in that jurisdiction, so as to handle a specific legal matter.

The above discussion sets forth only the minimal, technical requirements for becoming a lawyer. The practice of law and the task of becoming a satisfied and skilled lawyer will require much more in the way of preparation, education, ambition, experience, attitude, interest, and sheer love of the law. The remainder of this chapter will focus on how a prospective student can best prepare for law school and life as a successful lawyer.

WHAT SKILLS ARE NECESSARY FOR EFFECTIVE LAWYERING?

Chapter 1 addressed the many roles that lawyers play, sometimes in a single day. Lawyers function as advocates, detectives, business advisors, negotiators, counselors, and actors, to name just a few of their responsibilities. To be proficient in these and many other important roles, the lawyer should work toward developing certain skills and aptitudes. Any book about how to prepare for a career as a lawyer must therefore necessarily begin with a description of some of the most important requisite skills and aptitudes so that prospective lawyers can start to focus on developing them as soon as possible. The prospective lawyer can thus examine the opportunities that are available to her in terms of formal coursework, outside reading or study, and life itself, with an eye toward becoming a successful and well-rounded legal professional.

A lawyer must have the ability to analyze facts and appraise situations objectively. *Objectivity* requires that an individual either reserve judgment or refrain from drawing a conclusion until sufficient facts are brought to light that will enable her to form a well-founded opinion. One way a prospective lawyer can develop objectivity is by participating in formal or structured debates, especially ones in which the same participants are forced to argue both sides of the issue. Another is by virtue of life experience. This might come about through a situation in which the outcome of a dispute was very different from that the individual anticipated. This experience can be particularly powerful when it reveals a situation contrary to that person's strongly held beliefs.

Advocacy, a characteristic that is as central to lawyering as is objectivity, can be either a learned skill or a natural gift. Although it is important for a lawyer to weigh the facts and maintain an open mind, it is also important for the lawyer to advocate for his clients, advancing each client's interests in an appropriately persuasive and effective manner. Clients expect their lawyers to act as advocates, using argument and persuasion to bring a jury or corporate officer around to the client's point of view. Many prospective lawyers may not recognize that common life situations often present excellent opportunities for the refinement of advocacy skills. An individual who is pursuing reimbursement of medical bills from an insurer that refuses to pay must act as an advocate for herself. A parent seeking assistance for a child who is struggling academically must advocate for her child. Looking back at experiences such as these and figuring out what persuaded, or failed to persuade, the insurance company or school superintendent enables the future lawyer to refine these skills. Long before a person enters law school, she can look for opportunities to develop these skills she will need as a lawyer.

One of the attorney's main tools in advancing a client's interests is *writing*. It is through the written word that attorneys accomplish much of the day-to-day work of client representation, including keeping clients informed. An attorney's ability to write well is fundamentally important, regardless of her area of practice or level of expertise. An attorney never ceases to refine her ability to write clearly and persuasively. Writing skills can be improved through formal coursework, through work experience, and sometimes even by simply taking the initiative to maintain a varied and challenging personal program of outside reading.

An attorney represents her clients through a process of *communicating*, both with the outside world and with each client. An attorney might be engaged, for example, to negotiate the terms of a business deal on the client's behalf. As part of the service she provides, the attorney will discuss her negotiation strategy with the client before, during, and after the negotiation. The attorney must discern her client's wishes and communicate them to the opposing side. The attorney must also be able to communicate any relevant terms of the transaction, or agreements or instructions about the transaction, to other attorneys, secretaries, paralegals, experts, and co-counsel working on the matter. As her audience changes, the attorney must change the way in which she presents the information, taking care to ensure its accuracy each time. Thus, articulating thoughts properly and unambiguously is fundamental to successful lawyering. Some individuals are born with a natural ability to convey thoughts clearly and succinctly. Others, however, must rely on formal instruction, constructive criticism in work or school, and life lessons learned from situations in which communication was ineffective and negative consequences resulted. Future attorneys must be aware of the importance of effective communication and should look for opportunities to refine those skills.

An attorney must also have well-developed *listening skills*, which are integral to effective communication. Poor listeners may fail to understand their clients' concerns or miss facts that would make or break the client's case. Attorneys who fail to listen also sometimes fail to recognize which hat the client needs the attorney to don at the moment: that of therapist, strong advocate, or business advisor. In addition, like most people, the attorney's clients sometimes will be untruthful. Attorneys must listen carefully so as to determine whether a client or witness is telling the truth. Listening skills are perhaps best developed, and sometimes even improved, by participating in relationships in which bi-directional communication is important. It does not matter whether the relationships in question are personal or professional ones—rather, what matters is that they work. Listening is fundamental to the success of any relationship, including that between lawyer and client.

An attorney ideally should possess *broad knowledge*, so that he can not only converse with clients and colleagues about legal and non-legal subjects, but also bring that knowledge to bear in examining a client's needs and providing advice. Being well-read, or at least having some exposure to current and historical events, different political systems, and diverse cultures, is all part of developing a breadth of knowledge that is helpful in providing effective representation. This perspective is a result not only of formal coursework, but also of reading widely and, perhaps most simply and most importantly, of learning from experience.

Although intellectual ability and legal training are both very important to the practice of law, learning to *think logically and methodically* is at least as important. This kind of thinking is a learned ability that can be refined and strengthened with practice. Students of the law are, for example, encouraged to tackle legal questions by engaging in a four-part process: (1) identifying the legal issue to be examined; (2) stating the rule of law to be applied; (3) applying the law to the relevant facts; and (4) drawing a conclusion based on the foregoing analysis. This approach is often called the "IRAC" approach, an acronym that stands for "Issue, Rule, Analysis, and Conclusion." The IRAC method is a useful tool because it forces one to think methodically and logically. Long after graduation from law school, lawyers use analytical constructs such as IRAC to work through legal questions. Pre-law students can also be taught to employ this methodology. This form of analysis may bring new structure and clarity to the way in which pre-law students and those who are currently employed as non-lawyers approach their work.

Professionalism, in the legal world, describes the level of conduct that is expected of an attorney in all dealings with clients, opposing counsel, the court, and colleagues. Professionalism includes poise, confidence, maturity, judgment, discretion, and integrity. This concept requires attorneys to adhere firmly to a code of personal morality and to act with integrity, even when the attorney's client may not be doing so or when the attorney can achieve greater advantage for a client by declining to do so. Because an attorney represents the legal system to everyone she encounters, she should take care in how she presents herself in her public and private life. Some facets of professionalism, such as poise, are learned skills for many lawyers. Others, such as personal morality, generally are developed very early in the prospective lawyer's life, even in childhood.

Sometimes, in the course of advancing a client's interests, the attorney will find that she must expend an incredible amount of time and energy to do the job right. Indeed, professionalism may require that an attorney who has promised to handle a matter for a fixed fee end up losing money on the matter by taking more time than she expected to take. It may require that she work until the early hours of the morning, on occasion, to finish a legal document to be filed later that day, or that she marshal additional resources, even at her own expense, to complete the work that she has promised.

Attorneys sometimes handle cases that last for five or more years. At times, just having the mental stick-to-itiveness necessary to think creatively about a case requires *stamina*. Stamina will also help the lawyer to maintain her level of interest in and commitment to a matter as it progresses and changes.

In addition to developing technical skills, a lawyer should have a basic understanding of *business etiquette*. This is as important, for a couple of reasons, for the lawyer who represents individual clients as it is for the lawyer who represents corporations. First, the attorney is making an impression on a prospective client from the moment at which the attorney speaks with the client on the telephone or shakes hands with her. Second, the attorney represents the client in dealings with others; as a practical matter, the client is often painted with the same brush as the attorney. Therefore, the attorney's conduct must be beyond reproach so that his client is effectively represented. Appropriate business etiquette includes, for example, introducing people who may not have met previously, even when those individuals are on different sides of a transaction or litigation. Etiquette also suggests that the attorney should speak with individuals without using a speakerphone, unless, of course, the conversation in question is a conference call with multiple participants in one office. Etiquette may dictate that the attorney avoid the practice of automatically complaining to the superior of a lower-ranking businessperson who has mishandled a matter, rather than speaking directly with the person who made the mistake. Simply stated, manners do matter, even in the legal world.

Attorneys are entrusted with enormous responsibility. An attorney maintains trust and fulfills the expectations people have of her by showing *respect for institutions and processes*. She discharges this responsibility by observing deadlines, following accepted procedural practices, and otherwise acting in a manner that is consistent with the trust placed in her.

Handling matters with appropriate respect requires *discipline*. Clients expect their telephone calls to be returned in a timely fashion, for example. Papers to be filed with the court take time—sometimes weeks or months—to prepare. To function effectively, an attorney must budget his time, manage client expectations, manage calendar deadlines, and supervise associates and staff. The attorney can keep matters balanced and moving forward by being disciplined and by paying attention to the details.

Sometimes, a lawyer finds that practicing law, or even leaving the practice of law at an appropriate time, requires a measure of *courage*. If, for example, the lawyer learns that her client improperly altered evidence, she must have the courage to confront her client. To the same effect, the attorney may realize that, for a variety of reasons that may be personal, professional, or both, he is not functioning well emotionally. Under these circumstances, he must have the courage to admit that there is a problem and take appropriate action. Sometimes, doing so may even require that the attorney recognize that it is time to leave the practice of law, and perhaps take up another profession.

DEVELOPING THESE SKILLS: COURSEWORK AND DIRECTION OF STUDY

The prospective lawyer, as an undergraduate, has a veritable banquet of interesting and useful courses from which to choose. Many of these classes will later prove helpful in dealing with clients both as people and as clients. Although no specific class or major is required for law school, an undergraduate student may, through careful course selection and thoughtful attention to extracurricular activities, provide herself with an excellent foundation for her future career as a lawyer.

Some colleges and, less commonly, some high schools, offer pre-law programs. The scope of these programs is defined variously. Many pre-law programs, however, include courses on the court system, on writing, and in liberal arts such as psychology, mathematics, sociology, geology or the physical sciences, and philosophy. Although few schools have a separate pre-law department, many designate a faculty member to oversee and advise participants in the program. Some pre-law programs include extracurricular activities that complement participants' in-class study. They might, for example, have debating teams or, less commonly, moot-court programs. The competitions may be intramural, or regional or national. They are intended to be a practical application of what is taught in the classroom.

College students can also craft their own pre-law program and should not be too concerned if their school lacks a formal one. Such students, working with or without a pre-law advisor, generally focus on choosing courses that traditionally are regarded as preparation for law school, such as political science, history, and economics, in addition to those mentioned above.

Students who have completed a traditional pre-law program should not, however, become overconfident about their substantive knowledge of the law. College-level mock-trial experience or undergraduate business-law or constitutional-law classes are likely to be very different from their law school counterparts. The student should appreciate them for what they are—an orientation—rather than expect them to confer a significant substantive advantage in law school.

A student who is working with a pre-law advisor should recognize her own responsibility vis-à-vis that of the advisor. The advisor is not responsible for determining the course of the student's schooling or ensuring that the student is exposed to the various disciplines that will be of assistance to her as an attorney. The advisor, rather, is simply that: an advisor, who provides guidance in that capacity. The advisor's role may include conferring with the student about course selections and helping the student to obtain information about test dates, scholarship and application deadlines, and law school programs in general.

Students should not feel overly restricted in their choice of major or coursework in preparation for law school. It is difficult to determine exactly which courses will offer any given student the best preparation for law school. Instead, the focus should be on developing the skills and aptitudes discussed earlier in this chapter. Most law schools are looking for diversity of thought when selecting a student body. Thus, admissions officers actively seek out people who, through life or professional experience, may bring an interesting perspective to the study of law. Often, these different viewpoints make for lively classroom discussion. In a law school seminar, for example, students may become engaged in discussions about the merits of affirmative action. Students often have diverse opinions on this subject, and those opinions are not necessarily split along racial lines. Instead, they are likely to be the result of life experience.

Students should focus on subjects they enjoy. Both in school and in professional life, people tend to perform at a higher level when they are doing something that is of great interest to

CHAPTER 2
Pre-Law Preparation

them. When a student enjoys a subject, she becomes immersed in it, is receptive to learning, and cares about her performance. Often, this positive attitude and enthusiasm translate into higher grades, which are, as discussed in Chapter 3, important when the student is applying to law school.

Formal schooling offers a wonderful (and fleeting) opportunity to learn how big the world is—students should therefore not be too quick to specialize and to focus so narrowly that they lose out on the chance to explore. One student who double-majored in political science and economics chose to take one unrelated course each semester of college—from literature to Spanish to mythology to basic sociology—just to keep her horizons broad. These are the courses she enjoyed most and, ten years later, these are the courses she remembers best.

The prospective law student might also consider choosing a major that would allow her to enter another profession or otherwise to be marketable in the event that she either does not attend law school or delays her law school matriculation. Pre-law students sometimes major in journalism, marketing, accounting, finance, nursing, or education before attending law school. A great number of lawyers leave the practice of law, some to pursue long-held interests in subjects they studied as undergraduates.

Some courses provide particularly solid preparation for law school. Those that emphasize writing are a good example. College-level writing courses will provide the pre-law student with the invaluable opportunity to get constructive criticism and comprehensive feedback on his writing. They also make it possible for the student to master some of the skills he will need for legal writing. Too often, students leave undergraduate school without having done any scholarly writing. Some schools will allow students to opt out of English courses or will give them college credit for high-school English courses. Although avoiding a college-level English course or writing requirement may seem like a victory at the time, doing so can turn out to be a mistake. The practice of law involves so much professional writing that a prospective law school student should seriously consider taking advantage of every undergraduate opportunity to improve his writing skills. This said, the value of an English major can be overstated; being a strong creative writer, for example, does not necessarily lead to success in law school. Indeed, the kind of writing that is required in law school often frustrates English majors. Creativity does have a place in effective lawyering, but employing this skill appropriately and to maximum effect requires significant experience. Majoring in English can, however, provide a prospective law student not only with the benefit of being familiar with important works of literature, but also with broad exposure to varied ideas and cultural backgrounds.

In addition to writing well, it is critical that lawyers read and comprehend the written word well. Attorneys spend an enormous amount of time reviewing documents and reading contracts, correspondence, reports, and court decisions. They must often assimilate information and then make decisions quickly, based upon their understanding of those documents.

The prospective law student might also consider courses such as philosophy and logic, which will assist her in developing analytical abilities. Rhetoric does not wholly comprise law; rather, at its best, the law is also logical and precise. Therefore, being able to understand a philosophical argument or parse a theorem is excellent practice for dissecting a court's analysis or an opponent's argument. Moreover, these courses may assist the prospective law student in preparing for the portion of the LSAT exam that tests logic and the ability to reason. Political philosophy is also a valuable introduction to those schools of thought that form the basis for much of the modern American legal system. Studying the writings of Abraham Lincoln, Alexis de Tocqueville, Jean-Jacques Rousseau, and John Locke, for example, may provide an important perspective for the study of law.

Similarly, history courses provide an excellent context for understanding the law. As discussed in Chapter 1, a historical understanding of the development of the law is fundamental to America's precedent-based legal system. History provides examples of how people interacted and made decisions; it elucidates the morals and values of a group of people at a given moment in time. All of these factors affect the evolution of the law. Indeed, an understanding of history may be the best preparation a future law student can have for comprehending the fluid nature of American law.

In psychology courses, students learn to understand the emotional development of individuals. Because the law is a series of stories about human experience, these courses can offer valuable insight into the motivations of individuals and can assist future lawyers in understanding human behavior in the context of the law. Many law students, especially future litigators, find this background to be useful.

At first, it might seem counterintuitive that math and science courses would prove useful for the study of a discipline, such as law, that may seem relatively inexact. In fact, however, these courses are likely to be quite helpful. Sometimes the clear thinking that characterizes good legal practice requires the level of precision that would be exercised by a mathematician or scientist. Students who majored in these fields are generally proficient in identifying critical issues and relevant facts. Students with technical backgrounds may also find that they have a relative advantage in speaking concisely and precisely. In law, as in the hard sciences and mathematics, words often have technical meanings and precise definitions; therefore, using a single word improperly can change, even destroy, an entire argument. Math and science courses are particularly good preparation for those law school courses that are based primarily upon rules or statutes, rather than common law. Scientists and mathematicians often find that parsing a statute or attacking a problem methodically comes naturally to them, given their technical background. Students who study science or mathematics should, however, also take elective courses, such as literature or public speaking, that will help them to develop their communication and writing skills. Otherwise, these students may be at a relative disadvantage when they begin to study law.

Generally, any courses that include a survey of the American court system, the criminal justice system, or the political and formal divisions of government are very useful for future attorneys. For many prospective law students, having a basic knowledge of this material demystifies some of the procedural aspects of the law. In addition, understanding the context in which the law is made gives students some perspective on how politics influences policy decisions and vice versa.

Proficiency in a foreign language can be useful in law school, as well as in the later practice of law. Law students often describe the process of learning to think like a lawyer as being much like learning a new language. Attorneys who are bilingual or multilingual may also be able to provide services to clients who cannot communicate in English.

GRADUATE DEGREES

A graduate degree is certainly not a prerequisite for law school. A number of students, however, enter law school with this background and find it to be beneficial. Some of these students have found that the analytical and writing skills that were required of them in graduate school served them well in law school. Particularly if the graduate student worked with a faculty team or an individual advisor in developing and preparing a dissertation, thesis, or other scholarly paper, she is likely to have been required to communicate her ideas with precision and to defend her conclusions persuasively. In addition, the graduate student might have had the opportunity to teach at the university level, or at least to work as a teaching assistant. As discussed in Chapter 1, all lawyers must function as teachers, of their clients, their peers, and the judges before whom they practice. Finally, having a master's degree in another discipline may make the student more marketable as an attorney if the degree is in a field that employers regard as being helpful for the practice of law. Students who hold a master's degree in business administration or an advanced degree in taxation or accounting might be particularly attractive candidates for business-law positions, for example; those with medical degrees might have a relative advantage in medical-malpractice law; and those with a background in international studies might use that experience to seek employment in international law.

INTANGIBLE FACTORS FOR PRE-LAW PREPARATION

Successfully navigating undergraduate school, and maximizing the value of the courses offered there, requires more of the future lawyer than simply the ability to achieve good grades. Future lawyers must develop an attitude of learning. They should anticipate that each professor, pre-law advisor, informal mentor, or legal professional with whom they interact or discuss their career plans can teach them something worthwhile.

The love of learning goes hand in hand with the expectation of learning. Lawyers never stop learning; those students who do not enjoy this process, but prefer a more static environment, may therefore find the practice of law to be unsettling. A lawyer never knows what kind of needs her client will have. Each day of law practice presents an opportunity for the practitioner to learn something new. This phenomenon makes the practice of law particularly exciting—and challenging.

Another way for the future law student to nurture a love of learning is to check his ego at the door. The law is properly conceived of as a service industry, rather than simply a business, and the lawyer should consider himself to be a public servant. With the power and prestige that are attendant to the practice of law comes responsibility. Thus, the lawyer should seek to be a pillar of the community, or at least an involved and committed participant. Being involved in this way will ensure that the lawyer remains well-rounded and connected enough to function effectively as an advocate.

The future lawyer's level of personal maturity is another factor that may affect the lawyer's success in law school and in her career. To develop the maturity that both require, some students take time off from their studies, after their undergraduate work is complete, to work or travel abroad before going to law school. A family business, the Peace Corps, or the military can all provide varied—and valuable—experience and perspective. Sometimes, the connection between this experience and the future lawyer's career plans is direct: One student who hoped to become a union organizer worked on an assembly line before law school. Other times, the benefit is more indirect, revealing itself through the student's general level of maturity.

Finally, although a prospective law student should recognize that major challenges lie ahead in the form of, at a minimum, at least three years of law school, she should feel confident that hard work and dedication generally do yield positive results. Any student who truly wants to attend law school should be able to accomplish this goal. In considering whether to apply to law school in the first place, however, the student should keep her expectations in line with reality. Law is not a magic ticket to getting rich—it is a profession and a calling.

ACADEMIC HONORS AND AWARDS

A student's past academic performance will be a very important consideration for the law schools to which she applies. Academic honors and awards are objective manifestations of the kind of scholastic excellence that law schools are likely to find impressive. Membership in Phi Beta Kappa, other field-specific honor societies, the Dean's List, the Honor Roll, and the National Honor Society may be valuable in helping the student gain admission to the law school of her choice. In addition, an applicant's past receipt of merit-based scholarships often favorably impresses law schools.

EXTRACURRICULAR ACTIVITIES

Students should consider participating in extracurricular activities and internships that will help them to develop the skills and aptitudes mentioned earlier in this chapter. Many of these opportunities will provide valuable exposure to the law. When time and resources are limited, students may want to focus on activities that complement their pre-law coursework. This is a good way for future lawyers to develop a strong work ethic and habits that will remain with them throughout their academic life and beyond.

Many future lawyers find undergraduate social sororities and fraternities to be valuable. These organizations not only provide their members with a network of social and professional contacts around the country and around the world, but also give those students who serve as officers in them the opportunity to develop leadership and organizational skills.

As discussed earlier, although college-level mock-trial and debate programs are generally different from the competitions in which law students participate, they may provide a valuable introduction to the legal process. Even if a school does not have a formal trial or debate program, a student may be able to put together a team and solicit a faculty advisor anyway. This effort may require that the student figure out for herself how to fund and organize the team, and how to ensure that the team is in compliance with the relevant national rules. If the student will take this initiative, however, the experience not only provides an excellent pre-law exercise and an opportunity to receive recognition, but also demonstrates leadership, commitment, and a strong interest in the law.

Some law schools recruit heavily from college-level mock-trial and debate programs. Indeed, some sponsor high school or college mock-trial competitions at the law school to give participants a chance to look around the school. Some of these law schools even offer special scholarships to students who matriculate following these competitions or offer automatic early admission to the top performers.

When a prospective law student is assessing her pre-law-school employment options, she is likely to find that particularly fine opportunities are available to her if she can afford to work for little or no money, at least at first. Government agencies, law firms, courts, and public-interest programs such as AmeriCorps often provide excellent opportunities for future lawyers to view the legal process from an insider's perspective.

Serving as a law-firm runner, case clerk, or paralegal may be the most common type of pre-law employment, and many future attorneys find this experience to be very valuable. In each of these positions, the prospective law student can observe the schedule and the conditions under which lawyers work and can make an informed decision if he chooses a career in the law. These positions also expose the future lawyer to those less glamorous tasks—such as photocopying, document compilation, and courier service—that support the practice of law. Indeed, many future lawyers, having served in this capacity, vow never to undervalue their support staff.

Working in the recruiting department can be helpful as well. Doing so is a good way for a prospective lawyer to see how law firms recruit students and how they look at applicants' résumés and other credentials.

Doing volunteer work for a political campaign is also a good idea. If the student wishes to go into politics, he might volunteer for the campaign of a congressional representative, senator, or governor. Alternatively, those who anticipate a more traditional law practice may benefit from assisting a state-court judge or county district attorney in campaigning. These volunteer positions can provide not only exposure to a different side of the law, but also a valuable network of connections, and possibly a mentor. Other future law students work in state or federal legislature internships in college or serve as legislative pages while they are in high school.

For some future law students, a relationship with a mentor will develop as a natural outgrowth of employment, personal contact with lawyers, or relationships with family friends. Others will find themselves actively seeking a mentor. Some law schools provide formal or informal mentoring programs, and some students meet mentors through the state bar association or through a college alumni network. Students with special interests or who belong to minority groups may also find mentors through groups of individuals who share their needs and interests.

REFERENCES

References, which are discussed more fully in the next chapter, are important, not only for admission to law school, but also for later employment and for admission to the bar. Even before her first day as an undergraduate, the student should think about who might be willing to give her a reference. If she is dedicated and conducts herself with integrity, she will be in a strong position when seeking a reference. It is also very helpful to have the support and guidance of an advisor or professor, either formally or informally. The student should seek to develop relationships with mentors in both high school and college—and not just with lawyers. When the student does choose a lawyer as her mentor, she should look for one who understands that the law is not just about money and prestige, but also about personal responsibility. She should seek to develop close relationships with those who will guide her personal and moral growth as well as her intellectual pursuits. The best mentors are generally those who know, and value, the student well enough to have her best interests in mind.

PERSONAL CONDUCT AND INTEGRITY

In addition to academic performance and a well-rounded undergraduate education, personal conduct is very important. To maximize her success as a law student and, later, as an attorney, the future lawyer should conduct herself responsibly, both in school and in her personal life. She should seek to have a flawless record of academic integrity: no suspensions, honor-court or discipline-board hearings, or expulsions. A spotty course history, including incomplete courses and late-dropped courses, may suggest a lack of care. She should also have no criminal arrest record. A future lawyer's work history will be important, too; therefore, she should keep accurate records of her employment and approach every job, however menial, as if it matters—because it does. Being fired, even from a fast-food restaurant, is a burden the future law student does not wish to carry on her employment record. The student may also find, at some point, that she needs to use her former employers as references for law school and for the bar-exam application. Especially in the latter case, former employers may be asked a detailed list of questions about the student's integrity and performance, even if the student's work for that individual had nothing to do with the law.

KNOWING THE DEADLINES

From the very first day that the student decides to pursue a career in the law, he should have a personal timetable in place. This timetable will help him to determine when to take the LSAT, gather his references, and prepare his application forms, all of which are discussed in detail in the next chapter.

PREPARING FINANCIAL MATTERS

Throughout their undergraduate careers and beyond, future lawyers should strive to keep their personal debt load as low as possible. Law school is an enormous expense for those who must finance it themselves. Those students who borrowed money for their undergraduate education or to finance the lifestyle they chose to lead before law school may especially find that what they make as attorneys may not be sufficient to repay the debt they have incurred. This can be the case even if the law student secures particularly lucrative employment with a private law firm. Thinking ahead, even as an undergraduate, will help the future lawyer to navigate some of the big decisions that lie ahead.

PLANNING WHERE TO APPLY

The prospective law student should try to determine, as far in advance as possible, where she wishes to pursue her legal education. This can be especially helpful when it comes time for the student to apply to schools and to seek financial aid. As further discussed in Chapters 3 and 4, students who express their interest in a given law school very early may improve their chances of being admitted and, if admitted, of receiving financial aid. Therefore, the prospective student should visit several law schools. An undergraduate might do so over the course of her college education. Some prospective law students turn these trips into enjoyable family vacations or tack these visits onto vacations that have already been planned. Handling this process in a deliberate fashion provides the student with an opportunity not only to demonstrate a strong commitment to the school of her choice, but also to get an early glimpse of the campus life there.

INFORMATIONAL INTERVIEWS

Informational interviews with lawyers, judges, and other legal professionals are a good way to learn about the practice of law. Prospective law students often find that these individuals are quite forthright with them because, unlike job applicants, the students are not asking for anything but advice.

During such interviews, future lawyers might ask about the career path of the individual with whom they are meeting, including the classes, majors, and undergraduate and law schools he chose. Other good topics of conversation might include his regrets and triumphs, the best and worst days in his career, a typical day in his law practice, any difficulties he had with the transition from law school to practice or from one kind of practice to another, and his proudest moment as a lawyer. If this person is willing to allow the prospective law student to go along with him to a hearing, deposition, or simply a day at work, doing so can provide a valuable context for understanding any advice the attorney may have given the student. Prospective law students can also go and watch oral arguments on their own at a local court. The public is generally admitted to these proceedings, absent compelling circumstances that militate in favor of excluding all but the parties.

ADDITIONAL PRE-LAW PREPARATION FOR RETURNING STUDENTS

Those students who are attending law school after another career or after having worked as a stay-at-home parent often wonder whether they can resume the mind-set of a student without making drastic changes. They may well find that they need not make any such change; indeed, perhaps they do not want to return to "student mode," whatever that phrase means to them. Rather, having managed a professional life or a household itself is good preparation in terms of discipline, time-management, organization, and communication. Also, as discussed below and throughout this book, approaching law school as a job is an excellent way to stay organized, to remain focused, and to keep law school in proper context.

Having said this, however, a prospective law student who has been out of school for a long period of time might wish to practice the mechanics of being a student. This might include becoming accustomed to a large volume of reading and to the discipline that is required for completing writing assignments within a deadline. In addition, some returning students may find that they need to hone their listening skills and their ability to follow directions, especially if they were in positions of authority in their former work life or home life.

Many returning students succeed by treating law school as the next stage of their continuing career. For some of these students, this means setting—and maintaining—regular hours; keeping an eye on promotion to the next level; finding mentors; asking questions to ensure that they maximize their experience in law school; dressing appropriately; and treating classmates as professional associates and colleagues. In many ways, these individuals often find themselves at a competitive advantage during law school because they better understand the process of active learning and often are more mature than other students about grades and other law school pressures. Many returning students also benefit from having a context in which to put what they will study in class. Having paid bills, taxes, and perhaps a mortgage, for example, or perhaps having participated in a lawsuit filed against a former employer, can provide a valuable context for classroom learning. In addition, many of these students find that their concerns about their skills—such as writing—having fallen into disuse are unfounded. Indeed, some returning students find that they study harder and more effectively than their classmates because they can appreciate the comprehensive cost—and benefits—of a legal education more than their less experienced counterparts.

It is a good idea, however, for these students to have a very clear idea of why they are returning to school. A law student who has had another career should know whether she is attending law school to further that career, to leave that career behind, or to seek a connection between that career and the practice of law. One returning student found that his previous job experience enabled him to see ways to use his law degree that would not otherwise have occurred to him.

OTHER WAYS TO PREPARE

All prospective law students can use their life experience, however limited or full it might be, to provide context for their study of law.

Whether the prospective lawyer is currently in school or employed, there are several simple ways that she might develop her lawyering skills through her everyday life or work experiences. She might, for instance, engage in critical thinking as she reads the newspaper, following up on stories that are of interest to her and challenging the assumptions that are expressed there. One lawyer has done something similar with his children: because he doubts that the greenhouse effect and global warming work as some scientists say, he has taught his school-age children to think critically by reading materials beyond those that are assigned to them in school. Because of this exercise, his children are equipped to ask sophisticated and probing questions of their teachers. Future lawyers should look for ways to think more critically about the world around them, and to examine more analytically the information upon which they rely when forming opinions or discussing matters with others.

Some students prepare for law school by doing background reading. Many schools provide recommended—or required—reading lists for first-year students. Prospective law students should not put too much stock in anecdotal accounts of or novels about law school. There is no single model of law school, just as there is no single model of a successful law student. It is best for the student to investigate each school in which she is interested, rather than forming generalized, uninformed opinions based upon the viewpoints of others, many of which may be out of date. Some students choose to ignore books and movies about law school and the practice of law such as *One L*, *The Paper Chase*, and *Double Billing*. Others find them to be amusing, even comforting, after they have successfully conquered their own first year of law school or practice.

Keeping up with current events in the world in general and the law in particular is another good way for prospective lawyers to keep their perspective. It is often easy for students, especially during college, to become disconnected from current events. As this chapter has emphasized, it is important for any prospective lawyer to understand the context into which the law fits, and keeping track of current events is one way to do this.

In attempting to stay abreast of current issues in the law, the student might choose, for example, to subscribe to the free e-mail alert service for decisions of the United States Supreme Court. Some state-level and lower federal courts also provide this service. In addition, the prospective lawyer might benefit from viewing the local legal newspaper online, at least occasionally, or from reviewing the materials contained on the American Bar Association's Web site. Student rates for legal periodicals are sometimes available to college and high school students as well as to law students. *Anderson's Directory of Law Reviews* is available online at andersonpublishing.com. There, various law reviews can be found by name or by specialty. This provides prospective law students with the opportunity to keep track of some of the emerging issues in the law, as presented by law students and academicians. The student might choose, for instance, to look at the most prestigious law reviews, to review those at the schools she is most likely to attend, or to examine those in areas in which she believes she may be interested in practicing. This effort gives the prospective student something to talk about during the aforementioned informational interviews and on law school applications. More important, keeping track of developments in the law is a good way for the future lawyer to begin to feel some connection with the law.

This book can help the student to navigate the basic requirements for obtaining a law license, and can even illuminate some of the intangibles that make for a successful career in the law. Only the student himself, however, can realize his potential as an attorney by bringing to bear the lessons he has learned through his professional and personal experiences. Taking life lessons to the next level—actually learning from them and making solid decisions based upon them—is a skill that can be developed and refined. This chapter presented a number of tools for connecting real life to the law. This process does not begin during the pre-law preparation process, nor does it end when the student graduates from law school. Rather, this is a lifelong endeavor, highlighted by periods of increased maturity, by a history of sound and rational decisions, and by a healthy amount of self-confidence—all of which are essential to the development of a satisfied and skilled lawyer.

CHAPTER 3

The Process of Selecting and Applying to Law Schools

This book has described what lawyers do, how they do it, and the important role that law school plays in the lawyer's professional development. What this book has not yet discussed is how a future lawyer actually gets into law school. This chapter is about the law school selection and application process, which requires a great deal of hard work and careful planning. With endurance, the prospective law student will complete the steps this chapter describes and will begin law school, an experience that is likely to bring about significant changes in the individual's life and way of thinking. Although this time can (and should) be exciting, especially for someone who has long desired to become a lawyer, this experience can also be somewhat overwhelming. There are deadlines to consider, various fees to be paid, essays to write, recommendations to secure, and matters to be coordinated with the Law School Data Assembly Service (LSDAS). Furthermore, all of these steps must be taken with care—the applicant must ensure that no slip-ups, such as essays sent to the wrong school, or miscalculation of application fees, jeopardize her chances of acceptance.

Navigating this process requires the applicant to focus on refining many of the skills that he will later employ as a lawyer, including the ability to organize, to multi-task, to communicate clearly, to ask for help, and to act as a professional. In addition, from the application process forward, this effort requires applicants to gather, organize, and analyze facts.

The applicant should regard this process as a crucial step in her professional life and should approach it with the same care and dignity that will be required of her when she begins to practice law. How she presents herself to admissions officers and to those whom she asks for recommendations is just as significant as how she will later present herself to the board of state bar examiners. Indeed, there are similar consequences, at each stage, for intentional misrepresentation: both may affect the future attorney's admission to the state bar of her choosing.

TIMING ISSUES

Timing is important, too. The applicant must determine, for example, when to take the tests that are necessary to apply to law school, as well as when to submit the applications and supporting information that will be required of her. The prospective student should also consider whether the time is right to attend law school at this point in his life and his career. Some students find it beneficial to hold a job before they enter law school. As discussed in Chapter 2, students who return to school after holding a job often find that the perspective they have gained from the experience can be valuable in putting their legal education into context. In addition, by living and working in the state where the student wishes to attend law school, she may be able to establish residency and thereby to take advantage of reduced, in-state tuition rates.

On the other hand, some prospective law students who work for a year or two simply for the sake of getting work experience may come to regard that time as having been wasted. If, for example, the year spent working is not especially productive or does not provide significant, tangible benefits in terms of helping the student to set aside money for law school or providing exposure to a business or professional environment, then she may have simply delayed her career as an attorney. Another potential drawback of taking time off before returning to school is that making the transition from being gainfully employed to being an unemployed student again can be difficult. This adjustment may put a significant strain on the student, or on her family, especially if she has taken on financial obligations—such as the purchase of a home or a car—from which she cannot now easily extricate herself. For other students who opt to take time off between their previous studies and law school, life events such as marriage or divorce, pregnancy, or illness may make deciding whether to attend law school afterward more difficult.

Once a student has decided to apply to law school, he must consider the amount of time that will be necessary to prepare for and take the Law School Admissions Test, subscribe to the LSDAS, discussed below, research prospective law schools, budget loans and savings, secure recommendations and other supporting materials, and obtain and complete law school applications. This process could take an entire year, perhaps from January of the year before his planned law school matriculation to the following January, at which time the applicant will have submitted most of his applications and will be awaiting admissions decisions from the law schools of his choice. Planning the process to require nearly a full year will allow the applicant to be fully organized and, more important, to be fully educated about the options that are available to him. Law school is likely to be one of the largest financial expenditures in most applicants' lives, especially when funds are borrowed that must be repaid with interest. Taking the time to understand how the money will be spent and to make careful decisions is a valuable investment at this early stage in the process. An educated applicant has a clear advantage in choosing a school that fits her and that will best assist her in beginning what should be a satisfying and fulfilling career.

Some people decide to apply to law school rather late in the game. Either they had not previously considered becoming a lawyer or had considered, and rejected, the idea and then revisited it, often after being laid off from or leaving a job for some reason. These individuals can, with some effort, compress the application process into six months, perhaps fewer if they have already taken the LSAT. Parts of the application process can be accelerated with relative ease and no additional expense. For example, at many schools, applications may be submitted electronically. Other steps of the process may be expedited as well, if an applicant can afford to do so. Transcripts may be sent by overnight delivery, or the LSAT may be taken in a distant location that requires the applicant to travel and incur the costs of transportation, and possibly hotel, food, and related expenses, rather than waiting for the next test date in a place closer to home.

Other aspects of the application process generally should not be rushed. For example, an applicant who hurries to take the LSAT without adequate preparation may receive a lower-than-desirable score that will negatively affect her chances for admission to the law schools of her choice. Applicants should also understand that, even if they are able to submit their applications at or before the deadline, a relatively late submission might put them at a competitive disadvantage. At some schools, for example, although the application deadline might be February 1, the admissions committee may already have extended offers to those who applied through the early-decision program, discussed in more detail below, long before February 1. In addition, as early as December, the school may have begun to review candidates from the general application pool, and to make admissions offers to some of them. Each school has a limited number of students it may admit, and each admissions committee is seeking to fill its entering class with students possessing a broad range of experience. Therefore, late applicants are, by definition, in the less-than-optimal position of competing for fewer spots than are available to those who apply early in the process. Many law schools employ a rolling admission system whereby they extend offers of admission to applicants as the committee completes its review of an application or a set of applications. One practical result of such a system is that the school might choose to admit a student with lesser qualifications early in the process, when many places are available in the entering class, but not later. Therefore, prospective law students should give themselves every advantage by starting the application process as early as possible.

Another timing factor to consider involves the early-action programs at many law schools (also called "early decision" or "early admission"). Such arrangements allow applicants with a strong interest in a certain law school to apply for admission sooner—usually by mid-November—than the majority of applicants, and to receive a decision sooner than other applicants. At many schools, applicants agree that, if they are offered—and accept—admission through this program, then they must withdraw their applications from other law schools. Normally, an applicant who has been offered admission pursuant to an early-decision program must notify the school early—often by January—whether he intends to accept. Applicants who have participated in the general application process, by contrast, may be able to communicate their acceptance or rejection of a school's offer of admission in April or later.

Some schools employ stricter admissions standards for early-decision applicants than for those in the general application pool. Because these applicants are being extended an offer of admission before the admissions committee has had a chance to review the entire pool of applicants, the school has a less comprehensive frame of reference in which to evaluate them. A student who seems like a borderline candidate in November may become a standout as the remaining applicant pool is reviewed through March and the school finds that there are fewer strong candidates than were expected.

Other schools apply the same level of scrutiny throughout the acceptance process. At such schools, relatively weak applicants will not be at a competitive disadvantage if they apply for early decision. In addition, most schools will allow an early-action applicant to be considered as part of the regular applicant pool if he or she is not given an early offer of admission. Applicants who believe they might be interested in an early-action program should consider taking the June LSAT exam the year before they plan to begin law school.

There are many benefits to participating in early-action programs. Perhaps most important, if the applicant is fairly sure about which school he wishes to attend, then there is little reason for him to wait for a decision when he could find out sooner. Having an offer of law-school admission in hand will allow him to breathe a sigh of relief and actually enjoy the remainder of his undergraduate or other graduate program or perhaps the last several months of a job. Having this security may allow the applicant to spend a spring or summer semester abroad or to travel, both of which would be difficult if he were awaiting admissions decisions throughout January, March, or even April. For someone who is placed on a wait-list or hold-list, the uncertainty can stretch into August. Moreover, a successful early-decision candidate will not incur the expense of having to apply to other schools. Having his acceptance in hand early will also allow him more time to visit the law school to explore the city where it is located, and perhaps to find suitable housing as well.

The drawbacks of these programs, though few, can be significant and therefore require that the potential early-decision applicant carefully consider whether to participate. At many schools, the decision to accept an early-admission offer is binding. Therefore, if the applicant has also applied to a "dream" school to which she does not expect to be admitted, and receives an offer of admission there just one day after she has accepted an early-admission offer from another school, she may find herself unable to attend her first-choice school. She may also find herself in a difficult position if the financial-aid package from the school to which she applied for early admission is unappealing. Not having received offers of admission and financial assistance from other law schools, the applicant may be less than fully educated, at this early stage, about the scholarships, loans, and grants for which she might be eligible at other schools. Sometimes early-action applicants become so enamored of certain schools that they fail to consider objectively other institutions that might provide a better education or that are more suited to their needs. Another potential drawback, as discussed above, is that some law schools employ more rigorous admission standards for early-admission applicants than for those who participate in the general application process. This phenomenon ultimately may not present a problem if the school allows an unsuccessful early-decision applicant to be reconsidered with the pool of general applicants. In fact, this turn of events could work to the applicant's benefit because the admissions committee already should be aware of the applicant's strong interest in the school.

The following sample timetable illustrates why a law school applicant should set aside adequate time for the application process. The timetable begins in January of the year before the student wants to attend law school (for example, an undergraduate's junior year of college) and ends during the spring before the student's intended fall matriculation. This schedule assumes that the applicant has decided to take the June LSAT so as to leave open the possibility of either re-taking the exam, if necessary, or applying for early decision once she has fully researched her options.

January-March: This is the best time for the applicant to think critically about being a lawyer and what a legal career requires, and also to consider his own reasons for wishing to attend law school. If he ultimately decides to investigate other options, there is still time to change course without having invested much time or money. At this same time, the potential applicant should begin to gather information in preparation for the LSAT, including the dates when private LSAT-preparation classes generally begin, and when and where the June LSAT will be offered. Once he has identified law schools in which he is interested, he should begin to research the application process at each, including how and where to acquire applications. If the applicant is currently a student, he should double- and triple-check the steps he must complete to obtain his present degree, so that his law school matriculation will not be delayed. At this point, the applicant has only two full semesters remaining, plus one summer if necessary, to complete his degree requirements if he wishes to matriculate as a law student the fall after his graduation. This is also the time for the applicant to make an appointment with his school's pre-law advisor to learn as much as possible about the application process, the law schools in which he is interested, and the resources that he will need. Even if he has already graduated, his alma mater may make this service available to him upon request. The prospective law student should also consider seeking lawyer-mentors at this point, whether formally or informally, for advice on the application process and on a legal career generally. This advice may be especially useful for someone who does not have access to a pre-law advisor. Finally, the applicant may want to consider preparing a system to organize the incredible amount of paperwork and numerous checklists that he will need in the upcoming year. The applicant may want to prepare folders that include room for the following:

- ◆ research on schools of interest to the applicant;
- ◆ résumé information;

♦ potential references, including contact information;

♦ copies of recommendations, if they have been made available to the applicant;

♦ copies of honors, awards, or any published material to which the applicant wishes to refer in her application;

♦ employment information, including business cards for various positions the applicant has held;

♦ drafts of narratives, essays, or personal statements; blank and duplicate essay forms;

♦ final versions of narratives, essays, or personal statements;

♦ relevant financial information, including copies of recent tax returns, copies of check stubs, and a credit report;

♦ duplicates or photocopies of applications;

♦ LSDAS materials and the most current *LSAT & LSDAS Registration and Information Book;*

♦ information related to the LSAT, including a secure place for the applicant's admission ticket if she has not yet taken the exam, and the contract with any private LSAT-preparation provider with which the applicant decides to do business;

♦ folders for each individual school to which the prospective law student applies, including room for the actual application, correspondence to and from the school, and any school catalogs or brochures;

♦ miscellaneous research or materials about the cities where various law schools of interest are located;

♦ copies of the applicant's most current transcript;

♦ financial-aid applications and information;

◆ a basic budget outline or financial statement, listing assets and debts; the budget will be filled in with more detail as the start of school gets closer;

◆ records from any other services the applicant has chosen to engage, including résumé- or personal-statement-editing services or a private consultant; and

◆ miscellaneous materials (some schools require a recent physical examination or vaccination records, for example).

February-March: During this time, the applicant should finalize her review of LSAT-preparation courses and decide whether to take one. If she chooses to do so, she might submit a deposit at this time if one is required. A discount may be available for those who sign up early. Alternatively, tuition may be waived if the student agrees to act as an on-campus representative for the program.

March-April: The potential applicant should register for the June LSAT and ensure that she receives all confirmations and informational material in a timely manner.

May-June: During these two months, the applicant should finalize her preparations for the June LSAT. At this same time, the applicant might begin approaching potential references. If, for example, the applicant did well in a spring course, he should ask the professor for a recommendation immediately. By fall, the professor may not remember the student as well and therefore may not be able to provide a strong or specific recommendation.

June-July: During this period, the applicant should take the LSAT exam and receive her test results. She should register with LSDAS, keeping in mind that her LSDAS subscription will expire in twelve months. To receive the full benefit of her subscription, the applicant should become familiar with everything that the LSDAS offers, and its rules and deadlines.

July-August: The applicant should gather her law school applications and research her online application options. If she decides to apply online, she should make sure that she has the necessary computer software. Now is also the time to devise a calendar of all of the relevant deadlines, so as to ensure that applications are submitted on time, including any early-decision deadlines. The applicant should begin to draft or update her résumé, and continue to do so, as necessary, throughout the summer and fall as her grade point average, employment history, or other credentials change, or as she receives any additional honors or awards.

September-November: During this time, the applicant should secure any recommendations that she still needs from professors or employers. She should also ensure that each college and graduate school she has attended submits transcripts to the LSDAS as soon as spring grades are available. This process generally requires that the applicant order and pay for each transcript, then follow up to ensure that the LSDAS receives them. The applicant might also consider attending a law school forum in the nearest large city. There, representatives from various law schools will be available to answer questions about the school or participate in panel discussions on some aspect of the admissions process. An undergraduate applicant should also take the opportunity to talk with admissions officers and other law school representatives who might be visiting her campus. Many law schools report that their admission-committee members are on the road intermittently from July through November. Some larger universities may either hold a "law school visitation day" or jointly sponsor such an event with one or more other colleges or universities. At this time, the applicant should also begin to draft her personal statement and the other components of her application to each school, especially if she wishes to participate in one or more early-decision programs.

October-November: During this period, the applicant should submit applications to any law schools to which she is applying for early decision. In preparing her applications to other schools, the applicant should continue working on the personal statement and other required essays, including any that may be required for scholarships or grants.

November-December: The applicant should submit her remaining applications at this time, well before each law school's deadline.

December-April: While awaiting his acceptances from schools, the applicant should chart the relevant dates for financial-aid decisions. He might also consider obtaining a personal credit report and, if he will be applying for a loan to finance law school, asking any potential co-signer or co-borrower to do the same. The applicant should pay off his consumer debt, to the extent that he is able to do so. Many applicants work during this period of time, so as to pay off their debts and set aside money for law school expenses.

April-through end of summer: During this period, the applicant should review her acceptance offers and make decisions about her matriculation. If she has the time and the resources to do so, she might visit those law schools to which she has been accepted, especially if the school in question has organized a formal visitation period for prospective students. Once she has made her decision, the applicant must indicate to the law school of her choice her intention to matriculate. In so doing, the student should keep in mind each school's deadlines and any deposits that she must pay to hold her place in the entering class. In addition, those applicants who are on a wait list or a hold list with one or more law schools should continue to monitor their status with each school, submitting additional information if it is appropriate to do so. Once the student knows where she will be matriculating, she should complete the process for obtaining financial aid. She should also begin to think about where to live and whether to have a roommate.

August: If the student must move to attend his new school, now is the time to do it. This is also the time to register for the first semester of law school, to purchase textbooks, and to obtain any initial reading assignments. If possible, the new student should take a break before school begins, to celebrate his successful completion of the exciting, but challenging, application process.

Some prospective law students take law-school-application courses. Whether these programs are worth the time and expense is something that each applicant can determine only for herself. In making this decision, applicants might consider whether the information provided in such a course is available elsewhere, perhaps even free of charge. For example, the student could attend a university-sponsored law school informational seminar, obtain materials at a local library, or encourage a pre-law advisor to hold an informal meeting for the purpose of guiding students through this process. If the applicant finds, however, that he needs the level of structure that such a service provides, he might consider whether law school is the right place for him. Much of a lawyer's career is spent organizing and assimilating large quantities of data and drafting written materials, with careful attention to detail, all while managing a personal life. A prospective law student who is overwhelmed by the application process may find similar challenges in the practice of law.

THE LAW SCHOOL ADMISSIONS TEST

The Law School Admissions Test (LSAT) is administered four times each year, usually in June, October, December, and February.

The LSAT tests a person's ability to comprehend written material under time pressure, as well as his logic and reasoning skills.

Test sites are located throughout the United States and in many other countries. The test is not, however, administered in each location every time. A limited number of individuals may take the test in a given location each time. Therefore, the student should consider registering early for the exam to ensure that she is assigned to the test location of her choice.

When a prospective applicant does not take the LSAT examination for which she has registered, this information is included in the LSDAS report that is sent to the law schools to which she has applied. Although there may certainly be legitimate reasons for needing to reschedule, an applicant who has a record of failing to show up for the LSAT is likely to find that this has a negative impact on her chances of admission to the law school of her choice.

Applicants often wrestle with the question of when to take the LSAT. The conventional wisdom is that the applicant should have completed at least three full years of undergraduate work before taking the examination. By this time, the student should have taken upper-level courses in his major, requiring critical thinking and fairly sophisticated analysis. The best time, therefore, for many applicants to take the LSAT is after completing their junior year of college. Doing so allows the applicant enough time to re-take the exam if necessary. By taking the exam in June, nearly a year before the typical fall matriculation date, the applicant should have time to decide whether she wishes to apply to any school for early decision. This schedule will also give her time, once she has received her LSAT score, to determine which law schools are most likely to admit her.

Applicants often ask whether they should re-take the LSAT in an effort to improve their scores. For some applicants, this strategy works: the *LSDAS and LSAT Registration & Information Book* publishes a chart showing the rate of improvement in scores for those who choose to re-take the exam. Any applicant who is considering this option, however, should keep in mind the fact that all of her LSAT scores—not simply her highest score— ultimately will be reported to the law schools to which she applies. In addition, there is always the possibility that a subsequent score will be lower than the first one. Although the information provided by the Law School Admissions Council (LSAC), as referenced above, indicates that many test-takers do find that their scores improve with subsequent testing, the average test-taker realizes only a relatively small increase in score. If the applicant re- takes the examination and does not do significantly better than she did the first time, she may come to feel that the additional time and expense were wasted. Those who are considering re-taking the LSAT may wish to weigh some or all of the following factors: If the applicant tried his best, but still fell far short of the scores he achieved in practice exams under simulated conditions, then he might seriously consider a second attempt. If, on exam day, the applicant's ability to perform was impaired because of illness or a family emergency, then he might strongly consider taking the examination again. If, however, the applicant tried his best, but simply earned a relatively low score, then, without specific information suggesting that additional tries would raise his score, he probably will not benefit from re-taking the exam.

An applicant who decides to re-take the LSAT should employ at least the same high level of energy that she marshaled when she took the examination the first time. She should avoid falling into the trap of believing that, because she has already invested a significant amount of time in preparing for the test, she does not need to do any more work. Instead, an individual's performance on an exam of this type is often affected by that individual's ability to master the mechanics of the exam, including working at a fast pace, a skill that many test-takers develop only through prolonged and regular practice. A test-taker can lose this conditioning after even a few weeks off.

It is important for the applicant and her family to keep LSAT scores and other milestones in perspective. Although the LSAT score plays a very important part in admission to law school, it is certainly not a determining factor in the level of success the future lawyer will enjoy or how highly regarded she will be as both a person and an attorney. Often, during the first few weeks of law school, students will compare LSAT scores and even speculate about their classmates' scores. New law students are encouraged to avoid these discussions. Instead, now that law school has begun, students should focus on developing the skills that will make a difference in their lives as attorneys. What matters most is becoming a credit to the profession. The LSAT score has very little predictive value—perhaps none—in assessing how a future lawyer will conduct herself in difficult professional situations. Instead, the test is a tool that, along with undergraduate grades, provides admissions officers with an educated guess about how a given applicant will perform in law school. After the applicant has been admitted to law school, her LSAT score is of very little importance. Indeed, law students should neither list their LSAT scores on their résumés nor mention a high score during an interview unless that information is specifically requested. Instead, the Law School Admissions Council regards the LSAT score as private information that should be used for admissions purposes only, and law students are encouraged to adopt the same approach. Those who did not excel on the LSAT should take heart: now that they have been admitted to law school, it is their performance there that matters most as they begin their legal careers. Along the same lines, those who scored high on the LSAT should avoid being overconfident: a new, and more important, task has now begun.

Taking practice exams is an important part of preparation for the LSAT. Practice exams, however, are only part of the preparation, and the applicant should avoid becoming too focused on these exercises. During the actual LSAT examination, unlike the practice exams, the applicant will not have access to test answers at the end of the booklet. Some test-takers find that they become dependent on consulting these answers, and are disoriented on test day when the answers are unavailable. Moreover, some applicants take so many practice exams that they reinforce bad habits or unproductive ways of tackling a problem. For these and other reasons, private LSAT-preparation courses control the practice-exam experience by providing instruction on test-taking strategies, as well as the opportunity for students to take, and evaluate their performance on, practice exams.

In evaluating the various commercial LSAT-preparation courses, applicants should remember to be educated consumers. Before making a decision, applicants may wish to speak with representatives from the company offering the course and to review any information posted on the company's Web site. Information about how often the material is updated and who teaches the course may provide useful insights about each program being considered. Insofar as program faculty is concerned, the applicant may wish to know whether the course simply employs its own former students who scored well on the LSAT or, instead, hires individuals with formal teaching experience. It is important that the applicant ask incisive questions, because there are many companies and individuals offering LSAT preparation or coaching, and these companies range in size from a single law student to thousands of professional teachers. The applicant might also consider calling the local better business bureau to find out about the company's history. An Internet search to investigate the owner's professional background and experience, especially if the company is small or newly established, might be a good idea, too.

Actual test-taking strategies for the LSAT are beyond the scope of this book. The LSAT exam, however, is important enough to the law school admissions process that the applicant should consider taking a preparation course rather than simply relying on a history of doing well on multiple-choice exams. The score that an applicant earns on the LSAT can directly affect where he is admitted to law school, as well as how much scholarship assistance is made available to him. Good LSAT-preparation companies can teach the applicant ways to approach each kind of problem to save time and can provide exam study tips. Many applicants, wanting to avail themselves of every advantage in the law school admissions process, find these courses to be valuable.

REGISTERING WITH THE LSAC AND SUBSCRIBING TO THE LSDAS

Virtually all law schools that are approved by the American Bar Association, as well as some that are not, require that law school applications be submitted through the Law School Admissions Council (LSAC). The LSAC uses a subscription service, the LSDAS, to streamline the application process and thereby to save admissions-committee members from having to spend time making sure that applications are complete. As described above, prospective law students subscribe to the LSDAS for a twelve-month period, in order to coordinate the handling of transcripts, letters of recommendation (sometimes), and LSAT scores and the accompanying, non-scored writing sample, through the LSAC. The LSDAS gathers the material and prepares a report for each applicant. Upon the law school's request to the LSAC, the LSDAS forwards the report to the law school to which the student has applied. The report contains the following information:

> (1) A summary of all undergraduate courses and grades, broken out by semester. This summary includes

courses from which the student has withdrawn, as well as schools from which the applicant has taken only a few courses. The LSAC converts the summary to a 4.0 scale for ease of analysis.

(2) Photocopies of all undergraduate, graduate, and professional-school transcripts. The applicant must have a transcript sent to the LSAC from each school attended, even if the student attended the school for only a few courses at night or during high school for college credit. If the student already attended one or more law schools, for instance, then the transcripts from those schools would be included here as well.

(3) All LSAT scores (up to twelve), not simply the student's highest LSAT score, as well as the LSAT writing sample. The report will also indicate whether the applicant canceled an LSAT exam.

(4) Letters of recommendation, if the applicant chooses to have them provided through this service.

(5) A notation indicating whether the applicant has been the subject of any investigation for misconduct.

The LSAC does not make admissions recommendations to a law school, nor does it rank applicants or provide an assessment of any applicant. Rather, the LSAC, through its subscription service, the LSDAS, simply uses a uniform method to coordinate and deliver information to individual law school admissions committees.

The process of registering with and providing information to the LSAC requires the same level of candor and accuracy as will be required of the applicant later in applying for admission to a state bar. Any irregularity in this process, such as failing to provide necessary information or providing false or misleading data, can subject the applicant to disciplinary measures or even prevent the applicant from being admitted either to law school or to a state bar. The LSDAS report will be forwarded to every state bar to which the applicant later applies for admission to practice law. The information contained in the report will be compared with the information provided by the applicant on the bar application, as well as any additional information discovered through the background check that is performed on behalf of the state bar for each candidate for admission.

As the timeline provided above indicates, the applicant should familiarize himself, early in the process, with the rules governing subscription to the LSDAS service. This information can be found in the most current edition of the *LSAT & LSDAS Registration Information Book*, which is published each year around March. Applicants sometimes overlook important information contained in this booklet, such as the fact that the LSAC provides other admissions-related services, sometimes free of charge. For example, applicants can register with the LSAC's free Candidate Referral Service. This service makes certain information about applicants available to law schools that are seeking candidates who meet specified criteria. A law school might, for example, want to increase its minority enrollment and might therefore wish to contact minority applicants through the Candidate Referral Service, to encourage them to consider the school. This service can be of benefit to an applicant, but the applicant must be aware of it to participate. The booklet also contains other information of a more technical nature, including specific procedures to follow in the event that the applicant's biographical or other information changes. It is critical that the applicant maintain a file that is up-to-date and accurate. Thus, this information booklet should be considered required reading.

Applicants need not know the specific schools to which they plan to apply before subscribing to the LSDAS. Rather, each applicant pays the LSAC a certain sum of money for the number of schools to which he or she will apply. Then, the schools themselves contact the LSAC for the applicant's report once the application file is complete. A law school will not request this information from the LSAC unless and until the school has received every other item necessary to complete the application, such as the application form and essays that the student submits to each school directly. The applicant, therefore, should at least have a general idea of the number of schools to which she will apply when she subscribes to the LSDAS. She can, however, always pay to add schools later.

Foreign-educated applicants may not be able to coordinate their application through the LSAC. These individuals should review the *LSAT & LSDAS Registration Information Book* for specific instructions, but should expect that they will have to notify the schools to which they are applying that they are foreign-educated and therefore will have transcripts and recommendations forwarded directly to the schools. Some law schools require that foreign-born applicants take the Test of English as a Foreign Language (TOEFL), a standardized examination of the foreign applicant's proficiency in the English language.

RESEARCHING AND SELECTING A LAW SCHOOL

Narrowing down a list of law schools to which to apply is not an easy task. In handling this process, applicants are strongly urged to consider criteria beyond law school rankings, particularly the annual rankings published by non-legal, national magazines such as *U.S. News & World Report*. These rankings can be useful, especially if the applicant uses the information they provide as a basis for asking her own, focused questions of the schools in which she is especially interested. The applicant should not automatically assume, however, that a top-ranked law school is necessarily a "better" choice for her than a lower-ranked school, especially if the rankings are relatively close to each other. One law school might be a better choice for advocacy training; another might provide a more personalized legal education for a student with learning disabilities. Neither consideration is likely to be reflected in a general system of rankings, although either might be of great importance to an individual applicant. No law school, no matter how highly ranked, is right for every student.

Applying to law school is not only time-consuming, but also expensive. Most law schools charge an application fee, although this fee may be waived on the basis of financial need. Some schools charge a fee for the application itself, whether it is downloaded or sent to the applicant through the mail. There is also the cost of postage to send the application and other correspondence to each school. Visiting prospective schools or even making long-distance telephone calls to speak with school representatives is an additional expense. Furthermore, as discussed above, there is a fee associated with sending an LSDAS report to each school. Due to constraints of time and cost, many applicants choose to focus on a limited number of schools, sending applications primarily, or even solely, to schools where they have a reasonable chance of being admitted.

One applicant developed a list of fifteen schools. At three schools, her chances of getting accepted were slim because of the schools' very selective admissions criteria; at three others, she was very likely to be accepted, based solely on objective criteria. The remaining schools fell somewhere in the middle. This applicant chose to focus, almost exclusively, on getting into the highest-ranked school possible. Looking back, she feels that she chose the right law school, although she now believes her focus on rankings was overblown.

The following are some suggestions for researching and selecting schools to which to apply.

Many applicants begin their law school search with at least some idea of where they ultimately want to live. These preferences may stem from a desire to be near family or simply from having an interest in a certain area. Attending law school in the geographic area in which the applicant wishes to practice is an excellent way to develop connections with other lawyers there. After graduation from a local law school, the new attorney can remain active with her school, whether through an adjunct faculty position or through a leadership position in the alumni association, and enjoy the contacts that doing so provides her. In addition, if the school has a strong local reputation, the lawyer will find that her degree gives her instant credibility with judges, clients, and other lawyers in the area.

One applicant narrowed down her list by region, based on many of the factors discussed above. She knew generally where she wanted to live and thoroughly researched the law schools within a certain number of miles from that area. She then applied to all of the law schools that met her geographic criteria, including a few that were "dream" schools to which she did not expect to be admitted. This approach kept the process simple, but still gave her some options in the event that she did not get into most of the schools to which she applied.

As an alternative approach, many applicants use the Boston College Online Law School Locator (25th to 75th percentile scores) as a beginning point in choosing law schools to which to apply. This tool allows the applicant to enter her LSAT range and GPA range and thereby determine, based on those objective criteria, schools at which she is most likely to be accepted. The Internet site provides links to individual law-school Web sites, as well as other helpful information. Applicants should keep in mind, however, that scores and grades are only one factor to consider in deciding where to apply. The Boston College matrix does not purport to help the student evaluate any of the other very important factors, such as reputation, student life, location, specialties, cost, and the availability of in-state tuition discounts.

Another way for a student to begin her research is to speak with a pre-law advisor, specifically discussing the academic environment in which the student tends to perform best. The advisor is likely to have the benefit of having counseled others who have gone on to law school and reported back about their experiences. Some pre-law advisors are very proactive, actually visiting law schools and speaking at length with admissions-committee members at law school informational fairs. Having access to this kind of knowledge will give the applicant at least a starting point for his research. In relying on this kind of field research, applicants should remember that, although other students may have had good or bad experiences with a given school, the experience will not be the same for every student. Moreover, the culture at a school may change, sometimes dramatically, when, for example, a number of long-time faculty members either leave or retire and a new group comes to power.

The current version of the *Official Guide to ABA-Approved Law Schools* is another useful tool for prospective law students. This book provides up-to-date information on all law schools approved by the American Bar Association, including data relating to tuition, admissions criteria, financial aid, and any special programs that each school offers. Because the information is presented in a uniform manner, applicants can compare schools based on similar criteria. For example, the guide includes the annual tuition for each school, although some schools might publish this information themselves in terms of the amount that is charged per credit hour.

The guides or charts discussed above, although they provide helpful information, can sometimes cause an applicant to focus too much on school rankings or GPA and LSAT scores as the main determinants of where ultimately to apply. Many prospective law students spend significant amounts of time poring over these numbers and sometimes make major decisions based simply on them. As discussed below, there are a number of other factors that applicants should consider as well.

Whether the applicant uses online resources, print media, or word of mouth to gather information about specific schools, having a convenient list of each school's application requirements will help her to stay on track throughout the process. In addition, many applicants find it to be helpful, even at this early stage, to speak with practicing attorneys about their own application decisions and any lessons they learned when choosing a law school.

The applicant may also wish to visit the schools she is considering. Many law schools organize an official visiting day for prospective students. At some schools, an applicant can also enlist the assistance of an on-campus student coordinator who might be able to organize a full day of events for her. When visiting a law school, however, the applicant should keep in mind that she is not in familiar territory. One prospective student caused a mild classroom disturbance by taking a student's seat when she visited a class, not realizing that seats had been assigned and were limited.

Some applicants find it helpful, when considering a given law school, to ask the same question of different people. This exercise might be equally helpful if the applicant gets very similar, or very different, responses from those of whom he asks each question. Consistent answers might suggest a "stock" answer or homogeneous school culture. Alternatively, if the applicant gets vastly different responses from different sources, he knows that he has identified something on which he should follow up. The student may perhaps wish to check in at online comment boards, including the Princeton Review discussion forum. There, students offer varying opinions on particular schools or the admissions process.

The applicant also might consider the quality of the career services office of schools in which he is interested. Many a student will require the assistance of this office in securing his first job after law school. An applicant might consider, for instance, the level of knowledge and experience of the dean or director of the office. He might also find it useful to know something about the number, and the variety, of firms, companies, and agencies where the office has helped to place students. An applicant might inquire about how the school's employment data are calculated. For example, when a school reports that 98% of its graduates are employed nine months after graduation, does this figure include graduates who are employed in non-legal jobs or in paralegal or secretarial positions? In reviewing statistics relating to a law school's recent graduates, an applicant should read critically. When considering statistics on graduates' average salary, for example, the applicant should note whether these statistics include the entire graduating class, the top 10% of the class, or only those students who are employed full-time as attorneys. In addition, the applicant should find out whether the career-services office prescreens the firms and organizations that recruit its students or whether it prescreens the applications and résumés of students who wish to apply for the positions posted by the office. At some schools that do prescreen résumés or allow employers to do this, not all students will have an equal opportunity to interview for jobs.

Geography is another major consideration in the decision-making process for many applicants. An applicant might, for instance, be considering both law schools that are regionally focused and those with a national reputation. An applicant who knows where she wishes to practice might be best served by attending a regionally focused law school, especially if the school has an active alumni network that can assist graduates in securing employment. An applicant who has no idea where he wishes to practice law, on the other hand, might be better served by attending a law school with a national reputation, so that he can move as needed. Personal considerations can be important factors, too. Many applicants choose schools based upon their proximity to the applicant's family and other support systems. This consideration can be particularly important to law students with dependents or other personal obligations.

Some schools take special measures to assist applicants in making their decisions. In addition to the visiting days discussed above, some schools put together a mock class for prospective students, assigning reading beforehand so that applicants can experience the preparation and participation that will be expected of them. Alternatively, a school might hold a reception for prospective students, in conjunction with a local law firm. Such a reception not only provides a forum for the school to answer prospective students' questions, but also allows the law firm to establish name recognition, early on, with these students.

The relationship between students and faculty is another important factor for an applicant to consider in selecting a law school. Some useful information about this dynamic, such as the ratio of students to faculty, is objective and relatively easy to find through public sources such as a national guide to law schools or a school's Web site. Other information, such as the nature of student-faculty interaction and the extent to which faculty members are available to students outside of class, may ultimately be more revealing and is more difficult to gather. Word of mouth from current students and graduates is perhaps the best source of reliable information on these matters. In addition, the formal materials that are provided by a school may contain some clues about the school's culture. A small, regionally based law school that prides itself on its personal interaction and nurturing atmosphere may provide more student-faculty interaction than a national law school that touts its renowned faculty scholars.

Some applicants view a school's bar-passage rate as another important factor to be evaluated. Although one school's having a higher bar-passage rate than another may be significant, it does not necessarily mean that the school with the higher rate provides a better legal education. A nationally oriented school that does not emphasize any particular state's law in the classroom may have a lower bar-passage rate than a regional school where most students study state law and procedure. The students at a regional school may, therefore, be better prepared for practice in that particular state. The students attending a school with a national focus may, however, have received an excellent, perhaps even superior, general legal education. An applicant should perhaps be more concerned if she learns that a nationally oriented school has a low bar-passage rate compared to other such schools. This information may suggest that the school is not providing its students with an adequate foundation in subjects that are typically regarded as a solid, general background for a new lawyer. If so, then that particular school, although prestigious, may not be doing a very good job of preparing new lawyers for practice, which is, after all, the point of law school for most individuals.

Some prospective law students know that they plan to focus exclusively on a certain area of the law or kind of legal practice. These students might have applied to law school for the purpose of furthering their own, established careers or taking over a family member's legal practice or business. Others enter law school knowing that they want to do *pro bono* or public-interest work. For these students, a school's areas of specialization, certification, or concentration may be an important factor, perhaps even a determining factor, in their choice of school. One northeastern law school, because of its unique program in which students alternate between classes and internships, attracts students who have an early, strong interest in working in the public sector. Other schools have reputations for strong advocacy programs, and send graduates primarily into trial practice. At such schools, both the classroom experience and the extracurricular activities are intended to prime students for a career in litigation. The benefits of choosing a school with a strong focus include having access to the expertise of faculty members in areas that are relevant to the students' own aspirations. The reputation of their alma mater in the student's primary field of interest also helps students when they seek or change jobs. Some students change their minds about the area of law they wish to pursue after school has begun. If a student has chosen a school that focuses on an area of law that is no longer of interest to her, then she may have a difficult time finding enough relevant courses to continue her legal education there. For example, sometimes a student's financial situation changes such that a public-interest position is out of the question, at least for the short term. In addition, students often discover that other areas of law interest them more than those that motivated them to choose a particular law school in the first place. Students should take some comfort from the fact that this scenario is very common, even among practicing lawyers. If the student has chosen a school where she can pursue more than one area of interest comprehensively, she should be able to switch gears with relative ease, should she decide to do so.

A prospective student may also actively seek schools where there are professors who are known for their research and publications in a certain area of the law. Opportunities for future employment in that field of law may open up as a result of working closely with these professors. Students should, however, keep in mind that professors sometimes leave schools, whether for personal reasons or in the interest of career advancement. Therefore, a student should not choose a law school based solely on a certain professor's affiliation with the school. If, however, a school has a strong institutional reputation in a particular area—such as law and economics, which is an major area of focus for a number of law schools—then it is likely to attract other important scholars in the event that a professor with a national reputation leaves. In these circumstances, it may make sense for a student to choose this school if she has a strong interest in this area of the law.

A student who is considering a career in public-interest law or another area of the law that tends to be less lucrative than private practice might also consider whether the schools in which she is interested have programs to assist students who choose relatively low-paying areas of practice. Some law schools, for example, provide scholarship money to these students. Others offer tuition-reimbursement to their graduates, with eligibility based upon students' debt-to-income ratio. Alternatively, a student might choose to attend the least expensive law school to which she is admitted, so that she can pursue such a position with comfort.

PART-TIME OR EVENING PROGRAMS

Increasingly, law schools are offering part-time programs that allow students to attend law school on a reduced-hour basis. The students typically complete law school in four years, and generally no more than five or, if a leave of absence is taken, six years. Students take anywhere from eight to twelve credits per semester. The classes may be scheduled during the evenings only, mornings only, or even on a more custom-tailored basis. Part-time students work toward their degrees by attending classes during the fall, spring, and at least two or three summers. Overall, students take a similar number of credit hours as their colleagues in the full-time J.D. program, although there is some variation, depending on the school and program.

The admissions requirements for these programs are generally similar to those for students matriculating full-time, although a few unique programs have more stringent requirements, which are discussed below. Some schools have separate admissions applications for the part-time program, while others have all students fill out the same application and then give them the option, once an offer of admission has been made, to choose either the full-time or part-time program at that school.

A few schools have instituted part-time programs that are specifically aimed towards parents, including single parents who are the sole caretakers for their children. In these programs, students are required to complete their course work in a more independent fashion than other law students, in return for more flexible scheduling and fewer hours spent on campus. Therefore, these programs may have more selective admissions criteria than other part-time or full-time programs. Only a limited number of students may be accepted for these types of flexible programs, but they are well worth investigating for those individuals who want to attend law school, but face personal obligations that limit the time they can spend away from children or other dependents.

The class size for the part-time or evening program is generally much smaller than that in the full-time program, and the students, on average, may have more work or life experience than the average student in the full-time class. The small class size allows for more student participation and interaction with one another.

There are other advantages to a part-time program for those who wish to attend law school, but for whatever reason cannot do so full time. For some, a part-time program allows the student to work full time (so long as the student does not enroll for more than twelve credit hours) and maintain the salary, insurance, and vacation benefits that would otherwise be unavailable. This schedule allows students to maintain a family home, reduce the amount of money borrowed for school, or care for children during the day. There are career reasons to consider such a program, too. The student can maintain a relationship with an employer, who may be paying for the J.D. degree, and use the degree and the courses taken to enhance a business career.

Students participating in these programs should, however, examine a number of other factors, as well, including some potential drawbacks. For example, students should inquire about the faculty members who are teaching the core and elective courses. Are they the same, full-time faculty members who teach in the full-time J.D. program, or are they primarily practicing attorneys and adjunct professors who are brought in for the purpose of teaching night programs? In addition, the degree to which part-time students have the opportunity to be involved in various aspects of student life is important to explore. For example, do part-time or evening students have access to the same programs, seminars, special events, or student activities as do the full-time students?

Access to student bar associations, including the criteria for running for office, is another area that prospective students may wish to investigate. Similarly, participation in law review, moot-court competitions, and other high-profile extracurricular activities is generally made available to any part-time student who has the time and otherwise meets the criteria for involvement, but the prospective student may wish to verify this with the school in which she is interested, before she enrolls.

Part-time or evening students often feel that they lack the time to be as involved in student life as they otherwise might be. These students must remember that, in addition to attending class in a compressed time frame, and attending to work or family obligations, they also must prepare for class in the same manner as the full-time students. A reduced credit-hour load does not necessarily mean that the course load or content is reduced. Often, the personal, professional, and educational demands placed upon the part-time student leave little room for extracurricular involvement.

Balancing job responsibilities with law school and family is another area that can be rife with difficulty. The student's employer will expect the same level of performance from the student as before the student started school. That dedication may mean staying late to complete work assignments or bringing work home. For the part-time student, any additional work responsibility can easily cut into class time or time that should be spent on class preparation or family responsibilities. Missing class repeatedly to attend to personal or professional obligations is simply not an option for participants in most programs—many law schools have attendance policies. In addition, the amount the student is paying per credit hour should be sufficient incentive to attend each and every class. Another potential issue for part-time students is that the student will be required to spend significant periods of time outside of class reading material that is challenging and dense, to say the least. It may be hard to concentrate on the volume of material that must be read and understood after a long day of work or attending to other responsibilities.

In sum, being a part-time student requires much dedication—at least as much as full-time students must bring to bear, and probably more—and the ability to establish and maintain firm boundaries with an employer. As discussed throughout this book, managing the expectations of both employer and family is paramount to successfully navigating the four or so years that it will require for a part-time student to complete her J.D. Legal employers do, however, recognize the tremendous dedication that is required to complete a part-time program and work full-time (in the home or workplace). Thus, the student who chooses to attend a part-time program, and who does so successfully, should emphasize her accomplishment as she prepares her job-search materials. Even more than the graduates of a traditional, full-time J.D. program, the part-time graduate has had the opportunity to refine, during law school, those time-management, stress-management, and task-management skills that will serve her well in the practice of law.

In choosing a law school, prospective students often fail to consider the level of competition among students. At many law schools, competition among applicants does not end once admissions offers are made and accepted. Instead, the culture of competitiveness may continue to grow throughout the first year, when all of the new students are vying to achieve top grades. The pervasiveness of this phenomenon will depend on the culture of the school and the types of student it attracts. The applicant should not rely upon generalizations; for example, a small, private law school attracting students who intend to practice in a discrete geographic area might tend to generate an environment that is particularly collegial—or particularly competitive. Thus, the applicant who is considering this school would be wise to ask specific questions and to make her own observations. The level of competitiveness among students might also depend on whether (and how) the school ranks students or assigns them numerical grades. Some law schools have done away with ranking systems completely or identify only the top student in each class. Instead, the school might provide its students with an estimate of their standing within the class—such as indicating that a student is in the top 15%—for purposes of putting each student's GPA in context for potential employers. Other law schools issue precise numerical rankings for each member of the class. Still others employ a combination of these approaches, giving numerical rankings to students in the top portion of the class, and providing the rest of the class with estimates of their relative standing. At its best, competition pushes each student to do her best; at its worst, however, this dynamic can alienate students from one another and create a culture of rancor rather than collegiality.

If a prospective student has political aspirations, she should consider the degree to which the law schools in which she is interested are known for advancing graduates' political careers. This factor may be important, regardless of whether the student wants to work behind the scenes in national or state politics, or to run for office herself. She should think about the degree to which her affiliation with each institution, as well as her participation in extracurricular activities such as student-body leadership and student political organizations, is likely to better her chances of political success. Some law schools, for example, generate a disproportionate number of national leaders. Others tend to place leaders at the state level. One state law school prides itself on having educated every governor of that state for the past hundred years. At these schools, serving as student-body president or chairperson of a student political organization is often a stepping-stone to a position of considerable power.

The law school's endowment is a factor that few applicants evaluate, but that directly affects student life. An endowment is created when alumni or other donors give money that is intended to be invested, rather than spent when given, for purposes of improving the school's curriculum, physical plant, and special programs. Endowed schools generally spend, for their current needs, only the interest that is generated by the endowment corpus. Law schools with little or no endowment must finance all of their expenditures—long-term and short-term—with tuition and annual gifts. Thus, the budget of a tuition-driven law school can be greatly affected by short-term fluctuations in the number of students choosing to attend the school. Endowment funds may be used for myriad purposes—to fund clinical programs, to establish chaired professorships so as to attract new, nationally recognized scholars or reward those who are already affiliated with the law school, or to provide need-based or merit-based scholarship assistance to incoming students.

Prospective students should also review the required and elective curricula of each law school in which they are interested, noting the range and depth of courses that are offered each semester. For example, an applicant might consider whether practical courses are available to help her develop negotiation skills, learn the basics of local trial practice, or set up her own firm. Ideally, these courses would be offered each semester—or almost every semester—so that the student would have multiple opportunities to enroll in each course. This consideration can be particularly important if the courses in which the applicant is most interested tend to be popular, and therefore quickly oversubscribed. Increasingly, law schools are providing future lawyers with instruction in business skills as well as legal skills. For those students who intend to establish their own practices, either immediately after graduation or later in their careers, these skills can prove to be valuable. Most lawyers, and especially most sole practitioners, will have a client base that consists, either in whole or in part, of individuals who cannot afford high or even mid-level hourly rates. Although this work is not *pro bono*, it is lucrative only if the lawyer can practice with great efficiency and without compromising the quality of the legal services she provides. The attorney may, for example, need to learn to research and draft a high-quality complaint in six hours rather than twenty-five. Some law schools provide specific, practical instruction along these lines. Others offer more general practice-preparedness courses that give students a glimpse of the business end of law practice. Some schools also offer courses that tackle specialized, emerging issues in the law, such as genetics, which may be of practical benefit to someone with an interest in law-and-science or intellectual property work.

The applicant's minority status, or interest in learning in an environment that is socially accepting of his or her sexual orientation, may be another consideration in choosing a law school. An applicant who is of Latin descent, for example, might wish to attend law school in an environment that includes at least some students with the same background. The prospective student might also look for a school that can provide a network of graduates with the same background and interests. These connections can be of great assistance to the student when he is seeking advice or employment. Many students of color or minority status feel that law school is difficult enough without having to break new ground or to forge alliances and networking relationships wholly on their own. For prospective students with these concerns, research is especially important. The applicant may wish to take a close look at student life, both at the law school and throughout the larger campus, if the law school is part a university. The applicant, for example, might research whether the school has a student association that is geared toward her interests. She might also review the faculty biographies on the law school's Web site to determine which faculty members are of a minority background.

An applicant may also have the opportunity to direct questions to a law school or student representative. Sometimes, prospective students can submit inquiries anonymously. For many students, this interaction—whether it occurs anonymously or through personal contact—is their first opportunity to form an impression of each school. Indeed, some applicants choose their law school, at least in part, based on each school's response to their inquiries. For example, an applicant might form an impression from the way in which a law school representative responds to a question to which she does not know the answer. Does she find out the answer and report back to the applicant in a timely manner? Does she help the prospective student to find the answer for himself? Does she fail to follow-up? Although these factors are likely to be important to a prospective student in forming an initial impression of each school, the student should keep in mind that the admissions staff may be overwhelmed with inquiries and paperwork, particularly at times of the year when applications are arriving in droves. Even though these individuals might give short shrift, at times, to applicants' questions, this response may not be indicative of the school's attitude, nor is the admissions office the only source from which the prospective student can seek answers to her inquiries. Instead, if a question is sufficiently important, the student should query a faculty member, dean, or other administrator as well. Besides, once the student has matriculated, her contact with the admissions department will be minimal or non-existent at most law schools.

As always, graduates and current students, especially those of similar backgrounds and interests, can provide applicants with valuable advice. If the prospective student does not know who she can ask questions, then she might seek out former students or upperclassmen. The admissions office can be of assistance in this effort. Even if the prospective student finds that there is no support network currently available on campus for students who share her background or interests, she might choose to start such an organization once she matriculates. The student may be able to enlist a national organization to back up her efforts with resources and support. In addition, the law school or university may be able to provide her with backing. Some students find the dean of student affairs to be a useful ally in such an endeavor.

The prospective law student should strongly consider involving her family, especially her spouse or those who depend on her for support, in her choice of law school, as she would in any other major decision. Student life at some law schools, more than others, is inclusive of those students with strong personal obligations. For example, a law school might organize activities to which students commonly bring their children and other family members. Giving students' families the opportunity to interact with each other can create an environment that benefits the student as well as her family. Family members often express appreciation at being included in the law-school culture and having the chance to form friendships with others who are similarly situated. Not having these opportunities can make family members feel alienated and ignored.

Some prospective law students take advantage of opportunities for distance learning or attend law schools that are unaccredited, provisionally accredited, or tenuous in terms of accreditation. Students make these choices for a variety of reasons that may include everything from limited admissions opportunities to an attempt to accommodate part-time employment or the needs of family members. In evaluating each of these options, the prospective student should consider the reputation of the program, how long it has been in existence, and the placement and bar-passage records of its graduates. When a student chooses a law school that subsequently loses (or fails to achieve) accreditation, she faces difficult decisions, particularly if she wishes to practice law in a state that refuses graduates of unaccredited schools the opportunity to seek admission to the bar. Under these circumstances, she is likely to depend not only on the support of an alumni network, but also on the school's own attempts to correct the accreditation situation. Ideally, the student would have considered these factors, and planned for these contingencies to the best of her ability, when she made her decision to attend the law school.

ADMISSIONS AND ADMISSIONS COMMITTEES

A law school's admissions committee typically is made up of members of the administration, the faculty, and the admissions office. Many law schools also employ a dean of admissions to oversee the process. Once an individual's application is complete and her LSDAS report has been received, some or all of the members of the committee will review her application. They may do so independently, and then discuss the application with other members, or they may do so collectively. Applicants should assume that every word of their application will be read, whether by a staff member who provides committee members with a summary, or by the committee members themselves. Thus, the prospective student should exercise great care in preparing an application that represents her best work. Committee members may engage in a discussion about an individual applicant's strengths and weaknesses. The committee may choose to defer its decision on certain applicants to compare them to the full pool of applicants closer to the admissions deadline. Some admissions committees will automatically admit students who are at or above a particular grade point average and LSAT score.

As discussed in Chapter 2, law school admissions officers evaluate students on some objective criteria—but also on many subjective factors—following their review of the student's application, résumé, and undergraduate record. One objective factor that they consider is each applicant's LSAT score. The LSAT is considered to be a relatively strong—although not foolproof—predictor of academic success in law school. Studies indicate that an applicant's LSAT score is even more accurate as a predictive tool than an undergraduate grade point average. The LSAT does not measure all of the skills that are necessary for success in law school, but it does test an applicant's proficiency in performing certain analytical tasks and evaluating material critically. The LSAT's primary value is that it measures each applicant's aptitudes in a uniform manner and thus provides the law school admissions committee with an easy way to compare candidates.

Because it measures only certain skills and aptitudes, the LSAT is not the only factor that the admissions committee considers. The student's cumulative grade point average, or GPA, is another important, objective factor in each candidate's chances of acceptance. The law school admissions committee may use a formula to combine the LSAT and GPA, so as to avoid putting undue weight on one over the other, and also to give a more balanced picture of the applicant's overall skill level. This system lessens the negative impact that an especially low GPA or LSAT score might have on an otherwise strong application. In evaluating an applicant's GPA, law schools generally take into consideration the reputation and level of rigor of the undergraduate school or schools the applicant attended, as well as the difficulty of the courses she chose to take. Admissions-committee members generally are familiar with the curricula of the schools from which most of their applicants come and understand the level of performance that each grade point average represents, in that context. For example, a student with a B-level GPA from an architecture program at an Ivy League school may be a more attractive applicant than one with an A-level GPA from another school. In addition, an experienced admissions officer is likely to be aware of any significant institutional grade inflation or deflation at a particular school. As discussed below, references sometimes can assist applicants if they mention the student's high level of performance, particularly if the student's grades might not seem impressive to an outsider who lacks information about the program. The person providing the reference might choose to reinforce this positive impression by providing statistics, if she is able to do so, indicating the average GPA range for students in a particular program.

Admissions officers will also attempt to get a feel for each applicant's writing ability and other communication skills. Committee members may, for example, look at the applicant's personal statement, other essays, and LSAT writing sample, as well as take note of specific comments, in letters of recommendation, on these abilities. The technical merit, style, and substance of the essays may also be important factors in the school's decision-making. Furthermore, the committee might be favorably impressed by the fact that an applicant who has earned a graduate degree or is currently enrolled in a graduate program will have additional writing experience from having completed a master's thesis or doctoral dissertation.

The admissions committee may also be impressed by an applicant's demonstrated leadership ability and other intangible personal qualities such as dedication, commitment, problem-solving ability, integrity, and maturity. Because the committee will have little or no opportunity to observe these characteristics for itself, it will look to the applicant's résumé, the personal statement and other essays, and perhaps most important, the letters of recommendation, in evaluating these intangibles. Reviewing the applicant's résumé, for example, committee members might note that the applicant achieved positions of responsibility in the extracurricular activities in which he was involved. The fact that an applicant was entrusted with the leadership of a group or organization, especially a well-known organization such as a national fraternity or sorority, communicates to the admissions committee that others regarded the applicant as worthy of holding a position of responsibility. An applicant's work history may also demonstrate leadership skills. This information may be particularly telling if the individual has worked for a significant period of time before applying to law school, such that he has had the opportunity to advance within the company, or companies, that employed him. The committee might consider, under these circumstances, the individual's history of promotions, as well as his demonstrated abilities in supervising others. In addition, the applicant's academic history may reveal a wealth of information. Absent other explanation, a significant number of withdrawals, incomplete courses, or low grades may reflect negatively on the student's level of commitment and maturity.

A student's racial, ethnic, or cultural background may also be relevant to the admissions committee's decision. This factor might be considered in one of several ways. First, the applicant may have chosen to identify himself, on his application, as being a member of a minority group. The committee may therefore consider that information, as well as the rest of his application, in deciding whether to admit him to the incoming class. Second, information about an applicant's race, ethnicity, or cultural background might come into play through an affirmative-action policy. A law school might, for example, set aside a certain number of seats in the entering class for persons of color or those with a particular ethnic background. Third, more informally, the committee might determine that a candidate's application merits a second look or additional consideration because of his status as a member of a minority group.

Finally, some law schools consider an applicant's state or country of residence in making admissions decisions. For example, a school might set aside a certain number of places in an incoming class for residents of the state in which the law school is located. An applicant who otherwise meets the objective admissions criteria set by the school might therefore be ruled out or in based on residency. A school might also seek to attract individuals from other countries, so as to encourage discussion of, and exposure to, other legal systems.

THE APPLICATION PROCESS

Near the beginning of this chapter is a suggested timetable for preparing to apply to law school. At the beginning, this process involves obtaining application forms and organizing other resources before the applications are due. Ultimately, however, it comes time for the applicant to roll up her sleeves and complete the applications. Actually putting pen to paper (or fingers to the keyboard) is an exciting process that gets easier for many candidates after they have completed one or two applications. To minimize errors, candidates should consider making at least one photocopy of each application form and filling in the required information exactly as it will appear on the final version. This process will allow the candidate to practice answering questions in the space provided and will also provide her with a master copy against which to proofread the final version of the application. Each essay, of course, should be finalized and carefully proofread before it is copied onto the actual application.

In choosing an application with which to begin, the prospective law student should first consider any schools that participate in an early-decision program. Next, the applicant should complete the forms for the schools in which she has the greatest interest. This is the time when her skill in organizing a calendar of deadlines will come into play. Someone applying for a joint-degree program, for example, may be required to complete two applications for a single school or a single, longer application that encompasses both programs. Setting up a master calendar, with each application deadline noted, and then establishing her own, personal deadlines for each step of the process, might be useful. For example, although the deadline for an application might be February 1, the student might decide to have her application in by January 7. Applicants may also find it useful to tell family members or friends about personal, internal deadlines so that external pressure can be brought to bear, if needed. From time to time, family members can inquire about specific applications or about the process generally. Many practicing lawyers utilize a comprehensive, internal deadline-setting procedure as part of their daily routine.

Prospective law students can obtain applications in a number of ways. At many schools, they can be downloaded from the school's Web site, although there may be a fee for this. Some applications can be completed and submitted online. Some applicants use a program such as LSACD-ROM, which allows the student either to apply electronically, sending the application to the LSAC for forwarding to the law schools of her choice, or to print out the application and mail it to each school. The Windows-compatible LSACD-ROM package includes official applications for all ABA-approved schools, as well as searchable data and links providing comprehensive information about many of these law schools.

In addition to these computer-based approaches, all law schools will provide a written application form upon request. Some schools will respond to a telephone request for an application, while others require that requests be submitted in writing. For this reason, the *LSAT & LSDAS Registration Information Book* provides postcards that applicants can send to law schools, requesting information and applications. This source also provides contact information for all ABA-approved schools. Law schools also make applications available onsite for those applicants who visit the campus in person.

Online applications bear particular mention, not only for their convenience, but also because the ease with which they are obtained and submitted may tempt some applicants to adopt a lackadaisical, informal approach in completing them. Some applicants, for example, answer the required questions and compose their essays while online, then simply submit the application without giving it further attention. It is generally unwise to adopt such an informal approach. Instead, prospective law students should treat these applications with the same care that they would employ in completing a written application to be submitted through the mail. In addition, even when the individual submits an application form online, there is often some part that she must mail. The school may, for example, require a hard copy of the signature page. Remembering this final step is important, because the school will not deem the student's application to be complete until it has received all components of the application, even those that the applicant might believe to be unimportant—like a signature page

The Personal Statement and Other Essays

Most schools will require a written personal statement or essay as part of the application. Sometimes, the application includes specific directions about the information that is to be contained in the essay. For example, the school might ask the applicant to describe why he wishes to pursue a law degree, or to discuss those people or events that have influenced his life in a significant way. Law schools consider the personal statement in a variety of ways. The admissions committee wants to see that the prospective student can write a coherent, organized, and thoughtful essay. As this book has emphasized, solid writing skills are crucial to law school performance and to success in the legal profession. By reviewing each applicant's personal statement and other essays, law schools can determine whether the applicant meets at least some threshold level of competency as a writer. The admissions committee may also use the personal essay to eliminate students who do not pay attention to details (such as spelling, punctuation, and basic grammar) or who are seriously deficient in certain technical writing skills.

The essay also provides a glimpse into the personality and values of the applicant, important qualities that often are not otherwise apparent from the data supplied in the application. Admissions officers might be interested in the applicant's goals, motivations, and priorities. A personal statement is the applicant's chance to distinguish herself as an individual, impressing upon the admissions committee those aspects of her life and personality that make her unique, and demonstrating that she will make a positive contribution to the intellectual and social environment of the school. The personal statement, which generally should not exceed two typed pages unless the school directs otherwise, might discuss significant personal experiences that have shaped the applicant, might state why the applicant wishes to go to law school, and might explain why the applicant wants to attend this law school in particular.

Whatever its general direction, each essay should have an identifiable theme. This theme should unify the whole essay, should be communicated in the first sentence, and should be supported by specific points and examples, just as if the applicant were writing a term paper. It is best, however, that the applicant not give too many examples or attempt to make too many points in the short space of two pages. The essay's conclusion should restate its theme. An applicant who is having difficulty getting started might, as with other types of writing, begin by listing her ideas. At this stage, she should simply brainstorm and should avoid rejecting ideas as inappropriate or imperfect. She might begin with the reasons why she is applying to law school. A particular event or individual might have influenced this decision: the applicant might, for example, have watched her parents or a close friend deal with an unfair situation in which a lawyer was able to help. An applicant should attempt to delve beyond the general reasons that are often given for wishing to attend law school—such as a desire to assist the less fortunate—and should provide specific support for her motivations—such as why and how she believes a law degree will help her to achieve her goal.

Once the applicant has spent time brainstorming, she should begin to eliminate some ideas and expand upon others. Writing a chronological life history, for example, is generally not advisable. First, such a history generally fails to convey a cohesive theme. Second, such an essay might be duplicative of the biographical information provided elsewhere in the application or on the applicant's résumé.

Even when personal information is directly relevant to the theme of an essay or personal statement, applicants should exercise sound judgment about the amount and nature of the personal information that they divulge. For example, if the matter is handled correctly, it may be appropriate for the applicant to discuss a divorce or other difficult life event that provided her with insight into the workings of the law. Indeed, many individuals are motivated to attend law school after such an experience. Others believe, more generally, that the best way to avoid being in a position in which they would have to pay a lawyer is to become one. Personal information, however, can easily cross the line of appropriate disclosure. No matter how difficult a former spouse was or how underhanded a former business partner was, the applicant should avoid attacking that person. Instead, she should focus on herself, describing how these events affected her and shaped her desire to pursue a law degree.

Next, the applicant should prepare a rough draft of the essay. At this stage, he need not slow down the process by engaging in self-editing. Later, he can ensure that his word choice is exactly right and that he has used parallel construction. Many practicing attorneys prepare their written work in this way: one attorney begins each major brief or other piece of work product by employing the simplest of structures, writing sentences as elementary as "See Jane run." At this early stage in the writing process, it is more important for the applicant to put her thoughts down on paper than to focus on refining what she has written. Many people find that, once they have given themselves permission to write badly, their ideas will flow freely. Once the applicant has completed a rough draft, no matter how rough it might be, she might consider treating herself to a short break to get some distance from the essay before polishing it.

One attorney reports that she spent six months crafting her admissions essay. She agonized over striking the right tone and highlighting the right information. Finally, in frustration, she scrapped her previous work and, in one evening, wrote an essay that she then submitted after careful proofreading. She reports that this lesson carried over into her practice: there are times when spontaneity yields a better result than does sheer force of will. Going with a spontaneous approach, however, does not excuse the applicant from ensuring that her syntax, punctuation, and grammar are perfect. Indeed, they must be.

In addition to the standard personal statement, the law school may either require or allow other essays. These essays, which may be on a specific topic determined by the law school or one of the applicant's choosing, are sometimes used, along with the personal statement, for making admissions decisions. Sometimes, however, these essays serve a different purpose: most commonly, evaluating the applicant as a candidate for scholarships and grants if he is admitted to the law school. Additional essays may also be required of an applicant to a joint-degree program. The applicant should ensure that these essays do not contradict, in tone or in substance, his personal statement. To prevent such a conflict, the prospective student should read all of his essays together, especially if they were written several months apart, and consider what the written essays, taken as a whole, communicate about him.

Because the content of a prospective law student's application can be central to the admissions process, a cottage industry has emerged in which individuals and companies provide assistance to law school applicants in preparing their applications, résumés, and essays, and in seeking letters of recommendation. Some of these companies walk a fine line between writing material for the applicant, which the applicant is then to revise before submission, and simply providing the applicant with editorial guidance. An applicant who is considering one of these services must remember that no third party can or should write a personal statement or essay for her. She should assume that the law schools to which she is applying would frown upon such a practice if the schools were aware of it. These services can be expensive, and providers vary greatly in terms of their experience and competence. The applicant should know exactly what she is getting for her money, when the services will be provided, and what happens in the event that she is unhappy with the end product. For example, some organizations will provide supplementary editing services to fine-tune the final product, but may limit the extent to which they will do so.

Recommendations

Another important part of the law school application is the written recommendations that are submitted by people who know, and are in a position to evaluate, the applicant. The role of a personal reference is to vouch for an applicant by explaining how she will make a positive contribution to the law school community. Law schools often require two recommendations, and some specify that both must be academic references. Other schools permit or require more recommendations, but require that at least two be from a professor or teacher. The law school may indicate how it will treat recommendations beyond the required number. If the applicant chooses to include additional recommendations, then she should ensure that they truly add something to her application.

Securing academic recommendations might prove to be difficult for applicants who have been out of school for many years. These applicants should make every effort to obtain academic references but, if it is not feasible to do so, might be permitted to seek recommendations from past or current employers instead. If the applicant must use professional references, he should choose someone who is in a position to comment on his intellectual capacity and analytical ability, and perhaps also to give specific examples of projects that the applicant handled successfully. For this reason, unless a law school specifically requests them, letters of recommendation from personal friends or family members are not usually appropriate or helpful.

Sometimes, the person who is supplying a recommendation will ask the applicant to prepare a statement for him to sign. In such a case, the applicant might first provide the person who is serving as a reference with a copy of her résumé and personal statement. Then, before preparing a draft recommendation, the applicant might ask the person what he would be comfortable saying about her. The applicant should be sure to prepare the draft, and submit it to the person who is providing the recommendation, well in advance of the due date. The draft, of course, should be error-free and ready to be signed and submitted to the school.

Even if the person who is serving as a reference does not request that the applicant herself prepare a draft recommendation, the applicant should supply him with a copy of her résumé and her personal statement. Doing so will ensure that he has access to pertinent, up-to-date information so that he can be specific and accurate in making his recommendation. This information may be particularly helpful in refreshing the memory of a professor who taught the student either some time ago or as part of a large class. The applicant might also consider giving him a copy of her transcript, a list of the schools to which she has applied, and perhaps even a copy of each school's request for recommendations. With this information in hand, the person who is supplying the recommendation will have a clear idea of what the admissions committee wishes to know about the applicant so that he may address these subjects fully. A thoughtful applicant might also prepare a cover letter that highlights particular items about which the person providing the recommendation can speak directly, such as the length and breadth of his acquaintance with the applicant.

A letter of recommendation should set forth the provider's professional background and the nature and extent of his knowledge of the applicant. For example, he may have employed the applicant and supervised her performance on a particular project. The employer might specify, for example, that the applicant worked for him for more than two years and that he had the opportunity to observe her work ethic, writing ability, and business skills. Next, he should focus on the particular characteristics or abilities that make the applicant a strong candidate for law school. As with the applicant's own personal essays, specific examples carry more weight than a list of generalizations, however glowing. Thus, the person who is supplying the recommendation should avoid using general descriptions that could apply to most applicants. If he is in a position to comment on the applicant's fitness for the legal profession, he should be encouraged to do so. Finally, it will assist the admissions committee if the person who is making the recommendation can provide a frame of reference for the applicant's achievements. For example, if he is a professor in the applicant's major, then he can give some background about the level of difficulty of that program, and can compare the applicant's performance to that of the applicant's peers.

Résumé

Most law schools will require each applicant to submit a current résumé with his completed application. From the résumé, the admissions committee will get a feel for the applicant's work history and level of employment responsibility, academic honors and awards, extracurricular activities, and community involvement. The applicant should take great care to provide specific, useful information on the résumé. This résumé may be lengthier than that which he would submit to a potential employer: unless the law school specifically states to the contrary, applicants should not be overly concerned with keeping the résumé to one page, as they might when seeking employment. The applicant can therefore use this opportunity to highlight interests, achievements, and experience that might not otherwise be brought to light.

Personal Consultants

Increasingly, companies and individuals have begun to offer their services as personal consultants to law school applicants. Most of these consultants have some personal experience with the admissions process, whether as an admissions-committee member, a former dean of admissions, or an employee of the admissions office. A lawyer who worked for the admissions office while she attended law school owns one such company. Some benefits of these services include receiving a high level of personal attention and an insider's view of the admissions process. As with essay-consulting services, the applicant might consider the possibility that the law schools to which she is applying would look with disfavor upon the close involvement of a third party, if the schools were aware of it. Even if the law school did not object to this assistance, the applicant should assume that her own reputation is tied to that of the consultant, who is essentially acting as her agent, even though the consultant may be doing so behind the scenes. The applicant should therefore take care to choose a consultant who is credible and who is not known to "package" applicants so as to mask problematic underlying issues.

The Completed File

The next step is to finalize and submit the application. Many schools provide applicants with a checklist, either in hard copy or online, to remind them of each item that must be included to complete the application file. Regardless of whether such a checklist is available, however, it is up to the applicant to ensure that her application to each school is complete. For example, some schools might require, in addition to an undergraduate transcript, a certification from the undergraduate dean indicating that the applicant graduated in good standing from the institution. Although this detail might seem to be unimportant, without it the application file is incomplete, and will not be considered by the admissions committee. In addition, an applicant who waits until the last minute to request this certification—or her undergraduate transcript—might discover that she owes the undergraduate institution money. (Overdue library books or parking tickets are frequent sources of this particular woe.) Many schools will refuse to provide the requested information until the balance is paid.

Many law schools will notify applicants when their admissions file is complete, indicating that the application will then be under active consideration. The applicant should file this confirmation away, in case it is needed later should any questions arise about the timing or completeness of her application.

Wait List

Sometimes, a law school will place an applicant on a wait list or hold list. These lists operate differently at different schools. At some schools, being on a wait list might mean that, should other applicants to whom an offer of admission has already been made decline to enroll, then the wait-listed applicant may be admitted. In such a circumstance, the wait-listed applicant might not find out until August whether there is room for him in the class. This uncertainty, of course, may put him in a precarious position in terms of securing financial aid and housing, purchasing books, and making personal plans. Other schools have a hold list whereby they defer decision on certain applicants, pending the receipt of complete statistics on the make-up of the applicant pool as the application deadline approaches. It may be that the school does not want to admit too many Caucasian males with a degree in political science, for example; thus, depending on how the applicant pool shapes up, a student on the hold list may find that his application returns to active consideration.

An applicant who is notified that she has been placed on either list should consider keeping the admissions committee abreast of any significant achievements or awards that she receives after her admissions file is complete. These letters should be brief, but should highlight each recent accomplishment and reaffirm the applicant's continuing interest in the school. In addition, an applicant who is on a hold list might choose to write a brief, supplementary letter addressing any weakness in her record, such as a period during which she earned low grades. She should not, however, simply reiterate information already contained in her application; these materials will likely be read again anyway if the admissions committee reconsiders her application. Furthermore, an applicant who has been placed on a wait list or hold list might wish to submit an additional letter of recommendation. If she does so, she should ensure that the letter adds something new to her file, rather than duplicating comments that have already been made. It might be particularly helpful if the new letter highlights a recent achievement.

Acceptance

An applicant may communicate his acceptance of a law school's offer of admission in writing, verbally, or in any other manner indicated by the school. The acceptance, however, may not be effective until the applicant pays a deposit. The deposit holds a place for him in the entering class and is often credited toward tuition. The applicant should strongly consider accepting an offer of admission early so that he can begin to focus on securing appropriate financial aid. As discussed in Chapter 4, there is generally more money available, in the form of scholarships, grants, and loans, at the beginning of the admissions process than toward the end. In addition, an applicant who accepts an offer of admission early may have an advantage in finding good living accommodations either on-campus or close by, and perhaps in selecting a roommate.

TRANSFER STUDENTS

Sometimes, whether for personal or academic reasons, a student may wish to transfer to another law school to complete his second and third years of study. Generally, law schools have a separate application process for transfer students. The school will be especially interested in how the student did in his first year of law school, as measured by his GPA and the reputation of the school from which he is transferring, as well as the reasons why he wishes to transfer.

The school will also consider the availability of places in its second-year class. This variable may be affected by the school's own attrition rate. The transfer student will need an official law-school transcript, a letter of good standing from the dean at his current school, letters of recommendation, including at least one from a professor at his current law school, and an active file with the LSDAS containing his LSAT score and other information.

There are both positive and negative aspects of transferring. The advantages generally revolve around the student's reason for requesting the transfer in the first place: perhaps the student wanted to attend a nationally known school but was unable to secure admission until she attended another school and improved her class rank. If she is admitted to her first-choice school as a transfer student, she will now be exactly where she wanted to be, albeit via a circuitous route. On the other hand, the student may not feel that she is truly part of her new class, since so many close law-school friendships are formed during the stressful first year.

The admissions procedures for a visiting student, also called a transient student, generally are similar, but less onerous, than those for a transfer student. A visiting or transient student attends classes at another law school for a period of time, typically one semester or one year, but still receives a diploma from his "home" school. A student might do this, for example, to take courses that are of particular interest to him, but are not available at his current law school. Alternatively, a student might take this step in order to study with a well-known professor at another law school.

Often, students wonder whether it is appropriate to discuss personal or family reasons for requesting a transfer. So long as the reason is not trivial, but is a serious, concrete one, such as the transfer of a spouse, or a child custody situation, personal reasons are acceptable grounds for transfer and are among the most common reasons that students make such requests.

This chapter covers a lot of ground, which is simply a reflection of the significant amount of information that must be sorted through and evaluated by a prospective law student. It is important to maintain a "present-sense" orientation throughout the process: this period, as stressful as it may be, is not just about pre-admission or pre-law activity—this is the applicant's life. Life does not begin once the applicant has been admitted to law school, has successfully earned the J.D. degree, or is admitted to the bar. Thus, striving to keep life choices in perspective and achieve a healthy balance is just as important now as it will be later in law practice.

CHAPTER 4

Loans, Scholarships, and Other Ways of Financing Law School

Determining how to pay for law school should be one of the very first considerations for a would-be law student. For most people, however, financing their J.D. degree ranks so low on their list of priorities that it will be considered only after completing an undergraduate or master's program, taking the LSAT, and finishing the application process. Some even wait until they have been accepted to the two or three top law schools of their choice before figuring out how to pay tuition and living expenses. Financing law school is a challenge for many prospective law students of any age.

Compounding the problem are factors somewhat outside the students' control. Undergraduate costs have increased greatly, so more people are applying to law school with substantial undergraduate debt. Moreover, parents of current twenty-something-year-old college and law-school students were not necessarily focused on saving for college in the early 1980s, as are many parents of children born now. Then, Americans did not have the wide range of educational-savings or tax-deferral vehicles that are available today, nor did many parents anticipate that education in the twenty-first century would be so expensive. As a result, prospective law students, and sometimes their parents, have a formidable financial task ahead of them, marked by preparation, planning, and finessing. Compared to other graduate-school programs, law schools offer fewer grants, scholarships, and stipends for tuition and living expenses. In addition, many students find that working is a less-than-desirable option for full-time students that is even prohibited by some schools during the first year. Even after the first year, many schools limit the number of hours that a full-time student may work in outside employment. Law students are left with few choices other than borrowing the money and applying for every available scholarship or school grant.

There are options, of course, and this chapter examines the process for obtaining financial aid, and suggests some sources of funding that may merit further inquiry. In addition, the chapter discusses the relative value of attending a less expensive, and potentially less prestigious, law school as compared to a more expensive, but higher-ranked school. Although each individual ultimately must make this decision for himself, weighing personal considerations as well as financial ones, there are practical factors that may help guide the decision.

Approximately 80% of students finance their law school education by borrowing money. To state the matter plainly, this money must be paid back, with interest. There may be some exceptions for those who become disabled, for example, or who are eligible for loan forgiveness because they have chosen a career in the public sector or with a public-interest group. Each loan program has its own exceptions, and some loan programs may not have any exceptions or loan forgiveness at all. The repayment terms for loans vary, but typically students can defer payment of the principal and interest for a period of time, usually a few months, following graduation from law school. In addition, some companies allow borrowers to pay only interest for the first six to nine months after graduation. Besides family, there are three main sources for loans: the federal government, private lenders, and individual schools. Students generally combine one or more of these sources to make up for any amounts not covered by scholarships or grants.

GRANTS AND SCHOLARSHIPS

Students can also finance a portion of, and in some cases all of, their law school tuition with grants and scholarships. The best source for these scholarships and grants is the law school the student is planning to attend. Schools generally offer some combination of the following: need-based scholarships, need-blind scholarships, and scholarships based on a student's minority or qualifying disadvantaged status. Some scholarships are sufficient to pay a student's entire tuition bill, as may be the case when a school is trying to attract a top candidate. Indeed, some scholarships include books, living expenses, and spending money as well. Others may cover only a portion of the tuition, or only living expenses. Schools recognize that top students will have other options in terms of attending a more prestigious school, but may consider a less highly ranked school if the right amount of scholarship money is offered. Applicants should keep in mind that some schools are better endowed than others and thus have more money available to give to students. As discussed earlier, this is a reason why the school's endowment, although not considered by popular rankings, is one of the factors a student should examine when deciding upon a school.

When a successful applicant receives her acceptance letter, it may state the amount of money the school is willing to give and/or loan to the student. If the applicant is considering enrolling at the school, she may want to set up a telephone interview immediately with a school financial advisor, or, if so directed by the school, an admissions officer, to discuss the financial package that has been offered to her. Acting quickly is in an applicant's best interest: more scholarship and grant funds are available, and schools have more room to expand the lending package, if appropriate, for applicants who express their interest early.

The admissions or financial aid officer will be the applicant's best source of information on how to obtain money from the school, once the applicant has been accepted. The limited availability of these resources—both monetary ones and the time, energy, and attention of admissions officers—is another reason why applying for admission and financing, and accepting an offer early, can work to the student's advantage.

One first-year law student discovered that her new roommate had a higher LSAT score and higher grade point average, but less scholarship money, than she did. The difference was that this student, unlike her roommate, had applied to both the school and private sources for everything for which she was eligible, and did so early. She noted that some students did not even realize that scholarship aid was available, even from the schools the prospective students were planning to attend.

Schools provide both formal and informal loan counseling; students who are borrowing money should take advantage of this resource. Administrators can, for example, help applicants work through a budget and can provide a better understanding of the cost of living in the area where the law school is located. Moreover, administrators can tell the applicant what other students have experienced in terms of the cost of books and other living expenses. During these conversations and meetings, the applicant should keep in mind that she is making a first impression on these officers and administrators at her prospective law school. The applicant should always be polite and express appropriate appreciation for the assistance received. The applicant may also wish to inquire as to whether she can apply for grants or scholarships in addition to any financial aid package already offered to her and, if so, what the relevant deadlines are for those applications.

Some schools will invite students to interview or compete for certain scholarships. Often, the scholarships are prestigious full scholarships that are awarded to just a few members of the entering class. The school might provide scholarship-focused essay materials to be completed by all applicants once they have been accepted. The essays might, for example, focus on why the student deserves or needs (depending on the criteria for the award, which might be merit-based or need-based) that particular award or grant. Certain students may be selected for an interview based on those essay responses or simply by virtue of having certain grades and an LSAT score at or above a certain level. The interview may occur in one of a few ways. The school may have a scholarship weekend, during which it invites a select group of prospective students to visit the school and interview for the scholarships. The school will generally pay for travel, lodging, and meals during the course of the visit. Applicants attending such events should take care to be friendly, rather than competitive, with other interviewees they encounter during the visit, remembering that these individuals may be their classmates for the next three years. Alternatively, the school may arrange for a telephone or in-person interview. In either case, applicants may speak with members of the admissions committee, which could include professors and administrators, possibly even those at the dean level. In addition, applicants may meet with and be interviewed by second- or third-year law students, themselves often recipients of the very scholarships for which the applicants are interviewing.

Preparation is necessary for any scholarship interview. An applicant may not be sure of his own level of interest in a school, especially his "safe school," but that does not mean that he should approach the financing or scholarship process casually. Indeed, the safe school may offer him a package that would be difficult to turn down. Before being interviewed, the applicant should learn something about the school and its philosophy, and should be able to articulate solid reasons why he is considering attending the school. Scholarship applicants should be sure to review their initial applications so as not to contradict anything set forth there. Most important, applicants should learn why a particular scholarship was instituted and how it is funded. For example, a scholarship may have been established to honor a distinguished graduate of the school. Learning something about the award's namesake and why the donor thought he or she was worthy of such an honor will demonstrate the applicant's level of interest as well as his resourcefulness. In addition to honoring important individuals in the life of the law school, scholarships may be funded by an alumni group or even a local special-interest foundation. The applicant should research the basic criteria for the scholarship, both financial and academic, and, at some point in the process, find out whether the scholarship is awarded every year and whether the student can lose his funding, if, for example, his economic situation changes or he does poorly in school. Some of this information will be set forth in the materials produced by the school, and some might be obvious, such as in the case of an award that is named in honor of a former Supreme Court Justice who is a graduate of the school. Additional information may be garnered from school administrators, others in the admissions office, or previous recipients of the award. This is all part of the continuing dialogue that the applicant should have with the school. These scholarships, especially those that provide full tuition or more, are prestigious and impose a responsibility on the recipient that goes beyond doing well academically. Recipients of "flagship" scholarships, as the most prestigious scholarships are sometimes called, are expected to reflect the ideals, virtues, and standards set by the namesake, or, at the very least, not embarrass themselves or the school, both while attending law school and after graduation. In addition, it is appropriate for the recipient of a scholarship to acknowledge his debt of gratitude, both by writing a simple and timely thank-you note to the person or organization funding the award, each time the award is renewed, and by contributing to the law school, to the best of his ability, throughout his career.

An applicant who is being interviewed in person should be sure to bring both formal interview clothes and business-casual wear. A suit may be required for the formal interview. Although the school is likely to clarify this matter ahead of time, it is nevertheless wise to bring the suit as a precaution, just in case it is needed, to ensure that the applicant is not embarrassed by being inappropriately dressed. When a suit is not required, men should wear khakis or casual dress pants, and a shirt with a collar, or other business-casual wear. Women have a bit more leeway, but should avoid tank tops, spaghetti straps, short skirts, denim of any type, or other clothing that could be considered inappropriate by a conservative interviewer.

Once a school finalizes its list of scholarship recipients, the recipients may be invited to the school for a different type of "scholarship weekend," a gathering of prospective students who have been awarded scholarships and are considering or have accepted an offer of admission. This is an excellent opportunity to meet potential (even likely) classmates in an intimate setting. Also, attendees will have the opportunity to interact on a one-on-one basis with professors, administrators, and upperclassmen with whom they are likely to develop relationships once they have enrolled as students. Some schools schedule these trips when classes are in session and allow prospective students to sit in and listen. Again, the prospective student's dress and demeanor are very important. This is often the first opportunity for the student to make an in-person impression on future classmates and professors. One student remarked that, at a scholarship weekend she attended, several women dressed inappropriately and seemed not to realize the importance of the event. Even though attendees at this second kind of scholarship weekend have already been awarded scholarships, they should prepare as if that were not the case. It is respectful and appropriate to know something about the school and the particular award and to review, at least once, the student's own admission materials. Attendees should be prepared to ask thoughtful and detailed questions about the school and student life; the factors for school selection that are listed in Chapter 3 provide some ideas along these lines. Learning what areas of scholarship interest each participating professor, for example, might provide a basis for interesting discussion. Along the same lines, attendees might ask professors how they came to the school to teach and whether they attended law school there. Just as when the student is later searching for a job as a lawyer, these are important opportunities to gather information and should not be passed up lightly.

Besides law-school-based scholarships and grants, there are very few other sources of scholarship money. This situation is very different from those facing students applying to undergraduate or other graduate school programs, where alternative sources of funding are more readily available. Given this situation, students are encouraged to pursue foundation scholarships, interest-based grants, or corporate scholarships from either a parent's employer or a corporation located in the student's hometown. For example, some major employers draw their workforce from a relatively small population area. Such employers often give back to the community by offering scholarships or sponsoring competitions, both of which are opportunities that may be available to prospective law students. This type of financial aid requires leg-work on the part of students; such aid is generally not advertised on the major scholarship-source Web sites, although it may be reported to local high school or college counselors. Another example of alternative funding might be a public-interest group that wants to encourage students to pursue a law degree with an emphasis in a particular field. To be eligible for the award, a student might be required to take classes in a certain area of the law or at least express an early interest in the field. Special-interest bar groups sponsor scholarship competitions for law students that may provide additional money during law school. For example, one bar organization that is open to lawyers of a certain ethnic background sponsors a writing competition for law students and awards a monetary prize.

The Loan-Application Process and Organizational Tools

Applying for loans, both federal and private, requires the same level of diligence as seeking scholarships and grants. A methodical and informed approach is the best way to tackle financing law school through this source of funding, as well. Chapter 3 discussed the importance of having a calendar to mark all appropriate deadlines, including test dates, application dates, and follow-up dates. All relevant financial deadlines belong on that same calendar. For example, applicants for federal loans, and generally for school-funded loans as well, must complete a Free Application for Federal Student Aid (FAFSA). The FAFSA can be obtained online, or from any law school or college. Anyone who is even thinking about applying to law school should visit the Web site http://www.fafsa.com to get information about relevant deadlines. Reviewing that site will at least provide the individual with a sense of the type of information that will be needed and when it must be submitted. Two other organizational tools may be of assistance as well: (1) a chart with room to fill in the lending criteria and terms for each type of federal, private, or school loan; and (2) an estimated budget. The chart could have headings such as the following:

> (1)   Lender and contact information;

(2)   Type of lender (for example, federal government, private company, or bank);

(3)   The maximum amount that can be borrowed per semester or per year;

(4)   The combined maximum amount that can be borrowed over the course of the student's legal education;

(5)   Any minimum amount that must be borrowed;

(6)   The amount of any application fee or transaction fee;

(7)   Criteria for eligibility (for example, having to exhaust federal loans first, the need for a co-signer, a minimum number of credit hours, or United States residency);

(8)   Any events that might change a student's eligibility, such as dropping to part-time status, marriage, divorce, or receiving an inheritance;

(9)   Any requirement of a credit check for the student and for any co-signer;

(10) Any minimum ratio of debt to income and other assets;

(11) The application deadline;

(12) The dates on which disbursements are made (to ensure that payment will arrive in time for enrollment each semester);

(13) The interest rate and, if the rate is variable, how that rate is calculated;

(14) The loan-repayment term;

(15) Any penalty for early repayment;

(16) The length of the post-graduation grace period, if any;

(17) Whether deferrals are available and, if so, under what conditions;

(18) The availability of any interest-only programs, which allow the student to delay the repayment of principal;

(19) The availability of programs that allow the borrower to skip a monthly payment, often called a "payment holiday";

(20) The availability of loan consolidation, a matter that is likely to be of particular importance to students who obtain funding from more than one source;

(21) The availability of loan forgiveness for students who enter public-interest fields, or in the event of the disability or death of the borrower;

(22) Whether payment is guaranteed if the student becomes disabled;

(23) Whether reapplication is required each year and, if so, whether the student's financial picture and scholastic performance will be evaluated anew each time;

(24) The terms under which a borrower will be considered delinquent; and

(25) Any interest tax deductions available for this type of loan.

The second tool, the budget that is discussed in Chapter 5, should be kept on hand for all discussions with financial aid officers. Early on in the process, the applicant will not have all the information necessary to fill out these charts or the budget. As she researches information on the Web and talks with various financial aid counselors, however, the chart and budget will get fleshed out. The applicant should keep these tools handy and should use them to ask the right questions and to stay focused. To keep the tools current, and therefore useful, the applicant must be sure to update them as needed on information about the loans themselves or any change in the student's personal or financial situation.

An early step for a student preparing to finance a legal education, perhaps even before the student prepares the organizational tools discussed above, should be getting her financial house in order, as well as that of any potential co-signers for a loan, generally a parent or other family member. Private lenders, especially, may require a co-signer. The prospective student should also decide early whether she will be emancipated from her parents for tax purposes and, if so, must then be sure that her parents follow through when they file their yearly taxes. The benefit to parents of using a law student as a tax deduction may be outweighed by the later cost to the student; i.e., less financial aid may be available to her if she is treated as a dependent for financial aid purposes. Next, the prospective student and her potential co-signers should each order a copy of their respective credit reports. There are many free online sources from which to obtain copies, but the student and co-signers should be sure to secure reports from one of the three main credit reporting services and should ensure that these requests themselves do not show up as multiple inquiries on their credit histories, a situation that may make it difficult to obtain credit. For example, experian.com and myfico.com provide information from all three bureaus. Upon receiving the credit reports, each party must double-check every item to be sure to clear up all mistakes, no matter how minor. That process could take weeks, even months, and should be initiated as early as possible.

While putting these organizational tools together, it is important that the prospective student pay off as much consumer debt as possible. He or she may need to get an extra summer job or work overtime to do so, and might even move in with parents if this option is available. It is important to whittle down this debt now, before law school begins. One student started law school with $1,600 in credit card bills. She was unable to pay this amount off all at once, so she made minimum payments until she graduated and started working as a lawyer. The cost to her of items she purchased for $1,600 nearly tripled by the time she paid off the debt.

During this early stage of financial planning, the prospective student should consider making an appointment with a college pre-law advisor, even if the student graduated from college many years ago. These counselors can be valuable sources of information and advice—after all, it is in the school's best interest to see its graduates succeed so as to bring the school recognition and eventually to allow students to contribute financially to the school. These counselors may know of good sources of financial aid to which they can direct prospective students, and can also introduce students to other students who have obtained funds from alternative sources. There is no need for an applicant to generate all of this information independently— finding out where others have obtained money in the past and applying to these same sources can be excellent time-savers.

Next, the prospective student should update her résumé. Private lenders, particularly banks, may require a résumé. The applicant should also gather her tax records, most recent W-2 forms, and, if she is currently employed, any recent pay stubs. This may be a good time to fill out the FAFSA application and get a PIN number as all of these documents will come in handy when preparing the application for aid.

Then, the applicant should step up the level of her research. She should look at the specific requirements for the federal and private loans that she is considering. There are significant differences between them, a few of which are discussed below. The most comprehensive and accurate information, however, can be found on the Web. Aid programs are constantly being expanded, interest rates change frequently, and students today have options that were not available even two or three years ago. The following sites and telephone numbers should provide a good start:

www.FAFSA.org
www.salliemae.com
www.GradLoans.com
www.nelliemae.com or
www.nelliemae.com/loancenter/loan_overview.html
www.accessgroup.org
www.wiredscholar.com
www.alternativestudentloan.net
www.academicedge.chelafinancial.com
www.fastweb.com

Other resources are the Fleet 1st Loan (888-FLEET-GO), TERI Alternative Loan (800-255-8374), and Nellie Mae EXCEL (800-634-9308) programs.

The federal government provides loans such as the Stafford Loans to undergraduate and graduate students. These loans generally have low interest rates and flexible repayment options. In addition, interest may not accrue while a student is still in school. Furthermore, these loans do not require a credit check. A FAFSA is required, however, and a new FAFSA must be filled out each year if the student wishes to re-apply for these loans. There is a maximum amount that a student can borrow under the Stafford program and this maximum includes undergraduate federal loans. Loan eligibility may change during the year, perhaps as a result of marriage, divorce, or inheritance, and this could affect a student's ability to secure federal loans.

There are some significant differences between federal and private lenders, some of which may make one option more or less desirable for any given student. Private lenders typically require that both the borrower and any co-signer or co-borrower be creditworthy. These loans will affect the co-signer's debt to asset/income ratio until they are paid off. Any default or late payments by the student will also directly affect the co-signer, who will receive ample notice if the student has failed to make payments. Private lenders ultimately will look to the co-signer for repayment of the entire loan in the event of a default. Some private lenders, like the country's largest, Sallie Mae, require that a student exhaust federal sources of loan money before seeking a private loan. Other lending criteria vary by lender, particularly in the case of a bank or smaller lending institution.

Law schools provide loans to students as well, including emergency loans to students who require money immediately. The repayment term may be shorter for these loans, but the interest rates are generally favorable. Also, some students have found that schools are somewhat more forgiving than third-party lenders when a loan payment or two is missed. Schools, for example, may wait longer than third parties would before reporting a delinquency to a credit bureau. As schools will remind borrowers, however, these grace periods should not be abused. Repayment directly affects the school's ability to provide loan funds for other students. The financial aid office can walk an aid applicant through each of these borrowing options as part of an overall financing plan.

THE IMPACT OF DEBT AND CONSEQUENCES OF DEFAULT

Many students fail to realize that the indebtedness they incur in law school is likely to affect their lives, and their options, for five, ten, or even twenty or more years after graduation. More than a few law students have entered school with aspirations of working as public defenders, public-interest attorneys, judicial clerks, or district attorneys, only to be forced to abandon those dreams, sometimes forever, by the financial pressures their high debt levels impose upon them. Such choices can be even more difficult if the student has a family that has sacrificed for her to attend law school and is now looking forward to living more comfortably once the student has graduated. One lawyer, married to another lawyer, has described the couple's large monthly payments to their respective student-loan companies as "a mortgage without the house." Similarly, students with high loan balances should expect their borrowing power to be limited until the loans are repaid. These limitations may include purchasing a less expensive home or car, or not being able to purchase a home or car for some time, or at all. A monthly payment that seems manageable may become onerous once the student realizes that that is the *minimum* sum he must pay each month for the next several years. Many students comprehend this reality for the first time only when they receive the fat packet of repayment coupons in the mail, several months after graduation.

Default is to be avoided at almost all cost, and there are many ways to do this. Most important is regular and frank communication with lenders. Suppose, however, the unthinkable happens—the student defaults! The situation might evolve as follows: Letters with escalating threats begin to arrive from the lender, and there are daily telephone calls. The situation may deteriorate such that the borrower is afraid to open the mail or to answer the phone, so she does neither. One day, a package arrives in the mail from a law firm. The letter begins, "You are now in default on your student loans. . . ." The letter demands immediate payment of a sum with too many zeroes. The recipient does not have that much money. In fact, she does not have much money at all. Her heart sinks. What can she do now?

First, the borrower must realize that she is not alone. Unfortunately, the default rates on law-student loans are simply staggering. Second, she must swallow her pride and deal with the situation. Normally, default means that the lender has required another institution, called the guarantor, to make payment on the defaulted loan, such that it is now the guarantor, rather than the original lender, who owns the debt. Although many guarantors will contact defaulting borrowers to discuss the situation, the borrower must not assume that this will happen, but should take the initiative to find out who the guarantor is and to contact the guarantor.

Some borrowers will find that collection agencies or private law firms, rather than the guarantor, make contact first. Defaulting borrowers who are being harassed by collection agencies would be well advised to research relevant state and federal laws to find out what their rights are, as borrowers. For instance, there are circumstances under which a defaulting borrower may insist on dealing directly with the creditor. In addition, state and federal laws provide some protection for an individual's privacy and may protect the borrower from calls at work, calls to friends and relatives, and other embarrassments.

When the borrower has contacted the guarantor, the borrower should indicate her intention and willingness to pay her debt. She should also expect that the amount of her debt has now increased—default generally triggers additional fines and perhaps even a higher interest rate. (Readers who are outraged and disheartened by this fact will usually find that they agreed to these very provisions when they applied for the law school loans.) If the initial contact was by telephone, the student may wish to follow up by mail, even certified mail. If possible, the borrower should establish a working relationship with a single contact person who represents her creditor. In addition, when the borrower promises payment, she simply must follow through, every time, on time. Making contact and establishing rapport and trust is critical to repairing a damaged credit history.

Sometimes, defaulting borrowers will be permitted, after a certain period of making timely payments post-default, to enroll in a loan-rehabilitation program. Although the terms of each program vary, these programs can offer an excellent opportunity to rehabilitate credit. The borrower must be patient: one defaulting borrower was allowed to enroll in such a program after just a few months, after having been in default for a very long time. Another borrower in the same household, however, having defaulted more than a year later, waited almost two years to enter a rehabilitation program, patiently making her loan repayments as promised each month until she was accepted by the program. (In fact, when this borrower first contacted her creditor post-default, she was dismayed to learn that there was no rehabilitation program in place at that time. Her patience eventually bore fruit, but the process was a slow and difficult one.)

In sum, there is life after default, and borrowers who have defaulted on law-school loans can and do go on to get past the experience, to rebuild their credit, and even to purchase homes. The process, however, requires much time and effort, as well as tremendous patience and honesty, both with the creditor and with oneself.

ADDITIONAL OPTIONS

Some students have opted to pay for law school by taking out a home-equity loan. There may be tax advantages to doing this, which are less novel now that interest on certain federal student loans is tax deductible (provided that a graduate is within the eligible tax bracket). The bottom line, however, is that following this plan means that the student's house is on the line in the event of a default. Missed loan payments in the first few years after graduation and immediately following a job change are relatively common, and a home-equity lender may not be nearly as forgiving as educational-loan providers tend to be. The stakes are high for these types of loans and, given the wide range of educational-loan products that are now available, prospective students should consider home-equity loans as a last resort.

The United States military offers several education programs that a prospective law student may want to consider in financing her legal education. Although these programs offer excellent financial and training advantages, only prospective law students with a genuine interest in being lawyers for the military should take advantage of them. Under these programs, the student, upon graduation, will serve in the armed forces as a military lawyer for a period of perhaps three to six years. He or she may initially be assigned to work as a prosecution attorney or as a defense attorney, and usually ultimately will do both over the course of his or her career. One military lawyer, who actually handled only prosecution matters, gained extensive trial experience in a short, three-year period. During that time, this lawyer handled all phases of matters going to trial, including locating, interviewing, and preparing expert and lay witnesses. Some of the trials involved either high-profile matters or, more typically, matters in which a person's liberty was at stake. He finds that his trial-preparation experience as a military lawyer is directly relevant to his current civil practice. He acknowledges, however, that not all civilian lawyers value his experience as highly as he does. Thus, he found that his plan for financing law school ended up being an excellent move for his career development.

An excess-leave program may be a good option for prospective law students who are currently on active duty in the military and are of relatively high rank. Under such a program, an officer may receive a pro-rated share of military pay and benefits while attending law school. For example, the officer might be paid for every day that he or she is not in law school (Saturday, Sunday, holidays, and summer), which would mean that the officer would make more money and receive a greater share of benefits during the second and third years of school when he or she is not in class every day. In return, the officer would be expected to work during the school year, perhaps at a local recruiting office. During the summer, the officer would work as an intern at a military base, assisting the military lawyers there.

Another option available through the military is a funded law program in which an officer (generally one who has served for two to three years) attends law school as his or her sole job for three years. In this program, the military pays all tuition costs and the officer receives full benefits. After graduation, the officer becomes a military lawyer for a period of perhaps six years.

Students who are not yet enlisted but are nonetheless considering military careers can take advantage of other programs through which the military will provide financing for their legal education. As young lawyers, they will leave school with little or no debt and will be equipped with excellent training for later careers in civil or criminal law if they decide to leave the military. One lawyer who received post-law-school legal training in the military remarks that the education he received there was very good. He notes that a federal judge, a former military lawyer himself, taught courses to the military lawyers in the program this lawyer attended.

Outside the military, a student's current employer may be another option to help finance law school. Some larger companies provide funding for employees to pursue graduate degrees, even law degrees. Often, these options are available at companies that are large enough to accommodate an employee who is making a professional change. The company might, for example, have a large legal department and think highly enough of the employee in his or her current position that it may be willing to finance all or part of the employee's legal education. Generally, in such a situation, the employee must commit to work for the company for a period of time, or risk having to pay back the tuition money. The employee may be required to work during the day and attend law school at night or part-time. Students taking advantage of such assistance must not, however, run afoul of school and ABA restrictions on the number of hours students are permitted to work. Another option is for an employee to use a law degree to enhance the job he or she currently holds. For example, it may be in a company's best interest to send one of its scientists to law school in order to handle patent filings in-house, or at least to assist or to supervise the patent lawyers in that process. Prospective law students should not rule out funding from smaller employers, either. One oil company executive felt confident that a law degree would advance his employer's interests, even though the company was relatively small. His continuing dialogue with his employer has been positive. If an employee is sure that he wants to attend law school, and is willing to divulge that information to his employer early enough to establish a plan for the employee's continued involvement with the company, then it may be appropriate to ask the employer for tuition assistance, even if no such formal plan is in place. The employee should be sure, however, that he has marshaled the facts in support of his position and can show how and why his getting a law degree would benefit his employer. In return for such assistance, the employee should be prepared to agree to work for this employer for a certain period of time, during or after law school, or both.

Another way to finance a law school education, at least in part, is to work and attend school part-time or work while attending school full-time. Part-time programs are discussed in detail in Chapter 3. Chapter 14 contains some suggestions for students who are attempting to study for the bar exam while working part-time or full-time; many of these same considerations are applicable to the student who works while attending law school.

Applicants to law school are sometimes faced with fortunate, but difficult, choices when they are admitted to more than one institution. Chapter 3 discussed many of the factors applicants may wish to consider in making choices about where to apply and where, ultimately, to enroll. Financial considerations may also come into play in an applicant's decision. Many students, for instance, find themselves choosing between a large state university's law school and a smaller, private university's law school. Some of the differences that may exist between these schools were presented earlier—the level of personal attention, class sizes, interaction with faculty, and so forth. The financial component of this decision-making process is also an important consideration. A student who is able to get an in-state tuition rate at a large university is likely to be saddled with less debt, sometimes far less debt, than her counterpart at a private university. In addition, this student may not face the expense of relocating to attend law school. Even tuition at a large, out-of-state university may be less than the tuition charged by a private law school. Thus, an applicant might be wise to consider choosing a state university, in circumstances in which money is an important limiting factor, over a private university, even if the private law school has a higher ranking.

Likewise, and as discussed above, most law schools will offer merit-based scholarships to some of their top applicants to encourage them to enroll. These law schools know that top applicants will be offered admission at higher-ranked law schools, but hope that a full or partial scholarship will convince the applicant to enroll. Applicants who are offered such scholarships are well advised to consider them seriously. Some scholarships even include stipends for living expenses and for books, items that can otherwise drive up the cost of a legal education considerably. In addition, some schools provide special events or other privileges for merit scholars. Furthermore, applicants offered merit scholarships are generally those students whom the law school most expects to be successful students and, later, successful attorneys. These predictions are often, although not always, correct. Chapter 9 discusses many of the extracurricular activities that are made available at most law schools. Some of these activities are limited, at least in part, to students whose grades place them at the top of the class. Therefore, if the law school's early prediction of an applicant's success is an accurate one, the student may find that she enjoys opportunities that would perhaps not have been available to her if she had chosen to attend the higher-ranked school without a scholarship.

Financing law school is a subject that deserves as much attention from the student as does the initial decision to attend law school. The reason is simple: how the student chooses to pay for his legal education is likely to influence greatly his quality of life and the nature of his practice as a lawyer. Financial considerations often influence, for example, where an attorney is employed and for how long, as well as the types of matters he handles. Thus, this chapter has encouraged prospective law students to educate themselves, early in the application process, about the available options for financing law school. These include traditional means such as scholarships, grants, and loans, as well as less-traditional options, including funding some or all of law school through the military, with the assistance of an employer, or by working full-time and attending law school part-time. Moreover, this chapter has stressed that researching and applying for scholarships, loans, and grants early will increase the student's chances of obtaining the most optimal funding, and also give the student an early perspective on which law schools are within her financial reach.

CHAPTER 5

Making the Transition to Law School

Thoughtful preparation before school begins can make the difference between a productive first semester of law school and one that is harried and distracting. The transition to law school begins as soon as the student receives her acceptance letter and begins planning to enroll. Some students will be coming directly from undergraduate school or from another graduate program, while others will be returning to school from the workplace. Recent college graduates may have the advantage of fresh study habits, but are often surprised by the level of commitment and professionalism that law school requires. Those who are coming to law school from another career may have the comparative advantage of greater discipline and an understanding of the concept of opportunity cost, but may find some difficulty in readjusting to the different rhythm of an academic schedule. This chapter will help both groups prepare for law school.

PROFESSIONAL TRANSITIONS

New law students who are leaving behind jobs should take care to make that transition as smooth as possible, both for themselves and for their former employers. Some students will have a particular incentive to handle this situation professionally, especially if they plan to go back to the same employer or same industry after graduation. It is not uncommon, for instance, for a private-firm paralegal to attend law school and then to return to his firm as an attorney. In some situations, the student may continue to work for the firm during school. Even those students who do not expect to return to their employers—or even to the same line of work—should navigate this transition with professionalism.

Taking care to wrap up loose ends will not only make the employee look good, but will also minimize the number of disruptive telephone calls and e-mails she is likely to receive once school begins. Some students find the transition to be easiest if their replacement has been hired before they leave. Even if the student leaves without knowing who her replacement will be, she should organize the files she is leaving behind, prepare memoranda to let the next employee know the status of her work, and notify clients, if appropriate, about who their new contact person will be.

If possible, a new law student who is leaving behind a job should take more than a week off between the end of her employment and the beginning of school. Although it may be difficult for many students to do this, both financially and logistically, this brief reprieve can provide valuable time for rest and mental preparation. This short break is likely to be one of the few times in the new law student's life when she has the luxury of *not* living under the specter of work that needs to be done.

FINANCIAL PLANNING

All new law-school students should prepare a reasonable, comprehensive budget before beginning school, regardless of whether their legal education is to be financed through private savings or through loans. Students who are leaving behind jobs are perhaps more likely to have significant savings than those who are fresh from other academic programs; at the same time, however, those students who are accustomed to being gainfully employed may need to be more disciplined in scaling back their lifestyles to meet a student budget. Shopping and dining out are two activities that many new students find most difficult to curtail. This can be especially difficult for those who find both activities to be particularly tempting when they are under stress.

The student who is financing her legal education through loans should not automatically borrow as much as the lender will permit. Too often, students think of borrowed money as "free" and forget that they must pay every dime back, with interest, for many years to come. The less the student borrows, the less she must pay back. In addition, many law-school graduates find that their employment choices are limited by their debt load; some enter law school hoping to take public-interest jobs only to realize, three years later, that they are in so much debt that they must take the highest-paying job available, rather than the one they really want. Budget planning can help the student minimize her debt load—and maximize her freedom of choice in employment after law school ends. For the same reasons, students should seek to minimize or eliminate revolving debt such as credit-card payments before law school begins.

The student must set out to prepare a budget that she can live with for the next three years; although she is likely to fine-tune her budget as the years progress (textbooks almost always cost more than expected), the basics are likely to remain relatively constant—food, shelter, and tuition. Creating a budget that includes *everything* from a computer to holiday gifts can be a daunting proposition; thus, the following list of possible budget categories may be of assistance:

Tuition
Mortgage or rent, including deposits and application fees
Renter's or homeowner's insurance

Utilities—electricity, gas, and water, including deposits

Moving costs, such as truck rental

Groceries and personal needs

Clothing, including appropriate interview clothing and accessories

Books and supplies

Computer and related accessories

Car payments and car insurance

Car maintenance, gas, registration, *ad valorem* taxes, and parking fees

Health insurance

Student-loan payments

Other consumer-debt payments

Telephone (including cellular telephone) and Internet service provider

Travel expenses

Entertainment (cable television, movies, dining out, gifts)

Child-care and costs associated with children, such as diapers, formula, clothing, toys, and tuition

Emergency funds ($500, for example)

LOGISTICAL PLANNING

With regard to some of these items, including health insurance and computer supplies, the student may find that she can get a more favorable price through the law school than would otherwise be available to her. Many schools contract with private insurance providers, for example, to give their students competitive rates. Some law schools also work with one or more computer manufacturers to develop a package, including both hardware and software, that is well-priced and tailor-made for their students. In any case, the school is likely to be an excellent source of information to help the student prepare a budget. Some schools will provide their students with basic information such as names and telephone numbers of apartments owners/brokers, utility companies, and local grocery stores. Even so, most students who are new to a community find that they benefit from having a few days to a week to become familiar with their new surroundings and to unpack before school begins.

COMPUTERS

In deciding whether to purchase a new laptop computer for law school, the prospective student should first consider any package or special deal that the school may offer. As stated above, some schools contract with computer manufacturers to make custom-built machines available to their students. In addition, some law schools actually require that students purchase laptop computers. Even where this is the case, however, the extent to which the student uses the computer on a daily basis is likely to depend on her own preferences, including her skills as a typist. Students who are attempting to figure out their own hardware and software needs for law school should not only speak with a representative from the school about the school's requirements or recommendations, but should also inquire as to whether they will be permitted to take their examinations on computer. Students should also think about whether they expect to take their class notes on computer or by hand. The pros and cons of each are discussed in Chapter 7. A student who wants to take notes on her computer in class might opt for a light-weight laptop, while a student who chooses to use her computer only outside of class might either choose a more powerful, less portable laptop, or might spend the same money, or less, for a high-powered desktop computer with a large screen to minimize eye fatigue. Again, the prospective student should assess her own study habits and preferences when making this decision.

Many students are already proficient in computer use by the time they begin law school. Even so, law school has its own software and databases, such as LEXIS and Westlaw, two computer-based legal research systems, and eAttorney, a Web-based legal-recruiting-management service and software, that students must master. There are also a number of Internet law-school resources, many of which may be made accessible to the students through the law-school or law-library Web sites. Some of these may be available off-campus, while others may be limited to on-campus or intranet use. Valuable law-school Web site resources may include faculty biographies, course Web pages and listservs, interview and employment information, information about guest speakers and lectures, calendars of academic and extracurricular events, links to other law- and entertainment-related sites, tips for handling examinations or getting oriented to law school, and library resources.

PROJECTING A PROFESSIONAL IMAGE

In preparing for school, the student should also gather her official contact information. She is likely to be asked to provide the name of an emergency contact person, along with that person's address, telephone number, and e-mail address. The student should choose a contact person whose telephone number and relationship with the student are unlikely to change—a parent is often ideal. When possible, the student should select an address where she will feel comfortable receiving report cards and official correspondence from the school for the next three years, as well as alumni publications after her graduation. The same rule of thumb applies to the telephone number that the school will have on file for her.

Finally, in selecting an e-mail address, the student should choose one that is appropriate for official purposes, and for her résumé and job applications.

A ROOM OF ONE'S OWN?

For many students who are moving to a new community to attend law school, selecting a place to live is a major part of the transition. In assessing housing needs, a student from out of town is likely to rely heavily on information supplied by the school. Some students will have the option of living on-campus. On-campus housing is often less expensive than that available in the private market. Many students find it convenient to live in a dormitory, especially if a meal plan is available, and especially during the first year of law school, when the student's time is likely to be particularly limited; indeed, many students who must live off-campus choose apartments that are close to campus for this very reason. Students who live on-campus or close by benefit from having more law students nearby for study purposes, from the camaraderie that develops among students who spend time together, and from spending less time commuting. However, those who commute by rail or subway often find that they can study en route. Some students prefer to live away from other law students in order to have an escape from the high-stress environment of law school.

Choosing whether to live with another law student is a very important decision for single students. Many students enjoy living with others who are in the same position, and roommates often become close friends. Furthermore, the financial benefit of shared living expenses is obvious. At the same time, many first-year students are likely to find themselves experiencing more stress than they have before, for a sustained period of time, and they may not wish to share this experience with another person in the same position. Strangers who live together sometimes have truly horrible experiences with a roommate's misbehavior, unpleasantness, noise, or differing values. Some schools will assist students in meeting others who are likely to be compatible as roommates (which is also a good way to connect with classmates in advance of school), offering questionnaires and other means of identifying similar likes and dislikes; other schools will leave this matter for students to handle on their own. Regardless of what the student ultimately decides about having a law-student roommate, this matter is one that should be carefully considered.

LAW-SCHOOL ORIENTATION AND PRE-LAW "BOOT CAMPS"

Some schools offer a law-school preparation course, either free of charge or for an additional fee. Indeed, some schools either require all students to attend or require those students who were admitted with grade point averages or LSAT scores below some cut-off point to attend. There are also commercial law-school preparation programs available from companies such as Law Preview and Bar/Bri. Some run for only a single day, while others run a week or more.

Although each course is different, most include some or all of the following components: a preview of core law-school courses, lectures on study skills and other tactics to ensure day-to-day law-school success, and practice examinations. These courses may acquaint students with some of the "nuts and bolts" matters discussed in Chapter 7, including note-taking, outlining, briefing cases, time-management skills, and the basics of legal research and writing. The courses also often offer valuable suggestions, pointing out the merits of reading ahead when possible, for instance, and informing students that, contrary to what they may have expected, longer exam answers are not necessarily better than short ones. In addition, insofar as the courses offer a substantive preview of law school, their organizers often take special pains to attract professors who are both interesting and skilled in presenting the material at a basic level. Most courses are intended merely as an orientation, not as instruction that would in any way substitute for the classroom learning that awaits the student in law school; indeed, the organizers of some courses take care to warn participants not to become over-confident. Furthermore, each student must ultimately tailor her learning and class preparation to her *own* professors and law school. Nevertheless, this kind of orientation may help students in navigating their first semester of law school.

First-Year Core Courses and Other Required Courses

A typical first-year curriculum is likely to include some or all of the following courses. Each of these courses may last one semester or two, depending on the law school. If the course lasts for two semesters, there may be an examination each semester, or one exam at the end of the year. Even if an exam is given each semester, some schools count only the grade on the second examination. Some schools provide for first-semester or first-year students to take their classes on a pass/fail basis in order to reduce the level of stress.

Civil Procedure. In Civil Procedure, students learn the mechanics of managing a civil suit, from choosing a forum and filing the complaint to final entry of judgment. Most civil procedure courses focus on federal courts. Although some courses address the appellate process, the primary focus is often on proceedings at the trial level.

Criminal Law. In Criminal Law, students often focus on both the Model Penal Code and the common law, also known as judge-made law. Students are introduced to the elements of a variety of crimes, along with the mental state that is required to convict a defendant of each. In addition, many criminal-law courses focus on the purpose of criminal punishment.

Torts. The very word "tort" is a new one for many first-year students. A tort is a non-criminal wrong. In other words, when a person commits a tort, she will not be prosecuted by the state and subject to criminal penalties such as a fine or imprisonment. Instead, she may find herself as the defendant (the person or entity being sued in a lawsuit) in a civil action brought by the injured person or that person's legal representative. If the plaintiff (the one initiating the lawsuit) prevails, normally the defendant must pay a sum of money that is determined by the jury or other fact-finder. Intentional torts and negligence are usually the major categories to be considered.

Contracts. Civil Procedure, Criminal Law, and Torts are all matters of public law; students learn about the standards that have been set by society in each of these areas. Contracts and Property, by contrast, deal with the law governing private agreements. Although the courts and legislatures intervene at the margins, where the parties have agreed to a transaction that violates public policy, for instance, the primary role of the courts in this area is to discern and enforce the transaction to which the parties agreed, not to create a transaction for them.

Property. There is significant overlap between Property, the second of the private-law core courses, and Contracts. Both apply to the purchase or lease of a home, for instance. Property law usually covers such issues as possessory rights in personal property, real property, future interests in property, marital property, and landlord-tenant relations. This course may also examine public-choice issues such as restrictions on the sale of body parts, discrimination in land use and sale, and noxious or dangerous uses of land.

Legal Research and Writing. Legal Research and Writing is a critical part of the "basic training" that law students receive in preparation for practice. This course provides students with the tools they need to put what they have learned from doctrinal courses into action. Chapter 11 provides a comprehensive introduction to researching and writing on legal issues.

Many law schools also require students to take some or all of the following courses during their law-school careers:

Legal Profession or Professionalism. This course is one of the most useful ones in law school. Students learn how to handle some of the thorniest issues they will face in practice—those involving the relationship between attorney and client. In this course, students are introduced to the basic standards of professional conduct that will be expected of them, under relevant state law and the American Bar Association's Model Code of Professional Responsibility or Model Rules of Professional Conduct. Students learn how to handle client money and confidences properly, how to avoid conflicts of interest when representing multiple parties, how to withdraw from a case when necessary, and how (and whether) to represent a client who has been untruthful.

Constitutional Law. This is one of the courses that students often anticipate with pleasure because it includes so many famous cases and gives students an opportunity to discuss the very bedrock of our legal system—the United States Constitution. Students will learn the principles of federalism, including which powers reside in the federal government and which are given to the states. In addition, students learn the functions of all three branches of government. Other major areas of focus include some of the most important constitutional concepts, such as due process, equal protection, and judicial review. At many schools, extensive treatment of the First Amendment and the many amendments relating expressly to criminal law is reserved for other courses.

Business Organizations or Corporations. In this course, students examine the law of the formation, operation, and dissolution of business interests, including such important business concepts as agency, partnership, corporations, and limited liability companies.

Evidence. Evidence is one of the most practical courses for a student who is interested in a career in advocacy. The course may focus solely on the Federal Rules of Evidence or may encompass relevant state law as well. In Evidence, the student will learn how to put together his case for trial, assessing each aspect of testimony and each item to be introduced, for its relevance, admissibility, and weight. The student will also learn how to make objections, as well as how to respond when objections are made to his own evidence.

Trusts and Estates. This course introduces students to estate planning, wills and will substitutes, the consequences of the failure to make a will, trusts made during life and for administration after death, and fiduciary duties.

Federal Income Taxation. This course focuses on the federal government's taxation of income. Students learn the basics of earnings, deductions, exemptions, and credits.

Commercial Law. Commercial law covers some or all of the ten articles of the Uniform Commercial Code, or "UCC." The Uniform Commercial Code is a joint project of the American Law Institute and the National Conference of Commissioners of Uniform State Laws, both influential private groups that include well-known private practitioners, professors, and judges. The UCC has been adopted, in some version, by every state legislature in the country and provides the basic laws by which companies do business, including contracts for the sale or lease of goods, checks and promissory notes, documents of title, and secured interests in personal property.

Even those law schools that do not require these courses may list them as "recommended" courses or "bar-preparation" courses. The entering student should understand, however, that she is not really taking these classes to prepare for the bar. Rather, as discussed in Chapter 14, the bar examination has its own guidelines and is best approached with its own strategies.

KEEPING THE FIRST YEAR IN PERSPECTIVE

Although law students sometimes lose their perspective on this matter, they are not taking courses to earn grades. Grades may indeed be a means to an important end—finding satisfying employment as an attorney—but it is important not to confuse the means with the end. Many students enter law school excited about the practice of law, only to have their enthusiasm dulled by the daily pressure of class preparation and the pervasive pressure to earn grades that are good enough to help them get the jobs they want. Although this book contains a great deal of information that is targeted at helping the student navigate these intermediate goals, the student is encouraged not to lose sight of the ultimate goal. Indeed, this concept is what the practice of law school is all about: law school is ultimately for the student. Although she must, during her three years of law school, complete a number of tasks (including required coursework, class preparation, and exams) because the school requires her to do so, she should remember to keep her own goals in mind at the same time. If the student is interested in advocacy, legal history, jurisprudence, or international human rights, then she should seek to tie whatever she is learning to her own interests. Even if this endeavor requires additional time on the front end, it is likely to help the student learn the information more comprehensively; most people learn best when they have some personal reason to remember what they have learned. It is important that the student be able to look back on her three years of law school and see not only tasks she accomplished at the behest of someone else, but also a list of skills she acquired and experiences she enjoyed for her own pre-professional development. Some students are best able to keep this focus during law school by writing down some goals before school begins. A student who has asked herself, "Why am I in law school? What am I spending tens of thousands of dollars per year to learn?" is likely to look for ways to get her money's worth each day. Even during the busy and hectic first year, a student can attend lectures on campus given by prominent speakers, look up the occasional interesting law-review article that is noted in a textbook's footnote, talk with classmates about how the law is represented in current events, or simply make an appointment to talk with her professor about her own professional interests and aspirations.

SETTING ONE'S OWN MORAL COMPASS

A prospective law student must prepare herself in ways that go beyond finances and logistics: students must also take charge of their moral and ethical development as it relates to the practice of law, even before law school begins. A student who tries to check her own morality at the law-school door is likely to find herself extremely dissatisfied, both with law school itself and with her own day-to-day experience of being there. Practicing lawyers face the same difficulties and must, likewise, learn to go about their own daily work in a way that is consistent with their personal sense of ethics and morality. In addition to becoming aware of their own, internal moral sensibilities, law students must learn the external standards of ethics that will govern them as lawyers and put those into application. The practice of law requires a great deal of personal responsibility on the part of each individual attorney. Law students, like practicing lawyers, need not assume that the professors and practicing attorneys with whom they are in contact are necessarily acting with the utmost integrity and should not follow these individuals blindly. Instead, any future attorney must assess any questionable issues for herself, according to the internal and external standards of ethics and morality that govern her conduct.

BALANCING LAW SCHOOL AND LIFE

The face of today's law student is changing. The percentage of female law students now, for the first time, is greater than that of male students. In addition, today's law student is generally older, if only by a few years, than the law student of previous generations, and is therefore more likely to be married or have children. Especially for students with family obligations, the law-school experience requires superb time-management skills and purposeful planning to make matters go smoothly. The following are some thoughts gleaned on this matter from lawyers and law students alike. The strategies reflected here are not necessarily unique to law school, but they do represent choices that helped some law students achieve a measure of balance.

Although many of the suggestions below are directly targeted to individuals with children and/or a spouse, these considerations are important to every law student. Students who are responsible for the care of an aged parent, are in other committed relationships, or are living near family or close friends may find direct analogues between the scenarios mentioned below and their own situations. Even those students who are responsible only for themselves must remember to balance law school with outside interests. In fact, it is perhaps easiest for those who are not beholden to other people to lose themselves completely in law school.

The student should focus, early in law school, on keeping his own expectations, as well as those of family members, in proper perspective. The student must dismiss as unrealistic any thought that he can attend law school full- or part-time and simply put family responsibilities on hold for three years. A student who chooses to approach law school this way is likely to find that he puts his family on hold for many, many years to come as a practicing attorney, because his level of stress will grow, rather than dissipate, over time. Many lawyers remember believing, in law school, that the prospect of having some free time was always just around the corner: If I can just get through moot-court rounds, *then* life will be easier. When interviewing season ends, *then* life will be easier. When my law-review comment is completed, *then* life will be easier. In law school, as in the practice of law, a new short-term or medium-term deadline will always emerge and will command as much attention as the student or attorney will allow himself to give it. Therefore, the law student, like the practicing attorney, must realize that life cannot revolve around the law, nor can it revolve wholly around the family member who is a law student or a practicing attorney. Law school, like the practice of law, is but one aspect of life, both for the student and for the student's family. The family will still need everything that a healthy family needs: leadership, attention, time, discipline, affection, and recreation, to name a few of these needs. The law student should anticipate that her family's needs will sometimes impinge on her law-school work, and sometimes be inconvenient. In fact, she should expect that there will be times when this balance does not seem to be manageable. The student will deal with these same issues as a practicing attorney; thus, expecting, and planning for, some degree of chaos during law school will give the student an advantage as a new lawyer, while others are wrestling for the first time with how to achieve the necessary balance. The student will feel guilty, at times, for neglecting her work, her family, or both; these feelings are normal. As a law student or a practitioner, there is always something that could or should be done, whether for family, for the home, or for school or work. The student should both expect this guilt and take measures to minimize guilt by establishing reasonable boundaries and adhering to them, two goals that are discussed below.

A student should also manage the expectations of her family or spouse. She might start by explaining to the family that an adjustment period is normal and that it may take a few tries before things are running smoothly. It will take a few weeks, at least, for the student simply to become accustomed to the rhythms of law-school life. Children as young as three years old can understand that the family routine may change and that mom or dad is going to school. The student should reassure her children and her spouse that they will remain her first priority, even when it may seem that she is devoting an enormous amount of time to law school. And she should communicate this reassurance by actions as well as words; in other words, the student must follow through on what she says she will do. Therefore, the student should try not to over-commit or to make promises to the family that she cannot keep. She should not tell her children that Thursday evening will be family game night if she knows that upcoming moot-court rounds will make doing anything on Thursday impossible. When the student fails to manage expectations well, this failure breeds resentment and hurt feelings. The family, and especially the children, should not be made to believe that school is a higher priority than they are. The student might take her children or spouse to the school when class is not in session and show them where she attends classes, even letting them sit in her customary chair. This simple exercise will help the children (or partner) to

169

visualize where she is all day and will establish a connection for all family members that might otherwise be difficult to create.

A student should take care to manage the expectations of his school colleagues, as well. Students often find it easy to become over-committed to extracurricular activities or to a study group. Although there is nothing wrong with becoming involved, it is important that the student be honest with himself and his colleagues about the extent of his involvement and time commitment. When others, like school colleagues or professionals from outside the school, are depending on the student to fulfill promises, misunderstandings may cause them to form the opinion that the student is unreliable, not thorough, or even duplicitous.

The law student should establish boundaries, setting limits on those areas upon which law school will not be permitted to encroach. Law school must not overrun every aspect of the student's life. The student remains a spouse, parent, or family member, and must take affirmative steps to ensure that these important relationships do not become secondary to his status as a student. One suggestion is to establish time boundaries: a student may carve out a three-hour block of time, for example, perhaps before and after dinner, to spend with family. One student treated law school like a job, arriving on campus each day at 7:30 A.M. He reviewed the day's material before class, spent time between classes preparing for the next day, and continued preparing until he left school at 5:00 P.M. He then went home, spent uninterrupted time with his family, and then, after the children were in bed, finished his preparations for the following day. His time was budgeted closely but was more than ample for high-quality preparation. This student graduated with the second-highest GPA ever accumulated at his highly regarded law school.

The student may also want to keep a close eye on the coping behaviors he employs during law school. Anecdotal evidence suggests that many individuals handle law-school stress in the same way that they later handle stress as practicing attorneys. For example, students who self-medicated with drugs or alcohol in law school often continued these self-destructive behaviors in their careers. It is therefore very important that the student get sound advice on handling stress during law school, rather than waiting to address the issue later when the consequences may be even more severe and when assistance may be more difficult to find. The student may also periodically question whether her reactions to stress are normal, or whether she finds herself becoming more agitated than her peers by similar stressors. This behavior might signal to the student a need for stress-management assistance.

Simple though it may sound, perhaps the most important piece of advice is that the student spend time with his spouse or significant other, and, if he has them, his children. The student might even find ways to include a spouse or child in her preparation for school. Even a young child can hold flash cards or participate with the student in memorization exercises. One lawyer would give her preschooler an animated explanation of her oral arguments—this exercise helped her to memorize the material and also became fun time for her to spend with her child. The same tactics can be used in law-school preparation. A willing spouse might provide an objective set of ears to hear an outline summarized out loud and might ask questions that elucidate holes in the student's preparation. In addition, many law students find it a useful exercise to explain the origins of a particular legal doctrine in layperson's terms. This practice will also demonstrate to the student the value of the "knowability" of the law, a concept discussed in Chapter 6. Other students practice moot-court arguments in front of family members, even allowing them to ask questions as if they were the presiding judge. From time to time, the student might also simply ask her spouse or children if they want to hear more about what she is learning.

Law students with family obligations often find it to be important and useful to connect with other law-school families. Seeing how others cope with situations is helpful and gives everyone involved the sense that they are not alone in this situation. Maintaining these friendships is also a way to stay involved in the law-school social scene, while at the same time involving one's spouse or children. These bonds can be helpful when an emergency arises and the student needs another family to pitch in. This can be particularly important if law school is the first time that a family has been away from their extended family. When the student does not have the security of having grandparents or aunts and uncles available for assistance, other students with families may be able to help out. Some students find that switching on and off for babysitting each month is a good idea, especially if the children are already well acquainted with one another and with the other family.

Some law students will also need to secure day-care arrangements. This process may involve a few false starts before the student finds a child-care situation with which she is completely comfortable. If necessary, arrangements can always be changed: a student may find that she needs to hire a new caregiver or switch from a babysitter to institutionalized day-care, for example. In selecting child-care, students should apply the same type of investigational and lawyering skills that they use in seeking employment. A student who is considering hiring a nanny or an in-home caregiver may want to run background and credit checks. A local private-investigation firm may be able to assist with this matter. The cost is generally under $100 for a background check that would include investigation of the candidate's credit, criminal record, and assets. Before conducting such an investigation, the student should secure the prospective care-giver's permission, as well as the person's Social Security number, date of birth, and contact information. The student should also call the references provided by the candidate and find out how well those people know the candidate, as well as whether they have any reservations about the person. If the reference is from a former employer, the student should find out, for example, whether *that* person actually called the references previously supplied by the candidate and whether the candidate missed an inordinate number of days of work for some reason. Just as she would do if she were conducting an interview as a practicing attorney, the student should investigate details about each candidate: she should find out, for example, how the candidate intends to deal with discipline issues, what kind of food the candidate enjoys making, and what the candidate believes are appropriate games and interests for children who are the age of her children. In so doing, the student should attempt to schedule more than one interview. Also, she should be sure to inquire about the candidate's health and any history of missing work due to health-related problems. In short, the student should be just as diligent in making child-care arrangements as she was in selecting the right law school.

As discussed above, the student must have her financial house in order before law school starts. These considerations, while important for all law students, are of particular concern to those with family obligations. The student might, for example, choose to devise a budget long before law school begins and spend a few months living within that budget, even if she is currently employed and making substantial money. This exercise will allow the family to see what standard of living will be attainable and may also lessen the family's shock at living on a student budget. The student who engages in such planning will begin school with a clear understanding of the time it takes to take care of the finances and will therefore be better able to factor this in when budgeting her time.

Before school begins, family members should also have a clear idea of each person's role. If a parent is planning to attend law school, then the family should know who will be running the day-to-day aspects of the household. Establishing a routine with respect to grocery shopping, laundry, free time, and handling the finances should help things run smoothly. In addition, knowing what to expect in advance with regard to household responsibilities may lessen resentment by a non-student spouse down the road.

The law student should become accustomed to expressing appreciation to the rest of her family. The family will be asked to endure stressful periods, especially during exams, and to adjust to a schedule that may be less regular than before. Although law school may be challenging for the student, it may be even more difficult for his or her family.

The student should also expect that his relationships with immediate and extended family, as well as with his friends, may change. Law school changes people; indeed, it must do so. Law school forces students to think more logically and more analytically than before, and the student may find that his law-school learning bleeds into the personality he adopts in his personal life. (One point of very specific advice: Even when she is in the midst of a semester of trial-advocacy class, the student must *never* adopt cross-examination as a model for communicating with her spouse.) The student is likely to find that his thoughts about the federal constitution and fundamental human rights will change as well. Many students find that their family members and friends recognize very quickly that they are looking at issues more critically than before. Law students sometimes find it hard not to respond in a very critical manner when a family member or friend makes a comment about Congress, politics, or the Supreme Court that is in conflict with the student's learning. Often, rather than attacking the friend or family member, the student might reasonably decide that it is not productive to engage in this particular discussion and might simply ignore the remark. Law students so quickly become accustomed to analyzing the statements of their peers and professors alike that they often find it difficult not to do the same with their loved ones. Many times, however, this incisive style is best reserved for the classroom rather than the family room. Finally, the student should be prepared for the fact that some friends or family members might resent the fact that the student has made a significant, and potentially very positive, change in her life. Others might, either consciously or subconsciously, transfer to the student any negative feelings they might have about attorneys or the practice of law. In any event, the student must learn to watch herself change in law school and must ensure that, at all times, she is proud of who she is becoming.

In making the transition to law school, many prospective students fear becoming overwhelmed by the wealth of legal knowledge they must master very quickly. They should take comfort from the fact that, in addition to the orientation programs described above, many schools provide comprehensive academic-support programs. The student should be aware of these resources as she begins her legal education. First, many schools provide student tutors, sometimes called teaching assistants or dean's fellows. These tutors, typically upperclassmen who did very well in their first-year courses, are available to help students with coursework, with learning to outline courses and to brief cases, and with logistical questions. At many schools, they keep office hours during which students can either simply drop in or make appointments in advance. Sometimes tutors are made available for legal-research-and-writing class as well as for doctrinal courses.

Second, many law schools offer academic-skills workshops or academic-enrichment programs throughout the semester. In these workshops, which are typically led by a professor, students receive formal training in class preparation, briefing and outlining, and exam-taking techniques. Some schools even address such real-life issues as etiquette and debt management. At some law schools, attendance at these programs is mandatory; at others, students may choose whether to attend.

Third, students who are experiencing anxiety, depression, extreme stress, or other mental-health problems are often given access to professional assistance, either free or at reduced rates. These professionals provide confidential counseling and other support. They may be employees of the law school or university, or they may be associated with the institution only through private contract. Although many students take advantage of this service during school, those who know themselves to be particularly prone to such problems may want to research this option before school begins. These issues are dealt with in greater detail in Chapter 10.

Fourth, some students may be eligible for assistance through the CLEO program. The CLEO/Thurgood Marshall Legal Educational Opportunity Program provides low-income, economically disadvantaged and minority students with the educational tools and financial resources to excel in school and pass the bar examination. A United States Department of Education grant funds this program, which encourages its graduates to consider public-interest law. Students may also wish to explore other options available through special-interest groups that have as their stated goal encouraging and supporting students of certain racial, ethnic, or religious backgrounds.

Finally, and in addressing more generalized concerns about law school, prospective students may find the following perspective useful. In many ways, law school is taught backwards, and a student who recognizes this fact may be better equipped to find meaning in the legal-education process than her classmates. In the student's first semester, she will encounter, depending on her school's curriculum, five or six of the most difficult concepts she must master in law school. The first is legal writing. As the student will learn, legal writing is different from other kinds of writing. The second is in criminal law, and its name is *mens rea*.

Mens rea describes the state of mind that the fact-finder must determine the criminal defendant had to convict her of a given crime. The third involves civil procedure, and it is called personal jurisdiction. Personal jurisdiction is the power that a court must exercise over a defendant to determine the defendant's rights and interests. The fourth is in property law, and it is called future interests. This addresses the division and alienation of certain, intangible property rights. The fifth is in contracts, and it is called consideration. Consideration, or the price of the promise being sought, is the central concept that courts use to determine which promises should be enforced. The sixth involves torts, and its name is proximate cause. Proximate cause is a policy-based determination that courts employ in deciding how close the relationship between a wrongful act and an injury must be before the court will impose liability. During the first semester (or first year) of law school, students are introduced to these concepts, and grapple with them intellectually, but often they have no idea of their significance.

Then, usually in the student's second year of law school, he begins an internship, participates in a *pro-bono* project, becomes involved in clinical work, writes a law-review article, or joins a mock-trial or moot-court team. At this point, for the first time, the student works on a "live" problem, and discovers that these difficult concepts taught in his first-year classes are actually very important because they can influence the course of events in the real world.

During the student's third year of law school, he has the opportunity to take some fascinating elective courses, many of which have "Law and" in their title. The courses offered might include "Law and Literature," "Law and Medicine," or "Law and Theology." In these courses, the student comes to see how her interests outside law school, possibly including the subject in which she earned her undergraduate degree, relate to the law.

Unfortunately, some students have forgotten the concepts they learned during their first year by the time they realize the "real world" application of those concepts. Other students get the formal opportunity to connect the law to their outside interests only after they have become so disconnected from those interests that they have ceased to look outside the law for learning and personal growth. First-year students can, however, recognize this pattern and take the time to discover, for themselves, how these difficult first-year concepts work in the real world and how the law is connected with their own values and interests. Students who do so are likely to find law school to be far richer, and far more enjoyable, than those who simply attempt to learn, without context, what is placed before them. Students who find a context into which to place their legal education are more likely to remember what they learned long after graduation.

To do this, a student might ask himself, at the beginning of his first semester of law school, why he should care about Contracts. The student can answer this question only for himself. A good way for the student to accomplish this in contract law, for example, is by having some contract in mind throughout the semester *that matters to him*. In this way, he will learn various concepts by imagining what significance they have in real life, in the context of a contract that is meaningful to him.

A student might, for instance, think of his own lease relationship with a difficult landlord, the negotiation of a purchase of a car, or a business deal that went sour. Each situation might include a contract that sets forth the student's rights and obligations. More philosophically, the student might focus on the fact that contract law is private law rather than public law. Unlike matters of criminal law and civil procedure, which are decided by the outside world, contract law is the law that people build for themselves, and this distinction gives the contracting parties great power. As discussed above, the first priority of a court is to determine what the contracting parties were trying to accomplish. The second priority is to examine whether the law permits parties to make such deals. Even more theoretically, on an international level, treaties are contracts that govern the relationships among sovereign nations. Thomas Hobbes, John Locke, Jean-Jacques Rousseau, and a number of contemporary scholars have written about the relationship between people and government, and have referred to this relationship as the social contract. Such a contract consists of the people's consent to be governed and agreement to abide by the rules the government creates. Some have argued that, in the United States, the social contract either has been breached or never truly existed, because several groups of people were excluded from participation in framing the government.

Students can go through this exercise for each of their first-year courses. In trying to put legal education more generally into context, students might wonder how their own pre-law education to date relates to the material they will learn in law school. Students should remember that law is not its own subject. Instead, law is a series of stories of disputes that arise among people out of human experience. Therefore, everything that is relevant to human experience is relevant to the law. In other words, every pre-law educational or professional experience can enrich the practice of law school, both for the student who had the experience and for her colleagues.

Now that the prospective student has thought her way through the first semester of law school, anticipating the stressors, orienting herself with regard to the resources that will be available to her, and getting some idea of the expectations that she will face, there is but one step left to take: Jump in with both feet. The student should remember, every day that she is in law school, that she is paying to be there, in time, effort, and money. Often, the student's family is bearing much of the cost, emotional as well as financial. In return for this investment, the student is given access to a wealth of opportunities and learning experiences. Each day, she should remind herself why she has chosen to be there and should strive to make the most of law school.

CHAPTER 6

Using Context, Policy, and Theory to Navigate Law School Like a Lawyer

Putting the law, and the process of learning it, in context is not necessarily a difficult task, but it is one that is easy to overlook. Law students often become so absorbed in the law-school experience itself that they lose track of the world outside the doors of the school while they are there. It is important that law students avoid this common mistake because lawyers do not practice in a vacuum, and law students do not learn best in one, either. Instead, both law school and the practice of law are most effectively understood, and best enjoyed, in context. So exactly how does a student strive to put law school in context? By taking the time to consider current events in light of the new body of knowledge he or she is acquiring every day. Along the same lines, law students should continue to read the newspaper, watch the news, or at least peruse the daily headlines online, as faithfully as they read their class assignments each day, and never hesitate to ask questions that tie the outside world into what is being covered in class. Simply stated, law students should look for a reason to care about what is being taught in class: The real-life implications of some courses, like criminal law, may be relatively easy to discern, because a person's life or liberty may hang in the balance of each case that is decided. For other courses, like the intimidatingly entitled Uniform Commercial Code, the student may have to search harder to make the material meaningful to her. This can certainly be done, however: The Uniform Commercial Code (or UCC) is the law that makes it possible for businesses across the country to work together. By creating a common law to govern business transactions, which was ultimately adopted, at least in some form, by each of the fifty states, the drafters of the UCC made it possible for businesses all over the country to coordinate their efforts and expectations with one another with regard to sales and leases of goods, the exchange of funds, and other important day-to-day commercial tasks. This body of uniform law makes it possible for businesses in California and Florida, for example, engaging in a transaction with each other for the first time, to know what to expect from each other. Therefore, consumers and business owners alike should care about the UCC because it is central to the effective functioning of interstate commerce in the United States.

In an attempt to make sense of the learning process that is expected of students in law school, the student may find it helpful to reduce basic steps to the following four maxims: (1) Identify the rules that govern the matter being studied (the "rules" are sometimes called the "black letter" of the law); (2) pull back from the rules and attempt to place them in context, considering where they fit in the context of the other material that has been presented in the course thus far; (3) analyze the rules, to discover the policy or historical considerations that are hidden beneath the surface; and (4) apply the rules to the facts of the matter being studied. To do this effectively, students must first have mastered some basic learning skills: reading comprehension, critical thinking, briefing, and an understanding of legal procedure. These are some of the "nuts and bolts" that will be discussed in Chapter 7. First, however, the student must understand the larger context in which she will learn the law. Only then will she be able to learn, analyze, and apply the rules properly.

INTERDISCIPLINARY STUDY: AN EXAMPLE OF CONTEXTUAL THINKING

One way in which students may gain perspective on law school and the law itself is through engaging in interdisciplinary study, both inside and outside of the classroom. "Interdisciplinary study" is a popular concept in law schools today, and it really means following the lead of the title of this chapter: putting law school in context. At some point in each student's legal career, whether in court, in conversation with colleagues or clients, in formal legal scholarship, or even in attempts to build a framework for understanding law school coursework, the student is likely to use what she learned before she came to law school in trying to make sense of the law, either for her own understanding or in the process of explaining the law to another person. Alternatively, both law students and lawyers sometimes enjoy exploring an area that is new to them, whether it be art and architecture or evolutionary biology, to expand and enrich their understanding of the law. This process is not only enjoyable, but also will likely make the participant a better scholar and a more effective advocate. In addition, many of these individuals find that a change of pace in the materials they choose to read for pleasure can be an excellent way to gain perspective on the law.

The interdisciplinary study of law is important not only to legal scholarship—something with which law professors and those law students who choose to participate in law review will be concerned—but also to classroom learning. Some professors enjoy supplementing the assigned textual reading with charts, maps, pictures, graphs, and discussions of history, for instance, to add depth and context to the lesson that is being taught. Professors do this for several reasons. First, this kind of supplementary material generally makes class more enjoyable and provides the students with some variety, which can be much needed, especially during the stressful first year of law school.

Second, and more important, however, these supplementary materials are learning tools that give students a reason to remember the lesson and, especially for students who are at the beginning of their legal education, provide some familiar hooks on which to hang the new information they are learning in class. Many students find maps and charts, for example, to be relatively easy to understand because they are common learning aids in undergraduate school and even secondary school. Sometimes, these familiar tools can make the unfamiliar material that is being presented at the same time—namely, the black-letter law— easier for law students to digest.

As many new law students can attest, learning the law itself, with all of its strange Latin terminology, as presented in enormous, expensive textbooks with no pictures and an unusual, very formal style of writing, can feel foreign at first. At the same time, however, each student enters law school with some twenty-odd years or more of life experience and education. During that time, each student picked up some knowledge of the basic principles of art and science and math and history along the way. Using some of this previous knowledge to make sense of the law— and to put the law in context, using interdisciplinary tools such as those some professors use in class, as discussed above—helps many new law students to find themselves at ease more quickly.

Therefore, as the professor is employing interdisciplinary tools in class, students may want to consider looking for ways to do the same, whether by bringing in ideas from their undergraduate work or previous graduate studies, by keeping up with current events, or by considering the application of the law to relevant events from their own life experiences. Much of this can be accomplished simply by remaining curious throughout law school. As this book discusses in some detail in Chapter 7, students are encouraged to look up unusual phrases in the cases they are assigned to read for class, even if the professor does not require them to do so. Along the same lines, as also discussed in Chapter 7, many students find that seeking additional information about a case—reading the rest of an opinion that may have been excerpted for the text, looking up financial information about the litigants, consulting a map, or building a small family tree while reading the case—will make the case come alive and ensure that the lesson of the case stays with the student, not just for the exam, but also for years to come as a lawyer.

As this chapter touched on earlier, interdisciplinary study plays a significant role in formal legal scholarship. Students who are at the beginning of law school may not expect that this kind of highly specialized, often theoretical writing will be of much interest to them. Although they may have some vague conception that their professors spend part of their time engaged in this kind of scholarly work and may understand that certain upperclassmen participate in creating something called a "law review," students may not understand the importance of legal scholarship as they enter law school. Simply stated, legal scholarship is important because it functions as a major vehicle for the development and reform of the law. Reading cutting-edge law-review articles and other legal periodicals is a good way for both lawyers and law students to gauge where problems are in the current law and to consider possible solutions. Sometimes, a law-review article will give a practicing attorney or a law student an idea for a unique argument to advance his client's interests. Interdisciplinary scholarship—scholarship that contains elements of both law and another discipline, such as medicine, theology, mathematics, or philosophy—shows how the law is connected to these other disciplines, such as those that many students studied prior to law school. As is discussed below, this material can provide an excellent way for new law students—and for non-lawyers—to see how the law connects with real life.

Indeed, interdisciplinary theory in legal scholarship can and should afford law students and other readers many of the same benefits already discussed with regard to interdisciplinary work in the law-school classroom. The *Oxford English Dictionary* defines interdisciplinary as "contribut[ing] to or benefit[ing] from two or more disciplines." Ideally, interdisciplinary work should both contribute to an understanding of each discipline and benefit from the state of the art in each. This chapter will return to that concept shortly. In layperson's terms, interdisciplinary studies often involve "Law and" another discipline, such as Law and Economics, Law and Literature, Law and Psychoanalysis, or Law and Architecture.

The *Oxford English Dictionary* also indicates that the word "interdisciplinary" dates back only to 1937, when it was first used in the Journal of Educational Sociology. Therefore, interdisciplinary study is a relatively recent development in our American educational system. Students who are considering this approach to law school may find it to be useful to examine some arguments that they may hear, both in favor of and against interdisciplinary study. This short discussion is intended to give the new law student something of an introduction to this kind of work, so as to encourage the student to look actively for ways to connect law school with the world outside.

Stanley Fish at the University of Illinois describes interdisciplinary work as the process of "expanding one's discipline by listening to others."[1] Law students, for instance, may choose to do their pleasure reading outside the field of law. Inevitably, however, regardless of whether the student chooses to read history, fiction, poetry, or even the latest cookbook by Julia

---

[1] Castello, "Almost a Pragmatist," 26 Seton Hall L. Rev. 967 (1996) (citing Stanley Fish, *Professional Correctness: Literary Studies and Political Change* (Oxford University Press 1995)).

Child, he will take something from that reading that will enrich his understanding of the law. Law students often find that the same is true of allowing themselves the leisure time that is necessary to keep up with current events: almost invariably, the student's understanding of the law will enrich her appreciation of current events, and vice versa. Scholars who engage in interdisciplinary research engage in just this sort of cross-fertilization in a more concentrated and intentional manner.

Substantive interdisciplinary study can improve lawyers' legal-research methods, as well. Authors of traditional law-review articles, for instance, spend a great deal of time in law libraries, researching case law, relevant statutes, and scholarly writings on the points that they are exploring. Scholars writing traditional law-review articles do not, however, typically engage in intensive field research as scholars in other disciplines often do—but maybe they should. One scholar, arguing for greater collaboration between the fields of law and anthropology, noted that traditional legal research generally involves what she called "grand and generalized assumptions without precise consideration of facts or fragments of facts." She therefore called for a different kind of method as a complement to substantive interdisciplinary collaboration. Perhaps, she seemed to be saying, legal scholars should look at fewer minutiae and more context. New law students may wish to keep the same considerations in mind. This awareness can be particularly important because, when students graduate from law school and must, on a day-to-day basis, apply the law to the real world, their livelihood may well depend on their ability to make the law comprehensible to non-lawyers, including clients and jurors.

The value of interdisciplinary research, however, can be much more extensive than the foregoing discussion would suggest. Professor Jack Balkin at Yale Law School has noted that each discipline contributes its own vocabulary, its own heroes and villains, its own history, even its own way of asking questions.[2] Exploring each of these attributes of another discipline can enrich a student's understanding of the law.

Law students and lawyers sometimes question the practicality of interdisciplinary work, and readers of this section may be asking similar questions of themselves: Can a lawyer make use of interdisciplinary theory in court? Is this technique effective in practice? The answer to both questions is "Yes."

Although it may seem unlikely that a lawyer would make an argument from outside the law in a brief, a wise lawyer actually might choose to do just that, given the right opportunity to make a convincing argument by analogy or to develop a theme. For example, the lawyer might employ the language of evolutionary biology in describing the way that the law has changed over time in response to changed conditions in the surrounding community. More commonly, a lawyer might use interdisciplinary theory in an opening statement to a jury or in explaining a legal problem and a proposed solution to a client. Why? Because interdisciplinary theory uses concepts that are familiar to the juror or client—like art or history or math—to help her become oriented in the discussion of law that is to follow, which is likely to be less familiar to her. As students often discover when their professors employ interdisciplinary techniques in their law-school classes, using familiar concepts makes it easier for the juror or client to remember what the lawyer has told her.

In addition, a lawyer might use law and economics theory in speaking with a potential client, in an initial interview, about the financial aspects of deciding whether to bring suit. For example, if the costs of litigation are likely to exceed the maximum amount that the client will win even if she prevails in her lawsuit,

---

[2] Balkin, "Interdisciplinarity as Colonization," 53 Wash. & Lee L. Rev. 949 (1996).

then it may not be a good business decision for her to proceed with the matter. The same considerations come into play when a lawyer is counseling a client who has been sued and is deciding whether to settle the matter or litigate the dispute before a court. If the costs of preparing a defense outweigh the amount that the plaintiff is seeking, for example, then the client may wish to consider an early settlement of the matter. If, however, the client anticipates that others may file similar lawsuits against it in the future, it may make good business sense for the client to take the present case to court and, if the client prevails in the present action, thus deter further litigation. Why would an attorney talk about economics with a client? The clients of an attorney who has a traditional commercial-litigation practice are generally businesspeople, and talking with them about economic efficiency is, in essence, speaking their language. Students may hear their professors say, in class, that one of the functions of the law is to be knowable—in other words, to be comprehensible and intuitive to non-lawyers. To the extent that the law is consistent with experience outside the law, where most of life occurs, it is more predictable and thus more knowable.

Another argument that law students may hear, or may raise on their own, is that interdisciplinary education is a distraction from a proper legal education. The concern is that, when law students spend too much time in courses like law and literature, they will never be able to write good briefs. Considering such an argument, Professor Barbara Bennett Woodhouse at the University of Pennsylvania Law School has come to the defense of interdisciplinary study in her own field, which is family law. She asserts that interdisciplinary study is actually very practical training, at least in that particular area. Because court opinions in family-law cases center on ephemeral concepts such as the best interest of the child, the psychological parent, and equitable distribution of property, she argues, future family-law attorneys must be exposed to psychology, economics, sociology, religion, and history, so as to be able to decipher these terms and thus to represent their clients effectively.

One final argument against interdisciplinary study may be a fear of dilettantism. Students may remember the truism that "a little knowledge is a dangerous thing." To do interdisciplinary work, it is important that the law student or lawyer not be afraid to be a beginner in a new field, and this learning process can be disorienting and difficult at first. A lawyer who wishes to employ the language of evolutionary biology in crafting an argument, for instance, should not rely on her knowledge of biology from college because the state of the art in that field may have changed in the years since her graduation. Moreover, quite frankly, she may not have been an expert in the field, even when the subject was fresh in her mind. So what should she do, if she believes this approach would be effective in preparing her case? As a starting point, the lawyer should locate an accessible, very recent book in the field, preferably one that was written by a recognized scholar in that discipline, read it thoroughly to get a foothold on the information and the basic vocabulary that is employed in that area, and then use the book's bibliography—an excellent bibliography is another must for this initial resource—to choose the next round of sources. Ultimately, the careful lawyer needs to ensure that she is using "the state of the art" in this borrowed field to enhance her legal argument. The student or lawyer should keep in mind that this legal form of cross-training not only can be very effective, but also can be a great confidence-builder when used successfully.

Many law students and lawyers find interdisciplinary work to be intimidating, especially the first time they try it. After the student or lawyer has done his "homework," so to speak, he should take this very simple advice: Give it a try! In scholarship, in law practice, or in class, lawyers and lawyers-to-be need not shy away from a field that is new (or that is seemingly unrelated to their areas of expertise) and that may have valuable insights to offer, simply because of the fear of being wrong. Again, Barbara Bennett Woodhouse at Penn addresses this concern in a way that may be useful to those who are considering interdisciplinary projects. She said, "Surely, the lessons of interdisciplinary study will be lost if lawyers or legal scholars become so timid about their ability to learn from and collaborate with colleagues in other fields that they abandon the project of incorporating interdisciplinary materials and insights into a legal perspective."[3] One experienced professor is known to encourage his students to "take on something that is almost too hard." This process can provide a great boost to the lawyer or law student's professional self-esteem, especially as the individual ventures into a new area and sees herself succeed.

At some point in his legal career, whether in court, in conversation with clients, in his scholarship, or even in his attempts to build frameworks for understanding his law-school classes, each student should consider using what he learned before he came to law school, or even taking on something new. This endeavor is likely to make him a better student, a better scholar of the law, and a more effective advocate.

USING POLICY TO PUT LAW SCHOOL IN CONTEXT

Any person who has watched the "reality-oriented" legal television shows has observed actors and actresses giving impassioned, policy-driven speeches in their roles as lawyers, both inside and outside the courtroom and in dealings with clients and other lawyers. Policy considerations—to better the welfare or prosperity of the state, the

---

[3] Woodhouse, "Mad Midwifery: Bringing Theory, Doctrine, and Practice to Life," 91 Mich. L. Rev. 1977 (1993).

community, or the citizens of either—underlie every area of the law. Indeed, because of the amount of media attention that is devoted to the policy implications of the law, this side of lawyering is relatively familiar to many students, even as they begin law school. Legal theory, on the other hand—the philosophical side of lawyering, which is introduced below—is less familiar to many students at the beginning of law school, but both its language and its role in influencing the direction of the law become important as each student begins the journey toward becoming a lawyer. Both policy and theory are fundamental to legal education; as is discussed below, each relates to what is called the "black letter" of the law, the set of rules that constitutes the law. Students may encounter professors who focus on any one of these three areas—policy, theory, or black-letter law—to the exclusion of the others; therefore, it is important to know the role of each.

Policy disagreements frequently engender spirited discussions, both during law school and in the practice of law. During law school, policy is most likely to be raised, and debated, in areas of the law to which students can relate—like matters of marriage, divorce, and landlord-tenant law, for instance—or areas of considerable political concern—such as abortion, the death penalty, and prayer in school. Policy arguments are both very powerful and easily misused. By their very nature, they are intended to appeal to the heart as well as to the mind. For example, courts will not enforce a contract to sell bodily organs because doing so is both contrary to the law and offensive to society's collective conscience. Considering the matter more generally, courts will not enforce contracts to engage in any illegal activity, not only because the activity contravenes the law, but also out of a belief that the state should not condone such activity. Often, effective policy arguments arise from personal experience, and this connection gives the proponent of the argument strong motivation to advocate for its adoption. Although strong feelings can give rise to exceptionally productive debate, they can also contribute to an atmosphere of anger and frustration that can polarize a classroom as well as a courtroom.

With these considerations in mind, how should a student wield such a powerful tool? One professor gives students the following advice on the first day of class and reiterates this advice when the class reaches an area of law that she knows is likely to generate strong, and potentially divisive, emotions: "Policy arguments are welcome in the classroom only when they are made hand-in-hand with legal arguments." In other words, this professor does not permit students merely to vent, making statements of opinion that are unsupported by the law, such as, "Allowing equitable division of the property of unmarried people *is wrong because it encourages nonmarital relationships!*" The professor does, however, encourage students to make comments that reveal the policy decisions that underlie a given law or ruling. For example, the student may make a significant contribution to the class by pointing out that a particular court's refusal to become involved in dividing nonmarital property *had the effect of leaving the property in the hands of the more powerful partner—historically, in a heterosexual relationship, the male partner.*

New law students may have difficulty seeing the difference. The first statement is a bare expression of opinion—fine for after-class discussion among classmates or between students and the professor, but not particularly productive in helping to understand the law. The second statement brings the law and policy together, recognizing that court decisions that might, at first, seem to be grounded purely in the law can have strong social and policy implications. Class discussions that are peppered with the first kind of statement may deteriorate into veritable shouting matches, while the second kind of statement is likely to contribute to the class, as a whole, demostrating a greater understanding of the policy behind the law. All law is created by human beings for other human beings, and each person, in seeking to understand the law, brings to bear his or her own value judgments. Therefore, regardless of whether the class is discussing a statute—law made by a legislature and then, typically, signed into law by a governor—or case law—often called judge-made law—it can be helpful to look "behind the scenes" at the people making the laws, and the values they were seeking to promote.

In approaching delicate policy issues, some students find it productive to ground strong opinions in the words of neutral third parties, rather than personalizing their disagreement by directing their comments at individual classmates who may have advocated for a different position. One professor, in devoting class time to considering current events from the perspective of the law, found this method to be especially helpful during the disputed election of 2000 and in the aftermath of the terrorist events of September 11, 2001. Both times, the professor prepared a packet of readings for the students, to guide the subsequent in-class discussion. She tried to include, within each packet, readings that represented a wide range of views, including some that were likely to be unpopular with most of the students in the class. Thus, when a student would express a particular viewpoint, the professor could respond by directing the class to a similar argument, made by a third party, in the packet of readings. This process not only legitimized each student's opinion, but also invited the class to focus on the position being advocated, rather than the personality of the student who had made the assertion. The articles were also useful for counterpoint. Rather than challenging a student's assertion as being invalid, the professor could show the class a differing opinion and invite the class to consider the relative merits of each. Students indicated that the exercise was useful to them, both in helping them to understand the legal issues being discussed, in each case, and in setting an example of how they might navigate an emotional discussion as lawyers. The professor also felt that taking this approach helped to defuse the tension that students often feel in introducing unpopular viewpoints, by shifting the focus toward the issues and away from any particular student. In preparing for a policy discussion, whether in class, in court, or before a supervising attorney or client, students and lawyers alike may find that "arming" themselves with the words of neutral third parties provides them with increased confidence and credibility, especially as new lawyers.

Using Theory to Put Law School in Context

Now this chapter introduces a second, and likely less familiar, tool for approaching the study and practice of law: Legal Theory. "Game Theory," "Law and Economics," the "Veil of Ignorance." Unlike impassioned policy-based arguments, these phrases are not often heard on network television but will become an important part of each student's life, both during law school and after. These are a few of the more prevalent theoretical approaches that lawyers use to understand, evaluate, and test the law. Like policy arguments, theory-based assertions are often most valuable, and most comprehensible, when they are used in explaining, supporting, or denouncing the rule itself—the aforementioned "black letter" of the law—rather than standing on their own. Some of these tools have elaborate names and explanations, while others are more a matter of common sense.

Dollars and Sense

In a course on Payment Systems, which is one component of the Uniform Commercial Code discussed earlier, the class might discuss extensive litigation regarding a tractor that was appealed several times to the highest levels of the court system. At the beginning of the discussion, before the class has begun to dissect the court's decision or even to consider the case's procedural history, the professor might ask the students, "Was it worthwhile to bring this lawsuit?" Many students find it easy, in law school, to focus so narrowly on the rights and remedies that are available to the parties in each case that they forget that not every lawsuit is worth pursuing. In addition, law students are often surprised to learn how expensive litigation can be. Many assume that the litigation simply must have been fiscally worthwhile for the parties to have pursued the matter to the appellate level, and for it therefore to be reported in their casebook. To prevent a loss of practical perspective, law students must consider economic issues like this one when they read the cases that are assigned to them. Similarly, in the practice of law attorneys cannot assume that their clients and potential clients have already considered the financial repercussions of litigation when they first approach the lawyer to bring—or defend—a lawsuit on their behalf. There can be significant, negative consequences of a lawyer's failure to consider this important issue up front, which may include a client's receipt of an unexpectedly large bill from the attorney and subsequent refusal to pay, thus resulting in the lawyer's hard work having gone to waste. The professor's question is intended to invite the class to consider all of these real-life concerns.

Students also come to realize, through such a discussion, that they need the client's assistance in formulating the answer: How old is the tractor, and how large is it? The class might end up discovering that the tractor may be worth as little as $1,000 or as much as more than $100,000 by the time the discussion has concluded. Obviously, then, the lawyer cannot determine whether it is fiscally responsible to recommend this litigation to her client until she has more information on the goods in issue. This exercise is intended to remind the students of the importance of asking incisive questions of the client. The client will not necessarily know what facts are important to his case so it will be important for the lawyer to inquire further so as to flesh out the relevant factual background of the matter, and to listen attentively to the client's answers. (Alternatively, the professor might conduct this exercise by pretending to be the client herself and asking the students to interview her about the case. Such an approach gives the class the opportunity to think through how they would conduct the client consultation in order to draw out the important facts.)

What if litigation does not make financial sense? Should the matter immediately be abandoned or settled? These are follow-up questions that the professor might ask the class to discuss. In considering these questions, students are introduced to the concepts of the "test case" and the "repeat player." In the tractor case, for example, the class might discuss the fact that a large manufacturer of tractors could be willing to litigate an issue involving a $1,000 tractor because of the company's interest in generating positive precedent in order to protect its interests in the future. Generating positive precedent can consist of either creating new law that promotes the client's interests or challenging existing law that is contrary to the client's interests. Through this discussion, students also discover that a successful "test case," in addition to appropriate financial backing, requires excellent facts and, where appropriate, a sympathetic location, also known in legal parlance as a sympathetic "venue." If all of these factors are present, then litigating a given case might be a good business decision for the client even if there is no immediate financial gain. The class might also discuss how, on the consumer side, groups of potential plaintiffs have joined forces—sometimes with backing from consumer groups—and brought lawsuits that otherwise would have been cost prohibitive, using a procedural device called a "class action," which allows them to bring suit as a unit rather than as individuals. These class actions may yield relatively few dollars for each consumer, but collectively may have the desired corrective effect on a company or industry.

Finally, the class might discuss how the nature of legal research itself is different when the lawyer is litigating a test case rather than a matter within an established area of law. In the first year of law school, students are assigned a variety of legal-writing tasks, including writing a memorandum—an explanatory piece that is normally used by collaborating lawyers or by a lawyer and client—and a brief—a persuasive piece that is normally exchanged between opponents and argued before the court. Both are discussed more thoroughly in Chapter 11. Whether the task at hand is to explain the law that exists in a given area (as in a memo) or to advocate a client's position (as in a brief), the first step is always excellent and thorough legal research. Simply stated, the law student or lawyer must know *what the law is* before he can explain it, much less advocate for some position. In a test case, because the stakes are significant, the level and quality of the legal research that is required to protect the client's interests is perhaps even higher than it normally would be. In preparing such a case, lawyers often find themselves not only presenting the relevant law in the area being litigated, but also researching and arguing any other law that could potentially be relevant or even analogous. In so doing, lawyers often rely on secondary sources such as legal treatises and law-review articles.

All of these factors are important in counseling a client on whether litigation is likely to be productive in any given case. In preparing to engage in this analysis as practicing lawyers, students might ask these questions of themselves as they read the assigned cases and prepare to discuss them in class: Did it make financial sense for these parties to litigate this issue? If not, is there some explanation for why these parties proceeded to trial and through the appellate process? Who is financing this litigation? Is this a "bet your company" matter in which, for example, the company must litigate a patent right—and win—or the company will be out of business?

THE CHEAPEST COST AVOIDER, OR BETTER LUCK NEXT TIME

When professors talk about the "cheapest cost avoider," they are asking the class to look at a situation as if on "instant replay," thinking through the facts that precipitated the current controversy as if they were happening once again, and could be changed. The cheapest cost avoider is a concept associated with the law-and-economics movement. The key word in a law-and-economics discussion is "efficiency." If this situation were to arise again, which party could most easily avoid the loss? Who could change his or her behavior most efficiently to prevent this controversy from arising again? The "cheapest cost avoider" is that person or entity that could best have prevented the loss on the front end. Importantly, the cheapest cost avoider is not necessarily the party that is "at fault" in the matter. In assigning liability for a controversy that has already arisen, some law-and-economics theorists believe that liability should be placed upon the cheapest cost avoider, not because that party was somehow to blame in the instant dispute, but, rather, in an effort to encourage *others in that person's position in the future* to take steps to avoid the loss in the first place.

Students may find it helpful to decide, early in law school, what their own, individual response is to law and economics, because this school of thought is extremely important in contemporary legal scholarship. Indeed, several law schools (most notably the University of Chicago, Chicago-Kent, and George Mason) are known for emphasizing this part of legal theory. Some students find that they are comfortable with its forward-looking approach, while others feel that justice would be better served by focusing on the equities between the parties that are now in court, rather than on some fictitious parties whose dispute has not yet arisen. Strong arguments can be made for both sides, and students may want to become familiar with both.

Students who studied economics as undergraduates might find that now is the time to dust off those Economics 101 and 102 microeconomics and macroeconomics texts to remind themselves of some of the vocabulary they learned at that time, revisiting concepts such as indifference curves, price discrimination, and equilibrium. Alternatively, those students who were not familiar with these concepts before law school should consider taking the time to learn the basics of economics, especially if they have enrolled at a school that tends to emphasize this way of looking at the law. Learning the basic vocabulary early will assist the student in keeping up with class discussion when it takes a law-and-economics turn and will help her to apply this important theoretical tool.

INCENTIVES, CLARITY, AND KNOWABILITY

The concept of incentives is closely related to that of the cheapest cost avoider and requires the student to put himself in the position of the judge. If the judge rules in favor of one party or the other, what conduct will she be encouraging on the part of similarly situated parties in the future? Some professors will ask students to consider such questions so as to encourage them to focus on the importance of creating laws that generate productive incentives for society. Like the concept of the cheapest cost avoider, this approach shifts the focus away from those litigants who are now in court, and instead considers potential claimants in years to come.

Discussions that invoke incentives can result in lively and productive debates about policy. Students often find it informative, in examining a court's holding, to consider both the incentives that the holding creates and whether the students believe such incentives are positive for society. In discussions about incentives, some professors will ask students to imagine that they are "behind the veil of ignorance." This phrase, the brainchild of political philosopher John Rawls, requires students to imagine that they are present at the establishment of a new society and have no idea what role they will play: each person could end up being President, for example, or each person could find herself homeless. In this state of ignorance, which Rawls calls the "original position," the parties are asked to build a society. Rawls believes that the hypothetical decision-makers engaging in this exercise, as rational actors, will form a government that makes life bearable for those who will find themselves, once the veil of ignorance has been lifted, to be at the margins of society. Rawls's theory provides one way of looking at the incentives that a given law creates: Does the law create a society that is humane to its poorest citizens?

In addition, law professors sometimes talk about the importance of a law's clarity. One way of evaluating the extent to which a given law meets this goal is by asking the following questions: If an article on this statute (or the outcome of this case) were published in tomorrow's newspaper, would a person of average intelligence be able to understand the law (or this court's opinion), absent a legal education? Would that person be able to apply the court's holding to his or her own personal behavior in the future, as well as to that of others? The concept of clarity explores the answers to these questions. Law professors may also ask the class to consider whether it is fair to expect citizens to abide by laws that are not clear. Students may have heard the legal truism, "Ignorance of the law is no excuse." Each student may wish to consider for herself whether she believes this standard to represent an appropriate weighing of the interests of policy-makers, lawyers, and the general public.

Finally, some law-school classes may require or invite students to consider the concept of knowability. Like the law's clarity, its knowability is assessed from the point of view of the person of average intelligence who does not have a legal education. If this person were asked to guess what the law is in a given area, how close would his guess be to the actual law? Knowability goes to the heart of the law's connection (or lack thereof) to the mores and culture of the community. The student may wish to consider the relative value of laws that are intuitive and those that are counterintuitive to members of the general public. The interplay between knowability and incentives can be fertile ground for exploration, as well: Can laws that are counterintuitive ever influence behavior in a way that prevents future litigation?

It is, of course, possible to have a single law that satisfies the three concepts of incentives, clarity, and knowability; another law that fails to satisfy all three; and any number of laws that fall somewhere in between. In evaluating a court's holding, or the rule of law that is established in a particular case, students often find it useful to consider the court's performance in each of these areas. If the court's decision in a particular case fails to satisfy these considerations, the student may ask how the law could be improved.

GAME THEORY AND THE ROLE OF LAW

Lawyers (and lawyers-to-be) sometimes overemphasize the role of law in human interaction. In an effort better to contextualize the law, professors may introduce a concept called game theory. Although game theory is a complex theoretical system, this brief introduction will focus on only one portion: the stages of a relationship, which typically include beginning-game, mid-game, and end-game behavior. Courtship provides a good analogy for understanding these stages. In the beginning of a relationship, parties are likely to be generous with each other without expecting reciprocation. This is done in an effort to build up good will and to solidify the relationship. The middle of an intact relationship is often characterized as involving "tit for tat" behavior, meaning that each party will respond in kind to the behavior of the other: positive behavior will be returned, at this middle stage, and so will negative behavior. "End-game" tactics come into play only when the relationship is irretrievably broken. At this time, knowing that the relationship is ending or has ended, a party may be willing to engage in negative behavior for which there is no precedent on the part of his or her partner. It is only in this "end-game" time in a relationship that the parties resort to the formal use of law. This is why, for instance, there is very little litigation in an intact marriage. Indeed, bringing lawyers into the equation is likely to result in the parties' relationship immediately coming to an end. Instead, while the relationship remains intact, parties' behavior is generally governed by custom and social norms instead of by the law. Robert Ellickson of Yale Law School is the best-known proponent of the importance of social norms.

DAMAGES AND INJUNCTIONS—MAKING THE CLIENT WHOLE

Many students (and clients) are surprised to hear that courts do not usually order parties to do (or to stop doing) some act. Instead, the normal award that is given to a prevailing litigant is some amount of money. In certain situations, however, courts will order behavior rather than requiring the payment of money—when, for instance, the litigation concerns unique goods or real estate, or when the prevailing party can show that the award of damages will be insufficient to make her whole. Ordering the losing party to do (or not to do) something is called awarding "injunctive relief." Just as there are circumstances in which injunctive relief is relatively common, there are situations in which courts will almost never award injunctive relief—for example, when personal services are involved, as this would involve Thirteenth Amendment, involuntary-servitude concerns, or when the prevailing party has lost only money.

In other situations, injunctive relief would simply be impossible to award—when, for instance, a litigant's loved one has been injured, and there is no way to undo that injury. Instead, if the litigant wins, he or she will get an award of monetary damages. Thus, the bottom line is that the litigant does not, when monetary damages are awarded, get what he wanted to begin with: instead, he gets some sum of money to compensate for the loss of what was desired.

Students may be well served to think through the implications of this aspect of our legal system: Will a litigant really be "made whole" by the award of money damages? If not, can the student conceive of an alternative way of awarding relief that would be more effective? Are there some cases in which money damages are more effective than in others?

Finally, as law professors sometimes ask the class to consider, there may not be a redress for every wrong done to a person or property. If one neighbor's tree falls on another's house, causing a fire that destroys everything inside, the neighbor whose home and belongings are now gone may wish to bring suit. However, unless the other neighbor should have known that the tree was likely to fall—for instance, if the tree was severely diseased or had been damaged from being hit by a car—then this may be a situation in which no legal recourse against the neighbor is available. Lawyers frequently find themselves having to explain to would-be clients that the law does not necessarily provide relief for every injury, as heart-wrenching or disappointing as the situation might be.

Although some professors will employ their own creative methodologies to introduce students to each of the concepts that have been discussed in this chapter, others will expect students to have some intuitive understanding of them or to become familiar with the concepts on their own. In either case, as the student navigates law school, he should keep context, policy, and legal theory in mind. These are powerful and important tools that, combined with a comprehensive understanding of the "black-letter" of the law, will enhance both the student's (and lawyer's) understanding of the law and one's ability to explain the law to others—and persuade others on clients' behalf.

CHAPTER 7

The Nuts and Bolts of Law School

Law school is the beginning of a lawyer's practical training. In law school, students are trained to think, act, communicate, and learn like lawyers. Like members of any profession, law students improve their skills and abilities by mastering five major aspects of the experience: the who, where, when, how, and why of what it means to be part of the legal profession. This chapter addresses the nuts and bolts of law school. The chapter begins with a discussion of the most significant interpersonal relationships, and then covers class preparation, reading and briefing cases, outlining, study groups, study aids, dealing with professors and colleagues, basic classroom etiquette, and pre-examination assessment opportunities such as mid-terms and practice problems.

WHO: THE LAW-SCHOOL COMMUNITY

The practice of law is fundamentally about people and their personal and business relationships with others. In many ways, law school involves the same dynamics. Students regularly interact with fellow students, professors, members of the law-school administration, and professional and non-professional staff members. The individual styles, prejudices, interests, motivations, training, and experiences of each person in the community play a part in the law student's total experience. This section considers by category those interpersonal relationships that are central to a legal education.

STUDENTS

At many law schools, students are grouped into two to four sections, each of which may contain fifty to 100 students. At schools that are organized in this fashion, students will take each of their core doctrinal classes with this same section. These sections are sometimes subdivided into smaller groups for legal research and writing; in addition, some law schools organize one core first-year doctrinal class in small groups so that the students can have more personal interaction with the professor who teaches that class. Because students remain with the same section for their entire first semester (or first year) of law school, the section will often become close-knit and may develop a strong sense of group identity. These bonds are made even stronger by activities outside of class. Section members often form study groups, engage in extracurricular activities, and socialize together much more than with members of other sections in the first-year class. They are even less likely to interact significantly with members of the second-year and third-year classes. At some law schools, section identity is so strong that alumni, even many years after graduation, identify themselves by section.

Later in the first year, students are likely to become more aware of the other students who populate the law school, including upperclassmen, visiting students from other countries, and students pursuing a post-graduate law degree such as a masters degree in law (LL.M.) or doctorate in the study of law (J.S.D. or S.J.D.). If the law school has its own building, or even its own campus, law students may continue to have little interaction, throughout law school, with undergraduate students and other members of the university community. In addition, whether members of the general public outside of the university have a regular presence in the law-school environment may depend on whether the school offers a legal-aid clinic or other services that cater to the non-legal community.

The first-year class, and even the larger law school, is a relatively self-contained community in which students learn, debate, volunteer, socialize, and sometimes even live. Because law school is so self-contained, the ability to get along, to be tolerant of different viewpoints and faiths, and to be accepting of different kinds of people is very important.

The insularity of the law-school community also requires that students be continually mindful of their professionalism, both inside and outside the classroom. Many students describe law school as a "fishbowl," a place in which personal behavior, even outside of school, is a matter of public knowledge. Many have described the experience of being in law school as more akin to the small community in which they attended high school or even junior high school, rather than the relatively large, anonymous community in which they pursued their undergraduate studies.

Professionalism requires that students be respectful of and courteous toward fellow students. Some people grasp concepts in class more quickly than others; students who do should nevertheless keep listening to the professor and realize that there may be more to learn about a subject. Similarly, students should avoid laughing when another student does not seem to understand the material or makes inappropriate comments. Students should also refrain from making audible comments about either the students reciting cases or the views expressed by those students. More generally, when criticizing or critiquing a colleague's argument or views, students should work hard to ensure that they criticize only the argument, not the student making the argument. Personal attacks are inappropriate. One student regularly voiced an unpopular position in matters of public policy. More often than not, he was simply playing devil's advocate. He rather enjoyed riling up the class, however, particularly when the responses other students made to his comments were personally motivated, rather than being directed at the arguments he made in support of the views he espoused.

Students should realize that their activities outside of the classroom are often known within the law-school community. They should expect that their colleagues and their professors know who regularly holds parties at his or her home during the week, who is engaged in the use of illegal drugs, and who is studying in the law library until closing time every night. Other students and professors form impressions based on this information, regardless of whether they expressly communicate those impressions to the student. In addition, students are often assumed to be similar to their friends and associates. Therefore, a student whose friends drink alcohol to excess or use illegal drugs should expect that his colleagues and professors may assume that he engages in the same behavior.

Being mindful of one's behavior in public is good training for the practice of law. Lawyers never know where they will encounter their clients outside the office. Lawyers have lost clients because of careless or even offensive statements, about either the client or other matters, that were overheard by the client herself or related to the client through an observer. Elevators, cellular telephones, and e-mail all pose similar hazards. In law school, likewise, much information that might otherwise be private is likely to become a matter of public knowledge, including pregnancies and births, marriages and divorces, and other very personal matters. Students should therefore strive to ensure that their behavior is consistent with the impressions they wish others to form of them.

Relationship dynamics are important in law school. Students should think carefully before dating their classmates, and should understand that their colleagues and professors are likely to know who the students are dating and may long associate them with those whom they dated in law school. Also, because some relationships do not work out, students should consider not dating other students in the same section or class.

The emotional strain of having to see that person day after day, all day long, could cloud what should otherwise be a wonderful learning experience. Students may also find that the new ways of thinking they learn in law school have an effect on their personal relationships. They may take on a greater sense of responsibility in the family, with people looking to "the lawyer," even though that person is still a student, to lead the family in matters of legal importance. Alternatively, some law students have found that family and friends seek to attack or humiliate them, in an effort to respond to any real or perceived arrogance on the part of the student. Sometimes, these responses have nothing to do with the personal behavior of the student, but instead are generated by outsiders' beliefs about what lawyers do and who they are.

It is important that the law student understand the tremendous emotional, psychological, and time pressures that she will face during her three years of law school. Indeed, students may find that the bulk of the stress associated with law school stems not from the intellectual challenge it entails, but rather from the vast amount of work and reading that will regularly be required in a short period of time. Those students who have children often face additional pressure, and may find support and encouragement from others in the same position. Suggestions for balancing family and law-school responsibilities are presented in Chapter 5.

Friendships from before law school are often difficult, but important, for students to sustain. It can be beneficial for students to maintain regular contact with non-lawyer friends as reminders of the world outside of law school. Indeed, doing so can provide a valuable non-legal perspective. At the same time, however, law students must understand that their old friends may grow angry or even embittered at the investment of time and energy that law school requires.

PROFESSORS

The relationship between professor and student can be one of the most stressful, but also one of the most rewarding, experiences in law school. Law students often find that their relationships with professors shape the way they perceive certain areas of the law. A professor may even be so charismatic and enthusiastic that he inspires students to pursue a career in the area of law that he teaches.

At the same time, and although this may seem unfair, students must remember that law school is not a democracy; rather, the professor controls the classroom environment in all respects. Therefore, although a professor may choose to conduct class in a light-hearted manner, and may even choose to poke fun at students, students must be serious (in the sense of providing thoughtful and supportable answers) and professional in responding. Student antics during class are seldom tolerated and may result in the student who is responsible receiving extremely negative and unwanted attention from the professor.

Professors expect that students will conduct themselves with a demeanor that would be appropriate in a courtroom or law-firm setting. Thus, many professors frown on students who wear revealing clothing, who show up in class with bare feet, who engage in frequent sighing, groans, or other obvious expressions of boredom or distaste, and who make informal responses such as "Yep" or "Nope." Some professors take particular offense when students engage in other work or surf the Internet during class. If the professor finds a student's behavior to be particularly offensive, the professor may choose to use the student as an example for the rest of the class. In addition, some professors make a habit of calling on students who are engaged in inappropriate behavior, such as private, in-class discussions with colleagues.

The student behavior that is perhaps most likely draw a law professor's ire, however, is disrespect, whether for the professor, for another student, or for a classroom visitor. One professor had a practice of praising students in class who had done a good job in case recitation. Near the beginning of one semester, when she had praised a student for his fine recitation, he turned to the rest of the class and said, "Well, give me a hand!" Somewhat hesitantly, his colleagues applauded. The professor promptly ceased praising students in class for the remainder of the semester and made it clear to the class that the misbehavior of that one student was responsible for her change in tone.

Students should expect professors to be aware of more subtle behavior as well, such as their body language and facial expressions during class. It is common for professors to respond verbally to students' behavior as well as to their words. For instance, a professor might respond to a student who has been yawning by saying, "I apologize if I am boring you, Mr. Thompson. Perhaps you would like to recite the next case." Although students may feel anonymous in a large class, they should remember that the professor, standing at the front of the room, generally is able to view all of the students fairly well, especially in a classroom with tiered seating. Furthermore, many professors walk through the classroom during class. Like all people, professors form opinions of students relatively quickly. Unpleasant looks, smirks, grimaces, sighs, and yawns are some of the negative behavior of which a professor may take note. The professor is also likely to notice a student's attentiveness, pleasant demeanor, and professionalism in the classroom, and to form a positive opinion of that student's attitude and level of preparedness. Students should remember, in the case of a four-credit class, that the professor observes each student's conduct for a minimum of four hours per week.

If a student has performed poorly in class or, worse yet, has been reprimanded in the classroom for inappropriate behavior, the professional response on the part of the student is to make an appointment to speak to the professor to acknowledge the mistake and to ask for advice if it is needed. Many a professor has formed a poor impression of a student initially, only to change her mind when the student took responsibility for his actions and apologized. The unprofessional response would be for the student to run out of the classroom when the class period has ended, and to avoid the professor or look away when she passes the student in the hallway. If the student believes the incident will be forgotten if he behaves this way, he is mistaken. Instead, the professor is likely to share her impression of the student with her colleagues, leading them to form a negative impression of the student as well.

Sometimes, when a student has developed a poor relationship with one of his professors and has been unable to remedy this situation on his own, he may want to seek the assistance of another professor. This is a delicate matter, and certainly should not be attempted until the student has first tried to correct the problem himself. Indeed, the student should expect the second professor to ask him what he has already done to approach the first professor. If, however, the student has made a good-faith effort to remedy the problem and has failed, the second professor may be willing to put in a good word to her colleague on behalf of the student if she herself has a strong, positive relationship with the student.

Professors expect that students will be prepared for class. Some law professors are stringent in reprimanding students for recitation mistakes and poor preparation. Others insist upon strict obedience to classroom rules but offer wide latitude when students are substantively wrong, so long as they are prepared and are able to present a considered opinion. Many professors respond in a much more negative way when a student pretends to be prepared than when the student simply admits that she has not done the reading. Obviously, in a courtroom, an attorney would want to admit immediately if he did not know the answer to a question the judge asked, rather than trying to fabricate a response on the spot that might later harm his client. Law-school students should be no less protective of their own interests during class.

In dealing with professors, students should keep in mind the fact that professors approach relationships with students in a variety of ways. Some professors, when they are approached by students outside of class, will be as formal as they are in class. Others will be more informal, allowing students simply to drop by the office when the professor is available, for instance, and calling students by first name outside of class. Some professors even make themselves available to students to discuss matters beyond that of the course being taught, including job searches, law-review or moot-court work, or even personal matters. Although students may wish to see the professor during scheduled office hours for routine matters or quick questions, it is often wise to schedule time outside of normal office hours if the student wishes to have uninterrupted time with the professor.

When a student discusses a grade with a professor, it is important that he do so constructively, seeking advice on how to improve his work, rather than challenging the professor about the grade he has earned. Many professors are offended when students do not accept responsibility for the grades they receive, but act as though the grades are imposed arbitrarily. One good rule of thumb is as follows: In discussing a grade with a professor, the student should speak of the grade she "earned," thus accepting responsibility for the grade, rather than referring to the grade as one she was "given," thereby attempting to shift responsibility to the professor for her own poor performance.

At many law schools, students are given the opportunity at the end of each semester to evaluate their professors. In so doing, students are encouraged to understand the following. First, they should know that most professors and law schools take course evaluations very seriously, especially as the law-school administration makes decisions about retention, promotion, and tenure. Therefore, students who choose to be vicious or punitive should know that their actions might cause real harm to the career of the affected professor. Second, most professors would prefer to know that a student is having difficulty with the class or with the professor's teaching style long before the end of the semester when the evaluations are given. In fact, the only way the problem is likely to be addressed during the semester is for the student who is affected to discuss the problem with the professor. Therefore, out of a sense of professionalism, students who find themselves struggling, either with the substance of a course or the way in which it is being taught, should consider speaking with the professor as soon as possible. Obviously, the student's timing and attitude are likely to influence the tenor of the professor's response.

In all law schools, it seems, there are scandals involving students engaged in inappropriate relationships with professors, or professors who are perceived as being problematic or biased. Sometimes these concerns are legitimate, and other times they are merely school mythology. Again, like all professionals, students must learn to respond only to real issues, and not to be distracted by mere rumor or speculation. Some professors may, for example, express extreme political views that make it difficult for some students to feel comfortable in their classrooms. Students are likely to find that professors are particularly sensitive to any intimation of bias, and that they deal with this matter in a variety of ways. Several female law students have noted that professors actually treated the women in class more harshly than the men in an effort to show a lack of bias. A detailed discussion of what to do when such situations occur can be found in Chapter 10.

Although there are many moral, professional, and personal reasons to maintain a positive relationship with one's professors, there is an instrumental reason to do so as well. Many times, professors are well connected in the local community and may be able to assist students in finding employment. Furthermore, professors are often in charge of clinical programs or internships, and may be in a position to make personal recommendations either for or against a given student's candidacy for one of these positions. One student so angered the professor in charge of judicial-clerkship applications that the professor vowed to do everything in his power to ensure that the student did not receive a clerkship. He carried through on that promise.

Along the same lines, students who are seeking clinical placements, summer-associate or permanent law-firm positions, judicial clerkships, or placement in a law school's honors program, for instance, may need a letter of recommendation from one or more of their professors. A student who wishes to approach a professor for a letter of recommendation should do so as far as possible in advance of the time when the letter is due. She should be prepared to remind the professor who she is, if necessary, and should be ready to supply the professor with a résumé and transcript, if requested, so that the professor can highlight the student's accomplishments with particularity.

The type of recommendation letter that the professor may write on behalf of the student is likely to vary considerably, depending on the length of time the professor has known the student, and the student's attitude, level of effort, and performance in the activities in which she has interacted with the professor.

The sample letters at the end of this chapter are intended to show how recommendation letters may vary for students who performed well in class and demonstrated great effort and those who performed relatively poorly in class but demonstrated a great deal of effort. (This professor declined to write letters of recommendation for those students who demonstrated either little effort or a lack of professionalism, regardless of the grade they earned in the course.) The sample letters are also intended to demonstrate the difference that a professor's level of interaction with a given student can make, whether the professor and student have worked together on an activity such as law review, the student has been the professor's research assistant, or the student has simply maintained contact with a professor through informal mentoring. In addition, the sample letters are intended to show how letters of recommendation may vary, depending on the purpose for which they are being used.

WHERE: DYNAMICS IN THE LAW-SCHOOL CLASSROOM

The law-school classroom is a more formal setting than that to which undergraduate students are likely to have been accustomed. Although the tradition of wearing formal attire to class has long since been abandoned in favor of comfortable clothing, students at most law schools are still expected to dress in a manner that is not distracting to those around them. As stated earlier in this chapter, bare feet and revealing clothing are probably poor choices. In addition, some schools (and some professors) prohibit baseball caps and other hats in the classroom. Law schools vary in their policies on food and drink in the classroom. Again, the student should remember that her conduct is likely to make an impression on her professor, either positive or negative. Many professors are comfortable with a student's bringing a cup of coffee to class, but bringing a full meal, especially if it is accompanied by a newspaper, sends the professor the clear signal that learning is not the student's top priority for that class period.

At many schools, students sit in assigned seats. A law student should give some thought to his choice of seat on the first day of class, especially because he may find himself assigned to that seat for the remainder of the semester. It is often a good idea for students to sit near the center of the classroom, in good hearing distance of the professor and of other students who may be reciting or asking questions. Some professors require that students sit as close to the front of the room as possible, reserving seats in the back of the room for late-comers, if late entry is permitted, and visitors. Some professors tend to call more frequently on students at eye level; others focus on those in the back of the room whose attention might otherwise wander. Even if seats are not assigned, the student should pick a spot with which he will be satisfied for the remainder of the course; students tend to become proprietary about their choice of seating at an early point in the semester.

The American Bar Association recommends, as part of its accreditation guidelines, that students be permitted to miss only two times the number of credit hours of each course; providing a maximum of four absences in a two-credit course, six in a three-credit course, and so on. Instead of, or in addition to a formal attendance policy, some professors include questions on the final examination that only students who attended class regularly are likely to be able to answer. These questions may include details that, although they may have seemed unimportant to the student who merely read the case on her own, were emphasized in class. If the professor takes attendance, she may have students sign an attendance sheet that is circulated, or she may take attendance herself. As is further discussed in Chapter 10, a student should never sign the name of another student; doing so may place the student in violation of the school's Honor Code.

Most schools strongly discourage first-semester and first-year students from missing class, except for religious observance or a family emergency. After that time, each school's policy will vary. Some schools have strict attendance policies like that recommended by the American Bar Association, while others are lenient about class attendance. In addition, many professors impose their own attendance policies that may be stricter than those mandated by the institution. In any event, students should ensure that any missed classes do not interfere with their learning any more than is necessary. Some professors are willing to audiotape or videotape a class if the student notifies the professor in advance that the student will be absent. Some professors will also permit students to audiotape the class for one another. No student, however, should audiotape a professor's lecture without first obtaining express permission from the professor herself.

Meeting with the professor, before an absence if possible, is an excellent way for the student to ensure that she does not miss out on handouts or other materials that are to be distributed. This interaction also gives the student an opportunity to tell the professor that her absence does not reflect a lack of interest in the course. Besides speaking with the professor, students should obtain notes from others who were present and should ask their colleagues to pick up an extra copy of any distributed handouts, if possible.

Policies about late arrival in class also vary from school to school and from professor to professor. Many professors do not permit late entry into the classroom; in fact, some actually lock the classroom door. Other professors prefer that students do their best to attend each class, arriving late if necessary. If late arrival is permitted, students should give one another (and the professor) the courtesy of being as inconspicuous as possible. Often, thoughtfulness would suggest that the student sit in the back of the classroom, rather than climbing over other students to reach her usual seat. The late-arriving student should also enter through a back door if possible, rather than distracting students who are facing the professor. Finally, a student who arrives late should never boot up a computer unless she is able to do so in absolute silence. The same policies (and the same etiquette) apply to early departure from class.

From time to time, a professor may have to cancel class. There may be personal or professional reasons for the cancellation, or the decision may stem from bad weather or a national emergency. Professors generally try to provide advance notice to students if they are able to do so. Many will schedule a make-up class toward the end of the semester. The make-up class may be used to cover course material, if the class is still behind at that point, or it may be used for exam review. Either way, students should understand that such unavoidable situations sometimes arise and should treat the make-up classes as if they were regularly scheduled classes. Students should remember that they are consumers paying a great deal of money for each class lecture and should therefore expect their professors to reschedule cancelled lectures.

Finally, the extent to which students are permitted to ask questions during class varies greatly from professor to professor, as well. Some professors do not permit questions during class, but provide time outside of the classroom for students to get additional clarification and instruction. Other professors entertain questions during class, so long as answering those questions does not require too much of a digression from the material to be covered. Often, if a question is particularly involved or requires revisiting material that was covered at an earlier point in the semester, the professor will request that the student see her after class to discuss the question in private.

When We Learn the Law: The Pacing of a Semester in Law School

One of the most difficult matters for many students new to law school to grasp is the pacing of a law-school semester. Traditionally, each student is given one final examination at the end of each course, and that single examination accounts for the student's entire grade in the course. When a course takes an entire year, as is the case for many first-year subjects, there may or may not be an examination at the end of the first semester, and any examination at that time may or may not be part of the student's final grade. Instead, students in year-long courses may be tested only once, at the end of the second semester.

Because only one examination is normally given per course, law students quickly learn the importance of discipline, pacing, and learning as much as possible from any mid-course assessment opportunities that may be given, including mid-term examinations, pop quizzes, and sample problems. At the beginning of each semester, law students typically spend some time becoming acclimated to their new courses, learning how the professor conducts the course and the kind of preparation that is expected. Students often particularly enjoy the beginning of the spring semester as an opportunity to slow down the pace of their studies somewhat, and to recover from the fall examination period.

At the end of the first month or so of school each semester, students find themselves fully engaged with classes and extracurricular activities. It is at this busy time that students should begin to concern themselves with the examinations that will come at the end of the semester. This is a good time to organize a study group, begin an outline (discussed later in this chapter), and meet with the professor to iron out any substantive difficulties that may have arisen thus far.

By the last month of each semester, the student should be well organized for the upcoming examinations. Upperclassmen should be winding up seminar papers, law-review articles, clinical assignments, job interviews, and other non-examination requirements far enough in advance of the examination period to allow them time to focus on exams. All law students should be fine-tuning their substantive knowledge of course material and finalizing outlines during this time, meanwhile staying abreast of new material as it is presented.

Few law students are able to succeed through procrastination. In addition, those students who have planned carefully throughout the semester often find themselves getting more sleep and experiencing less stress than their classmates who may not have managed their time as well. It is important that students maintain a healthy balance throughout the semester, enjoying slower periods and allowing themselves sufficient rest while making sure that they are progressing steadily toward their end-of-semester goals.

HOW WE LEARN THE LAW

As discussed in Chapter 1, professors have different teaching styles, just as students have different learning styles. Regardless of their individual teaching styles, however, at least one fact is almost universal: professors expect law students to be very well prepared for class.

Preparation for Class

What does it mean to be prepared for class? Although the definition varies somewhat from professor to professor, some aspects are consistent. Preparation for class requires that the student read the assignment thoroughly. This means, among other things, that the student must look up every word she does not know, even if the word does not relate to the law, and even if the word does not appear to be important to the court's decision. This exercise expands the student's vocabulary, both legal and non-legal, and helps the student to feel confident about discussing legal matters. Furthermore, in addition to reading each case, the student should have read the text preceding the cases, and any notes and problems that may follow the case. Finally, and as discussed more thoroughly later in this chapter, students should begin to anticipate how the professor will try to stretch their understanding of the materials beyond the facts set forth in the assigned reading, and should attempt similar exercises on their own, before class.

In a class that is using a case-based textbook, students should expect most of the professor's questions to revolve around the cases, but should also read each note and problem and consider each question posed therein. Although many professors will not discuss every note or problem in the text, students should be prepared to discuss all of them, unless instructed otherwise.

When using a problem-based text, by contrast, students should expect the case law and textual material to be fairly self-explanatory. Although there may be some in-class discussion of this preliminary material, generally the bulk of class time will be spent discussing the problems and notes. Again, the student should think carefully about the outcome of each problem and the answer to each question posed in the text. Obviously, because the notes and problems are the primary focus of a problem-based course, the student's preparation for these should be more thorough than would be devoted to the notes and problems in a case-law-based textbook.

First-year students are often bewildered by the extent to which their professors insist that students pay careful attention to the facts of each case assigned. Many students view this practice as nothing more than a law-school hazing exercise. It is important to understand, however, why the facts are at least as important as the law in the students' learning process. Simply stated, learning the facts as well as the kernel of law that each case represents gives the student an additional way of accessing the information she has learned. For example, although the student may not remember a precise term of art such as the "benefit-detriment theory of consideration" in contract law, she may be inclined to remember the facts of the famous case *Hamer v. Sidway*, in which an uncle promises his favorite nephew a sum of money if the nephew will refrain from drinking, smoking, and playing billiards for money until he reaches a certain age. Becoming familiar with the colorful facts of the case is likely to make it easier for the student to remember the rule of law that the case represents.

Understanding Legal Citations

The first case in a popular contracts text is *Rollins, Inc. v. Foster*, 991 F. Supp. 1426 (M.D. Ala. 1998).[1] This particular way of identifying a lawsuit, which includes abbreviated party names, identifies the court where the matter was heard, and provides a citation for the case reporter in which the court's opinion can be found, is called a *case style* or *citation*. Even before students begin to read the case, they can use the case style or citation to glean some basic information about the litigation.

The citation begins by identifying the parties to the lawsuit. In this litigation, the parties are as follows:

Rollins, Inc. is the *petitioner* in this matter. The petitioner is the party who is seeking relief from the court. At the trial-court level, the petitioner, who is sometimes called the *plaintiff*, initiates the lawsuit by filing a legal document called a *complaint*. When students read the case, they learn that there is a second petitioner, as well, Orkin Exterminating Co. Inc., which is a subsidiary of Rollins, Inc. There are often multiple petitioners and respondents in litigation; typically, only the first entity on each side is listed in the case style.

Foster is the name of the *respondent* to this lawsuit. "Foster" is the last name of an individual, Ms. Judy Foster. Both

---

[1] For the reader's convenience, each of the cases that are referred to by name in this book was selected from Knapp, Crystal and Prince, *Problems in Contract Law* (4th ed., Aspen Law & Business 1999).

individuals and business entities such as corporations can be parties to lawsuits. When business entities are parties, they are identified by full name; when individuals are parties, they are identified by last name only. The respondent is the party who has been sued. At the trial-court level, the respondent, who is sometimes called the *defendant,* must file an *answer* in response to the petitioner's complaint. The respondent may also choose to file a *counterclaim* against the petitioner or a *third-party complaint* to bring other parties into the lawsuit.

The next portion of the citation indicates where the court's reported opinion may be found in the official published collection of opinions that are called *reporters.*

The first number, 991, is the volume number of the reporter where the opinion is published.

F. Supp. is the official abbreviation for the Federal Supplement, which is the reporter in which cases from the United States District Courts appear.

The second number, 1426, is the page number on which the opinion begins.

The last part of the citation identifies the court that heard the lawsuit, as well as the year in which the opinion was rendered.

M.D. Ala. is the standard abbreviation for the United States District Court for the Middle District of Alabama. This court is part of the federal system that was established pursuant to Article III of the United States Constitution, which states as follows: "The judicial Power of the United States, shall be vested in one supreme Court, and in such inferior Courts as the Congress may from time to time ordain and establish."

1998 is the year in which the case was decided.

The second case in this textbook, *Ray v. William G. Eurice & Bros., Inc.*, 201 Md. 115, 93 A.2d 272 (1952), looks different from the first because there are actually two citations linked together. The *Ray* case is a product of the state-court system of Maryland.

The first citation is from the official reporter for the state court that heard the case. Md. is the abbreviation for the Maryland Reporter. The reporter for the highest court in a state will have as its abbreviation the standard postal abbreviation for the state. Thus, the reader knows that this case was decided in the highest court in the state-court system of Maryland. Many states call their highest court the Supreme Court; the highest court in Maryland, however, is called the Court of Appeals.

The second citation is from a regional reporter. A.2d identifies the regional reporter in which the case is published—in this case, the Atlantic Reporter, second series. The designation "second series" simply means that, after so many years, the numbering for the reporter-system was restarted, so as to keep the numbers relatively low. For example, volume 200 of the Atlantic Reporter is followed by 1 Atlantic Reporter, Second Series. The Atlantic Reporter includes not only opinions from the state-court system of Maryland, but also those from the state courts of Connecticut, Delaware, District of Columbia, Maine, New Hampshire, New Jersey, Pennsylvania, Rhode Island, and Vermont.

This way of identifying cases with two citations is called parallel citation format, and is used only for state-court cases. Back before the age of electronic databases such as Westlaw and LEXIS, lawyers could find the cases to support their arguments only in the published reporters. Because these books were both expensive and space-consuming, a lawyer (or a court) might choose to purchase the state reporter or the regional reporter, but perhaps not both. Because the lawyer needed to make it possible for the court to look up the cases she was citing, she would include the citations to both reporters where the opinion could be found. Today, each court generally will indicate, in its local rules, whether it expects lawyers to use parallel citations.

Participation in Class and the Socratic Method

The classroom environment in law school is different from that which students are likely to have experienced before. In some classes, the professor lectures and students simply take notes, much as they may have done in undergraduate school. More often, however, the interaction between professor and students is much more direct. In the typical law-school class, as discussed in Chapter 1, the professor questions students intensively, one at a time, before their peers, challenging the student's legal analysis and expecting the student to marshal factual support for each conclusion. This process, which is called the Socratic method, teaches students to think on their feet, whether literally (some professors do expect students to stand when reciting) or figuratively; to argue persuasively; and to think creatively under pressure.

The teacher may also rely on other resources, such as PowerPoint presentations, audio-visual materials such as films, and in-class simulation exercises, performed either by members of the class or by visiting professionals. Sometimes, a teacher may invite a guest speaker to address the class. Normally, the speaker must be a person of exceptional skill or renown before a professor will surrender valuable class time for this endeavor.

Professors have various means of choosing students to recite a case or to answer questions. The professor may, for instance, pick students randomly, may proceed alphabetically, or may focus on one part of the classroom at a time. Many times, students will have at least a few days' notice of being called on if the professor proceeds in an identifiable pattern. Furthermore, some professors may notify the class in advance, whether in an earlier class or at the beginning of the class period, of those students who should expect to recite during that period. Professors' policies vary as to whether class participation is a factor in determining students' grades. Some professors do not count class participation at all, while others count it as some percentage of the grade. Some professors count a student's performance only if it is particularly good or bad. Regardless of whether class participation is ultimately a factor in the student's final grade, students often find that they benefit greatly from the opportunity that class participation affords them to develop a better understanding of the assigned material.

DIFFICULTIES IN CLASS PARTICIPATION

Sometimes students are not fully prepared to recite a case or to be questioned about the material. This situation often arises when students half-read the material, but do not learn it thoroughly. Whatever the reason, students often wonder whether it is better to attempt to bluff their way through the material or to stop the professor and ask to be excused due to a lack of preparation. The best way to handle this situation is to approach the professor before class and ask to be excused, citing a valid (and true) reason for being unprepared, such as spending the night in an emergency room with a sick child. Students should not, however, expect the professor to be sympathetic to an excuse such as having too much reading assigned in another core course. Approaching the professor "before class" means stopping by the professor's office or speaking to the professor in person before class is scheduled to begin. If the professor indicates that e-mail communications are appropriate for this type of notice, then the student should send an e-mail as soon as she knows that she may be unprepared. Even so, the student who communicates her lack of preparation to a professor by e-mail or voice mail should follow up before class begins to ensure that the message was received.

Some professors allow students to take a certain number of "passes" during the semester without citing a reason. Many of the professors who employ this system require that the passes be exercised before the class period begins, so that the professor need not waste valuable class time finding a student who is prepared to discuss the material. (In addition to irritating the professor, such behavior can have a negative impact on classroom morale. One lawyer can still recall, twelve years later, the identities of a few unprepared students from her first year in law school.) Being caught unprepared is embarrassing for the student, who can sometimes find it difficult to rehabilitate her academic reputation after such a situation occurs.

Sometimes, students are well prepared but simply freeze when called upon. If this happens, the student should do her best to work her way through the situation. She might try to start with some basics of which she is certain. For instance, in a contracts case, if the student is asked to identify the consideration supporting a contract, she might begin by reciting the definition of consideration. Often, just beginning to speak will help the student overcome her discomfort, while remaining silent will allow the tension to build further. Some professors will jump in and try to be of assistance, while others will allow the student to flounder. In any event, any student who has this unfortunate and nerve-racking experience should immediately meet with the professor outside of class, discuss what happened so the professor knows the student was not unprepared, and seek advice on how to handle the situation in the future. It may be a good idea for the student to show the professor the material that she prepared before class.

Some professors, in dealing with students who are truly phobic about class participation, are willing to make special efforts to make this experience more comfortable for these students. For instance, some professors will give the student five or ten minutes advance notice, saying, "In five minutes, I will ask Ms. Smith the following question." Others will give the same sort of notice at the end of the hour, such as, "At the beginning of the next class, I will ask Ms. Smith the following question." Allowing advance notice gives the student time to prepare an answer.

Students are also encouraged not to overemphasize the importance of being correct in class. Sometimes, professors will simply be unwilling to allow a student to give the correct answer during class. Instead, the professor might poke holes in any argument the student makes so as to stretch, as far as possible, the student's knowledge and ability to argue persuasively. The student should realize that the ultimate goal is not to appear to be a superstar in class, but rather to understand the material comprehensively at the end of each class session.

Other students may struggle with in-class recitations, despite thorough preparation, due to substantive difficulties with the assignment. Although many professors do not mind students giving incorrect answers, law students must understand the level of personal responsibility that is required of them. Students who are truly confused by the material, after doing their best to figure it out on their own, should not hesitate to ask for help. If the professor is unavailable, there may be student tutors or teaching assistants who will be able to lend a hand to help the student make sense of the material. Although students are encouraged to develop a sense of appropriate confidence in their classroom participation, it is equally important that a student not become what other law students typically call a "gunner" or, for those who remember the term, a "brown nose." Furthermore, students who are perceived as simply liking to hear themselves talk are frequently ostracized by their colleagues and cut off at the knees by their professors, in the interest of classroom economy.

Professors will often ask questions to which the student who is called on does not immediately know the answer. How the student handles herself in this circumstance is of the utmost importance. Her behavior can be critical not only in making a positive impression on the professor and on her colleagues, but also in learning the law. Statements such as "Could you repeat the question?" are generally not well-received, while alternatives such as "I am not sure that I heard you correctly. I believe what you asked is the following: _____. Is that correct?" are much more appropriate.

There are other methods of class participation: a student may volunteer, instead of waiting to be called upon, if doing so is permitted by the professor. In addition, a student may offer (or may be requested) to look up information to be shared at a later class, especially if the class becomes stuck on a particular concept or word. Others may be given the opportunity to answer quick, detail-oriented questions posed by the professor, which may be designed to give the student who has been called on to recite the case time to think and to prepare her response. One professor refers to this mode of participation as "making a cameo appearance."

Students with learning disabilities or physical disabilities should address these issues before the school year begins, if possible. Most schools will have an assigned member of the faculty, professional staff, or administration available to work with disabled students. Accommodations may be available for a student's disability pursuant to the Americans with Disabilities Act. It is crucial, however, that students work within proper channels to see that accommodations are arranged appropriately and in a timely fashion. Some students resent those who receive accommodations and believe that the accommodated students receive an "unfair advantage." Handling the issues confidentially and through the proper channels should minimize these concerns.

LEARNING FROM A NEGATIVE IN-CLASS EXPERIENCE

At some point in each law student's career, he is likely to experience the consequences of a professor's belief, whether correct or incorrect, that a student is unprepared. The fortunate student will be able to learn from the experience of others rather than facing the situation himself. Regardless of whether the experience is first-hand or vicarious, however, the situation, even if painful, presents an important and valuable opportunity for learning.

The law school classroom is a controlled environment with relatively low stakes compared to those that the student will encounter in the practice of law. Therefore, experiencing the student's embarrassment and the professor's anger and frustration under these circumstances may be an important life lesson that prevents the student from putting himself in the same situation later, with much greater consequences, in the outside world after law school. The following discussion introduces some ideas that may be of assistance to students in avoiding this situation both in class and, more important, later in the practice of law.

Most law students are bright, capable, poised, well-spoken, and professional. Because of these characteristics, many professors have high expectations of their students. Indeed, sometimes students progress with such ease through material that the professor assumed would be difficult, that the professor continues to increase the pace of the course (and her expectations of the class) steadily. If, suddenly, one or more students perform poorly in class the professor may assume that this is due to a lack of preparation or poor time management.

Poor classroom performance can occur for a variety of reasons, including other time commitments, such as job searches, extracurricular activities, papers, and other classes; illness or exhaustion; confusion about the professor's expectations; difficulty with a particular text; and more general difficulty with the course

237

material. Regardless of the source of the problem, students who fall behind in a law-school course often find it hard to catch up without great effort and, perhaps, the assistance of a colleague or professor. Law-school courses are not only difficult, but also build upon themselves in a way that can be uniquely unforgiving when a student gets lost in one of the preliminary steps.

When a professor assigns certain material to be prepared by the class, students should treat the assignment as a deadline. Often, given other time commitments, students do not prepare the assigned material until just before it is to be covered in class. This strategy can backfire significantly when students discover that they do not understand the material well enough to formulate an answer or, at least, a considered opinion, in response to a question. In these circumstances, a student who is called upon may throw up her hands and say helplessly, "I am so lost that I do not know how to respond." In this situation, the class is likely to see the professor respond with exasperation, just as a supervising attorney might if a junior attorney gave the same reply when the deadline came for an assignment the junior attorney was to have prepared. The professor is likely to wonder why the student had failed to inform the professor of her difficulty before class and to seek additional substantive instruction.

Students can learn from this experience by taking some advice that is relevant both to law-school preparation and to the practice of law. Indeed, the reasons students are likely to perform poorly in class—exhaustion, substantive confusion, and other demands on the students' time—are all situations that attorneys encounter frequently, even daily. Students, like practicing attorneys, can (and should) take affirmative steps to prevent difficulty when a deadline is looming.

Students should understand a professor's expectations. Especially if the class has been performing at a high level and moving quickly through the assigned material, the professor may expect that the class will find an upcoming task to be easy too. Because many law-school graduates are well-spoken, poised, and very capable, they are likely to face the same high expectations in their careers as practitioners. In law school, as in the practice of law, a student may find it useful to make a quick, early assessment of any assignment to see if she can respond right away to any expectations that might be inappropriate. A supervising attorney might incorrectly assume, for instance, that, because a junior attorney had studied the Uniform Commercial Code's Article 2 on sales in law school, he would also be familiar with the entirely separate Article 7 provisions on bills of lading. Along the same lines, an attorney who speaks German and has a working knowledge of Spanish would not necessarily feel comfortable summarizing a German deposition for a Spanish client. Under these circumstances, it might be appropriate for the junior attorney to inquire as to whether he is really the right person for the task.

Other situations may give rise to inaccurate expectations as well. A supervising attorney may give a junior attorney a research assignment, indicating that it will be a "quick and easy" matter. Upon beginning her research, the junior attorney may find that the matter is one "of first impression," meaning that it has not yet been addressed in that particular jurisdiction. Research for a well-established matter of law is very different from that for a matter of first impression. When researching a well-established principle of law, a lawyer cites the seminal cases and any relevant statutes, and her research is completed relatively quickly. With a matter of first impression, however, the lawyer may find herself doing a survey of out-of-state law, as well as exploring secondary materials such as law-review articles. Alternatively, she may find that she must base her argument in another field of law and argue the point entirely by analogy. Either way, researching a matter of first impression is a much more difficult and time-consuming task than researching a matter of well-established law.

A junior lawyer will often find, in other words, that she must somehow communicate to the supervising attorney, "This is a harder legal question than you may have thought" or "This is a more challenging matter for me than you may have thought, given my background." How well that message is received often depends on when it is given. If the junior attorney communicates this information to her supervisor shortly after she gets the assignment, the supervisor may seek additional assistance for the project, may choose someone else for the task, may extend the deadline, or may offer the junior attorney additional guidance. If, however, this message is delivered when the research should have been completed, or even shortly before the due date, the supervising attorney is likely to respond with anger and frustration, just as the law professor did: "Why did you not tell me sooner?"

Sometimes, both in law school and in practice, the student or junior lawyer may feel uncomfortable expressing her lack of familiarity with an area of law for fear of looking foolish. Again, she must assess the situation for herself, but she should get clarification immediately if she finds that it is needed. When one new lawyer first joined a large firm, her first project involved a statute called "FIFRA." Because the partner who was giving the assignment simply rattled off the acronym, talking about the statute as though it were one with which the new lawyer should be familiar, the junior attorney assumed she should know what it meant. After about five minutes, she finally gathered the courage to say, "There seems to be a gap in my legal education where FIFRA should be," and the assigning attorney actually started laughing. He said, "I am so sorry. I have been working on this case for two years. Of course you do not know what FIFRA is, and no one learns this in law school. It is the Federal Insecticide, Fungicide, and Rodenticide Act. Here is the cite for it." In this situation, getting beyond a sense of embarrassment and false pride and asking a fundamental question early on defused the new lawyer's discomfort quickly and made it possible for her to focus on the legal issue at hand, rather than racking her brain to figure out what "FIFRA" meant.

Poor time management is another reason that many law students (and junior attorneys) do not communicate immediately with the professor (or supervising attorney) about any difficulty they are having with an assignment. Coupled with the high expectations that are placed on both law students and junior attorneys—which, although a compliment, are also a burden—is the matter of multi-tasking and managing multiple deadlines. The following practice may be helpful to both law students and practicing attorneys in managing their time. As stated earlier, whenever a student or attorney receives a new assignment, she should consider starting it immediately, doing just enough work to ascertain whether the task will be difficult for her. In class, for instance, when a review exercise has been assigned and the professor has indicated that she expects the students to give quick, concise answers in class, students might do the first one or two problems as soon as possible. If the students begin the assignment immediately and find themselves so confused that they cannot even formulate responses, then they can let the professor know of their difficulty before the deadline, so that the professor can clarify things.

After the student or lawyer assesses her own readiness for the task that she has been assigned, she faces the next issue—determining what is expected of her in terms of her level of self-sufficiency. How much should she do on her own before she asks for help? In law school, professors' expectations vary. At a minimum, however, most professors expect students to read the assigned material, either to brief the cases or otherwise to become familiar with the facts, rules, and analysis presented, and to formulate a reasoned response to each of the questions posed in the notes and the problems before seeking assistance. Some professors do not care whether a student gives a substantively correct answer, so long as he can articulate how he got there. In addition, many legal texts provide relatively little introductory material on each new concept, so that students do not have enough information to respond correctly to notes and problems that follow each case or even to understand fully each case presented. In these circumstances, some professors require students to do additional research on their own, while others provide students with supplemental information in class.

Even when the professor does not require that students do outside reading, many law students try to minimize their chances of giving a wrong answer in class by reviewing supplementary information on their own. There are several resources that may be useful for this purpose, including the cases that are mentioned in the end notes and review problems that are contained in many texts, and the cases that are cited in the text of the material that the students are required to prepare for class. The law librarian can help new students find these materials. In addition, students may wish to consult treatises or other outside sources. Professors will often indicate, either in class or privately to interested students, which supplementary resources they consider to be most authoritative. Even if this extra work is not required, taking these additional steps helps many students to feel more comfortable.

In practice, expectations vary widely. Some supervising attorneys are willing to review true drafts—work product with which the junior lawyer is still struggling and that reflects her preliminary ideas and concerns. Even under these circumstances, of course, the junior lawyer should ensure that the work is substantively her best effort and includes no typographical or syntactical errors. Others will insist that the junior lawyer go to a person who is senior to her but junior to the supervisor for assistance, and that that mid-level attorney review her work before it goes to the supervisor. A few supervisors will make themselves completely unavailable to the junior attorney, but will nevertheless expect her to produce top quality work product on her own. Sometimes, these expectations are quite reasonable. Obviously, being resourceful is important. One firm fired a first-year associate because of his failure to meet the firm's expectations of a new lawyer. The last straw was when a mid-level associate had given him a two-week assignment that required him to prepare a pleading; a week after the assignment was given, the mid-level associate asked him how he was doing, and he indicated that he did not know how to find the pleadings file. (The pleadings file was not missing; the junior attorney had simply failed to look for it.) This fundamental failure to act resourcefully cost the junior lawyer his job that day.

Other times, junior attorneys face unreasonable expectations. One lawyer's very first deposition was of an expert witness, and the supervising attorney was out of the country that week, having given instructions that no one was to call him. The junior attorney had no idea what she was doing. Happily, a very kind senior associate took the time to give her an informal, one-hour mini-lecture on conducting a deposition and provided her with a number of useful deposition outlines.

When a law student or junior attorney is confused about some aspect of a task, it is often helpful for her to explain to the professor or supervisor what she *does* know, to show her level of preparation and to demonstrate good faith. In torts class, for instance, a student might say, "I know this is an assault, but I just cannot figure out whether the five-year-old should be held responsible because of her extreme youth." In practice, a junior lawyer might say, "I have found the relevant law, but I am having a difficult time figuring out whether the facts are applicable to our situation, because the case I found involves a slip-and-fall in a grocery store, while our case involves a private home." These responses are likely to receive a more favorable (and more helpful) reply than a simple "I do not know" would.

Clarifying expectations up front is important, especially when deadlines are involved. When a supervising attorney gives a deadline, the junior attorney must make sure she knows what the deadline means. If what has been assigned is a pleading, is the date that has been designated as "the deadline" the date on which the supervisor wants the junior attorney to present her preliminary opinions on the merits of the matter? Is it the date on which the supervisor wishes to see a first draft? Is it, instead, the date on which the pleading is to be filed with the court? Obviously, a misunderstanding about the nature of the deadline can be disastrous.

If the junior attorney has been given a deadline that represents the date on which a pleading must be filed, she should make earlier mini-deadlines for herself for the formulation of her preliminary opinions and the creation of a first draft. It is often best, especially for a very junior attorney, if she agrees on those mini-deadlines with the supervisor. If the junior attorney does some of the research right away, as suggested earlier, then she can make sure she will be able to meet each interim and final deadline.

In addition to the difficulties discussed above about deadlines, the junior attorney should ensure that the final product is what is expected. Clarifying expectations—about both deadlines and the kind of work-product that is expected—by e-mail is an excellent idea. If the junior attorney gives only an oral report when a memorandum was expected, the supervising attorney will obviously be displeased. If she writes a memorandum when only an oral response was desired, the client may not be willing to pay for the extra work. Along these same lines, even if the supervising attorney requests an oral response, many lawyers find that it is a good practice always to send a substantive, confirming e-mail, too. That way, both the junior and the senior attorney have a record of the work that was done.

What if the student or junior attorney is totally overworked? In class, some professors permit students to take passes, as discussed above. In practice, although junior attorneys do not have that option, another approach may be of assistance. Sometimes, supervising attorneys have no idea how much is on a junior attorney's plate. This is especially true for junior attorneys who report to more than one supervisor. Junior attorneys should, at all times, maintain an up-to-date list of all projects and their deadlines. A junior attorney should take this list with her when she goes into a supervising attorney's office to receive a new assignment. Saying simply, "I am overwhelmed" is not likely to go over well with a supervisor. Being more specific, and less emotional, however, can often be very effective. If one supervisor has given a junior attorney multiple assignments, she might ask, "Should the *Jones* brief be dealt with before or after the *Smith* filing?" If she is reporting to more than one supervisor, and each has asked her to make a different task her first priority, she might say to one supervisor, "John has asked me to make his brief my first priority. Could the two of you determine which is more urgent?" This approach, in which the supervisors decide among themselves which project is to be handled first, often works much better than the junior lawyer's attempt to make this judgment call for herself.

GETTING THE MOST OUT OF CLASS

Once the student is prepared, she is ready to attend the day's classes. Students who use computers should set them up early to avoid creating a distraction once the lesson has begun. Many professors begin each new class by briefly revisiting material from the prior class, either by summarizing the material or asking for questions from the class. If a summary is given, students will want to listen carefully, making sure that they understand and make note of those items that the professor is now emphasizing. During class, students often try to take notes while listening to the professor and participating in class discussion at the same time. As a result, those students who take notes on their computers and who type quickly may find themselves simply transcribing everything the professor says. One professor has described this as "camcorder syndrome," comparing this behavior to that of a parent who is so intent on capturing his child's soccer game on film for posterity that he never truly gets to watch the game while it is being played. Law students, similarly, must make sure that they balance note-taking with listening, observing, and asking questions for clarification if permitted to do so. To do all of this simultaneously, students learn to make quick diagrams and charts and to jot down concise notes on the case briefs they prepared before class rather than writing down everything that is being said. For example, if the opinion being studied introduces a three-part test, and class discussion is centered on how that test can be applied to new situations, then the student should already have the test written down in the brief she prepared before class and should just add in its application to the new facts as presented in class. In addition, students often devise or adopt symbols as shorthand for often-used terms of art, such as "K" for contract, "π" for plaintiff, and "Δ" for defendant. Similarly, students need not necessarily take notes in the order in which the lecture is presented; rather, the student might consider for herself where the material being discussed fits into the assigned reading. Some students learn better by listening, rather than by contemporaneously taking notes and later reviewing them. One student, who had difficulty reading his own handwriting, concentrated on listening to the lecture. After class or later that night, he would assimilate the day's lesson into his typed outline. Doing so gave him perspective on the lecture material he had heard that day and forced him to focus on remembering the major concepts that were covered.

In addition to being sufficiently prepared for class, students should try to get the most out of their law-school education. Although it is not clear that curiosity is a quality that can be taught, professors often express a desire to cultivate and reward their students' pre-existing curiosity. Students, for example, sometimes find researching subtle nuances of their assigned reading to be rewarding. For example, one case commonly used in the first-year contracts curriculum, *Poel v. Brunswick-Balke-Collender Company,* includes a somewhat cryptic phrase, "fine upriver para rubber." As it turns out, "upriver" means "up the Amazon river," and Para refers to the city of the same name in Brazil that was central to the country's rubber industry at the beginning of the twentieth century. The case involves a contract for the sale of rubber that was to be used to line the pockets of the exquisite pool tables made by the Brunswick-Balke-Collender Company. After the contract was negotiated, the price of Brazilian rubber fell so steeply in light of the development of excellent synthetic alternatives that the purchaser refused to take delivery, claiming that the person who had negotiated the contract on behalf of his company had lacked authority to do so. None of this historical information, however, is apparent from a quick reading of the case. Rather, the student must take apart this cryptic phrase to discover the interesting history behind the case. Speaking more generally, the versions of cases that are presented in casebooks are often heavily excerpted, and many students find it rewarding to consult the full text of cases that are particularly interesting or difficult. Similarly, the cases that are cited in the notes following a principal case can be valuable sources of information for students who wish to know more about the topic or are confused by the information presented in the text. Sometimes, these "note" cases (as law students call them) provide information to help students put the principal case in context. In addition, law students, especially those who are visual learners, often look for ways to make the case law come alive and therefore be more memorable. If, as in the contracts case *Glenn v. Savage*, the student is trying to determine whether the plaintiff should be able to claim that rescuing the defendant's timber from a river was an emergency such that he should be compensated for his efforts even though the defendant did not agree to pay him, the student might consult a map to determine whether the river was particularly deep or precarious at that point. Along the same lines, a student who is having a difficult time keeping all of the family members straight in the family-dispute case *Greiner v. Greiner* might find the task easier if she draws a family tree; similarly, a student who is trying to navigate the complicated real-estate negotiations in the case of *Normile v. Miller* might benefit from a timeline. Finally, a student who is trying to determine whether she could make an argument that *Katz v. Danny Dare, Inc.*, a case in which a disabled man's pension is terminated, is a case representing "the little man v. corporate America," should consult the company's Dun and Bradstreet reports, which would reveal that the company has only three employees.

Students may also bring context to their legal studies by tying their classroom learning to their own particular interests. Those students who find themselves drawn to specific areas of the law, such as legal philosophy, legal history, intellectual property, or human rights, should look for ways to nurture those interests, even during the first year of school, when time may not permit exploration of such matters at any length in the student's core doctrinal classes. Students should remember that law school is ultimately *for them*, and they owe it to themselves to take the time to personalize their law-school experience by cultivating their own interests. Often, professors who know of a student's interest in a given area will be glad to recommend books, to let the student know when relevant lectures are being presented on campus, or simply to sit and talk with the student about non-first-year subjects that are of mutual interest.

SPECIFIC STRATEGIES FOR LEARNING THE LAW

Students have two major goals in each course: preparing for class each day and becoming substantively familiar with the material in order to do as well as possible on the final exam. How students accomplish those twin goals varies greatly and cannot be reduced to a simple formula. Rather, each student must determine what works for him or her. This process may take some time because students do not necessarily know how they learn best. Often, developing a successful strategy is a matter of trial and error. The following is a synopsis of various approaches to mastering law-school coursework.

Assessment Opportunities

One of the most frustrating aspects of law school, especially for first-year students, is the fact that, at most schools, students are graded only once per semester in each course, based on their performance on a single examination. Grades are very important in law school, and if, upon taking the examination, the student discovers that she has not prepared adequately, it is too late for her to do anything about her grade. Therefore, students should take advantage of all opportunities for evaluation that are presented during the semester and should use them to their maximum benefit. For instance, some professors give graded or ungraded mid-term evaluations. They may mark each student paper individually, or they may simply provide students with a model answer and an opportunity to speak with the professor one-on-one by appointment.

Alternatively, professors sometimes assign in-class or out-of-class problems that simulate the traditional law-school, complex-hypothetical-fact-pattern examination question. Again, professors may mark each paper individually, or they may simply provide a model answer and an opportunity for further consultation. In any event, for the exercise to be of benefit to the student, the student should give it her best effort. The student may wish to do such problems while simulating the conditions under which the examination will be given, including closed-text or time-restricted conditions, especially toward the end of the semester. In addition to reviewing each problem individually with the professor, students often benefit from speaking with the professor about their improvement as the semester has progressed. Typically, students should expect to see fundamental improvement in their analytical skills as their first semester of law school progresses. Some professors suggest that students first get comfortable with the basics of legal analysis—learning to identify each issue by its proper name, to state the rule of law, to identify the operative facts and apply the law to the facts, and to draw an appropriate conclusion. The next step for a student who has become adept at legal analysis is to hone her issue-spotting skills. Some professors invite or require students to turn in, along with their answers to a sample problem, a marked-up copy of the problem, on which the student circled the important facts and briefly identified why each was important. The last step in this progression would be for the student to attempt a sample problem under simulated examination conditions, as described above.

Should the student continue to get the same feedback consistently, such as, "Your answer is too conclusory" or "You are forgetting to apply the law to the facts," the student should ask for additional instruction and advice. Sometimes, students will ask a professor very early in the semester what grade a sample-problem answer would have earned had it been on a final examination. Professors are sometimes reluctant to answer this question directly, because they do not want to discourage the student. In many instances, although the student's work may represent a good effort for the first month of law school, it will bear little relation to the kind of answer that will be expected by the end of the semester. Thus, although a truthful answer from the professor might be that the student would receive a failing grade if this were a final exam, the professor might well decline to say so because most or all of the class will find itself in the same position at that time. A model first-year Contracts exam, along with a grading grid and samples of the individualized written feedback that the professor provided to students in the class, can be found in Appendix A. A model Evidence exam for second- or third-year students, along with a grading grid, can be found in Appendix B.

Briefing

Law students will sometimes be required or encouraged to "brief" the cases that are to be prepared for each day's class. Note that the word "brief" is used differently here from the way it is used with regard to the formal legal communication of the same name discussed elsewhere in this book. When used in this context, the term refers to a specialized form of written abstract that is intended to assist the student in dissecting the important parts of the case and to prepare the student to discuss and learn from the case in class. Typically, a case brief includes the following parts: the name and citation, collectively called the "style" of the case, the pertinent facts, the nature of the case, the issue presented, the history of the case before it was heard in this court, also called the "procedural posture," the holding, and the court's analysis. In class, a student may be asked to recite all or any part of his brief. In addition, the student will be expected to be ready to apply the rule of law presented in the case to new hypothetical fact patterns that may be presented in class.

Understanding the purpose of each part of a brief is useful, although students should understand that there is no one "right" format for briefing a case.

STYLE: This includes the name and citation of the case and may also include the name of the court, the level of the court (trial, appellate, or highest court), and the name of the judge. The case style often helps the student to understand the procedural posture of the matter.

FACTS: In briefing the facts of a case, it is easy for students to get off track by listing too many unimportant facts. Instead, students should stick to the essential facts, those that were important to the court in reaching its conclusion. In addition, the student should identify the plaintiff, the defendant, and any third parties involved in the litigation.

PROCEDURAL POSTURE AND NATURE OF THE CASE: This portion of the brief includes a concise description of the type of case and its procedural status or posture. The procedural posture and nature of a given case might be, for instance, "Appeal to United States Supreme Court of personal-jurisdiction issue."

CONCISE RULE OF LAW: Determining the concise rule of law is often one of the most difficult parts of briefing a case. In determining the rule, the student should not rely on the headnotes that appear in the full, unexcerpted version of the text that might be found in the library. As many practicing attorneys will attest, the headnotes are often misleading and are sometimes even incorrect.

ISSUE: In determining the issue presented in each case, students often find it helpful to ask themselves, "Why is this case included in the textbook?" The answer to that question usually directs the student to the issue that is presented for review. For instance, in property class, a case may be included in the text to demonstrate how courts view a person's property rights in his own body. The issues presented in that case, therefore, might be, "To what extent does this person have enforceable property rights in his own body," and, assuming those rights exist, "Can the person sell those rights to another person?"

HOLDING: The court's holding is the answer to the question presented in the issue. In other words, returning to the example of a person's property rights in his own body, the court might have held that the person had no right to sell his own organs. Thus, the court's holding is what the court ultimately decided about the issue presented for review. Sometimes, opinions also include statements that are not necessary to the court's opinion. These statements are called *obiter dicta,* which, literally translated, means "something said in passing." These statements serve as a useful gauge in determining how a court might address cases with different facts that might arise in the future, but would not be binding on future courts. In other words, *obiter dictum* is not part of the court's holding, but is an extraneous, if sometimes interesting and persuasive, expression of opinion.

DECISION: The decision is the actual procedural ruling or order of the court, which is typically stated at the very beginning or very end of the court's opinion, or both. For example, an appellate court might reverse the holding of the trial court and remand (or send back) the case for a new trial, with instructions to the trial court to consider evidence on some issue that was not fully explored in the first trial.

REASONING: The court's reasoning explains its holding. If, for instance, the court's holding was that a person has no property rights in his own body that would make it possible for him to sell his body parts, the reasoning would explain how the court reached that decision. The court might, for example, have focused on the fact that the sale of persons (or parts of persons) has Thirteenth Amendment implications because it might involve a form of slavery. Alternatively, the court might assert policy considerations as part of its reasoning. In the body-parts case, for example, the court might discuss its concern that allowing the sale of body parts would have a disproportionate, negative effect on society's poorest members, who might be more tempted than those better off to risk their own health or lives to gain money by selling their body parts.

Textbooks

Most introductory law-school classes (and many upper-level classes) use textbooks that are almost invariably expensive, heavy, and devoid of pictures. In addition to using the textbook to prepare for class each day, students may find their textbooks to be valuable study aids in other ways. The table of contents of a textbook provides an excellent baseline for outlining the course because it shows precisely how the textbook's author intended the material to be understood. The order in which the concepts are presented is likely to suggest a useful method of organization for the student in reviewing for the exam. In a contracts textbook, for instance, an author might begin by discussing the parts of a contract, continue by examining the enforceable substitutes for a contract if some part is missing, then discuss the meaning of the contract or contract substitute, next address legally valid reasons for failing to perform a contract, and end by considering the consequences of and remedies for a breach of contract. The student might find that adopting this same method of organization helps her understand each new concept and how that concept fits in with the course as a whole.

Along these same lines, when they are using a case-based text, students should look for at least one important lesson in each case and each major note case. A critical question to ask is, "What changed?" from one case to the next, from one subsection to the next, and from one chapter to the next. A second, related question the student might ask herself is, "Why did the casebook author put this case (or note) in the text?" In other words, the student should consider what each case or note is meant to add to her understanding of the law. Other good questions to ask include "How did the lower court get the matter wrong (or right) when it considered the case?" and "Is there an exception to the rule of law established in this case?"

The student can engage in the same analysis when using a problem-based text. Again, each problem is included to elucidate a specific matter of law, and the student should make sure she understands the kernel of law that each problem exemplifies.

Furthermore, many textbooks now have their own Web sites with supplementary information for professors and students. Many textbooks also include a written supplement. The supplement may contain statutory information that is too lengthy to include in the casebook, as well as new cases that may have been decided after the book was published. Students are often tempted to treat these supplements as optional reading, but should avoid that common mistake. First, the statutes contained in a supplement are likely to be central to the class discussion of many courses. Second, if the supplement contains the most up-to-date case law or statute on point, the student will be doing herself a disservice if she does not consult it, especially if the law has changed such that the material contained in the textbook itself is now out of date. Third, some supplements include extra materials that are likely to be of use to students during their preparation for examinations, such as an overview of the course, a sample outline for the course, or sample examination questions with or without model answers.

Used law-school textbooks may provide advantages beyond the obvious economic one: they may help highlight, quite literally, some of the more important concepts in the text.

Especially if the previous owner marked up the book when she was reviewing for finals, the highlighting may indicate what the professor believed was most important about each case. Conversely, of course, a student may find that she is better off with a clean copy of the text than with another person's distracting, and even misleading, highlights and notations.

Study Groups

Some students find it beneficial to study with a group of other law students. These groups are sometimes referred to as "study groups," and are especially common in the first-year class. Although the following discussion may help a student decide whether a study group is a worthwhile use of her time, each student ultimately must decide this for herself. Group study is not necessarily useful for everyone. A study group may not be useful, for example, for a student who knows that he learns better on his own; for a student who prefers one-on-one discussion, rather than group discussion; for a student who is difficult or eccentric and has not fared well in a group atmosphere in the past; or for a student who has other time commitments that might regularly interfere with his ability to participate fully.

In a study group, a small gathering of students meets regularly to discuss the assigned material for a class. If the students all belong to the same section, and thus have several classes in common, the group might discuss all of these classes. Study groups work best when their members read the assigned material thoroughly beforehand, and then at the group meeting discuss outlines, difficult concepts, hypotheticals, or exam questions, or drill one another on material that must be memorized.

A group is probably most effective if its membership is limited. If the group is too large, invariably smaller cliques will form within the group, and the chance for personality clashes will increase. Also, in a large group, each person will have less time to practice addressing the group and expressing his thoughts or opinions, which is often both a useful way for a student to learn and a benefit of participating in a study group. Moreover, trying to schedule a convenient time for everyone in a large group to meet is difficult, and can result in inconsistent attendance, with all of the frustration, anger, resentment, and other problems that can arise from that situation.

The group should establish some guidelines for study. Formulating the rules in advance will make it easier for the group to address problems mid-semester and also will put each member on notice about the amount of work and level of commitment expected of him or her. Often, when people are involved in the decision-making process and assisted in creating the rules governing a given situation, they are more apt to follow those rules. In addition, it is much easier to approach a problem student with clear rules to which the student agreed than to spend time figuring out the rules as the semester progresses. For example, the group may want to agree in advance as to whether someone who has attended less than half of the group meetings should receive a copy of the group-developed outline. Students may also want to develop a protocol for handling personality problems, such as when a student engages in personal attacks or dominates group discussions. The group may have an anonymous procedure for bringing the situation to the attention of the problem student, or may elect a leader to address such matters. Alternatively, the group may decide to handle both study and governance of the group in a much more informal manner, gathering when time permits and addressing any difficulties as they arise.

Students who have had good experiences with study groups noted that discussions in their groups generally were kept on an issue- or policy-level, rather than fixating on specific facts or degenerating into personal conversations. Others tried to reserve a few minutes at the end of each session to brainstorm about the class material and the direction in which the professor would lead the discussion. If, at any time, the group becomes confused or stuck on a particular legal concept, the members may wish to consult with the professor as a group.

Students should remember that study groups are not forums for extended discussion of political views or even the latest legal news. Often, groups get stuck on debates for which there are no right or wrong answers, or disagreements over facts in cases. Sometimes, it is appropriate simply to agree that reasonable people could disagree on the matter and move on.

If possible, students should resist the urge to join a study group in the first week of school. At that point, students generally do not know one another well enough to form an effective group. Personal dynamics are important and will often set the tone for the group. In deciding who to approach, students should not limit themselves to students who seem to be like themselves; rather, they may want to focus on those who seem diligent, prepared, and have pleasant personalities. They should welcome diverse viewpoints, especially because getting a different perspective can enhance a student's own understanding of the material.

Students should avoid the appearance of insularity and should attempt to remain low key about the group's self-image. Sometimes study groups give themselves names and turn legal study into an all-out competition with other groups or members of the class. Although a competitive spirit can be healthy, fellow classmates are likely to react negatively to a group that seems impressed with itself.

In short, the usefulness of a study group depends on the level of individual preparation of its members and the ability of the members to communicate with one another clearly. Students should not feel pressured to join a study group; they are simply not effective for everyone.

Outlines

New law students may be surprised at the extent to which they hear one, specific method of exam preparation—outlining—emphasized as being critical to learning the material in each course. Many students are unfamiliar with outlining as a learning tool and may wonder whether it is really necessary *for everyone* to outline in order to be successful in law school. The short answer is, "No, but there are very good reasons why outlining has become such a revered means of study." Outlining requires that the student take apart the substantive material presented in class, discern for herself what is important, and arrange that material in a way that shows how each concept is related to each other concept. By engaging in this process, the student makes the material her own. Indeed, one of the traditional means of claiming ownership of property was to show that the claimant had mixed her own labor with the property, thus making it her own. A person who had found, cleaned, and refinished to her liking a wooden chair that had apparently been discarded might claim that, because of the efforts she had expended on the chair, the chair should now belong to her, even if the previous owner appeared and demanded possession. Extending this analogy, when the professor presents material in class, the professor is acting as the owner of the material; she determines the order in which the material is presented, which facts, concepts of law, and matters of policy are emphasized, and how long the students spend on each concept. The student, in preparing for exams, must add her own labor to that of the professor's (the previous owner) to reflect her own way of understanding the material. Although the student must ensure that she understands the material as it was presented in class, students often benefit from re-orienting and re-organizing the material for purposes of outlining.

Many students find that the value of an outline is almost entirely in its *making*, rather than in *having* the outline. Students

THE PRACTICE OF LAW SCHOOL

are often surprised to find that they spend countless hours creating an outline, never to refer to it again. This does not mean that the outlining exercise was in vain. Rather, students often find that, having made the outline, they have digested and internalized the material and now remember it without having to consult the outline again.

One student, who excelled in law school after being admitted provisionally, updated his outlines on a weekly basis. For him, that was an appropriate amount of time in which to sit back and start to draw concepts together. He would revise the outline as the semester progressed by adding to it or deleting material from it. At times, he would move whole sections. The revision process was important, especially as concepts became clearer toward the end of the semester. This student loaned his outlines to others, and tried not to view doing so as giving his competition an edge. His outlines made sense to him because they reflected the way he thought. He got the general idea for his outlining process from an upperclassman with whom he had bonded because of their similar military backgrounds and who became a mentor for him.

Another top student used chapter titles and tables of contents from his textbooks to guide his outlines. He tried not to be bound by linear thinking; rather, he focused on bringing together broad concepts in a way that made intuitive sense to him. He, too, felt free to revamp or reorganize his outlines as necessary, later in the semester.

Some students use outlines that have been created by other people, either commercial outlines, which are discussed below, or outlines created by other students. The best use of such products is usually to check the student's own work, rather than to serve as the student's main source of review. Reading another person's outline is a passive activity, while creating one's own outline is an active endeavor. Therefore, it is relatively easy for a student to convince herself, falsely, that she understands the material if what she reads in the outline sounds correct and familiar. The truth, however, may be that the student herself lacks the knowledge to produce such an outline and therefore is not as ready for the exam as she might believe. In addition, students who choose to use outlines created by others, whether student-created or commercial, should always consider the source. Sometimes, the material contained in such an outline may be incorrect. Other times, the outline may focus on material that was not important to the way a particular professor organized his course. In any event, a student who chooses to consult outlines generated by others might be well-advised to adopt a little bit of appropriate arrogance, and value her own intuition when her understanding of the material differs from the outline, rather than assuming that the author of the outline necessarily understands the subject matter better than she does. Having said this, however, there are certainly some students, especially those who are excellent at memorization and who have a knack for on-the-spot legal analysis, who perform well by reviewing outlines created by others, rather than creating their own.

Finally, some students find that the outline format simply is not useful in bettering their understanding of the course material. Visual learners often find themselves in this situation, as do students who approach law from a philosophical perspective. These students should consider creating other review tools for themselves. Visual learners, for example, often benefit from creating comprehensive flowcharts or decision-trees to show how all of the information in the course comes together. One student purchased large poster-boards for this purpose every semester and posted them around her room for inspiration. A student who learns the law best by grounding it in philosophy, on the other hand, might find that focusing on legal process and theory—how the law evolved and what policies were being advanced at each stage—works better for her than a rigorous, even rigid, approach such as outlining. Again, the only purpose of an outline is to assist the student. A beautiful, well-organized, labor-intensive outline is of no use if it does not help the student to learn the material. Therefore, the student should take the initiative to determine the means of study that best fits his style of learning.

Study Aids

In addition to their required course materials, students often spend a lot of money on law-school study aids. Because grades in law school are very important, there is a huge supply of (and demand for) supplemental materials that are marketed as providing students with a competitive advantage in preparing for examinations. A few study aids are excellent, some are a waste of money, and almost all are expensive. Many students excel in law school without ever consulting any kind of study aid. Therefore, students should not assume, simply because these items are available, that they are somehow necessary or even helpful for everyone. Because the stakes are high and the material is difficult, however, many law-school students will take comfort from using study aids. If the student is considering purchasing one or more study aids, she should make that decision based on sufficient information to choose those that are most likely to be of assistance to her and to avoid any that may affirmatively harm her performance.

Students may find it helpful to think about the many study aids available as a box of tools. Much of the skill is in picking the right tool for any given task. Almost all law-school study aids have both an upside and a downside; this section will discuss their advantages and disadvantages.

Students should keep in mind, when considering study aids, that the publishers' main goal is to make money. Therefore, study aids are structured in such a way as to appeal to students all over the country, taking courses at the more than 180 accredited law schools throughout the United States. Each course at each of these law schools is, of course, unique. Because publishers are trying to appeal to a broad market, they are likely to make their materials very general, so as to appeal to a variety of students who are taking the course from many different professors who are using different casebooks and different approaches. Thus, students will seldom encounter a study aid that is specially tailored to the way in which their own professor teaches the course (unless, of course, the professor wrote the study aid, in which case it may be an excellent investment). In addition, students will find some study aids to be of little use because they are organized in ways that differ from that used in the casebook the students' professor chose for their class. (There are, for example, at least twenty major casebooks currently available for teaching first-year contracts.) Sometimes, study aids focus on cases other than those included in the students' own text, and may even use different vocabulary that could confuse the student, rather than enhance his understanding of the material. Even if the study aid tracks the organization of the casebook that has been assigned for the course, it may not reflect the way in which the student's own professor approaches the course.

Hornbooks and Nutshells are often good investments for students who want a resource that is not only a useful study aid in law school, but is also likely to be useful to them as practicing attorneys. A "hornbook" is just another name for a treatise. (The name actually refers to the way in which old-fashioned primers were attached to pieces of wood and sealed with a clear layer of horn for protection from fingerprints, age, and wear.) Hornbooks are usually hardcover and resemble textbooks in the way that they are bound and labeled. Many publishers use different colors to differentiate hornbooks from textbooks. Thomson West, for example, binds its legal textbooks in brown and its hornbooks in green. Hornbooks also resemble textbooks in price and are probably the most expensive study aids available. They are, as a group, however, also the most reliable source to which law students can turn for supplemental information, primarily because law professors or practitioners who are established scholars in the field always write them. In some ways, hornbooks are mirror images of textbooks—textbooks include cases for students to read, as well as notes asking additional questions about the material in the case; hornbooks, by contrast, contain only textual discussion. Thus, as many students see it, textbooks ask questions and hornbooks provide answers. There are several hornbooks available in most fields of study in law school. Students should feel comfortable asking their professors to recommend a hornbook when several are available. Indeed, professors consult hornbooks, too, just as practicing lawyers do.

A hornbook is an excellent tool for a student who is having difficulty with a fairly discrete issue. In criminal law, for instance, a student might want to learn more about "specific deterrence," which is one of the purposes a court or legislature may consider in attaching a certain punishment to a given crime. A hornbook is a good source for the student to consult for additional information about a narrow issue such as this one. If, however, the student is having trouble with a broader concept in criminal law, such as the requirement of *mens rea* (a guilty mind) as one of the prerequisites to criminal responsibility, a hornbook is not the best choice, unless he has an evening to give to the undertaking: one popular criminal-law hornbook devotes more than fifty of its 900-odd pages to this subject. As one professor has said, trying to get a basic understanding of a broad concept from a hornbook is like trying to get a drink of water out of a firehose: the student is likely to be knocked over by the sheer volume of information.

The better tool for a student who needs basic information on a broad topic like *mens rea* in criminal law or personal jurisdiction in civil procedure is a Nutshell. Nutshells are small, soft-cover books published by West Publishing Company. As an aside, students are likely to be surprised by the cost of Nutshells: these compact volumes often cost more than $30 each. They are, however, very good tools for a student who needs a manageable introduction to a broad area of law. Indeed, practitioners often use Nutshells to refresh their recollection of areas of law in which they have not worked for many years, or even to get a head start in researching an area of law that is entirely new to them. Nutshells are more conversational in tone than textbooks or treatises but are, nevertheless, very reliable. As is true of treatises, established scholars write Nutshells. In addition, because these volumes are concise, the reader can get the broad overview she needs very quickly. Indeed, many a practicing lawyer has read a Nutshell cover to cover in a single evening to get up to speed on an area of law for which she needs some introduction or review. Many a confused law student has done the same in preparation for an examination or in-class exercise. Nutshells provide both an excellent summary of law and a good sense of perspective, showing how broad concepts fit together.

Nutshells, like treatises, are excellent tools for the right circumstance. Like practicing attorneys, however, law students must remember that a Nutshell is an overview, and only an overview. The Nutshell does not give a student the level of detail he needs to pass a course, just as it does not give a practicing attorney enough information about the law in *her* jurisdiction to write a brief or argue a motion in court without further research.

Students who wish to make productive use of their time while commuting or working out may find recorded material to be useful. (Students who need a real break from law school, however, should probably avoid filling this time with more legal material. Sometimes, it is important simply to take some time off.) Many of the companies that manufacture these recordings go to some effort to make them as enjoyable as possible, using humorous mnemonic devices and songs to liven up the material and to assist the listener in remembering it. In deciding to what extent he can rely on a recording being accurate, the student should research the source. Some feature professors who are established scholars in the area. Others are scripted by individuals who create products in a variety of legal fields, but are not necessarily specialists in any of those fields. Recordings, like Nutshells, are usually best used as sources of overview or review, but generally do not provide enough material, on their own, for the student to master the course material. In addition, some are tailored to particular casebooks. If the student chooses recordings that were created for a casebook other than the one being used in her course, she is likely to be distracted and confused by references to cases she has not read.

Because outlining is such an important part of many students' law-school experience, there are a large number of commercial outlines available for those who either do not make their own, or who want to check their own work against that of another person. Common commercial-outline series titles include Blond's, Emanuel's, Gilbert's, Quick Review, Roadmap, and West's Black Letter Series. As is true of students who are considering the purchase of recorded material, students who are interested in commercial outlines should research the identity of the author before deciding to purchase the product.

There are a number of textbooks available for every foundational course in law school. Each text has a different focus, includes a different set of cases, and uses a slightly different vocabulary to describe the same concepts. Except for West's Black Letter Series, commercial outlines usually purport to correlate with one or more of the major textbooks. Obviously, no commercial outline can cover ten or more different textbooks thoroughly. Instead, necessarily, each outline claiming to cover more than one text will include some cases that students using any given text have not read, and will leave out some cases that the students have read. The more books a commercial outline claims to match, the looser that match must necessarily be. If the student discusses a case on her exam that a commercial outline mentioned but that was not covered in class, many professors will give the student no credit whatsoever for that portion of her answer. Thus, students need to make sure that they learn the course as taught in their own class, not the course as presented in some commercial outline.

Blond's Law Guides are often popular with visual learners because they include charts that can be of assistance to students who are trying to figure out how to organize a course. These guides are smaller than many commercial outlines and are often geared toward a single, specific text. A student whose professor is using a text that is covered by a Blond's guide may find the guide to be of some assistance, therefore, while the student whose textbook is not covered probably should not purchase this product.

Emanuel's, Gilbert's, Quick Review, and Roadmap are among the popular commercial outlines that purport to correlate with more than one textbook. If a student is considering any of these commercial outlines, he should first figure out whether the outline tracks his text. These brands generally include an easy-to-read chart near the front cover, showing the casebooks to which the outline claims to correlate. Students should look not only for the name of their text, but also for the proper edition. An outline that claims to map the second edition of a text that is now in its fourth edition, for example, may not be a good investment, as many textbook authors make significant changes each time the text goes into a new edition. One author of a major first-year textbook has indicated that she generally replaces one-quarter of the text each time she prepares a new edition. Once the student has determined that the outline does correlate with the appropriate edition of her text, she might look to see whether the outline includes the first ten or so cases in her textbook. (Most commercial outlines have an index of cases to make this exercise a relatively quick one.) Although each student must decide for herself whether the purchase is a wise one, she may be well-advised to reject a commercial outline that, for example, includes only one or two of the first ten cases covered. Indeed, some professors purposefully choose texts that include cases that might be unusual or particularly recent, believing those cases to be superior learning tools to those that are more commonly included. Sometimes, but not always, students find that commercial outlines published by the same company that publishes their textbook are particularly good matches.

One popular commercial-outline series, West's Black Letter Series, includes only black-letter propositions of law, without citations (hence the name). Students whose professor has chosen a textbook for which there are no good matches in the other commercial outlines may be well served to consider this one. Because the outlines in this series do not cite a single case, students will not become distracted or confused by reading about cases the class did not study. The books in this series also include a computer disk that contains an abbreviated version of the outline so that students can personalize the product by adding specific cases from their own class. Indeed, students who choose West's Black Letter Series should annotate the outline in this way, either on the disk or by hand in the book itself. Not only will this process aid the student in understanding the material as he finds the section in the outline that relates to each case covered in class, but many professors also require students to remember and cite specific cases on the examination.

Many students consider using bar-review materials in preparing for law-school exams. The companies that sell bar-review courses sometimes encourage this process. Often, these companies have representatives on campus who seek to get first-year students to sign up early and put down a relatively small deposit to lock in a certain, advertised price at which to take that particular bar-review course after graduation. As an additional incentive for students to sign up, these companies frequently provide subscribers with outlines for first-year courses. Most of these outlines, however, were not originally written to assist students in preparing for law-school examinations. Instead, most were created for distribution during the bar-review course itself. Taking the bar exam is very different from taking a standard law-school exam and, although these materials are often excellent for their intended purpose, they may not be a good choice for use in law school. Many professors feel that the sample questions asked at the end of these outlines are generally far more elementary than the questions the students will be expected to answer on a law-school exam. Nevertheless, study aids are expensive, and those students who have reserved a bar-review course and who are given these materials free of additional charge may find them to be of some use in preparing for exams.

Commercially produced flashcards such as Emanuel's Law in a Flash are also popular. These typically come in a box and are organized by topic. Often, the cards are numbered or color-coded so that students can choose cards to assist them with a given topic or, if the box is turned over, may put the cards back in order for later use. Some flashcards ask relatively straightforward questions of law, others include hypotheticals, and still others ask the definitions of important terms. Like commercial outlines and recordings, however, flashcards are often geared toward particular casebooks and may at times distract or confuse students by including hypotheticals that relate to specific cases not covered in class or vocabulary that is unfamiliar. Some students respond very well to learning with flashcards. This method can be particularly helpful when students wish to drill themselves on the elements of a given tort, for instance, or the facts of a given case, if the professor requires the class to memorize case names. In addition, using flashcards can be a good break from the monotony of other kinds of study. As with outlining, though, often half the value of a review exercise is in preparing the review materials, and many students, therefore, benefit greatly from making their own flashcards. Indeed, some find that the process of making the flashcards is such a good review that, once the cards are made, the student can learn the content very quickly. Obviously, the student who uses commercially produced flashcards will not get this additional review. One particularly comprehensive approach to the review is for a student to make her own outline, then go through the outline, identify important terms and case names, and create flashcards to drill herself on those items. This is a tremendous amount of work initially but ensures that the student reviews the material in at least two different ways—by reading her outline and by reviewing her flashcards. Nevertheless, students who do not wish to invest the time or the energy in such an undertaking may benefit from using commercial flashcards.

Another product that may be useful is a set of commercial case briefs. These briefs are tailored to particular casebooks and particular editions of those casebooks. Because many law professors attempt to discourage their students from purchasing these products, which are often informally called "canned" briefs, some students think they must be some sort of "magic bullet" that ensures success in law school. This is probably a poor assumption on the student's part. Instead, the very characteristics that attract law students to canned briefs are the ones that cause law professors to dislike them so much. In addition to learning the substance of the law in their foundational courses, first-year students must learn to engage in legal analysis and issue-spotting. Indeed, mastering these skills is more of a challenge for many students than learning the substantive law, and is perhaps the most important task the student faces in her first semester of law school. When an attorney listens to a prospective client explain the legal trouble he is having, the attorney is trying to determine what the issues are, so as to apply the relevant law; this is the real-life version of the issue-spotting that students are required to do in law school. When, after she has identified the issues, the attorney explains to the client the legal import of the situation, the relevant law, and how that law affects the client's situation, the attorney is engaging in legal analysis. In short, these two skills are central to what practicing attorneys do, and a student must not (and should not wish to) finish her first semester of law school without mastering them. Briefing cases is the student's main opportunity to hone these skills during the first semester of her foundation courses. This is because, as stated above, a comprehensive brief both identifies the issue and dissects the court's analysis.

Although developing these skills is extremely important, students are likely to be tempted to short-change this process, due to a fear of looking foolish in front of classmates, a desire not to put in the time that is required for proper briefing, or perhaps both. Given these temptations, students often consider using "canned" briefs rather than creating their own. In the short term, these briefs may seem to provide a quick solution to the pressing concern of being called on in class and being unprepared or giving an incorrect answer. Canned briefs do provide some information about the cases and, sometimes, about the important notes following the cases as well, so that a student who might otherwise perform poorly in class might be able to get by with a canned brief. So, students might wonder, what is the problem with canned briefs? The problem is two-fold: First, as stated before, law students spend a great deal of time, money, and energy in learning to be lawyers, and students who are not able to brief their own cases are simply not developing the skills they need to succeed as lawyers, period. Second, canned briefs are often the least reliable study aids available. Unlike treatises, Nutshells, and many commercial outlines, canned briefs are not written by renowned legal scholars who are specialists in the field being studied. Indeed, many canned briefs list no author whatsoever, and this omission is not accidental. Some canned briefs are actually written by current law students, not by people who have any particular expertise in preparing this material. In addition, a fairly recent review of one common source of canned briefs revealed an error in *every single brief*. While some of the errors were relatively minor, others went to the core of the cases being discussed. The message here is clear: students should think twice before relying on sources that may be flawed, especially when relying on those sources will actually short-change the student's own learning process. Theoretically, a law student could purchase canned briefs and use them for emergencies, promising herself that she will go back and do the reading later. As a practical matter, however, doing so might require more discipline than the student can manage, especially given the many demands on her time during the first semester. Instead, the student is likely to find herself relying upon potentially flawed materials for her understanding of the cases, rather than analyzing the cases for herself.

MULTI-TASKING

This book discusses the skills that are important to doing well in law school. For example, careful preparation, attention to detail, a good attitude, and skills such as legal analysis and issue-spotting are essential. Students should add "multi-tasking" to this list. As lawyers quickly learn in practice, having an upcoming deadline in one case is normally no excuse for requesting an extension of a deadline in another case. Additionally, having a deadline in one case is *never* an excuse for doing sloppy work in another case. The same standard applies to the student's work during law school. In fact, in practice, there is simply never any excuse for an attorney's doing sloppy work for any client. Why then, should a student, who is an advocate for herself in law school just as she will be an advocate for her clients in practice, ever do herself the disservice of doing less than her very best at any task? When a brief is filed or a memorandum of law is turned in, it will bear no disclaimer indicating, for instance, that the attorney was required to write it in thirty-six hours straight, without sleep, to meet an impending deadline. Instead, all the judge, the supervising attorney, or the client will see is the work product itself, so it is important that the work be of high quality. The same is true of the student's work in law school. As discussed further in Chapter 8, many law-school professors grade exams using a system of "blind grading," that is, without knowing which paper belongs to whom. Therefore, all the professor will see when she is grading the examination is the student's answer; she will not know that the student was distracted by another student's fidgeting during the exam, was exhausted from staying up all night with family problems or a sick child, or was suffering from a migraine headache during the exam. Indeed, it would be inappropriate for the student to indicate these problems on her exam paper. (A practicing lawyer, of course, would not inform the judge deciding her client's case of any of these factors, either.) Instead, in the case of a true emergency, the student should seek dispensation from the proper administrator; in any situation that does not rise to the level of an emergency, however, the student is charged with doing her very best work, without presenting an excuse. The same behavior would be expected of her as a practicing attorney.

Understanding that her exam paper, her daily class preparation, and any other assignment she does during the semester must stand by itself, on its own merits, the student should take great care, as an advocate for herself, to make sure that she puts her best self forward in each instance. This might require that she care for her physical and mental health, get sufficient sleep and exercise, and eliminate unnecessary distraction and stress wherever possible.

WHY IS LAW SCHOOL RUN THIS WAY?

Why is classroom decorum so important? Why do law schools employ an honor code? Why must law students observe such seemingly inane or archaic rules? The answers to these questions rest upon the fact that law school is a professional school. The practice of law is a powerful and difficult profession. Attorneys are hired for their judgment, and they are hired to communicate. They get paid for their time and their poise. There is a huge sense of responsibility and something of a heady feeling that many lawyers experience with the practice of law. There is nothing quite like the first moment that a new attorney realizes that she, privately, sitting in her office, can write down a number of hours, to represent the time that she spent on a client's matter, and somehow, if everything goes right, the client will pay the amount requested for the work the lawyer did. There is something empowering, but also frightening, to many new lawyers in the realization that others will, quite literally, carry their work product into court and ask a judge to follow the law and the conclusions that are presented there.

Lawyers must earn this level of respect and trust. Many law students are recent arrivals from very large undergraduate programs in which students felt anonymous. As undergraduates, students did not expect their professors to know their names, and often the professors could not identify the members of their class. Instead, each student was just a face in the crowd. Law school is a much smaller community, in which students are surrounded by colleagues and professors who are likely to know who they are, by appearance if not by name, and to form opinions of them that are likely to matter to each student professionally. One reason why law school classes are so much stricter than most undergraduate classes is the expectation that, if law students act as professionals in relatively minor matters such as classroom decorum and appropriate class preparation, they will be well-trained to act as professionals in more important matters such as providing proper representation for clients and billing them accurately. This is one reason why law professors are generally intolerant of inappropriate classroom behavior and are often very rigid, even unforgiving, about enforcing classroom rules. Law professors know that, however tired and bored students might feel at 3:15 on a Friday afternoon, at the end of their torts class, they are likely to face greater challenges with much higher stakes later. Indeed, they are likely to be just as tired and bored while listening to a client talk at great length, at the close of a long work day, about matters that are extremely important to the client but may be difficult for the attorney to care about at that particular moment. Sometimes, clients approach lawyers with matters that seem trivial to the lawyer but are of great importance to the client, and the lawyer must treat the client with humanity and respect. Under these circumstances, the attorney does not have the option of behaving as a bored law student might—sighing, groaning, looking at her watch, or packing up her belongings before the session has concluded. This behavior is as unacceptable in the classroom as it is in a client meeting, and professors do take notice of classroom behavior.

Law school is professional training in other ways, as well. If an attorney yawns loudly or his cellular telephone rings in court, he may find himself being escorted out of the courtroom by the bailiff. If this happens when the attorney is waiting to make an argument on behalf of his client, the client may be forced to proceed in the attorney's absence, without representation. The attorney will thus not only have embarrassed himself and his client, but also perhaps lost his case, and maybe even his job. To avoid such hazards, law professors not only try to teach their students the basics of the law, but also try to train them to act professionally.

Some students scoff at this portion of the first-year curriculum's agenda, deeming it to be unnecessary hazing or even an "ego trip" on the part of the professor. Some view the process of professional training during law school as unnecessary, claiming that they will pull their behavior together when it "really matters." Students taking this approach are sometimes heard to say, "This is just law school," and to respond negatively to what they perceive as attempts to make the law-school environment seem more consequential than it really is. The truth is, however, that few people change their behavior significantly once habits have become ingrained. Furthermore, the student's classmates and professors form impressions of him as he acts now, not as he promises himself he will act when he is in practice. A student who engages in bad behavior in law school, such as lying during a mock negotiation, may find that this reputation stays with him. Ten years after graduation, classmates may remember him as having been "the kind of person who lies during a negotiation." This kind of stigma is not easily overcome, even if it is undeserved.

Lawyers are given great power, and some of that power includes the ability to do harm. Lawyers who engage in inappropriate personal behavior with clients, falsify their hours, commingle client assets, or simply fail to represent the client's interests are much more common than law students might think. In addition, members of the legal profession experience extraordinarily high rates of depression, substance abuse, and divorce. The pressures of law practice are great, and it is difficult for many people to act like professionals when they feel they are paddling for dear life. Many law-school graduates may feel this way when they begin to practice law. Professors who emphasize professionalism choose to do so because they want their students to understand, even at this early point in their legal careers, just how high the stakes are, and just how important the students' chosen profession really is.

SAMPLE LETTERS OF RECOMMENDATION

LETTER # 1: For a student who earned a top grade in her first-semester course with this professor, got to know the professor well as an informal advisee, and later worked with this professor on the law review.

To Whom It May Concern:

I am delighted to recommend Anna Smith for the position of judicial clerk. I have known Anna for three semesters now: as an excellent student in my Criminal Law class, where she tied for the top grade; as an informal advisee, with whom I have talked at length about the various options in legal practice available to someone of her tremendous talents; and as a new member of the law review, of which I am one of the advisors.

Anna began her legal education by demonstrating great motivation and ability and unusual intellectual curiosity, and she has only strengthened an already-excellent reputation since that time. Anna is poised and extremely well-spoken, and both her oral and written legal communication skills are exceptional. Just today, she presented a draft of her law-review student-comment at a school luncheon. Her presentation was persuasive and demonstrated extensive research; she also fielded questions from both a faculty panel (of which I was a member) and students and faculty in the audience with grace and skill.

Anna is not only an outstanding student but also, perhaps even more important, a delightful and involved member of the law school community. Her impressive intellect is exceeded only by her determination to use her legal skills constructively for the benefit of others. I have no doubt that she will do so in a significant way. Anna will excel in whatever area she chooses to use her law degree, and I believe her academic qualifications, together with her communications skills and her commitment to the community, will make her an ideal judicial clerk.

Please contact me if I may provide any additional information in support of Anna's candidacy.

Very truly yours,

Assistant Professor of Law

LETTER # 2: For a student who performed well in her first year of law school and sought to transfer to another law school.

To Whom It May Concern:

It is with enthusiasm and great pleasure that I recommend Nancy Jenkins as a transfer student to the University of Washington. Nancy was in my Civil Procedure class in the Fall of 200_ and not only performed beautifully on the examination, but also was a joy to teach. She exhibited a rare intellectual curiosity throughout the semester, and her diligent preparation and excellent participation made her an asset to her peers. Setting aside Nancy's strong academic record for a moment, however, I believe it is Nancy's tremendous compassion and desire to use her legal skills to assist others that will most help her to be successful in whatever field of law she ultimately chooses. In our conversations about Nancy's desire to transfer to the University of Washington, Nancy has emphasized her interest in the law school's advocacy program. Given her excellent undergraduate debate record, her very strong performance in our law school's Spring 200_ Closing Argument Competition, and my own observations of Nancy's poise and her ability to communicate effectively on her feet, I believe Nancy will be an asset to the University of Washington in whatever way she may choose to refine her skills.

If there is any further information I can provide that would be useful to you in your consideration of Nancy's transfer application, please contact me.

Very truly yours,

Professor of Law

LETTER # 3: For a student who had some academic difficulty during his first year and wanted to transfer so as to be closer to his family. This letter was submitted to the Law School Admission Council, rather than to a specific school, because the student was considering several options at that time.

To Whom It May Concern:

I am pleased to recommend Charles Jackson as a transfer student. Charles was in my Fall 200_ Property class and was a joy to teach. He is a hard-working, diligent student, and his class preparation and participation were consistently strong. He often took the initiative to do additional reading and practice problems when I suggested them to the class, and we met on a number of occasions to review his work together. I was impressed, knowing the family problems that have weighed heavily on Charles's mind this year, that Charles was able to remain focused on his coursework as well as he did. Throughout the remainder of his legal education, and especially when Charles is able to return to the Southwest to spend more time with his family, I expect to see his grades rise to mirror more closely his level of commitment and effort. His strong intellect, coupled with his kind, compassionate nature, make him a natural advocate, and I believe he will achieve great success in whatever area of the law he ultimately chooses.

Very truly yours,

Associate Professor of Law

LETTER # 4: For a student who had not performed particularly well during his first semester of law school and was seeking to enhance his opportunities by applying to the university's dual law-and-business degree program.

To Whom It May Concern:

I am writing to recommend Mitch Curtis for admission to the Master of Business Administration Program. Mitch was in my Spring 200_ Property I class and is currently enrolled in my Property II class. Although Mitch had a difficult first semester, he is taking steps to improve his academic performance. Mitch is a hard-working, diligent student, and his class preparation and participation are consistently strong. He takes the initiative to do additional reading and practice problems when I have suggested them to the class, and we have met on a number of occasions to review his work together.

Over the remainder of his professional education, I expect to see Mitch's grades rise to mirror more closely his level of commitment and effort. Mitch's strong intellect, coupled with his kind, compassionate nature, make Mitch a natural advocate, and I believe he will achieve great success in whatever area of law or business he ultimately chooses.

Very truly yours,

Assistant Professor of Law

LETTER # 5: For a student who was applying for a judicial clerkship and who served as the recommending professor's research assistant.

To Whom It May Concern:

It is with enthusiasm and great pleasure that I recommend Matthew Baker for a judicial clerkship. Matthew excelled in my Fall 200_ Legal Writing class, consistently demonstrating extraordinary preparation and motivation that have been reflected in his performance on his first-year exams. Indeed, I was delighted that Matthew's work resulted in his being invited to join the law school's honors program in his second semester. In addition, during his first semester of law school, Matthew learned that I was working on a paper in the area of international environmental law and asked me about it several times. Impressed with the depth of his questions, I ultimately gave him a draft of the article to read. A few weeks later, he returned the paper with several pages of his own ideas about the draft, beautifully written and carefully considered.

At the end of Matthew's first semester, being tremendously impressed with Matthew's analytical abilities, diligence, and intellectual curiosity about the law, I invited him to serve as my research assistant on the international-environmental-law project. He and I worked together for three months. Matthew's research and analytical skills, even as a first-year student, compared favorably with those of the best junior associates with whom I have had the opportunity to work in private practice. Due to Matthew's strong intuition and creativity, his research quickly became largely self-directed. Matthew's written work was, without fail, precise, meticulous, and concise.

Since Matthew has joined the Moot Court Board, for which I am a faculty advisor, he and I have had the opportunity to work together once again, and this experience has been just as positive as the first.

Given his excellent natural abilities as a student and scholar, his maturity and discipline, and his obvious enthusiasm for the law, Matthew will excel in any area in which he chooses to use his law degree. I cannot imagine a student who would be better qualified to serve as a judicial clerk if he is given the opportunity to do so.

Very truly yours,

Associate Professor of Law

LETTER # 6: For a high-performing student who was interested in pursuing a very prestigious public-interest position.

To Whom It May Concern:

It is a privilege to recommend Elizabeth Hope-Davis for the Community Service Fellowship program. Elizabeth did very well in my Contracts I class, consistently contributed in a significant and valuable way to class discussion, and was a delight to teach. More important, however, Elizabeth is steadfastly committed to devoting her considerable talents to public service, and I have no doubt that she would make an ideal Community Service fellow.

Elizabeth has made public service both a vocation and an avocation: I am aware of significant volunteer activities that she has been involved in for at least the last seven years.

Elizabeth's intellectual curiosity and keen legal mind are matched by her passion for *pro bono* work. This commitment was recognized early by the law-school community: Elizabeth quickly became deeply involved with the school's Association for Public Interest Law, serving as its Treasurer her first year. She also organized a large and important fund-raising event, and created the organization's Web page. Elizabeth has now been elected the organization's president.

Elizabeth somehow manages to find time for significant service to the College of Law community as well. She is currently an honor-court justice and a teaching fellow for the school's legal-writing program. Finally, but certainly not least, Elizabeth is a member of the moot-court team and was honored as the best oralist during the tryout competition.

I enumerate Elizabeth's many activities and achievements to give you a sense of the extraordinary, well-rounded woman she is. As her record shows, when Elizabeth commits to something, she gives it her very best effort. It is this wonderful combination of her inspiring strength of character, her excellent analytical and communicative skills, and her extraordinary drive and dedication that make Elizabeth such an exceptional law student and will, no doubt, make her an exceptional lawyer as well. I cannot imagine a student who would more richly deserve the Public Interest Fellowship and more ably and enthusiastically represent the sponsoring foundation if given the opportunity.

Very truly yours,

Associate Professor of Law

LETTER # 7: For a top-performing student seeking admission to the law school's Honors Program.

To Whom It May Concern:

I am writing to recommend Catherine Clark for admission to the Honors Program. Catherine was the top student in my Fall Torts section, and her excellent work, diligence, and intellectual curiosity have continually impressed me. In fact, I was so impressed with Catherine that I invited her to serve as my research assistant in her second semester of law school, and we have now been working together for three months in this capacity. The project on which we are working is highly theoretical and involves particularly difficult research—there are no headnotes to trace and no specific searches to run that would capture the information I have asked Catherine to find. In spite of this, Catherine has found more useful sources in the past three months than I would have expected a student to uncover in a year's hard work. In fact, her work has been of such excellent quality that at this time her research is largely self-directed. Catherine's comprehensive interest in and enthusiasm for the law and mastery of the mechanics of legal research and writing have made Catherine a joy to work with.

I believe that Catherine will both be of benefit to and benefit from the Honors Program if she is admitted. I have no doubt that she will devote the same great care and meticulous attention to the program that she has devoted to the research she has done for me. In addition, given Catherine's strong intellectual curiosity and excitement about the law, I believe she exemplifies the kind of student who will most benefit from the opportunity to explore the law's jurisprudential and philosophical foundations.

Please contact me if I may provide you with further information in support of Catherine's request for admission to the Honors Program.

Sincerely,

Assistant Professor of Law

LETTER # 8: For a single mother who got a good (but not excellent) grade in the recommending professor's class and who was considering transferring to a law school nearer to her parents for assistance with child-care needs.

To Whom It May Concern:

I am delighted to recommend Jan Stephens as a transfer student. In my experience, every professor wishes for a class full of students like Jan—bright, capable, motivated, personable, and focused. Jan was in my Civil Procedure class in the Spring of 200_ and now is in my Advanced Civil Procedure class. Jan performed quite well on the examination, and her diligent preparation and consistently excellent participation make her an asset to her peers. In addition, she is highly motivated. On a number of occasions in each semester, Jan has completed additional readings and practice problems that I have recommended to the class (or has found—and completed—such problems on her own) and has brought them to me for review and discussion.

Jan's strong academic skills and determination will ensure that Jan is successful in whatever field of law she ultimately chooses. Her creativity and the excellence she achieved in her undergraduate education in the hard sciences suggest that she is likely to use her degree in a manner that is as wonderful and as unique as Jan herself.

If there is any further information I can provide that would be useful to you in your consideration of Jan's transfer application, please contact me.

Sincerely,

Associate Professor of Law

CHAPTER 8

Exams and Grades

One aspect of law school towers above the others in striking fear in the hearts of first-year students and continuing to worry upperclassmen: the traditional law-school exam, a single test by which the student's entire grade for a course is determined. Although first-year students may have difficulty getting accustomed to the rigors and occasional humiliations of the Socratic method, to the degree of preparation required for class, and to the finer points of legal writing, it is the law-school exam that is likely to be of most concern. This chapter will assist both first-year students and upperclassmen in preparing for law-school examinations, in taking the exams with greater confidence, and in making the post-examination review a constructive learning experience. The chapter will close by discussing the logistics of grade appeals and providing some perspective on the importance of law-school grades.

FIRST STEPS

Just as a practicing attorney may begin to plan for trial the very moment she meets with a new client for the first time, so the law student must, on his very first day of class, begin to prepare for the examination. At this stage, the student should try to find out what will be expected of him at the end of the semester: Will this be a closed-book or open-book exam? If it will be an open-book exam, does that mean that *any* resources will be permitted? (Some professors restrict students from bringing in commercial outlines or other commercial study aids, even those that the student has herself heavily annotated, but will permit students to bring the textbook, their class notes, course handouts, and any student-created study materials.) Will this examination be administered at school, or will it be a take-home exam? Does this professor typically give an objective examination containing multiple-choice or true-false questions, a subjective examination consisting wholly of essay questions, or some of each? This information will assist the student, from the very beginning of the course, in determining how he should study. If the examination is closed-book, he will need to memorize everything he wishes to use during the exam; alternatively, for an open-book exam, the student might choose to tab his casebook and statutory supplement for quick reference rather than memorizing the names of cases and the exact wording of statutes.

The beginning of the semester is also the time when the student has an opportunity to deal with any larger issues that might affect his performance on the exam. Are there personal problems that need to be settled so that he can focus on his studies? Has the student learned from past experience that his writing style is poor? Some professors subtract points for poor writing. Others may simply have difficulty in following the student's train of thought if his writing is disorganized; this, too, can cost the student valuable points on an examination. Good writing takes practice, and the semester only gets busier as it progresses, so students with these kinds of problems should seek advice in managing them as soon as possible. Some schools offer seminars on taking law-school examinations. There are commercial exam-taking programs available, too. Particularly with regard to the latter, students may wish to ask upperclassmen or their professors whether these courses are worthwhile.

MID-SEMESTER

When outlining a course, the student should keep the examination in mind. Although law students should learn the terms of art introduced in each class as a matter of course, these terms may be tested with particular thoroughness if the examination includes an objective component. Students facing such an exam should therefore include definitions of these terms in their outlines. In addition, when taking essay examinations that consist of complex hypothetical fact patterns, students must be able to spot the facts that give rise to particular issues that were covered in the course. For this reason, students who are preparing to take such an exam might be well advised to include in their outlines thumbnail sketches of the facts of each case covered. These short factual blurbs will serve as prompts to the student, when reading an exam question, as to the kinds of facts that often give rise to particular kinds of issues. In a torts class, for example, the presence of a person of peculiar sensitivity may indicate that the student should look more closely to see whether this person might be an "eggshell-skull plaintiff." In a contracts class, similarly, if the facts suggest an emergency, the student should consider whether the doctrine of restitution might provide a remedy in the absence of an enforceable contract.

ENTERING THE HOME STRETCH

During the last month of class, the student must sharpen her focus on the upcoming examination. This is probably the best time to work through any old examinations that might be available, either from the professor or on reserve in the law library. Sample Contracts and Evidence exams are provided in Appendices A and B. If the student attempts to take an old examination too early in the semester, she is likely to be frustrated by her lack of knowledge of the course material. Alternatively, if the student waits until the reading period just before exams begin to try an old examination, she might find that the professor's schedule is so full that getting an appointment to review her answers is very difficult. If the examination is open-book, a wise student might already have tabbed her casebook and statutory supplement by this time so that she can test her referencing system in class during this last part of the semester rather than waiting until the exam to see whether it is useful. The student should finalize her outline during this last month of class so that she can focus on review, rather than assimilating new material, during the reading period.

The final month of the semester is also the time for the student to finalize some logistics; if she is planning to take the examination on a computer, the school will probably require her to sign up in advance to do this. There are pros and cons of handwriting as opposed to typing an exam. Many students find that they can type more quickly than they can write. Some students, due to their poor handwriting, should probably type if possible, especially because some professors have a policy that they will not grade anything they cannot easily read. On the other hand, computers can (and do) fail during examinations, leaving the student with no paper to turn in at the end of the exam session. Even if the computer does not fail, the student may accidentally delete her answer, as one student did, by inadvertently selecting the entire text with her built-in mouse and erasing her exam with a single keystroke. Pens and pencils, on the other hand, never crash. In addition, student concern about churning out as many pages as possible during an examination is often misplaced; indeed, many professors find that their best student papers are almost invariably the most concise ones. Thus, the student might actually be better served by the slower, handwritten approach than by a blur of hasty typing. As a matter of fairness, many schools require students who type their exams on computers to install and run "Examinator," "ExamSoft," or other software that blocks access to the Internet and to word-processing features like spell-check. The fact that this software must be installed is one reason that many schools require students to sign up in advance if they wish to take the exam on a computer.

THE FINAL PUSH

The Reading Period

During the reading period, the student should divide her time carefully to ensure that she prepares thoroughly for each upcoming examination. Some students find it helpful to map out the entire reading period and the entire examination period, counting the days that remain before each exam and dividing them up, deciding in advance what is to be studied each day.

A student, for example, may find herself with a reading period that lasts from Wednesday, November 27 to Tuesday, December 3 and examinations that run from Thursday, December 5 to Monday, December 16. Thanksgiving is November 28. Assume that examinations are spaced as follows:

Thursday, December 5: Contracts
Monday, December 9: Civil Procedure
Wednesday, December 11: Criminal Law
Friday, December 13: Property
Monday, December 16: Torts

How will she divide her time, assuming that all examinations are at 9 A.M. and that classes are worth three credit hours each and therefore will count equally in determining her grade point average? Should she skip Thanksgiving dinner? How can she get through *twelve* days of exams without losing her sanity?

In answering these questions and attempting to formulate a plan, the student may feel that she has encountered an LSAT logic question. A few rules of thumb may be of help in such an endeavor: First, many students find that two subjects is the *very most* they can study in a single day. Second, first-year students should take some comfort from the fact that most law schools try to ensure that students will have at least one day between exams and try to schedule exams as uniformly throughout the examination period as possible. Their colleagues in the second and third years often face a much more uneven schedule, and may even have to take two exams on a single day at some law schools. Third, many students find that they must take the evening off after completing one law-school exam before beginning to study for the next one. Allowing herself the luxury of a movie or just some relaxation before switching to another subject is likely to help the student pace herself throughout exams, maintaining her energy level until the very last test is complete. Fourth, in the absence of very strong reasoning to the contrary, students should allot equal time to courses with equal credit value. Fifth, many students find that they cannot study a single subject more than two days in a row. Sixth, although this point might seem obvious, the student should always devote the day before an exam to review of that course.

With these basic principles in mind, our first-year student might create the following schedule for herself:

Sunday	Monday	Tuesday	Wednesday	Thursday	Friday	Saturday
			Nov. 27 Study Contracts	Nov. 28 **Thanksgiving** Study Criminal Law	Nov. 29 Study Civil Procedure	Nov. 30 Study Torts
Dec. 1 Study Property	Dec. 2 Study Property	Dec. 3 Study Contracts	Dec. 4 Study Contracts	Dec. 5 **Contracts Exam**	Dec. 6 Study Criminal Law	Dec. 7 Study Civil Procedure
Dec. 8 Study Civil Procedure	Dec. 9 **Civil Procedure Exam**	Dec. 10 Study Criminal Law	Dec. 11 **Criminal Law Exam**	Dec. 12 Study Property	Dec. 13 **Property Exam**	Dec. 14 Study Torts
Dec. 15 Study Torts	Dec. 16 **Torts Exam**					

Note that the student now has exactly three days to study for each course, is studying each course the day before its exam, studies no material more than two days in a row, and need not study the night after she finishes any exam. In addition, because of the pacing of her exams, it was not necessary to split any of her study-days in half between two courses to provide each with equal time. Finally, although the student is assigned to study criminal law on Thanksgiving, she should eat dinner with her loved ones, too!

During his review for each class, the student should focus on the fundamentals first, making sure that he has in mind a basic approach for covering every concept learned in each course. In criminal law, for instance, the student will want to know the elements of each crime. If the exam is closed-book, he should have these elements memorized. In addition, if the class has discussed theoretical material such as various societal motivations for punishment, the student may wish to consider how he might incorporate this information in an exam answer.

If the exam is closed-book, the student might want to consider developing a mnemonic device, an easy-to-remember word, phrase, or sentence that reminds him of all of the major concepts that were covered in the course. Many students take comfort, on such an exam, in writing down the mnemonic device as soon as they receive the exam, so they can look for each major topic on the exam. This is often a good way for a student who has completed the exam and has a bit of time remaining, to go through, one more time, and make sure that she has not missed any issues. A student taking an open-book exam might use the textbook's table of contents for the same purpose. If she plans to do so, she should tab this page for quick reference.

During the study period, the student should be systematic and efficient in her approach. One good rule of thumb is that, some time in her review, the student should "eyeball everything," including the text, her notes, the outline, any handouts, and so forth, once, before focusing on the outline for intensive review. This approach is likely to enrich the student's memory of the matters that were covered in the outline. Some students have found the explanatory text and notes at the beginning and end of each chapter in the text to be of particular assistance in putting the material in context at this point. Discussions with others, such as the members of the student's study group, are likely to be helpful, but only after the student has done some review on her own. This way she can be confident that she is not merely relying on someone else's perhaps flawed understanding of the material.

Students should remember that there is no one right way to prepare for a law-school examination. Some students close down the law library every night; others find the atmosphere on campus to be far too stressful and spend their time studying at home. Some complete a battery of practice problems and exams; one top student never did so, although he did take care to learn the elements of each cause of action.

The Day Before the Examination

The day before the exam is usually best spent in a calm, moderately paced review of the student's outline, perhaps followed by drills on important definitions or the elements of the causes of action that were covered in the course. Many students find that flashcards, especially self-made cards, are useful with regard to this latter task. Some students benefit from doing one last review problem at this late date, while others decline to do so out of reasonable concern that, to use a baseball analogy, they do not do their best hitting in batting practice. In other words, the student should approach exam day *primed* for the exam, not too exhausted or tapped out to do her best.

Before going to sleep the night before, the student may wish to set *two* alarm clocks, just in case one fails. She might also benefit from having everything for her exam in one place, ready to go in the morning, to avoid the last-minute hassle that might result if something is misplaced. In addition to wearing comfortable clothes, the student might consider bringing a highlighter, several writing instruments, a watch (with the alarm function turned *off*), a calculator (just in case the professor includes some tricky numbers), and, if she is taking the exam on computer, all of the necessary supplies for her laptop. Some schools allow students to bring in beverages or even snacks during exams. As a matter of courtesy to others, however, students should avoid bringing anything that will create noise when it is opened or consumed. What about Bernard, the stuffed dog the student has brought to every major test since first grade? Well, the student should take comfort from knowing that, if she takes Bernard to the exam, she certainly will not be the only student who has chosen to bring along a good-luck charm. In fact, the exam room is likely to be strewn with Bernards and other lucky charms, some displayed prominently, and others discretely tucked away, with just an ear peeking out of the student's backpack.

EXAM DAY ITSELF

Before

Having set two alarm clocks, the student should wake up in plenty of time to arrive at the exam site with time to spare. Some students choose to arrive at the law school early but not to enter the test room (or to set up their materials and then leave the test room) until a short time before the exam begins. Especially during the first year, students may find that they feel calm, cool, and confident until they walk into the exam room, an hour before the test, and encounter all of their stressed-out classmates. In a civil-procedure exam, for example, a classmate might run up to a student, begging her to explain a finer point of personal jurisdiction at this, the eleventh hour. Should she? Alternatively, a member of her trusted study group might rush up to her and wail, "We did it all wrong on our outline. Let me tell you how subject-matter jurisdiction should really work." Should she listen? The answer to both questions is, *probably not*. Instead, it is usually the best policy, in the first instance, for the student to decline to take another person's stress upon herself at the last minute. If the other student really does not understand such a central concept in civil procedure as personal jurisdiction, he should have sorted through this matter before now. In the second instance, it is probably best for the student to rely upon the understanding of the material that she developed at a time of greater composure. Time will probably reveal that the group's considered approach to subject-matter jurisdiction actually was the correct one. But how will she resist the temptation to have her concentration broken by either scenario? Many students find that the best way to do so is to avoid the situation; rather than camping out in the exam room for an hour or more before the test, the student might simply choose to arrive later.

During

Despite careful study and any efforts students have made to work through practice exams, "the real thing" often overwhelms them when they first open the exam. Indeed, the packet itself is sometimes so thick that it makes an intimidating thud as it hits the student's desk. Just as the student took the calendar apart piece by piece and planned her exam-study period, so she should take the same approach on the exam itself. She should figure out immediately how much time is available to her per question. On a three-hour exam consisting of three essays worth equal credit, for example, the student has one hour per question. Of this time, she might choose to spend fifteen minutes per question reading and organizing her thoughts, and forty-five minutes per question writing her answer. Many professors will make this kind of information available to the class before exam day so they can do some advance planning along these lines.

Once the student has allotted time for tackling each question, she should stick to the schedule she has made for herself, period. If she has decided to spend the first fifteen minutes reading and thinking, she should do so even though she is certain to hear the pens of others around her scratching at the page immediately. Indeed, many professors urge students not to cheat themselves of this critical time to organize and prepare to write. Students who read the question too quickly, in an effort to begin to write immediately, are likely to miss very important issues. The traditional law-school exam requires students (1) to spot issues and (2) to analyze the issues, applying the law to the facts. Obviously, the student cannot possibly analyze issues that she failed to spot, and her grade will reflect this fact. Some professors recommend that students mark up the exam paper itself as they read, reading each sentence of a complex hypothetical fact pattern individually, circling or highlighting the facts that give rise to an issue of law, and briefly noting each issue that is raised with a word or two before moving on. Students who take this approach are likely to spot more issues than those who read through an entire question and *then* try to remember the important issues.

The student should expect the exam to include some issues that are easy to spot, as well as others that are subtler or more difficult. The student should remember that points earned for easy issues often are worth just as much as those earned for more difficult ones and should not fail to tackle the easy issues on the way to handling the more sophisticated ones.

What if the student has an emergency during the exam? Her computer might crash, for example, or she might have a medical or mental health emergency. Under such circumstances, school policy is likely to dictate the student's options. In any emergency, the student must notify her proctor and follow that person's instructions, which may include forbidding the student from mentioning the emergency to the professor, so as to avoid any interference with blind grading.

After

After the exam, the wise student probably should *not* dwell on it, standing outside the exam room with colleagues and comparing mental notes: "What did you answer on the first essay? What about the eleventh multiple-choice problem?" Many times, students who find themselves involved in a discussion such as this one will leave school feeling as though they must have failed the exam because their answers bore no resemblance to those of their classmates with whom they conducted this post-mortem review. First, the student should remember that her classmates do not grade her exam; the professor does. Indeed, her classmates' answers may well have been incorrect. Second, the student who is convinced that she totally forgot to cover an issue may realize later that she actually covered that issue thoroughly; because law-school exams are stressful, students often find that their minds play tricks on them such that they really have *no idea* what they wrote on the exam. Third, even if the student actually did fail the exam, which is probably not the case, dwelling on this fact will only hamper her performance on her other exams. Instead, she should take the night off, then redouble her efforts for the remaining exams.

THE POST-EXAM REVIEW

Once the student receives her grades, she may wish to review her examinations with her professors. Many students find that they benefit from reviewing exams on which they did well, as well as those on which they did poorly. Appendix A includes samples of individualized written feedback that one professor provides to her students. In either case, the professor may require a "cooling-off" period before she will meet with students to discuss the exam. Some professors also require that students attend a group review, conducted either by the professor or by a teaching assistant, before they will engage in one-on-one exam reviews with students.

Some professors will post a list of the grades (usually without names), so that students know, before meeting to discuss a paper, how they did relative to other students. In addition, some schools require, or suggest, that professors follow a grade-normalization policy (or "curve") to ensure consistent grading among all sections. Some professors will also make sample answers available to students, sometimes even immediately after the exam, so that students can, before meeting with the professor, get a sense of what a good answer would have addressed. Others achieve the same purpose by putting the top student papers on reserve in the library, with all identifying information removed. Along the same lines, one professor requires that each student review the best paper in the class (again, with all identifying information removed) before discussing his or her own paper with the professor. He finds that this gives the students some perspective on how they could have done better on the exam. Showing the students that a classmate excelled on the exam can also be useful in dispelling any belief that the exam was unfair or inordinately difficult.

When a student reviews an examination paper with a professor, her attitude really is the single most important factor in determining whether the session is constructive. Even the student's choice of terminology is significant. A student who asks to review a "grade" is signaling to the professor that her only interest is in the bottom line: her grade. A student who asks to review an "exam paper," on the other hand, is indicating that she is interested in learning about the quality of her work, rather than simply discussing the grade. Along the same lines, as discussed in Chapter 7, using language such as "I got a 2.0" indicates that the student is attempting to shift responsibility for his poor performance to the professor, while stating, "I earned a 2.0" shows that the student has assumed personal responsibility.

Common mistakes on exams include process errors and logical errors, in addition to substantive errors. Process errors are failures of exam-taking skills, while logical errors illuminate problems with the student's analytical skills. Substantive errors demonstrate a flaw in the student's understanding of the material covered.

Perhaps the most common process problems are due to hurry or inattention. Students frequently fail to read a question properly or fail to follow instructions. A mistake such as this, made in an instant of carelessness, can cost the student dearly on her grade. A student might misread a fact, for instance, and thereby send her analysis in entirely the wrong direction. Alternatively, the student might fail to read an instruction that says to argue only *in favor of* a certain position, and waste valuable time on the exam arguing both sides rather than more fully fleshing out the one perspective that was requested. A final, and very common, process problem is running out of time. Students must budget their time during a law-school exam. Even if one question is going so badly— or so well—that a student wants to "borrow" some time from a remaining question to spend extra time on the one she is currently writing, she should not do so. Simply stated, a student should spend equal time on equally weighted questions, period. If the student adheres to the schedule she made for herself when the exam began, process errors due to running out of time should be eliminated or, at least, greatly minimized.

Logical errors relate more directly to the substance of the material being covered. A student taking a contracts class, for example, might erroneously jump into an analysis of Uniform Commercial Code Article 2, a series of statutes applying only to the sale of goods, without first determining that the fact pattern being tested actually involves a sale of goods. The student should, instead, first have asked herself the threshold question whether the statute applies to this fact pattern, before going through this analysis. Alternatively, the student might have used such imprecise language that the professor could not tell exactly what point the student was trying to make. In a torts class, for example, a student who refers only to "causation" on the exam may lose points for failing to indicate whether he was referring to the concept "legal cause" or to "proximate cause." A third common logical mistake is mixing the elements of two causes of action. On a civil-procedure exam, a discussion of personal jurisdiction should include the concepts "minimum contacts" and "concerns of justice and fair play"; whether the individual is a proper party to the lawsuit in the first place, however, is better reserved for a discussion of the separate concept "joinder" and related issues.

Fourth, and most common, students may forget to complete any one of the four major parts of the legal analysis of any single issue. Students may hear the four components of legal analysis referred to as "IRAC," which is an acronym for Issue, Rule, Analysis, and Conclusion. First, the student should identify the issue being addressed. In a contracts question, for example, the issue might be, "Was there an offer made?" Then, the student should go on to state the rule that applies to offers: "An offer must be sufficiently certain to create in the offeree the power of acceptance, thus empowering the offeree to finalize a contract through his acceptance." Next, the student should identify the relevant facts: For example, "There may be an offer here when the church indicates to the city its interest in purchasing the library property. Alternatively, however, because the parties have not yet settled on the price, these discussions may simply be part of preliminary negotiations." Finally, some professors will require that students draw an affirmative conclusion such as the following: "The better argument here is that the parties are still in preliminary negotiations because the discussion was not sufficiently definite to constitute an offer." If a student's answer recites only the important facts—"The church has indicated to the city its interest in purchasing the church property"—without analysis, the professor is likely to inform the student that her response was merely "narrative, rather than analytical." In other words, such an answer identifies the important facts, but fails to indicate why they are important. If the student's answer consists only of a conclusion—"The better argument here is that the parties are still in preliminary negotiations because the discussion was not sufficiently definite to constitute an offer"—the professor is likely to tell the student that her answer was faulty because it was "conclusory." In this situation, the student addressed only the bottom line without engaging in legal analysis. Answers that focus only on the rule of law or only on the analysis are equally incomplete, but less common. Another common way that students get off-track is to engage in mere "commentary" rather than doing legal analysis. Returning to the contracts example, for instance, a student might write, "The city was foolish in relying upon the statements of the church." Although the student might have gone through the IRAC analysis in her own head, the answer she wrote is likely to earn no points for her whatsoever, because it includes no issue, no rule of law, no analysis, and no legal conclusion. Rather, the student has engaged in mere commentary.

Finally, the student may find that her exam contained substantive errors. Her property professor might tell her, for example, that her examination demonstrated a misunderstanding of the Rule Against Perpetuities. If the student finds that substantive errors predominated on her exam, she should seek additional instruction before moving on to something else. This task is especially important if the student has completed only the first semester of a two-semester course, as is the case with first-year classes at many schools.

CHALLENGING A GRADE

Sometimes, professors do make errors in grading. Because the student's career may be on the line, especially if the grade she received was extremely poor, the student might consider challenging the grade. Under such circumstances, the student should make sure that she follows her school's policy to the letter. She should not even consider appealing her grade until she has first discussed the exam with the professor; many students have felt that the low grade they earned must have been a mistake until they met with the professor and learned how their paper had fallen short of the professor's expectations.

Other times, the professor may agree with the student that he made an error. One professor willingly changed a grade after discovering that he had overlooked an entire examination "blue book" that a student had turned in; another changed a grade after realizing that she had made a simple mathematical error. At some schools, however, even a professor who agrees that a grade should be changed must ask for affirmation from the Dean, from a committee of his colleagues, or even from the full faculty before the registrar will enter the change. Thus, students should understand that grade changes are a major undertaking and are made relatively infrequently.

If, however, the student has met with the professor, has gathered the relevant facts, and believes that she must continue the grade-appeal process, she should do so with the utmost professionalism. She must always be courteous, both in her dealings with the professor and in speaking with others about the matter. The student is on much more solid ground when she is asserting facts rather than stating opinions or conclusions. Statements such as "My friend wrote a worse paper than I did and got a better grade than mine" are likely to be ineffective and very poorly received. The student probably lacks the professional judgment and experience to make such a statement. A more factual, objective approach, such as "I believe this question could reasonably be interpreted as asking for a discussion of springing executory interests [on a Property exam] rather than shifting executory interests" is more likely to receive serious consideration.

PUTTING GRADES IN PERSPECTIVE

This book's dedication of an entire chapter to law-school examinations reflects an important reality: in law school, grades matter a great deal, probably more than in the student's previous academic career. Students who receive top grades are likely to be the targets of heavy recruitment on the part of hopeful employers. This open discrimination based on grades is likely to come as a shock to those students who find themselves at the low end of the curve in law school, who are unaccustomed to being in this position, and who may therefore find themselves with many fewer job opportunities than their higher-ranked classmates. Indeed, the very importance of law-school grades has prompted many schools to discourage, even to prohibit, first-year students from engaging in outside employment during the school year. In addition, many schools strongly advise new students to focus on studying and working hard, rather than on extracurricular activities (even those associated with the law) or on job-hunting, especially during the first semester.

Not only job offers, but also various law-school opportunities, are available to students based upon their grades. Some law schools have honors programs with special seminars that are open only to top students. Many schools provide two ways for students to become involved in law review, moot court, and mock trial: First, students may participate in an intramural competition for inclusion based upon their performance; second, students may be invited to join, even if they did not compete in the intramural event, based on their high class-ranking. High grades are also recognized through inclusion on the dean's list and/or honor roll and, upon graduation, through induction into the Order of the Coif, a national legal honor society, or other school-based honor societies. Further, many schools give what is alternatively called an "American Jurisprudence award," "AmJur award," or "book award" to the top student in each course or, at some schools, in each required course. At some schools, this "award" is really nothing more than a bragging right and a résumé credential; the student can say she "booked" the class if she got the top grade. At other schools, the student really does receive a book— typically, the hornbook in that particular course—or, at least, a certificate of accomplishment. The importance of grades is also a major motivating factor in many schools' elaborate system of blind grading, thus ensuring that students receive grades based upon their performance on the examination rather than on more subjective considerations.

Although students should be conscious of the importance that others are likely to assign to their grades, they should not become obsessed with them. Indeed, law-school graduates usually find that the playing field is leveled very quickly in practice. Thus, once they get their first job, students should not be overly self-conscious of poor grades, nor should they be overly confident if their grades were high. Instead, the job at hand will be to focus on the next big task—navigating the first year of employment, post-law-school. Even the student's professors are unlikely to place as much stock as the student does in the student's grade as a measure of her competence. Many students are surprised to learn that their professors usually remember them, not for the grade earned on the examination they took at the end of the semester, but rather for the positive (or negative) contribution they made in class on a daily basis and to the law-school environment generally.

Grades are likely to come into play at a few points in a practicing attorney's career: when the attorney is making a lateral move, especially to a specialty, or "boutique," firm; when the attorney is pursuing a Masters of Law; or when the attorney is seeking to become a professor or a lecturer in law. Other than these limited situations, practicing attorneys seldom discuss their grades. In fact, some firms either prohibit or discourage attorneys from displaying diplomas or honors such as Order of the Coif in an effort to communicate equal confidence in each attorney.

So what should the student take from this chapter? Law-school exams are very important, and students should do everything reasonably within their power to maximize their performance on them. In addition, after the exam, students should try to learn from the experience by analyzing what they did wrong (and right) so as to hone their skills for later exams and, ultimately, for the practice of law. Finally, the student is encouraged to put grades in perspective, and understand that they are but a part of her success in law school and in life.

CHAPTER 9

Other Ways to Gain Distinction, Develop Skills, and Get Experience

During the first year of school, law students may feel as though they are all racing toward a single goal: Grades. Because, by definition, top grades are elusive, first-year students may believe that making good grades will be the sole factor in their success as law students and, eventually, as lawyers. As with all other aspects of law school and lawyering, however, students must remember to keep grades in perspective. That grades are important is indisputable, but law school is not a zero-sum game revolving around this single variable. Instead, there are many other ways to succeed in law school. In addition, excellent grades are no guarantee of post-law-school success: grades can help a new lawyer get his first job, but only his actual on-the-job performance will help him keep that job.

Following is a discussion of some of the many opportunities that are available in law school. Although many are offered only in the second and third years, law students should begin to consider, during the first year, those activities that may be of interest to them, and should begin to get involved in those activities.

BAR ASSOCIATIONS AND OTHER STUDENT GROUPS

The "bar" is the term generally used to describe any body of practicing attorneys, whether it be a city or state bar association or a group that defines itself along lines of interest, ethnicity, religion, or other grounds. The official body of practicing attorneys in the United States is called the American Bar Association (ABA). Thus, the Student Bar Association (SBA) is the model student bar association. The SBA is the official student leadership on campus, and it is involved in many aspects of student life. The President of the Student Bar Association is often considered the official representative of the law-student community. The SBA may be responsible for activities ranging from planning social gatherings to assisting with interviews of new faculty members to approaching the faculty and administration with ideas and concerns. SBA students devote tremendous energy to activities that affect very directly the experience their classmates have during law school. Participating in the SBA is not only important, but also often prestigious. Many future politicians have begun their careers by being involved, and becoming known, among their law-school classmates.

There are also student chapters of the American Bar Association and the relevant state bar associations. While the SBA is concerned primarily with intra-law-school affairs, students who participate in the ABA or a state bar association gain valuable experience by becoming involved, while they are still in law school, in some of the major professional organizations in the legal field. This involvement is likely to include getting to know local practicing attorneys, contact that can provide important resources and connections for later professional life.

Another important aspect of student leadership on campus is the Honor Court. Integrity and discipline are central to the legal profession, and the students on the Honor Court are focused on maintaining both in the life of the law school. Theirs is the difficult, but crucial, work of disciplining their peers for infractions of the school's code of honor. For example, at one law school, materials on which all the first-year students needed to rely disappeared from the library shelf. The school Honor Court became involved in the matter by publicizing the incident and publishing a petition for students to circulate reaffirming that the students wanted to continue to uphold the students' reputation for collegiality. Moreover, in a less public way, the members were involved in interviewing students with knowledge about the incident. Some schools also employ student prosecutors and student defense attorneys to ensure that the disciplinary process is comprehensive and fair, especially because the stakes of Honor-Court proceedings may affect a student's future as an attorney.

An increasing number of schools have an Inns-of-Court chapter on campus or a close relationship with a local, bar-sponsored Inn of Court. These organizations, the most prominent parent entity of which is the American Inns of Court, represent the legal profession's commitment to professionalism and civility among lawyers. These groups provide an informal mechanism for experienced jurists to teach and mentor those who are newer to the profession and those who are about to enter the profession. Each Inn of Court may be organized around a specific type of law practice or centered in a particular locale. Its membership may include judges, experienced and newer lawyers, law professors, and law students. Typically, these organizations sponsor programs that are intended to mentor young attorneys or law students by teaching them how to handle specific situations that they may encounter in practice. The members regularly gather for dinner. Sometimes, one group of members makes a presentation to the others at these dinner meetings; other times, the members simply socialize. An invitation to participate in an Inn of Court is an honor and can provide an excellent opportunity for a young attorney to network, while refining some practical lawyering skills at the same time. In describing the benefits of participating in an Inn of Court, members often cite the opportunity to develop strong professional relationships, to seek career guidance, and to improve their understanding of the level of professionalism to which lawyers should aspire.

Other on-campus groups are those that promote certain areas of the law, like the business-law, entertainment-law, maritime-law, or sports-law societies. At some schools, one of the major functions of these groups is social. For example, at one school, each society plans a major, school-wide social event each year. In addition, however, these societies serve a more important purpose by bringing together students with common areas of interest. Often the groups bring in guest speakers during the year or hold networking events. By doing this, these societies promote mentoring between experienced attorneys and law students, which can be one of the most valuable associations a new lawyer can experience when getting started.

Legal fraternities, most commonly Phi Delta Phi and Phi Alpha Delta, are national organizations with school-based chapters. Unlike undergraduate social fraternities, most law-school fraternities are coeducational and open to any persons who wish to join. Legal fraternities provide important opportunities for students to get to know one another outside of class and may also assist students in forming connections with alumni. At some law schools, legal fraternities sponsor school-wide events, speakers, and even competitions.

Faith-centered organizations provide encouragement and support in an area of life that is sometimes hard to nurture in the midst of going to school. Most law schools have a variety of faith-centered organizations that make it possible for students to get to know others with the same background and belief system. Especially those students who are far from home may take comfort in being able to commemorate with others events critical to their faith.

Student delegates to the National Association of Public Interest Lawyers (NAPIL) serve the important purpose of reminding the law-school community that law is not just about money. Indeed, it is difficult to imagine a more urgent message for new lawyers than that one. These students may provide services to needy persons in the surrounding community and may coordinate assistance efforts on campus, such as food or clothing drives. In addition, the public-interest group provides an excellent network for students who are interested in finding jobs in this important field. Usually, the career services office will have a director or other professional with particular expertise in this area who will work hand in hand with the student groups to that end. Some schools have public-service fellowships or scholarships for students who are interested in this area of the law. As discussed in Chapter 4, students with public-interest aspirations should be particularly vigilant in managing their finances during law school to make it possible to pursue these important (but often not as lucrative) opportunities.

The Black Law Student Association (BLSA) and the National Bar Association (NBA), along with the Hispanic Bar Association (HBA), provide excellent social and educational opportunities, both for the African-American and Hispanic law-student communities and for the school at large. Some of these organizations take very active roles in promoting diversity on campus as well as community action, and in providing organization-wide and school-wide opportunities for socializing and networking. Some groups, for example, sponsor job fairs that are attended by employers seeking to hire minority lawyers.

Many schools offer students the opportunity to work with student tutors, who are sometimes called Dean's Fellows or Teaching Fellows. These are upperclassmen who have successfully navigated first-year courses, legal research and writing, and upper-level required courses, and are chosen by the school to assist others. Some schools will assign struggling students to work with an upperclassman in such a program, while others provide this assistance on a strictly voluntary or informal basis. These upperclassmen are usually professional, caring, kind, and constructive in dealings with classmates and may provide a more approachable audience than law professors when extra help is needed. Working in such a program may give students who are interested in a future in academia an opportunity to see what it would be like to teach.

Many professors employ one or more research assistants and teaching assistants each semester. Research assistants help professors with the preparation of works of legal scholarship, while teaching assistants help with class preparation and, sometimes, marking papers. Working as a research or teaching assistant gives a student an excellent opportunity to develop a close working relationship with a professor who is likely to provide a strong reference, as well as be a good source of future contacts and advice.

Groups for women law students and the Lambda Lawyers Association, which often includes lesbian, gay, bisexual, and transgendered students, provide support and encouragement to students who have not always felt welcome in the practice of law. Groups also exist for African-Americans, Jews, Catholics, Latinos, Asian-Americans, and other minorities. In addition to social interaction on a group-wide and school-wide basis, these groups often provide opportunities for networking, mentoring, and social action.

Some schools choose student ambassadors or guides to serve as their official representatives to visiting outsiders such as prospective students, their families, and visiting speakers. These ambassadors devote their time to helping the law school present its best face to these groups of visitors and are often responsible for leading guided tours and answering a variety of questions about the school. Strong interpersonal skills are a must for these positions, which are often enjoyed by extroverts.

Political organizations such as the Young Republicans, the Young Democrats, the Greens, the American Civil Liberties Union, and others remind the law-school community of the important roles that attorneys play in the political process and the constructive ways in which each lawyer can be involved in shaping the law. Attorney-activists have been a big part of the history of this country and continue to serve, in large numbers, in all three branches of government at the state and federal levels. Political organizations often provide opportunities for lively on-campus debate and are important in "getting out the vote" during each election cycle, reminding students of the importance of exercising this civic duty and privilege.

LEGAL CLINICS

Many students choose to work in law clinics, interacting with "real world" clients. These students are on the front lines of the practice of law, even while in law school. Because these students often find that, once they put that first toe out into the real world, it wants to pull them all the way in, students in clinical programs must ensure that they balance the needs of real-world clients with other obligations, including coursework. Many professors will allow students to miss a class or two for a trial or hearing, but others will resist doing so. Students should not expect this special treatment, and should do their best to schedule clinical obligations accordingly. Clinical work provides law students with a great opportunity to contribute to the legal community, even before crossing the stage at graduation. It can take an incredible amount of time, however, so many students choose to relegate clinical work to their final year of law school, when their course work is likely to be at its most manageable.

Many students have found clinical work to be enormously satisfying, providing an outstanding learning environment as well as practical experience beyond that which a first- or second-year attorney is likely to gain. Because clinics are so valuable, they are often quite popular, and schools vary in the ways in which students are chosen for clinics. Some schools make decisions based on grades or interviews, while others simply choose students by lot, although there is often a minimum-grade qualification as well. Students participating in clinics are likely to gain practical experience in a variety of areas, such as domestic violence, indigent defense in misdemeanor cases, landlord-tenant disputes, or adoption. Often there are clinics in the surrounding community in addition to those with formal ties to the law school. Based on her experience working in a clinic, one student, when she graduated, felt competent to handle some wills and simple bankruptcy matters, to help foreign students with immigration matters, and to help persons obtain protective orders. Her clinical, hands-on training with a practicing attorney not only assisted her in choosing an area of practice, but it also provided an excellent foundation for her subsequent domestic practice.

Clinical work generally is unpaid, and some students find that they need to find paying jobs, or an unpaid internship that may lead to paid employment. Before working in a non-school-sponsored program, students should check the school's policy on outside employment. This may require a consultation with one of the deans to determine (1) whether work is permitted at all, especially for first-year students, and (2) whether there is a maximum number of hours per week that students will be permitted to work. A twenty-hour maximum is not uncommon.

The practical experience, networking opportunities, and financial rewards of working during law school are compelling, but students taking advantage of this experience must, like students in clinical programs, ensure that their outside work does not interfere with their law-school performance. One practicing attorney, eight years out of law school, reflected that she wished she had taken advantage of more on-campus opportunities during law school rather than becoming so involved with a law firm that she had little social or intellectual exposure to the other students during her last two years of school.

WORKING AS A CORPORATE REPRESENTATIVE

One option that allows some students to balance the financial and practical advantages of work with the obligations of life as a law student is working as a representative for Westlaw, LEXIS, or a bar-review course. Students who have taken advantage of these opportunities not only earn money, generally without ever leaving campus, but also get to know other students and often receive free perks. These perks may, in the case of a bar-review company, include a free bar-review course worth well over a thousand dollars.

FAMILY-ORIENTED GROUPS

Students with families, although they are seldom recognized as an official campus group, enrich the law-school community with their unique perspective and, at the same time, provide a touch of outside reality to an environment that can seem to be insular. These students deserve special recognition because they work hard to balance family obligations with law school. They remind the larger community that the most important part of life—even as students—often takes place beyond the law-school campus. Although first-year students with families sometimes worry that their family obligations will put them at a competitive disadvantage, many find that their better-than-average time-management skills, as well as the enjoyment and "real-world" perspective that the family affords, are actually positive factors in their success as students and as future attorneys.

INTRAMURAL SPORTS

Another way that some law students keep their perspective and relieve stress is by participating in intramural sports activities. At some schools, these groups are a major part of the social life of the institution. Intramural sports also give students an opportunity to close the books at least once in a while and to have some fun with their peers.

LAW REVIEW OR LAW JOURNAL

At some law schools, the law review or law journal is considered the most prestigious activity on campus. In addition, a growing number of law schools have multiple journals, including one general-interest law review and one or more specialty journals. At such schools, the general-interest journal is usually considered the most prestigious of the group. Because of the importance that many schools and employers place on law journals, this chapter will discuss this activity at some length. Some schools require students to have a certain, threshold grade point average to be eligible for law review, moot court, trial team, or other activities that are discussed below.

      Some schools and employers consider law review to be the most important résumé credential a student can garner during law school. First-year students may be made aware of this, through the grapevine or from practicing attorneys, but they may not understand the special emphasis given to this activity. Law review provides an opportunity for law students to learn how private business functions and, indeed, to run an extremely important private business as students. This opportunity is unique to law school: law reviews are student-run and student-edited, but they publish articles written by professors and other top scholars (as well as some student pieces, which will be discussed below). Chapter 6 discusses the importance of legal scholarship: these student-run, student-edited law reviews are *the single most important* place where that scholarship appears. Again, this opportunity is unique to the law: in other disciplines, professors vie to have their scholarship published in what are called peer-reviewed journals, which are, as their names would suggest, journals in which scholars' work is selected and vetted by esteemed colleagues in the same fields. In the law, however, odd as it may sound, *students* choose, edit, and publish the work of *professors*, both from their own school and from other schools. Thus, law-review students are exposed to the professional work of other scholars and have the opportunity to be on the cutting edge of the development of the law. At the same time, law-review students prepare their own original, scholarly papers, some of which may be chosen for the honor of publication by the law review. Students who are interested in academic careers or appellate clerkships may compete heavily for these coveted publication spots.

Professional scholarship is the second major responsibility for law professors, the first being teaching. Indeed, success and promotion for professors depend heavily upon getting their work published. Therefore, they will compete for selection by top journals, and journals develop reputations for accuracy, rapport with faculty, promptness, and other important business skills. As a result, law journals guard their reputations jealously, and the single most important way they do this is by ensuring that the articles they publish are of stellar quality. Journals do this by (1) choosing authors carefully, (2) checking the source of *every single assertion* in *every single article* (more on that later), and (3) ensuring that the article, as a whole, is original and substantively correct.

Because law reviews are entrusted with this important aspect of the development of the law, they provide an excellent forum for the development of a number of business skills. The first is keeping time: Many practicing attorneys are required to keep track of what is called their "billable" time. Billable time is, just as it sounds, that time which is spent doing work that is targeted toward a specific client's specific needs and that should, therefore, be billed to the client's account. Billing hours is how many law firms get paid. (The other major way that lawyers are paid is on contingency, that is, recovering some percentage of the client's total award or settlement, if any, plus expenses.) Even many attorneys who are on salary with a law firm are required to keep track of their billable hours, so that the firm can recover the money with which it paid the attorneys. When attorneys must keep track of their time, doing so with precision and integrity is of the utmost importance. Harsh as it may sound, the following formulation may be helpful in understanding why this task is so crucial: Overbilling is, pretty clearly, stealing from the client; along the same lines, however, underbilling is depriving the firm of the fruits of the attorney's labor. Because this function is so central to many lawyers' success, it is very important—and can be very stressful. Thus, getting comfortable with this task is critical. Law review gives students an opportunity to learn how to do this when the stakes are different from those in the outside world: the hours "billed" may govern how many credits a student receives for law-review work and may also affect the student's law-review grade.

A second major skill that law-review work helps a student to develop is attention to detail. Again, the reputations of law reviews depend on the fact that the articles they publish are accurate in every way. Thus, law-review students must take apart every single statement in every single article and ensure that (1) the statement is accurate and (2) the statement is properly attributed. This process is as important as it can be tedious. Students must check citation form, and check the author's grammar, style, word usage, and composition. This hard work is invaluable because these are exactly the skills that a practicing litigator uses in preparing a brief of his own—or reviewing an opponent's brief to look for errors. Along the same lines, a transactional attorney will use these skills in preparing contracts that are precise and watertight.

Further, law review assists students in developing what are sometimes called "soft skills," those skills that involve working well with others. A board of editors supervising a staff of law-review members (members are called candidates at some schools) governs the law review. The leader of the board is generally the editor in chief, and there may also be one or more senior editors, executive editors, and managing editors. For many law students, managing others is a new experience that will help give them some perspective on the practice of law. Students who start out in a law firm, typically at the bottom of the organizational chart, often comment that the management skills they developed as law-review editors helped them to understand the point of view of their supervising attorneys. As editors, law students are charged with delegating duties, training subordinates, sustaining organizational morale, cultivating appropriate social skills, evaluating and disciplining peers and subordinates, navigating the inevitable organizational politics, and managing deadlines and multiple projects. In addition, editors may find themselves attending meeting after meeting, just as they will in the practice of law. Many will quickly learn that a meeting can be an enormous waste of time—or a valuable and productive collaborative effort. Successful meetings generally require (1) a well-planned agenda, (2) a clear and capable leader, and (3) faithful attendance.

Members and editors of the law review have the opportunity to develop other business skills as well. Communication skills are, perhaps, foremost. Because they must run the law-review business, students become experienced at written and telephone communication. Law-review students quickly learn the value of timeliness and quality in communication. Good communication can defuse a difficult situation, just as bad communication can aggravate a difficult situation. Filing and organizing, working within a budget, negotiating contracts, and managing valuable relationships (with the law-school faculty, staff, and administration, with authors, with printers, and with subscribers), and being comfortable with electronic databases such as Westlaw and LEXIS, are also very important.

Because law-review students have an opportunity to develop each of these skills, being part of the law review can be a tremendous confidence-booster. Students learn to think on their feet and to trouble-shoot, both of which are essential to any lawyer.

If there is a downside to participation on law review, it is the tremendous expenditure of time and effort that is required of each student. So, if given the opportunity, should *you* do it? Some would emphatically say that the answer is "Yes," while others have mixed feelings. Some students participate in law review out of a sense that they are expected to do so if given the opportunity, and this sense may not be incorrect: One student who graduated first in his class found that choosing not to do law review was a handicap when it came time to look for a job. He had decided to focus on a clinic as a second-year student and devoted his attention to that endeavor, as well as to his course work. He felt that several firms rejected him on that ground alone. Indeed, some attorneys have voiced the expectation that top students will automatically participate in law review and have indicated that they assume that any student who turns down law-review membership is "lazy."

MOOT COURT AND OTHER COMPETITIVE TEAMS

Many law schools offer students the opportunity to participate in Mock Trial and Moot Court. The two are both similar to and different from each other. Mock trial simulates a jury trial and requires that team members learn to prepare witnesses, authenticate and present documentary evidence, and prepare opening and closing statements; in short, mock-trial members perform mini-trials, and often do so in competitions around the state, region, or country. The focus in mock-trial work is on advocacy and thinking on one's feet. Complete familiarity with the rules of evidence is crucial. One law school that is consistently recognized, at a national level, for the performance of its mock-trial team describes the experience of mock-trial-team membership as being like that of participating in a university's varsity football program in terms of excitement. At some schools, the mock-trial program is called the "trial team."

Moot court is similar to trial team in that it allows students to develop advocacy skills and practice effective public speaking, but different in that it simulates an appellate hearing before a panel of judges, rather than a full-blown jury trial. It is called "moot" court because there is no live, or justiciable, controversy being decided; instead, the legal issue being debated is what is termed "moot." The facts of the cases are fictional, but often based on real-life events and emerging legal issues. In addition, unlike trial team work, moot-court work involves both an advocacy component and a writing component; indeed, in competitions, student teams are graded both on their appellate brief, on which they spend weeks or months, and their oral advocacy. The brief is very important, and can constitute as much as one-third of the team's ultimate competition score. This brief can also sometimes be used for other purposes, such as a professional writing sample when members of the team are later seeking employment, especially if the student can separate out the part for which he or she was responsible. During the writing process, students find that it is especially important to work together with their teammates in writing and editing; there should be no obvious difference in writing styles or lack of continuity between various sections of the paper. In preparing the brief, students are well-advised to look at previous briefs that have been awarded high scores.

Like trial-team members, members of the moot-court board often have the opportunity to travel around the state, region, or country to compete against students from other schools. Also, like trial-team work, moot court requires extensive, often daily, practice in the weeks and months leading up to the competition. By the time of competition, the students' presentations are usually so polished that many judges, when scoring the students' work at competition, remark that the students' end product outshines the best work of many fine private practitioners.

A more recent development on law-school campuses is the formation of negotiation and client-counseling competitive teams. The development of these new competitive opportunities recognizes the fact that most cases are decided prior to trial. Thus, students who participate in negotiation and client-counseling competitions have the opportunity to develop skills that they will use daily in the practice of law. Much of what lawyers do hinges on their ability to communicate and to counsel, and the work these students do allows them to develop skills that will ensure that their clients are protected and well cared for on a daily basis. Again, like trial-team and moot-court participants, student members of these teams should expect to attend daily practices, at which their performances will be critiqued by other team members, a coach (who may be a student, a practicing attorney or judge, or a professor), and outside attorneys, judges, or professors. Many schools refer to this process as "benching," making reference to the judge or judges who sit on the bench during a trial or hearing.

Students who participate on competitive teams should expect to develop excellent practical and technical skills. Depending on the nature of the team, students can get experience in organizing, writing, editing, and proofreading a coherent argument, polishing presentation skills, fielding questions, and maintaining poise under intense pressure. Some employers, particularly in difficult economic times, look to hire students who have this practical experience, especially because, as new attorneys, the students may require less time (and, therefore, less money) to train.

In determining whether to participate on a competitive team, first-year students are well advised to speak with students who have gone through the program, to investigate the time commitment that would be required, and to learn more about the practical skills they should expect to develop. A particular benefit of such teams is that, through the benching and competition process, students get to interact with the practicing lawyers who serve as advisors, coaches and judges for the team. This is perhaps the best exposure students can get to attorneys who are obviously interested in working with them and with younger lawyers. In addition, these attorneys are often involved with summer programs at local firms, and such connections may lead to offers of summer employment or permanent employment. Competitive teams also provide students with an excellent opportunity to have experienced third parties critique their reasoning, persuasive skills, presentation skills, and, in the case of moot court, writing. Further, students on competitive teams are generally expected to prepare arguments on behalf of each party in the case and are often required to switch sides between competition rounds. This is a useful analytical exercise that few attorneys have the opportunity to experience in the outside world. This experience develops and demonstrates versatility and forces students to think critically and as advocates.

As with law-review work, students who participate on competitive teams should expect to devote a lot of time to preparation. The workload is likely to be especially heavy at the beginning, as students become familiar with a case file, conduct research, and, in the case of moot court, prepare a brief. The competitions themselves are also very time-consuming, particularly as the team advances to semi-finals and finals. Many students, however, report that they also find these competitions to provide enjoyable opportunities to travel and to meet students from other law schools.

In preparing for the competition, which is the ultimate goal, students should consider the following. Sometimes it is possible to discover who or what organization writes the questions for the competition, and thereby figure out whether there is an interest-based bias underlying the competition. Tailoring the presentation accordingly could provide an advantage.

Participants often find themselves spending substantial amounts of time practicing out loud, in front of mirrors. In addition, many students enlist friends, roommates, family members, or anyone else who will take the time to listen to their presentations. The presentation should be such that a smart non-lawyer can understand and follow it. Students participating in moot court or trial team indicate that this experience is much like speaking to a jury (which, of course, generally is composed of non-lawyers). Often, someone who is not trained in the law may be the best audience for testing whether the presentation is coherent and persuasive because that person will not be focused on the legal substance of the performance, but instead can comment on logic and clarity.

Some schools are equipped to videotape practice rounds. If this opportunity is available, students often find it useful to take advantage of it in preparation for the competition, and then do a critique afterward. Students may find that their perceptions of their own presentations are not accurate. Students are often surprised, upon viewing a videotape of the session, to hear how often they say "Um," tap a pen, look down at notes, or hunch their shoulders. These habits become obvious, however, when the student is able to view his or her performance on videotape. Throughout this rigorous preparation process, students should expect to see a great deal of improvement. Examining this process of improvement is good for the sort of self-analysis that will be important throughout an attorney's career.

In making the formal presentation, students should feel confident because of the many hours they spent in preparation, but should carefully avoid appearing cocky. Along the same lines, students must be respectful of and deferential toward the person acting as judge or mediator (often an actual judge), while still advocating appropriately for the client's position. Students should work toward a comfortable, conversational style that is neither stilted nor too informal. Providing the judge or mediator with an outline of the argument at the outset often helps that person to follow the flow of the presentation.

Some additional presentation tips follow. Students must dress appropriately, in a way that is professional and not distracting. During the competition, as in a trial, students should ensure that the desk before them is clean and uncluttered. The appearance of preparedness generally reflects actual preparedness. Some schools require that their students memorize each aspect of their performance to obviate the need for notes. Professionalism is at least as important as preparation: students must carefully avoid making faces during their opponent's presentation or otherwise reacting visibly. Such behavior not only displays a lack of professionalism, but also may actually encourage judges to go out of their way to give the benefit of the doubt to the opponent. Students must speak slowly and clearly. Although the student will have given the presentation dozens of times before the competition, she should remember that the presentation is entirely new to the judge. After misspeaking or jumbling words, a student should move on without apologizing or laughing. This will prevent the student from breaking her stride and her concentration, and it also displays poise. If the student loses her train of thought, she should briefly consult her notes or, if no notes are available, pause calmly to compose herself before continuing. When this is done correctly, the judge should not know that the student ever lost her place. In responding to questions, students should avoid offhand comments and flip responses, even if the questions from the panel are inane or incomprehensible. It is appropriate to ask a clarifying question if necessary. Along the same lines, students should remember that not all attorneys and judges who volunteer to assist with a competition team are experienced in asking questions or in steering the discussion where they want it to go. Students should keep this in mind in ensuring that they give thorough and comprehensible answers, but, at the same time, must not talk down to the questioner.

CONDUCT AND REPUTATION

In all of the activities discussed above, students are interacting with other people. Those people may be fellow students, teachers, administrative employees, clients in need of legal assistance, scholars from other law schools, vendors, technical people, and others. The manner in which the student conducts himself in *every* activity should be of paramount concern. People will remember students who showed up to meetings on time, were courteous to the administrative staff, handled difficult situations with outside professors and attorneys well, or, alternatively, cheated in the intramural softball game. One law student deliberately changed the intramural softball roster so that the better male players would take a turn at bat before the required rotation of female players. This was contrary to the school rules. An uproar ensued, which resulted in this student, now a lawyer in the same area as the law school, being remembered by his classmates years later for this lapse of judgment. Another student treated people badly throughout her three years of law school. Five years later, an attorney sent out a firm-wide e-mail inquiry about her new opposing counsel, which happened to be this same student. Within minutes, four other firm attorneys responded that they were classmates of this person and each cataloged numerous offenses supposedly committed by this person. As these examples show, every student's reputation and integrity are on the line each day, in every activity.

In short, a variety of activities is available to enrich students' law-school experiences. Many of these activities are not only enjoyable, but also provide valuable training and contacts for students' later careers as attorneys. Furthermore, students who participate in extracurricular activities that are of interest to them often find that they are able to bring those activities into the classroom and use them to generate interesting class discussion. Participation in outside activities can also bring otherwise abstract concepts like "personal jurisdiction" in civil procedure, "consideration" in contracts, "mens rea" in criminal law, and "proximate cause" in torts down to earth in a way that is memorable and concrete. Students often find that having "real life" experiences to which they can compare in-class hypothetical fact patterns makes law-school classes more enjoyable and more interesting. In addition, extracurricular activities often generate attorneys' fondest memories of law school.

CHAPTER 10

The Unforeseen or Unanticipated Issues: Specific Challenges During Law School

Students spend months and sometimes years preparing for law school. Some carefully tailor their undergraduate curricula to include a broad range of disciplines, or to develop writing and advocacy skills. Some students take classes to maximize their chances of success on the LSAT. Others read widely in advance of their first year in law school or even take law-school-preparatory classes. Some do all of the above. All of these efforts are made with an eye towards getting into the best law school possible, or at least being as fully prepared as possible.

Meanwhile, however, life happens. People fall in or out of love, become pregnant, disabled, or financially ruined. Some students question their career goals, intellectual capacity, or ability to cope with the pressures of a career in the law. Sometimes students become dissatisfied with the law-school environment or workload, or resent the demands law school makes upon their time. Some get called to active duty in the military; others have a run-in with the criminal justice system. These life events, both big and small, are difficult to anticipate and can be discouraging, can temporarily or permanently derail career ambitions, or can even cause the student to be in a place she never thought she would be—even, perhaps, out of law school.

The point is that many law students and prospective law students will be faced with situations for which they either could not or did not plan. They may seriously question whether they are able to stay in law school, or even whether they belong there. These decisions, of course, are ones that each student can make only for himself or herself. This chapter provides some counsel on how to prepare for the unexpected, guidance on some of the factors or options a student may want to consider, and suggestions about places to get help when it is needed.

SEEKING ASSISTANCE ON CAMPUS

This chapter begins with a look at the human resources available at the law school, starting with the school administration. Generally, the law school will have an associate or assistant dean of student affairs (or both). This dean may also be a professor at the law school or may hold another administrative position within the school community. This individual is usually the student's point person for all academic or personal issues and can either direct a student to the appropriate office or person, should it become necessary to do so, or may herself guide a student through the relevant decision-making process. She may also have responsibility for working with students with learning or physical disabilities and may oversee any special accommodation these students receive for test-taking or classroom-learning purposes. During orientation, this dean may provide an overview of the range of issues with which her office offers assistance; if not, students must figure out for themselves where to go with any problems or issues. Finally, this dean may have close contacts with on-campus and off-campus counseling and crisis professionals, for purposes of referral.

Some schools have a Dean of Academic Affairs, who would handle academic problems or other performance-related matters, as well as a Dean of Student Affairs. Because the line between an academic issue and a personal or financial problem can become blurred, all top administration officials are trained to get the student the appropriate help, regardless of whether the student selected the "right" administrator, and, if necessary, to direct the student to the appropriate person.

The school registrar also has responsibility for some academic matters, especially those that will affect the student's academic standing with the school. The registrar is the repository of a tremendous amount of very important (and often highly confidential) information about each student, including the student's contact information, grades, and other items involving his or her academic record. The registrar will know, for example, whether a student has taken a leave of absence, whether the student has been placed on academic probation, and whether the student has been disciplined by the honor court. Often, the only persons within the school's faculty or administration who have knowledge of a student's misconduct or misfortune are the registrar and the dean for student affairs or academic affairs.

Professors are another important resource for law students, even outside the classroom. The student should consider finding a professor who is willing to serve as a mentor. Having a mentor in law school is as important as it is in the practice of law. Students will find that each school has a collective reputation for how far it will go to help its students. At some schools, professors may, as a group, tend to be accessible and friendly. These schools, and the administrative and academic professionals who work there, clearly recognize that students are paying enormous sums of money to attend and that the school is making an investment in the students as well. At other schools, the faculty may seem aloof or might even seem to treat the students as a distraction from the scholarship that they deem to be their "real" work. In the former situation, the student's task in finding a mentor is a fairly simple one; in the latter situation, the student may encounter setbacks but certainly should not give up her search for this kind of valuable guidance.

Even at schools at which professorial mentoring is less common, the student can find a professor with whom he clicks and who will want to take an interest in his career. Often, students find that having a shared research interest, or even having an unusual hometown or alma mater in common with a professor, will be sufficient to start a mentoring relationship.

Some professors particularly enjoy mentoring, and may even invite students to come by and talk with them about non-course-related interests such as career planning, interviewing, or extracurricular activities. Students who are interested in doing so should not hesitate to take the professor up on such an offer. Other professors make a practice of taking students to lunch or dinner, often in small groups, or even inviting the students to dinner at their homes. Again, these invitations can provide an excellent opportunity for students to interact with their professors in an informal setting, as well as provide the foundation for later mentoring relationships.

For other students who may not have pursued a mentoring relationship as actively, simple hard work often results in a professor's taking an interest in the student's academic life. Many a professor who may seem intimidating at first will be favorably impressed by excellent classroom (and examination) performance. Some professors make special efforts to track those students who have done particularly well in their classes, and may even offer them positions as research assistants or teaching assistants.

Other students come to interact with professors through extracurricular activities, either those that are academic in nature, such as moot court, law review, mock trial, or an inn of court, or those that are based on other interests that the student and professor may have in common, such as political or faith-based organizations.

Furthermore, more than one student, recognizing the need for a mentor but not having a clear opportunity to develop such a relationship, has simply approached a faculty member and expressed an interest in getting to know that professor. The professor may or may not have actually had the student in class.

Many professors will be very flattered by such overtures, especially if the student can articulate a clear reason for wanting to get to know this particular professor, such as "I am interested in the area of law in which you wrote your last article," "I may want to do litigation and understand that you have a background in that field," or even "I think you would be a good role model."

In addition to members of the law-school administration and faculty, many students will find teaching assistants and other upperclassmen to be valuable resources. Often these relationships develop through academic or social activities in which students get to know one another. Students who have recently completed their own first year of law school are in a particularly good position to empathize and to offer valuable advice about individual classes and professors. One word of caution, however: if a student receives a piece of advice that seems contrary to her own instincts or to the advice given to her by a professor or administrator, she might be wise to seek at least one more opinion before proceeding on this advice. People learn differently, and what works for one student may not be helpful to another.

The career-services office is another resource for students. During their first year of law school, students will become familiar with the on-campus recruiting program. The work of the career-services office, however, can go far beyond coordinating on-campus interviews. Career-services professionals are also available to counsel students who simply do not perform well in interviews or who may even be regarded as "unemployable." The career-services staff can provide counseling on specific technical skills such as asking incisive questions, as well as more general aspects of interviewing such as poise and presentation. Some career-service offices will conduct mock interviews for students, which are sometimes videotaped and critiqued. In addition, and more relevant for purposes of this chapter, an experienced career-services professional can provide guidance on how to handle unusual situations that occur during summer employment, or difficult-to-address matters that may need to be revealed on a student's résumé, in a cover letter, or during an interview. For example, if a student's offer of permanent employment is withdrawn by a law firm or, alternatively, if the student did not receive an offer of permanent employment following the completion of a summer internship, someone in the career-services office can guide the student through various options to minimize the negative impact of this event on the student's chances of future employment, including talking with the firm about a potential letter of recommendation. In short, the career-services office offers a full range of resources with which students should become familiar.

The larger university community, if the law school is associated with one, may offer additional options to lend support to students experiencing either emotional or financial difficulty. Some schools have a counseling center or crisis center, which may be available to students free of charge. These professionals can also assist by directing the student to additional resources within the community. Depending on the nature of the problem facing the student, the student may want to speak first with the dean for student affairs so that the dean will be aware of the issue, and then be referred to the counseling center. There are some issues, however, that a student may be uncomfortable discussing with a law-school dean. Each student will need to make this determination for herself but should understand that resources are available to her, both at the law-school and university level.

DEALING WITH SPECIFIC CHALLENGES, BOTH PERSONAL AND ACADEMIC

Now that the student is familiar with the some of the main resources that are in place to see her through her legal education, this chapter will examine some specific challenges that may arise before or during law school.

Even before a student matriculates at the beginning of her first year of law school, issues may arise that affect her ability to begin her legal education. A car accident, a pregnancy, or an illness, any of which may involve either the student or a loved one, may change the prospective student's priorities, quite literally overnight.

If the student still wishes to enter law school, but wants to postpone this new venture for a semester or even a year, she may be able to do so. A school may outline the options that are available to students seeking to defer admission in its student handbook or other materials. In any event, it is a good idea for the student to call or visit the dean of student affairs in order to explain the situation and to relate to the dean what the student would like to do. The dean will likely direct the student to put her request in written form, including a brief explanation of the circumstances giving rise to the request. These requests are not unusual and are likely to be handled quickly by the school. The student may, however, need to update her admissions application or financial-aid information. To do so, the student should contact the financial-aid office for further direction, particularly if the student has already been granted financial assistance for the upcoming semester or year.

Sometimes, life events may affect a student's financial situation or criminal record. Regardless of whether these events occur before or after the student's matriculation, the student will need to update her admissions application immediately. Because law-school policies are likely to vary considerably as to when a student is expected to provide this information, the student should consult her student handbook and, if necessary, the member of the law-school administration who oversees this matter, to ensure that she complies with all reporting requirements. In any event, the student should notify the school if he or she has received a scholarship or grant that has been awarded on the basis of criteria, whether financial or personal, that he or she no longer meets. For example, a student may have been awarded a need-based grant and have subsequently inherited money.

Academic discouragement and disappointment often derail first-year students. Many earn, in their first and second semesters of law school, lower grades than they have ever received previously. This experience leads many to question their abilities and whether they belong in law school. In addition, the high-stress environment of law school leads some students to wonder whether their personalities are suited for a career in the law.

Students should take some comfort from a simple reality check: many of their colleagues and, more important, many now successful practicing attorneys, experienced the very same crisis of confidence at the beginning of their own legal careers. Because law schools, by definition, are populated with high-achieving, highly motivated students, the competition is intense. Consequently, many of these excellent students will receive relatively low grades, at least at first. Indeed, many students progress from receiving low grades their first semester to graduating from law school with honors. Such marked improvement may (and often should) be highlighted in a résumé or cover letter to a potential employer.

Having acknowledged the reality that many students begin their second semester of law school with grades that disappoint them, each student should seek to learn from the experience so as to improve her grades in the future. Most professors will be glad to provide the student with advice and constructive criticism, often in the form of post-examination reviews. These exam-review sessions are discussed at length in Chapter 8. The student's own attitude will be the strongest factor in determining whether such a meeting is successful. If the student needs to wait a few days (or even a few weeks) before speaking with her professor, so as to be ready both to take responsibility for her poor performance and to learn from the experience, she should certainly do so. Indeed, some professors will mandate a "cooling off" period before speaking with students about examinations. In addition, some professors will require that students who wish to review their examinations one-on-one attend a group review first to learn some basic information about the professor's expectations on the exam.

During one-on-one exam-review sessions, some professors will focus on the substance of the exam, while others will provide more general advice on exam-taking skills. In Appendix A, this book includes several model "prescriptions," provided to students who had completed their first-semester examinations, that include each type of advice.

After meeting with the professor in whose class the student earned a low grade, the student may wish to take advantage of some (or all) of his school's academic-support programs. In addition, the student may wish to speak with those professors in whose classes he performed well, to better discern what he did right in those courses that may not have transferred to the course in which he did poorly. Furthermore, the student may want to take this opportunity to re-acquaint himself with some of the activities listed in Chapter 9, which offer many opportunities to be successful in law school, and often do not require top grades.

Very few students flunk out of law school from a lack of ability. The ones who do fail generally do so, instead, because they choose not to attend class or otherwise choose not to participate actively in their own legal education. A student who finds herself with a disappointing grade report in hand, questioning whether she belongs in law school or feeling certain that the world now knows that she is a "fraud" who should never have been admitted to law school, should remember that the admissions committee saw something in her application and academic record that convinced them that she is capable of doing the work. No student would have made it this far, having been selected from a large pool of applicants, if the admissions committee did not feel strongly that he or she had the requisite ability to do well in law school.

Those students who are overwhelmed, either by academic or nonacademic challenges, are likely to find themselves disproportionately affected by the intensity of the law-school environment. Many students who have faced these same challenges have turned to counseling, meditation, and other forms of stress management. Indeed, understanding that law school can be so taxing, many schools make stress-management resources readily available, often at little or no charge to the student.

Students should keep in mind that their schools have an interest in keeping students enrolled and healthy, even if doing so requires extra help or counseling. Schools seldom want to lose qualified students, especially when issues like discouragement or too much stress are the cited reasons for leaving. As discussed above, many law schools, especially those that share a campus with a large university, provide counseling services. Often, at least the first several sessions are made available to the student free of charge. Those law schools that lack such on-site resources frequently are able to make referrals; again, these services are often provided to students at little or no charge. Finally, at least one law school, finding that its "official" resources were insufficient for the needs of one student, simply paid that student's therapy bills for a period of time so that the student could remain in school. Students may not find such a caretaking attitude at every school, but they will probably be impressed at how much the school can do to help a student who is in distress.

In addition to school-based resources or referrals, some law schools have strong relationships with the local bar association, which may include access to counseling programs staffed by other lawyers and be geared specifically to the needs of lawyers. Most state bar associations also have counseling programs.

MORE ON HEALTH AND WELLNESS

Before stress- or health-related issues arise, law students can take some steps to ensure their own well being. The step that is perhaps most important, but also perhaps most often overlooked, is obtaining health insurance. Indeed, so many students lack health insurance that many schools now require students either to provide proof of their own insurance or to purchase insurance through the school. Some students may be able to join the insurance program of a partner, spouse, or parent, or to extend their own health insurance from previous employment under COBRA. Others will need to purchase a private policy, either through the school or from another source. In any event, even a student with a relatively secure financial position can find her savings easily decimated by one single serious incident or illness. Thus, although the initial outlay of money may seem forbidding, securing health insurance in advance of law-school matriculation is simply essential.

Attention to the student's physical and emotional health is important on a continuing basis. Many students find that exercise can be an excellent stress-reliever. A number of law schools make it easy for their students to remain in good physical condition by providing exercise facilities, either in the law school itself or through the larger university, if the law school is affiliated with one.

Along the same lines, maintaining mental health is crucial. In addition to continuing with any mental-health care that the student may have received prior to law school, the student may find assistance in meditation, yoga, tai chi, biofeedback, or other means of mental relaxation, in his or her faith, or in reading for pleasure. Students find that, as they get caught up in the day-to-day work of learning the law, it is easy to overlook the things they enjoyed—and that therefore contributed to their good mental health—before law school.

ACADEMIC PROBATION AND EVALUATING WHETHER TO CONTINUE LAW SCHOOL

If the student has failed a course or has received such low grades that she now faces expulsion or academic probation, she may need to take steps in addition to those provided above. First, the student must gather the relevant information: What will be required of her now that this has taken place? If she has failed a course, may she repeat the course this semester? Will doing so have an impact on her anticipated graduation date? If she has earned very low grades, is there some minimum grade point average that will be required of her at the end of the next semester if she is to remain in law school? Is it possible for her to take a reduced course load this semester in an attempt to improve her grades? If she faces expulsion, is there an appeal—or readmission—process that might permit her to continue her legal education?

Once the student has obtained the necessary information and knows exactly the situation that faces her, she may find the facts sufficiently daunting that she needs, or wishes, to re-evaluate whether she will remain in law school. She may feel that a failing grade has so damaged her grade point average that she will no longer be able to find a job that will make it possible for her to repay the debt she would amass by the end of law school. If she has just ended a semester with a number of very poor grades, she may feel overwhelmed by the pressure of knowing that she must improve her grades substantially to remain in school. In some cases, schools have even counseled students that it is not mathematically possible for them to better their performance sufficiently in a single semester to continue with law school.

Whatever the student decides, she must remember that she is not being forced to stay in law school. Some students facing these kinds of difficult decisions find it useful to engage in a cost/benefit analysis. Sometimes, the student may find that it is a

348

good idea to discontinue law school, especially when better options beckon, either in other fields of education or in the form of employment opportunities. Even some students who have enjoyed a solid performance during their first semester have determined that law school is simply not what they had hoped it would be, or have found themselves longing for their former employment as nurses, real estate analysts, or computer programmers, for example.

There may be negative financial implications of a student's decision to leave law school, including any law-school loans that must now be repaid. The student's long-term professional and personal satisfaction, however, is likely to be infinitely more important than any immediate financial hardship. A student who is already questioning whether she wishes to pursue a career in the law should take heart from knowing that she is not alone in thinking that this career choice is not right for her. Indeed, many others who have left law school have gone on to exciting and productive careers outside of the law; a President and Chief Executive Officer of Hewlett Packard, for instance, quit law school. Others who enjoyed the "teaching" or "counseling" aspects of lawyering, but found themselves ill-suited to the profession in other respects, have found fulfillment in careers in the ministry, in health care, or in education, for example.

If a student is questioning either her commitment to or her suitability for a career in the law, but is not yet ready to make a decision, she may have other, less drastic, options available. Many schools will permit a student to take a leave of absence or, if she has not yet matriculated, to delay her admission. A student should consider using her time away from law school to become more familiar with the law and lawyers. The student should line up informational interviews, as discussed in Chapter 2, and seek out lawyers with whom the student has some connection—whether as a family friend or a "friend of a friend." The student may want to talk to these lawyers about the skills they believe are important to succeed in their respective areas of law. The student may ask them what they enjoy about their jobs, and what they do not enjoy. He or she should ask what these lawyers do on a daily basis—are they talking with clients, for example, or do they have very little contact with people? Ideally, this type of investigation should have occurred before the student enrolled in law school, but having the perspective of a year or semester might actually make the experience that much more useful.

Students who discontinue law school during a semester may, under certain circumstances, be eligible for at least a partial tuition refund. In addition, students who make this decision should explore with their educational lenders, if any, when the first installment of the debt they have amassed so far will become due. If the student is leaving law school for other schooling or to take a job with a relatively low salary, many lenders may be willing to discuss deferring repayment or allowing the student to make reduced payments.

HONOR CODE AND VIOLATIONS OF THE CODE

Other academic difficulties may be associated with an honor- or discipline-code violation such as cheating, plagiarizing, or harassment. Most, if not all, U.S. law schools have in place a code of conduct that addresses academic misconduct or dishonesty, or other inappropriate conduct that takes place at or away from the campus. These codes are meant to uphold the professional standards that are expected of practicing attorneys and to acquaint the students with the expectations to which they will be subjected as professionals. An honor code may take the form of a declaration that is sent to every applicant to the law school, which they are deemed to accept by virtue of enrollment. Alternatively, the code may be communicated to students by a short pledge that is to be signed by every enrolled law student, with an attached copy of the code. Many schools reproduce the honor pledge on each examination, requiring the student to initial the pledge each time she takes an exam.

The honor code itself will indicate its jurisdiction, as well as the scope of conduct it covers. Typically, an honor code addresses conduct that occurs on the university property or while a student is engaged in university activities or university-sponsored activities. Some honor codes address only academic behavior. Students should note, however, that some schools have honor codes with language sufficiently broad to include the breaking of any federal, state, city, county, or university law or regulation. Such an extensive honor code may cover conduct that occurs even five hundred miles away from the university, as in the case of lying or misrepresenting information on an application to *another* law school, or poor conduct associated with securing summer employment. For example, a student may have falsified his or her standing in class on a résumé for a summer position. Engaging in the proscribed activity may subject the student to discipline that includes some or all of the following:

(1) Expulsion from school, which may include being barred from attending, visiting, or ever applying to that school again. Expulsion may dramatically limit a student's opportunities to matriculate at other law schools (or even other graduate schools), as well.

(2) Suspension, which may or may not be permanent (as in the case of a suspended diploma). During any period of suspension, the student may be barred from participating in all law-school activities, either on-campus or elsewhere.

(3) A financial penalty in the form of revocation of any grant or scholarship money the student was to receive in the future. Some institutions will even require that the student make restitution of any sums already received.

(4) Denial of participation in any or all university or law-school events, extracurricular activities, honors, or offices.

(5) Denial of access to university or law-school facilities or resources, such as the law library or student center.

(6) A negative change of grade, or a determination that no credit will be given for a course, either of which may affect impending graduation or result in revocation of a law degree that has already been conferred.

(7) Withdrawal of an acceptance letter to a student who has not yet matriculated.

(8) A probationary period, the violation of which can result in the imposition of one or more of the penalties listed above.

Under the various versions of the honor code that are unique to each school, it is the responsibility of each student both to monitor his own behavior and to report any honor-code violations of which he becomes aware. Understanding that the latter requirement may subject students to considerable discomfort as well as to the wrath of their peers, many schools allow students making such reports to remain anonymous. Any suspected violations of the code should be reported to a designated faculty member or to a dean, typically the associate dean for student affairs.

Once a violation or suspected violation has been reported, the matter is likely to be referred to an investigative and prosecutorial body that may be called the Honor Court, Honor Board, or Honor Council. This body is given the responsibility of determining whether a student has violated the school honor code or pledge, serving as a court for trial of a suspected violation, and recommending an appropriate punishment if it finds that a violation has occurred. The honor court, board, or council is generally made up of current law students, whose decisions are reviewed by a faculty or administrative advisor. The number of students composing the body varies by school. The number may be as low as five, or as high as twenty-three. These students are usually elected representatives from each law-school class year. Some schools elect more students from the third year than from the first two, while others have an even distribution of students from all class years.

The hearing or trial before the honor court is generally a matter of some formality, although that too varies by school. A student may opt to have legal counsel present, or, as some schools allow, a non-lawyer advocate. Some schools provide "student attorneys" to assist their peers in these proceedings. These individuals, too, are often elected from the law-school population and are typically, but not always, upperclassmen.

The prosecuting arm (the honor court) and the accused student may present witnesses, submit documents or other materials, and present facts before the examining body. There are pros and cons to using a lawyer for this type of inquiry. On the one hand, much can be at stake; a student who loses an honor-court proceeding may be effectively shut out from the practice of law and may thereby stand to lose tens of thousands of dollars (or more), both in actual money borrowed and in the lost opportunity to practice law if he is expelled. For these reasons, having a lawyer present who has experience representing practicing lawyers in similar situations may be a good idea. On the other hand, having a lawyer present could convey to the trier of fact a false sense of guilt or, short of that, could inject such acrimony into the proceedings that constructive, less formal dispute resolution becomes impossible.

The investigation and subsequent proceedings are generally confidential. Any student who is involved in this process in any way, whether as an accused student, as a witness, or as a peer counselor or member of the dispute-resolution body, must act with the utmost professionalism in ensuring that the proceedings are kept private. Especially those students who do not find their own professional future to be at stake may find it easy to fall prey to casual gossip, forgetting the enormous negative consequences that may befall them, or their colleague, should they do so. It may be, however, that the punishment inflicted is impossible to keep secret, as in the case of expulsion or suspension. Finally, a student may be able to appeal a negative decision or request mitigation of a disciplinary measure by seeking to have the matter reviewed by the Dean of the law school.

To understand the weight of these proceedings, it is necessary to understand the impact that honor-code proceedings have on the student body at large. If a student is found guilty of an honor-code infraction, then many schools make a posting or public notice available to the law-school community. Although the notice will not include the student's name or other identifying information, it may include information about the charge and the punishment given. Often, an honor-code infraction is generally known in the law-school body as a matter of gossip, such that students are able to identify the person who was the subject of the inquiry. More important, the law faculty may also be made aware of the fact that a particular student was found to be guilty of an honor-code infraction and was therefore disciplined. The faculty member may disclose those facts in responding to a recommendation inquiry about that student.

In some schools, the fact that an inquiry was made and a student was found to be not guilty of an honor-code infraction might also be posted as a matter of public record at the law school. For example, in a situation in which it is widely known that a particular student is being investigated, in fairness to the student, a notice may be posted stating that an investigation was made of an incident involving certain conduct, and that no violation was found to have occurred. Indeed, a student who has been found not to be guilty of an honor-code infraction may consider requesting that this type of notice be posted, to rehabilitate her reputation following the honor-code proceeding.

The impact of an honor-code violation reaches far beyond law school. As a student prepares to take a state bar exam and to apply to the relevant examination board for admission to the practice of law, the student will be asked to identify any honor-code violations of which she has been found guilty and even any accusations that have been made against her. The student's law school will provide a written report to the appropriate board of bar examiners as well. The student may have the option of including a letter of response to any such charge or investigation in his or her permanent file, which will be sent, along with the dean's report, to the board. The student should use appropriate professional judgment in preparing any such letter. If the student has violated the honor code, then it is important that she acknowledge her mistake and accept responsibility for that violation. If the student believes that she was wrongly found to be guilty and has appealed that decision, then the letter should so state. Any student challenging a negative honor-court finding, however, must use care in framing her response; she should state the facts with precision and frankness and without vitriol.

The following are some practical scenarios with honor-code implications. One law school had a strict class-attendance policy. As part of that policy, professors required students to sign an attendance sheet, and professors would then use that sheet to call on students that day. One student regularly had his friend sign in for him so that he could skip class without losing credit for the course. Predictably, when the professor used the sign-in sheet to call on this particular student, his artifice was discovered. The misrepresentation constituted a violation under the school's newly adopted honor code. The student was disciplined, and the situation became a matter of common knowledge.

In another situation, a student plagiarized text from a former first-year student's moot-court brief. A teaching assistant noticed the resemblance to the earlier moot-court brief and reported the matter to the honor court. An inquiry was made, and witnesses were called to the honor-court trial, including the accused student's moot-court partner. The situation was resolved within a few weeks and resulted in harsh disciplinary measures: the accused student was found guilty, was barred from taking part in the competition, and was suspended from school for the remainder of the year. The student had to repeat the classes in which he was enrolled, although he had already completed part of a semester, and was required to pay for an additional year of school. All of this information was set forth in his permanent student record. Not only had the student plagiarized someone's work, but the student whose work was copied was also forever associated with this incident, even though she claimed to have no knowledge of it. The identity of the student who had plagiarized was known throughout the class, because a witness inappropriately discussed the matter with other "confidants." Moreover, the inquiry took time and resources away from the practice of law school for all the parties involved.

At another school, before the widespread availability of information through the Internet, a first-year student intentionally mis-shelved or removed all of the copies of an important article that members of the first-year class needed for an assignment. An inquiry was made, and the student was found guilty of violating the honor code. Unfortunately, and because incidents like this one were so rare at that school at that time, upperclassmen came to regard that particular first-year class as a whole as a new, especially cut-throat breed of student, branding the class as a group that would try to get ahead at all costs.

Although the formal sanctions for violating the honor code are certainly significant, students sometimes nevertheless question whether honor-code violations are taken seriously. Even though the very decision, on the part of a law school, to adopt an honor code demonstrates the school's interest in and concern for the professionalism of its student body, the extent to which students report potential honor-code infractions varies by school and by class within each school.

Other codes of conduct may govern the student's law-school life, as well. For example, the school may have a separate library code of conduct, the violation of which can result in a student's being banned or restricted from using the law-school library. Such a penalty could be devastating for a student who counts on this resource to complete first-year legal writing assignments, an upper-level seminar paper, or an extracurricular activity such as a law-review article or moot-court brief. Some schools also have a separate sexual harassment policy, the violation of which could result in some of the same sanctions as may be imposed for an honor-code infraction. Students who live in a dormitory may have rules to which they are expected to conform as residents, including restrictions on noise or overnight guests, for instance. Finally, the university as a whole may have a separate code of conduct that applies to graduate students. For example, if a student is so much as accused of committing a violent offense, then university rules may prohibit that student from entering the campus, including the law school.

DIFFICULTIES IN INTERPERSONAL RELATIONSHIPS

Another issue that may arise early in a student's legal career is getting off on the wrong foot with a professor. The student may have snickered inappropriately in class, given a flip answer, challenged the professor in a negative way, or shown up completely unprepared. This book deals at length with professor-student relations, especially in Chapter 7. The main point to keep in mind is that, although the saying may seem to be a cliché, students should keep open lines of communication with their professors. If a misunderstanding has occurred, or an act of classroom misconduct has developed into a "grudge match," then the student needs to take the lead and make an appointment with the professor. If the student has failed to prepare fully, or otherwise has shown the professor or one of his fellow students disrespect in the classroom, the student needs to admit his mistake, apologize, and lay the groundwork for a respectful relationship going forward. Accepting responsibility, even when the student is not convinced that he is entirely at fault, is a sign of maturity that will do much to repair the breach. This is also good training for situations the student may encounter later, in the practice of law.

There will be times when a professor has acted inappropriately in the classroom. If this occurs, the student who is affected (or who is concerned about the situation) should keep discussion with other students or complaints about the professor's behavior to a minimum. Instead, the student should analyze the situation objectively, perhaps even taking the time to discuss it with a family member. If, after reflection, and perhaps a day or two of thinking about the steps she wishes to take, the student feels that it is appropriate, she should speak to the dean for student affairs or the dean for academic affairs about the matter. If the student is satisfied with the dean's response, nothing further need be done. In unusual situations, an inquiry by the appropriate dean may be made, particularly when more than a few students report discomfort with a situation that has occurred in the classroom. Sometimes the dean of the law school will become involved if the matter is of particular gravity. In the case of a less serious situation that is of concern to the student, but does not rise to the level of requiring a dean's involvement, the student may find that speaking with the professor about the matter constitutes a sufficient solution.

Some students have problems with colleagues, an issue that may also arise in law practice. Indeed, students should regard the management of any difficulties in their interpersonal relationships with other law students as an important, early introduction to office politics. The student might find herself to be the object of gossip, whether justified or not. It may be a relatively small matter, involving rumors that the student drank too much at a party and acted like an idiot. Alternatively, the student may have been accused of behavior that affects her credibility, such as cheating on an exam or taking some other action that has now mobilized people in the class against her. For example, a student might be perceived as dominating class discussion or making distracting comments. A student may have taken an unpopular position in class discussion that led other members of the class, correctly or incorrectly, to form a negative opinion of that student's value system. One student made a remark in class that was perceived by many of his colleagues to be racist. Because most of the ensuing discussion took place outside the classroom and thus was beyond the professor's control, word about the matter spread quickly and had the effect of polarizing the class from that day forward.

The simplest answer to this type of problem is that the student should concern herself only with the things that she can control. She cannot control other people's opinions or proclivity to gossip about her. She also cannot control classmates who choose to believe gossip or misleading statements and subsequently to avoid her. She can, however, control her own actions and the statements she makes to others. She can also control the private information she chooses to share with fellow classmates. Some classmates are likely to become a student's good friends, particularly as a result of the camaraderie that is often associated with experiencing a challenging situation together. Students should be cautious, however, about revealing personal information too quickly, before these friendships have really materialized. Indeed, many confidences are best reserved for the student's long-time friends outside of law school who have shown that they can maintain a confidence.

OTHER PERSONAL ISSUES OR CRISES

Many students experience personal crises during their years at law school. These situations sometimes involve a family emergency, a student's illness or addiction, or financial difficulties that threaten the student's ability to stay in school. Students should recognize that the dean of student affairs sees these matters year in and year out and is experienced in helping students to become mobilized on both an academic and a personal front. Too often, students leave school temporarily to deal with crises without even thinking to notify the school or to make arrangements for classes to be taped or notes to be taken for them. One dean of student affairs reports that, when students do think to call, they often leave hurried voice-mail messages from the road, with sketchy or incomplete information. Instead of dealing with an important situation as a last-minute matter, when a crisis occurs, one of the first calls the student should make is to the dean of student affairs. The student should explain the situation, notify the dean of where the student will be and how to contact him, and then ask the dean what options are available to the student. If the student does not yet know all the facts about the emergency situation, he may need to call the dean back later to discuss the available options. The dean can then notify professors, if necessary, and can make arrangements for the student to keep abreast of his coursework and extracurricular commitments.

Criminal Matters

Periodically, law students get into criminal trouble. Most lawyers can recall at least one student in their law-school class who was arrested for driving while under the influence, for drug possession, or for petit theft or larceny. Although these situations are difficult for all involved, and students are likely to wish to keep this information private, the school must be informed of any matters involving the criminal justice system. The school may have an honor-code requirement that all instances of arrest, conviction, or violation of probation must be reported to the school within a certain number of days of the occurrence. Other codes of conduct, including those of any university with which the law school is connected, may require that all such incidences be reported to the university administration as well. This is particularly likely when a student is accused of a violent crime. The student should understand that the relevant codes of conduct may permit the school to take disciplinary and restrictive measures against the student, even if the student has not been convicted of the alleged crime. Moreover, the student's law-school application usually includes a continuing responsibility to update the application, in some instances *up until the student is admitted to a state bar*. All criminal accusations, investigations, arrests, convictions, or probation violations must be reported on that application. The application, and the consequences of leaving out such information, is discussed in more detail in Chapters 3 and 14.

In addition to the fact that the student has a duty to report such incidences to the administration and should therefore speak with the dean of student affairs, this dean may also be able to assist the student in securing a criminal lawyer or even in relaying information to the student's family. The dean may also have access to references for a counseling facility with which the dean is already familiar, and perhaps even a rehabilitation center, if either is needed. As discussed above, the dean will work with the student to make reasonable academic arrangements so that the impact of this matter on the student's law-school performance is minimized.

A law student must deal with the consequences of any arrest or conviction for a long time. The student may have difficulty obtaining permission to sit for the state bar exam or getting admitted to practice law in certain states. Some states will allow a student who is facing such a situation to secure a non-binding, advisory opinion from the character-and-fitness review board for the state in which the student intends to practice. This may be an appropriate option if the student has an arrest-and-conviction record from several years before but can demonstrate a clean record since that time. If, however, a student is convicted of a crime while he is in law school, then he is well-advised to consult an attorney who is experienced in handling such matters for lawyers, so as to protect his reputation, if possible.

Each student's permanent school file will include information related to any arrests or convictions and will be forwarded to the state bar in the state in which the student intends to practice. The student file usually also contains the student's application for admission to the law school, including information gathered by the LSDAS, any supplements or amendments to the application, the school's response to any such supplement or amendment, emergency contact information for the student, and a summary of any formal honor-court investigations involving the student. The file will reflect any disciplinary measures taken, and will contain a transcript of the student's grades as of the time at which the file is requested. The student file will not include information about informal honor-code inquiries, nor will it have detailed financial-aid information about the student. Information about learning disabilities or physical disabilities and measures taken pursuant to the Americans with Disabilities Act is kept in a separate file with the school.

The student will be required to answer many questions on her state-bar application, some of which relate to accusations of criminal behavior, arrests, convictions, or probation violations. Any discrepancy between what is reported there and the information contained in the student's permanent school file will be investigated and could result in a hearing being held on the subject of the student's fitness to practice law. Schools have been known to revoke a student's diploma after learning of a criminal conviction that was not disclosed to them by the student, but of which they learned later from the board of bar examiners. Ultimately, activity by the student that shows intent to mislead either the law school or the board of bar examiners can result in the student's not being permitted to practice law.

The student may also have to report information about accusations of criminal behavior, arrests, convictions, or probation violations to the registrar, and should consult the student handbook for details should this become necessary.

A more difficult question involves the information that the student must disclose to a law firm. Generally, the student should consider notifying his law firm, if, after he accepts a position with it, he finds that there is a chance that he will not be approved by the board of bar examiners for practice in that state. Some states conduct the character-and-fitness review before students are permitted to sit for the bar; other states handle these matters in the opposite order. Thus, the student may have information relevant to his ability to practice fairly early on in the employer-employee relationship. For example, if the board notifies the student that it will conduct a hearing before making any determination as to his fitness to practice law, then the student should understand that the process may not be a smooth one for him and should consider alerting the firm to this matter. In addition, if the student is required to fill out an application for the firm, then certainly all requested information must be disclosed, including any arrest or conviction. Sometimes, the student may be asked to fill out an application after he actually starts working for the law firm. If there is any matter in the student's past that is of concern, the student should first talk with a mentor or the human resources director at the firm to discuss how to handle the situation. It would generally be advisable to notify the firm of any potentially troubling matter in person, rather than through a written application.

Other Negative Activities

Lawyers, too, engage in activities that sometimes cost them their licenses to practice law or suffer from conditions that affect their ability to represent their clients. Some lawyers abuse drugs or alcohol, experience depression, neglect or abandon clients, or otherwise mismanage people and their money. Because of the challenging and stressful nature of practicing law, it is important that the student establish credibility with the firm and law school early, so that others can vouch for her down the road if she needs them to do so. If a student has built a solid record of personal credibility and later makes a serious error in judgment, her professors or colleagues may nevertheless be able to state confidently, in response to a subsequent inquiry by the board of professional responsibility or to the bar examiners, that she is usually conscientious and that the activity in question shows an uncharacteristic lapse in judgment. Similarly, attorneys may need to call on others to vouch for their personal and professional integrity. In order to do so, they must already have established a credible reputation for themselves with colleagues

Students must accept responsibility for mistakes in judgment and must honestly assess whether any given troubling incident reflects a continuing problem. Many people do not want to admit that they have an addiction or lack self-control, and these problems often resurface later in a person's career, sometimes with devastating results involving clients or other innocent third parties. Students should take particular notice when both friends and school officials are suggesting that counseling or rehabilitation is needed. In addition, students should not be afraid to seek help when they need it.

Pregnancy

Some personal issues like falling in love or getting pregnant are positive, but nonetheless affect a student's legal education. Pregnancy in law school is becoming a more common occurrence, especially as the average age of the entering class increases and as more women are attending law school. Some female law students choose to become pregnant while they are in law school, figuring that law school may provide an easier environment in which to be pregnant and have a baby than law practice would. Although this logic may hold true in some instances, a student may want to consider some complications that could arise should she make this decision. No woman can anticipate how easy or difficult her pregnancy will be. She may have had two easy pregnancies, and then a third may require extended bed rest and weekly doctor's visits. The mother-to-be may feel ill or be unable to keep down solid food for weeks, possibly longer. The stress of law school and her desire to take every possible precaution for the baby will often be at odds, as will be the case in practice.

There are some important differences between being pregnant and having a baby as a student and doing so as a practicing lawyer. As a lawyer, presumably the mother-to-be would have medical benefits, which could include disability benefits. These provisions would cover the mother financially (at least partially) should she become extremely ill or unable to work for a time. She would likely be able to recuperate at home (even for weeks at a time) and return to her job when she improves. As a law student, an absence of several weeks or months may impair her ability to earn proper course credit or to pass her courses with decent grades.

In addition, once the baby is born, the practicing lawyer may be eligible for a paid or partially paid maternity leave, an option that is simply not available to a student. The student may be able to secure a leave only if she withdraws for the semester or if the baby is born at the end of the school year or immediately thereafter, in which case the student's "leave" would be her summer break. Should the baby need extended care after the birth, the practicing lawyer would be able to take advantage of the Family and Medical Leave Act to care for the baby for an extended period of time. The Act does not apply to students.

Finally, being pregnant while interviewing for a job may, in all candor, limit the job prospects of the student. As much as interviewers try not to let a woman's pregnancy influence their hiring decisions, at the same time practicing lawyers know how difficult it is to strike a balance between family responsibilities and the practice of law. Law firms are not necessarily focused on making sure that first-year through fourth-year lawyers achieve a healthy balance between family and work; indeed, trying to strike that balance as a brand-new lawyer is not only difficult, but often is not encouraged. A student who is pregnant and going through the interview process should not apologize for her pregnancy, or in any way discount it or act defensively. She may want to address the issue head on: acknowledge the pregnancy, but then address the underlying concern: the lawyer-to-be's relative commitments to the practice of law and to family. She should avoid having the conversation center exclusively on the pregnancy, a situation that can easily take place, especially if the interviewer is pregnant or a parent. One advantage of being rejected for a job while pregnant is that it might tell the applicant that the employer is not one that values the contributions a mother can make, even as a new lawyer. If the student believes that she was not offered the job because of her pregnancy, she should bring it to the attention of the law school's career services office.

A student who becomes pregnant during law school should maintain frequent communication with her obstetrician and the dean of student affairs. If the student feels comfortable doing so, she should talk with the dean early on in the pregnancy about what arrangements can be made, if necessary. For example, if the student has not yet enrolled for that semester's courses, the dean may be able to help the student design a lighter load, or even a reduced load. A lighter load might include the same number of course credits that the student would otherwise have taken, but may substitute a skills course with no final examination for a "core" doctrinal course. The dean can help with these arrangements and can also offer some advice on what might be a workable course load.

The dean may also arrange for the expectant mother to have more frequent bathroom breaks during an exam, and thus more time to complete the exam, or may even arrange to change the exam schedule if necessary. Using the dean as the conduit for making exam arrangements minimizes the professor-student interaction on that front and also lessens the chance that the student's grade will be affected by bias, familiarity with the student, or other forms of favoritism. If the baby is due near the end of the semester, the dean of student affairs may arrange for the student to make an alternative arrangement, such as allowing the student to take the exam off-site, to take the exam early (an option that is somewhat less likely), or to take a modified exam. The dean, rather than the professor, must make all such arrangements so that anonymous grading is maintained.

Professors, however, may be of some assistance as well. Some professors may be willing to allow an expectant student to make up missed class time with written work that relates to the classroom exercises. When one expectant mother was put on bed rest for a number of weeks, the school was able to make advance arrangements for the lectures to be recorded, which allowed her to complete her courses. One dean, in describing a similar situation, noted that, prior to being put on bed rest, the student had a perfect attendance record, had notified the dean early about her pregnancy, and had otherwise established personal credibility with the school. Not every school will go to these lengths, but a student should always inquire as to any accommodations that might be available.

In addition, the student should familiarize herself with all appropriate deadlines for withdrawal, in the event that it becomes necessary or advisable for her to do so, and should thus be aware of the last possible dates by which she can get a full or partial tuition refund. She should also find out whether she can prevent her financial aid from being revoked, called in, or put on hold so long as she re-matriculates within a certain period of time. The registrar and financial aid office should be able to provide her with these facts. The timing issues are important: the student might consider whether she should take leave during the current or next semester, and gathering the pertinent information will assist her in making this decision.

Women will hear all kinds of stories about super lawyer/mothers who were able to put together a significant deal or write a brief while in labor or within forty-eight hours of giving birth. These examples are rare, and do not necessarily describe people that the student should strive to emulate. Right after the baby is born is the time to focus on the baby and the new family; few women want to think about anything else during that time, a situation that is exacerbated by the body's hormones in the weeks after giving birth. A student is likely to find that taking an exam during that time will be difficult, to say the least.

Finally, in the event that an emergency occurs, a pregnant student may want to provide the dean with all family contact and obstetrician information in advance.

Expectant and new mothers should inquire about the availability of a nursing room or day care on the campus premises. This is another example of how attending a law school that is connected with a larger university can be a benefit: the university campus will likely have child-care facilities associated with its early-childhood teaching program or school of education.

STUDENTS WITH LEARNING OR PHYSICAL DISABILITIES

Students with learning or physical disabilities will generally coordinate matters with the dean or top administration official who has been designated to handle such matters. Some schools have demonstrated great flexibility in accommodating students with disabilities, including designating student note takers within the class, or allowing students with disabilities to receive more time to take an exam. Administration officials, sometimes without the professor's even knowing that an accommodation has been made, usually handle these matters. For example, a professor may not know that a dyslexic student has been given extra time to write an exam. Alternatively, if a student must take an exam at a different time from other students, administration officials may keep back three or four other exams as well and deliver them to the professor together, so that the professor will not know which exam was given with an accommodation.

OTHER WAYS TO PLAN FOR A POSSIBLE CONTINGENCY

A student can plan in advance for some of the above-discussed contingencies. The student should consider obtaining medical and dental insurance, or, at a minimum, should have some type of catastrophic coverage plan in place. Catastrophic-care plans tend to be inexpensive and worthwhile; in the event that the student is seriously injured in an accident, for example, this resource may prevent financial ruin. Students who had previous health insurance through an employer should consider whether extending that coverage through COBRA is appropriate. The school, too, is likely to provide a medical plan for the student to consider.

Although many students find that finances are tight during law school, students should avoid budgeting to the last nickel. Instead, the student should always keep at least a few hundred dollars in reserve for emergencies, even minor ones like an unexpected car repair. A portion of the student's loan money can be reserved for this purpose, or the student may consider taking a second job just before school begins, so as to save some emergency money. As discussed in Chapters 4 and 5, a student should have his finances in order before matriculating so that unexpected financial hardships do not derail his legal education.

In addition, before law school begins, the student's living and personal situation should be evaluated with as objective an eye as possible. Some students attend law school with a significant other in tow. Many relationships, however, cannot withstand the stress associated with law school, and some partners simply choose to leave. In that case, the student may find herself solely responsible for rent, a car, utilities, and other expenses, all at a time of great emotional upheaval. Thus, the matriculating student should evaluate the stability and history of the relationship when planning for her future. Some students have used the first year as a time to live alone to determine the strength of the relationship, and have then made arrangements during the second year that depend more on the significant other. Either way, students should anticipate that relationships have ups and downs, and the student's investment in law school should not depend solely on another person's provision of financial support or transportation.

The student should also consider making preparations in advance when he or a family member is ill. The student may be awaiting news about the health of a loved one or may need to travel on short notice to attend to family matters. Under such circumstances, the student should give the dean of student affairs some notice that a problem that will require the student to travel may occur during the year. If the student provides the dean with all appropriate contact information in advance, then, if emergency travel does become necessary, these details need not be handled when the student is preoccupied with family concerns that may be taxing and emotional. A student who anticipates such a problem should also provide the dean with a course schedule each semester so that, if the dean receives a frantic call from a family member, she can find the student promptly.

Students with children may also want to make arrangements for schools, nannies, and other caregivers to have the name, direct telephone number, and other contact information for the dean of student affairs in the event that the parent is needed and cannot be reached. This, too, is a circumstance in which the student may wish to provide his or her course schedule to the dean.

A student with a medical condition that does not necessarily require an academic accommodation, but nonetheless is a matter about which someone in a position of responsibility should be aware, may also want to inform the dean of her situation. For example, a student may be severely allergic to bee stings or peanuts. If the student is stung or accidentally ingests food to which she is allergic, the school may be able to get appropriate help to her more quickly if the school has some record of the precise nature of the problem.

Every year, at every law school, students encounter situations that simply could not have been anticipated and for which no planning would suffice. A student can best be prepared for contingencies by exercising control over the things he can control, realistically evaluating family and relationship issues, and recognizing that early notice to the law-school administration of any serious personal or academic problem will increase the student's chances of getting proper assistance. The law school's resources are vast, and many schools are glad to assist their students with matters, both academic and personal, that students might never have thought to address with the school.

CHAPTER 11

Legal Research
and Writing

Legal research and writing is one of the most important classes students take in law school, and also perhaps one of the most underrated. It is important because lawyers get paid to communicate, and this class introduces the students to the major tools of written legal communication. Legal research and writing is therefore a critical part of the "basic training" that law students receive in preparation for the practice of law. It is frequently undervalued by students because it is ungraded at some schools, it is often worth less credit than the student's other foundational courses, and it teaches students skills that many believe they already possess.

Legal-research-and-writing programs vary greatly. In some schools, the program lasts a single semester, and students prepare one or two items—a memorandum of law and/or a brief—both of which are discussed below. In other schools, the program may last up to two years, during which students not only learn to research and write briefs and memoranda, but also prepare demand letters, client engagement letters, billing materials, and even time sheets. At the same time, many legal-research-and-writing programs provide students with the opportunity to develop their oral-advocacy skills through first-year, opening-statement or closing-argument competitions.

This basic training in legal research and writing gives students the tools they need to put what they have learned from their doctrinal courses into action. A knowledge of torts, criminal law, property law, constitutional law, contracts law, and civil procedure, for example—standard courses in many first-year law school curricula—is of little use if the student is unable to communicate what he or she has learned.

At some schools, legal research and writing is an ungraded course. It may be tempting for students to assume, in this case, that the course is not important. Such an assumption would be incorrect. Instead, those students who take legal research and writing as an ungraded course should use the opportunity to develop these skills to the best of their abilities without the added pressure of being graded. Some law schools find this to be a particularly appropriate approach because writing is such a personal experience and, to some extent, the standards for good writing may vary from professor to professor. Having said that, however, it is important to dismiss the often-repeated, but unfounded, belief of some students that legal-research-and-writing grades generally are arbitrary, reflecting the personal preferences of the professor rather than an objective standard of professional development. That this statement is so often repeated is probably due to the fact that mastering legal writing is an extremely difficult task, even for those students who have long prided themselves, or have even been complimented, on their writing ability. It is particularly important for English majors, journalism majors, and other students with previous training in writing, to realize the ways in which legal writing is different from non-legal writing. These students often feel frustrated as they go through the process of learning a new, more structured approach to writing after the formal training they have already received.

Legal writing is necessarily much more precise than the writing that students are likely to have done as undergraduates, regardless of their field of study. For instance, there are few true synonyms in the law. For that reason, new law students may comment that legal writing is "boring," as compared to the writing they did as undergraduates, because they are forced to be precise and to eliminate flowery language. Often, this very precision requires that writers repeat a single word, such as the name of a legal cause of action, many times in a single document rather than alternating that word with another that the student may mistakenly believe to be a synonym. For example, "consideration" is a legal term of art in the field of contracts. A student who is writing a memorandum of law on contract law may not simply substitute another word, such as "agreement," for consideration. Indeed, a student who does so will make her memorandum legally incorrect.

The precision that legal writing requires, however, does not totally stifle students' opportunity for creativity and individual expression. Rather, once students have learned to write a brief or memorandum of law that is legally accurate, they can then begin to tailor their legal-writing method to suit their own personal styles. Because legal writing is so important and may seem so difficult, and because students may try, in vain, to fall back on the ways of writing that satisfied their undergraduate professors, some legal-writing students find themselves making defeatist and blame-shifting statements such as "The professor just hates the way I write" or, sarcastically, "I guess I don't know how to write after all, even though I majored in English." Instead, students should simply focus on the task at hand: learning the ropes of legal research and writing. They should also take heart from the fact that generations of law students before them have had the same thoughts.

THE BASICS OF LEGAL COMMUNICATION

First, it is important for law students to understand some basic terminology. A memorandum of law (or a "memo") is, despite its informal-sounding name, a formal means of communication between attorneys for the same client, or between an attorney and her client. In a memorandum of law, an attorney typically (1) describes the relevant factual background, (2) states the question or questions to be answered, (3) provides a brief answer, and (4) sets forth a detailed analysis of the relevant law, applying the law to the facts at bar. A memorandum of law is an objective, even-handed document in which the attorney presents all of the arguments that either side could make, assessing the relative strength of each. Attorneys and their clients rely on solid, objective memoranda of law in making key strategy decisions. Because a memorandum of law is written for "insiders," it is important that it be straightforward and even-handed.

A brief, by contrast, is a document that is written for "outsiders" to the case, such as the judge and the opposing party. This document is intended to persuade these outsiders of the appropriateness of the client's position. Therefore, the lawyer acts as an advocate in presenting her brief: she must present her argument in a way that is true to both the law and the facts, but she will try to do so in a way that is as persuasive as possible, within the confines of the law and the facts. A typical appellate brief may include the following parts: (1) Title page, including the formal name, or "style," of the case; (2) Statement of Jurisdiction; (3) Question or Questions Presented; (4) Statement of the Case, describing the relevant facts and the previous history of the case; (5) Summary of the Argument and Citation of Authority; (6) Argument; and (7) Conclusion. A trial-level brief may include, in addition to the style, sections entitled Introduction, Factual Background, Argument and Citation of Authorities, and Conclusion.

BOOKS, BEAUTIFUL BOOKS!

In learning to do legal research and writing, there are certain resources with which students should become familiar. Students may be tempted, in this "information age," to downplay the importance of understanding how to use the printed materials contained in the library, relying instead on electronic legal-research databases like Westlaw and LEXIS, but it is important not to do so. Indeed, law students are probably best served by doing their initial research in the books in the library and following up with electronic research to confirm that all appropriate avenues have been explored. As students will learn, conducting effective electronic research requires great precision in their choice of search terms. For instance, going back to the earlier hypothetical on the contract-law doctrine of consideration, a search that employs the term "price" rather than the legal term of art "consideration" will not achieve the desired results.

In addition, it is difficult to engage, with electronic media, in the same sort of browsing that is possible in a library. Browsing is particularly important for research in an area that is new to the researcher because it allows the researcher to become comfortable with the authoritative materials on point and to determine the context of whatever she is reading. For instance, a student who is researching an issue of bankruptcy law for the first time is unlikely to appreciate the importance of the treatise *Collier's on Bankruptcy*, if she happens upon that treatise at all, while she is doing online research. If, however, she visits the bankruptcy section of her law library and sees the five, dog-eared copies of this multi-volume treatise dominating the shelves of that section, she is likely to take notice of it. This is important because an experienced bankruptcy practitioner who asks her about her research is likely to be disappointed if *Collier's* was not included in her efforts.

Furthermore, electronic research makes it extremely easy for any researcher, especially a beginner, to make a simple mistake that may lead her down entirely the wrong research path. For instance, it would be easy for a student to find herself looking through the *Federal Rules of Civil Procedure*, rather than the *Federal*

Rules of Appellate Procedure, where she intended to look. If the rule being researched happened to involve a matter such as the format and maximum permissible length of her brief, she would obtain incorrect and irrelevant guidance by consulting the *Federal Rules of Civil Procedure*, and, were this an actual court proceeding, her brief likely would be improperly formatted and therefore rejected.

Finally, even though they are provided free of charge to law students, electronic legal databases are very expensive, and some attorneys will not have access to them, or at least will not have the unfettered access to them that they enjoyed in law school. Therefore, it remains important, for these reasons, to know how to do research the old-fashioned way: in books.

With this in mind, this chapter invites the reader to relax, bring along a cup of coffee (in a spill-proof mug, please), and pull up a chair in his or her school's law library to examine some of the following important resources for legal writing: Please note that sources are listed separately for each category. In addition, there is significant overlap among the categories: many texts address both grammar and composition, for instance.

RESOURCES

Grammar and Composition

The rules of grammar teach students how to write coherent, effective sentences. Important grammatical concepts include the parts of speech, the parts of a sentence (including the difference between a subject and a predicate and between a phrase and a clause), the placement of modifiers, sentence structure, parallelism, and verb-tense consistency. Although other sources are listed that provide students with collegiate-level instruction in all matters grammatical, perhaps the most comprehensive treatment is presented in the weighty, 652-page *Oxford English Grammar*, a mighty book that not only includes the basics, such as how to diagram a sentence (remember that from elementary school?), but also addresses such grammatical exotic delicacies as hyponyms (a specific term, such as "kiwi," that is included within a general term, such as "fruit," which is then called the hypernym) and collocations (adjectives and nouns that have come to be so strongly associated with each other that the adjective often predicts the noun, as in "rancid butter" or "stale bread"). Ah, the joys of grammar!

The rules of composition teach students how to take thoughts and bring them together to build a cogent argument. Thesis statements, topic sentences for each paragraph, transitions between thoughts, proper document format, and appropriate citations to supporting authority are all elements of good composition. Revisions and proofreading are the ways that good writers refine their product when it is almost complete.

Grammar and composition sources include the following:

(1) Andrea Lunsford and Robert Connors, *The New St. Martin's Handbook* (St. Martin's Press, 1999).

(2) H. Ramsey Fowler and Jane E. Aaron, *The Little, Brown Compact Handbook* (7th ed., Addison-Wesley Educational Publishers, Inc., 1998).

(3) Laurie G. Kirzner and Stephen R. Mandell, *The Holt Handbook* (5th ed., Harcourt Brace College Publishers, 1999).

(4) Sidney Greenbaum, *The Oxford English Grammar* (Oxford University Press, 1996).

Style

Although there are not both "legal grammar" and "non-legal grammar" books, there are "legal style" and "non-legal style" manuals, and this section will introduce both. Capitalization, the formation of plural and possessive forms, the interplay of spacing and punctuation, and the use of parenthetical expressions are typical matters of style. Again, however, there is significant overlap among materials here: Strunk and White's classic, 105-page gem *The Elements of Style* manages to include elements of usage (discussed below) and composition along with its exposition of style.

In contrast to the lean *The Elements of Style* is the 921-page *Chicago Manual of Style: The Essential Guide for Writers, Editors, and Publishers*, another classic resource. In addition to the items contained in *The Elements of Style, The Chicago Manual of Style* includes extensive information about the appropriate treatment of names and terms of art, terms from foreign languages, abbreviations, and numbers and numerals. The manual also includes, for the use of publishing professionals, very technical information about the physical layout and assembly of a book.

As with its book of grammar, Oxford University Press has an elegant entry in the style category as well, *The Oxford Guide to Style*, which the cover modestly proclaims to be "the style bible for all writers, editors, and publishers." Like *The Chicago Manual of Style, The Oxford Guide to Style* includes technical bookmaking information as well as more traditional style-manual fare. In addition, *The Oxford Guide to Style* includes a particularly comprehensive section on the appropriate use and formatting of terms from languages that range from Amerindian to Welsh, should they ever be necessary to a student's research.

Some style manuals, such as the *United States Government Printing Office Style Manual* and the *Associated Press Stylebook and Briefing on Media Law*, are geared toward particular primary audiences, namely those who use and prepare government documents and newspaper articles, respectively, and contain additional materials that are extremely helpful, and also largely unavailable in other style manuals. The *United States Government*

Printing Office Style Manual, for example, includes not only the appropriate way to refer to every kind of government document that is published by the office, but also includes information about the names, chiefs of state, and legislative bodies of other countries, a lengthy recitation of the nouns and adjectives denoting the nationality of many citizens of other countries, the units of money used in many other countries, and the capitals and counties (or other geographic divisions) of each state and territory in the United States.

Along the same lines, the *Associated Press Stylebook and Briefing on Media Law*, which is organized dictionary-style, includes information on the handling of military titles, the names of unions, political parties, and philosophies, and many terms that are common to the law as well as to current events. The portion of the book that is dedicated to media law may be of particular use to students who have an interest in that field of practice. *The New York Times Manual of Style and Usage* offers similar features. As the title of *The New York Times Manual of Style and Usage* suggests, both media stylebooks also serve as fairly extensive general-purpose usage guides.

There is one manual that is specifically geared toward the law and lawyers, Bryan Garner's *The Elements of Legal Style*. In addition to addressing some matters of grammar, composition, and usage, in which this manual gives legal examples that are likely to be of special use to lawyers and future lawyers, *The Elements of Legal Style* highlights phrases, sentence constructions, and manners of speaking that are often used in legal communication, showing how each is properly used.

Some of the major style manuals are as follows:

(1) William Strunk Jr. and E.B. White, *The Elements of Style* (4th ed., Macmillan Publishing Co., Inc., 2000).

(2) *The Chicago Manual of Style* (14th ed., University of Chicago Press, 1993).

(3) *United States Government Printing Office Style Manual* (2000).

(4) *The Oxford Guide to Style* (Oxford University Press, 2001).

(5) R.M. Ritter, *The Associated Press Stylebook and Briefing on Media Law* (Perseus Publishing, 2000).

(6) Allan M. Siegal and William G. Connolly, *The New York Times Manual of Style and Usage* (Three Rivers Press, 1999).

An excellent manual on legal style is the following:

Bryan A. Garner, *The Elements of Legal Style* (Oxford University Press, 1991).

Dictionaries

Although dictionaries are likely to have been a part of each law student's personal reference library since the student first learned to read, these materials will take on new importance in legal research and writing, a practice of law school in which, as this chapter has already discussed, precision and accuracy in word choice are particularly important. Both general dictionaries and law dictionaries will be important resources in good legal writing.

First, non-legal dictionaries will take on new importance in law school. Many first-year contracts students read a case in which the central issue, in the dispute over the interpretation of a contract, is the appropriate definition of the word "chicken": Does it mean the more expensive "broiler" chickens, or does it include inexpensive "stewing chickens" as well? As this case demonstrates, clients will count on their attorneys' ability to use language correctly, both in drafting contracts and in representing them in litigation.

Many students will continue to rely on the same *Merriam-Webster's Collegiate Dictionary* that saw them safely through undergraduate school. Tucked into this dictionary are some useful features that students may not have used before: a pronunciation guide, chemical-element abbreviations and symbols, foreign words and phrases, biographical and geographical names, signs and symbols, and an abbreviated handbook of style. Less authoritative are online dictionaries of uncertain origin, and students may wish to be cautious about relying upon these sources.

Some students, and many professors, seek assistance from the *Oxford English Dictionary* for a particularly difficult, or particularly important, word. Many people consider the *Oxford English Dictionary*, an enormous, twenty-volume set that is also available in a single, microprinted volume or on CD-ROM, to be the definitive dictionary of the English language, so a definition from this dictionary, included in a brief, for example, is likely to carry considerable weight. Furthermore, unlike shorter, or abridged, dictionaries, the *Oxford English Dictionary* describes the history of a word, indicating its origins as well as its current meaning.

Second, a legal dictionary is likely to be the student's constant companion during law school. Like judges and supervising attorneys in practice, many law-school professors expect students to look up *every* unfamiliar legal term, even if that term does not appear to be influential in the outcome of a case. Although other legal dictionaries are published, *Black's Law Dictionary* is widely considered to be the most authoritative source. Indeed, practicing attorneys feel comfortable citing to *Black's* in briefs and in court, but would not do the same with other legal dictionaries that are available. Many of the definitions also include citations to specific cases in which the terms were first defined. Like a regular dictionary, *Black's* includes the pronunciation of each word, which can be particularly helpful for the many Latin terms that students will encounter. In addition, *Black's* includes a few extras in the back: a short table of legal abbreviations, a chart showing the justices of the United States Supreme Court throughout American history, the full text of the United States Constitution, and an organizational chart giving an overview of the system of government for the United States.

Besides these standard reference materials, some students are likely to make use of special-purpose dictionaries, including visual dictionaries and geographical dictionaries. These items are likely to be of particular use whenever a student needs a more in-depth understanding of a case, such as when she is handling the case herself in a clinic or preparing the facts of a moot-court argument. A visual dictionary, true to its name, includes pictures representing various objects and labels showing the various parts of each. A student—or an attorney—who is investigating a brain-injury case, for instance, may find herself needing to know the difference between the cerebrum and the cerebellum, and where each is located within the skull. A visual dictionary provides this information, and can be of particular aid to those who are visual learners.

Other times, again most likely when doing an in-depth analysis of a particular case, a student or practicing attorney will reach for a geographical dictionary to learn some information about the jurisdiction where the case is to be litigated or the location in which the incident in the lawsuit arose. In addition to pronunciation guides, which should save the student or attorney from mispronouncing the name of his or her venue, a geographical dictionary includes helpful maps, along with information about the population, major industry, and history of a place.

Useful dictionaries include the following:

(1) *Merriam-Webster's Collegiate Dictionary* (10th ed., 1998).

(2) *Oxford English Dictionary* (John A. Simpson and Edmund Weiner, eds., 2nd ed., Oxford University Press, 1989).

The best legal dictionary is the following:

Bryan A. Garner, Editor in Chief, *Black's Law Dictionary* (7th ed., West Group 1999).

Some special-purpose dictionaries are the following:

(1) Jean-Claude Corbeil, Editor in Chief, *The Macmillan Visual Dictionary* (Macmillan, 1992).

(2) Merriam-Webster's Geographical Dictionary (3rd ed., 1997).

Manuals of Usage

When a student or attorney encounters a word that is particularly difficult, or particularly important to her case, she may need information beyond what is provided in a dictionary. In these situations, manuals of usage are extremely helpful. Unlike dictionaries, which simply define a word and, in the case of the *Oxford English Dictionary*, describe its etymology, manuals of usage also indicate to the reader what the word does *not* mean, and how it is commonly misused. A usage manual, for instance, explains how stalactite and stalagmite are commonly confused, while a dictionary would simply define each. (And yes, the stalactite *is* the one that hangs *down* from the ceiling of a cave.)

In addition to standard manuals of usage, there is a legal manual of usage that explains words that are unique to the law, or commonly used in the law. This manual tells the reader that "jurist," for example, is not truly a synonym for judge but is commonly used that way. With their more conversational style and more comprehensive approach, manuals of usage provide readers with the additional information that is necessary to employ difficult words with confidence.

The following are well-known usage manuals:

(1) Bryan A. Garner, *A Dictionary of Modern American Usage* (Oxford University Press, 1998).

(2) Wilson Follett, Eric Wensberg (Compiler), *Modern American Usage: A Guide* (Revised ed., Hill & Wang Publishers, 1998).

A good manual of legal usage is the following:

Bryan A. Garner, *A Dictionary of Modern Legal Usage* (2nd ed., Oxford University Press, 1995).

Legal Citation Manuals

Attribution of proper authority is an extremely important task for law students in legal-research-and-writing courses and, later, in clinical work, in moot-court competitions, and in law-review writing, and also for practicing lawyers. Two major citation manuals are used in law schools at this time: The *ALWD Citation Manual* by the Association of Legal Writing Directors and Darby Dickerson, and *The Bluebook: A Uniform System of Citation* by the Harvard Law Review Association. Each student's law school will indicate which manual is to be used there, although students are likely to encounter both as practicing attorneys.

Both manuals have certain features in common: both address the general features of legal citations, including their structure and appropriate use, and provide models to be followed in citing various kinds of legal authorities from the United States and other jurisdictions, including cases, statutes, law-review articles and other periodicals, treatises, and legislative materials. In addition, both give precise directions on the formatting of citations, including spacing, footnoting and endnoting, capitalization, abbreviations, quotations, and the use of symbols. Each also includes extensive appendices that provide, among other information, specific guidance on the citation of materials that are associated with specific states, countries, and other jurisdictions.

Some students may find the entire concept of citation and attribution of sources to be a new one, while others may be familiar with systems such as that contained in the Modern Language Association of America's popular *MLA Handbook for Writers of Research Papers,* which is used in many undergraduate programs. Students who have advanced degrees in other fields, on the other hand, may be familiar with the *Publication Manual of the American Psychological Association.*

In any event, it is important for law students to understand the significance of citation to authority, within the legal system, and to understand that the system of legal citation is different from that used in other fields. In addition, unlike fields in which citation to authority may be reserved for scholarly work, practicing attorneys use legal citation daily, in everything from client-advice letters to briefs. Indeed, proper citation to authority, which must be both substantively accurate and properly formatted, is part of what makes any piece of legal work product "finished." By the time of graduation, law students should be so familiar with their school's preferred system of citation that they automatically write cases down in proper citation format, even in their class notes, simply out of habit. As one senior attorney has stated, many experienced attorneys believe that neat, clean, proper citation form is a signal to the client, the court, and the opponent that the document is substantively neat, clean, and proper as well. This same attorney noted that virtually every brief he reads that contains sloppy citation errors also contains sloppy legal arguments.

Legal citation is not, however, important simply as a matter of appearance. Instead, because of the American system of relying upon legal precedent—cases that have been decided before—attorneys must support each argument they advance on behalf of a client, by citing proper authority. Because it is so important that attorneys identify binding or persuasive authority in support of their client's positions, preferably by citing either a statute or case law from the jurisdiction where each client's case will be heard, students will learn that it is often preferable to use the words contained in the statute or case rather than attempting to rephrase them. Rephrasing often leads to inaccuracy; furthermore, the court or other decision maker is simply more likely to be impressed by binding authority than by the unsupported arguments of counsel, however cleverly crafted they might be.

The two major manuals of legal citation are as follows:

(1) Association of Legal Writing Directors and Darby Dickerson, *ALWD Citation Manual: A Professional System of Citation* (2nd ed., Aspen Law & Business, 2003).

(2) *The Bluebook: A Uniform System of Citation* (17th ed., Harvard Law Review Association, 2000).

Legal Research and Writing

In addition to any required text that is employed in the law school's legal-writing program, students may want to consider consulting some of the following resources. Some, such as *How to Find the Law*, focus simply on legal research; others are geared only toward legal writing. Many include some useful resources for both legal research and writing.

Early in the first semester, either during legal-writing class or outside of class, new law students are likely to receive library orientation. During this orientation, students will be introduced to a wealth of legal resources, including but not limited to case reporters, in which individual cases are reprinted; legal encyclopedias such *as American Jurisprudence* and *Corpus Juris Secundum*; and digests, in which abstracts describing a very large number of cases are arranged by subject matter. Often, because the students receive this orientation during a time when they (1) are overwhelmed with information and (2) are not yet in the process of doing legal research and writing, such that they would remember this information, it is quickly forgotten. *How to Find the Law* is a venerable book, now in its ninth edition, that has long been a favorite of law students who find themselves suddenly in the midst of legal research, having a hard time remembering the various resources that are available. The best aspect of this book, from the point of view of many students, is that it actually reproduces pages from various sources, such as reporters, legal encyclopedias, and digests, to jog students' memories, in addition to providing a comprehensive explanation of what each legal-research tool does.

Other books focus on legal writing, guiding the reader through the process of identifying the relevant issues of law: applying controlling case law and statutory law to the facts presented, and organizing, crafting, and explaining the conclusions drawn.

Several books, including *Scholarly Writing for Law Students* and *Writing and Analysis in the Law*, provide students with both helpful hints for research and guidance on the drafting of legal documents such as briefs and memoranda. Each is written in a readable style, and each is the recommended text for several law schools' research-and-writing programs.

The following are helpful legal-research manuals:

(1) Morris L. Cohen, Kent C. Olson, and Robert C. Berring, *How to Find the Law* (9th ed., West, 1989).

(2) Christina L. Kunz et al., *The Process of Legal Research: Successful Strategies* (3rd ed., Little, Brown and Co., 1992).

(3) J. Myron Jacobstein, Roy M. Mersky, and Donald J. Dunn, *Fundamentals of Legal Research* (7th ed., Foundation Press, 1998).

Helpful resources on legal writing include the following:

(1) John C. Dernbach, Richard Singleton II, Cathleen S. Wharton, and Joan M. Ruhtenberg, *A Practical Guide to*

Legal Writing & Legal Method (2nd ed., Fred B. Rothman & Co., 1994).

(2) Jill J. Ramsfield, *The Law as Architecture: Building Legal Documents* (West Group, 2000).

(3) Terri LeClercq, *Guide to Legal Writing Style* (2nd ed., Panel Publishers, 2000).

(4) Richard C. Wydick, *Plain English for Lawyers* (4th ed., Carolina Academic Press, 2001).

(5) Bryan A. Garner, *Legal Writing in Plain English* (University of Chicago Press, 2001).

(6) Tom Goldstein and Jethro K. Lieberman, *The Lawyer's Guide to Writing Well* (University of California Press, 1991).

Guides to both legal research and writing include the following:

(1) Elizabeth Fajans and Mary R. Falk, *Scholarly Writing for Law Students: Seminar Papers, Law Review Notes, and Law Review Competition Papers* (2nd ed., West/Wadsworth, 2000).

(2) Helene S. Shapo, Marilyn R. Walter, and Elizabeth Fajans, *Writing and Analysis in the Law* (4th ed., Foundation Press, 1999).

Thesauruses and Legal Thesauruses

A thesaurus is a useful tool for any writer. In seeking to vary their usage of non-legal terminology, many legal writers continue to reach for the classic *Roget's* single-volume thesaurus. When writing about legal causes of action, however, legal writers must be more careful: as this chapter previously stated, there are few true synonyms in the law. Therefore, a tool such as *Burton's*

Legal Thesaurus is likely to be of great assistance to writers who are seeking to vary their language without destroying the legal soundness of the document.

The best general thesaurus is the classic:

Roget's 21st Century Thesaurus: in Dictionary Form (Barbara Ann Kipfer and the Princeton Language Institute, eds., Barnes & Noble Books, 1999).

In addition, the following legal thesaurus may be helpful:

William C. Burton, *Burton's Legal Thesaurus* (3rd ed., Simon & Schuster, 1999).

Other Reference Materials

The New York Public Library Desk Reference, which is similar in many ways to a single-volume encyclopedia, provides a little bit of information on a vast number of subjects. The reader can find short biographical sketches of famous people, examine timelines of world events, learn something about each of the major world religions, and even peruse advice on basic etiquette. Legal writers are likely to find this volume useful in providing very basic information on an area that is completely new to them, helping them to become oriented so as to seek further information as needed.

Lauther's Complete Punctuation Thesaurus of the English Language is a unique resource that turns the classic grammar text on its ear in a way that may be helpful to some legal writers. Instead of looking up a part of speech, such as a comma or semicolon, in a typical grammar text, this resource invites the reader to browse through situations—formulating the beginning of a sentence, preparing the closing to a letter, or providing a mid-sentence interruption—and then introduces several means by which the writer's goal can be accomplished in a grammatically correct fashion.

Two alternative resources are as follows:

(1) *The New York Public Library Desk Reference* (Paul Fargis ed., 3rd ed., Hungry Minds, Inc., 1998).

(2) *Lauther's Complete Punctuation Thesaurus of the English Language* (Branden Publishing Company, 1991).

THE LEGAL-WRITING PROGRAM AND HANDLING ASSIGNMENTS

Schools are increasingly recognizing the importance of having a strong legal-writing-and-advocacy program, particularly for first-year students. In the past, some schools took the position that law schools should focus on teaching students *how to think* and law firms should teach them *how to write*. Those days are over. Law firms started taking notice that new associates from certain schools were better prepared than others for practice because they were more skilled writers than their peers at other schools. As a result, law schools now place great emphasis on these programs and have high expectations for the instructors who teach them.

The legal-writing program instructor will likely have practice experience, either as a practitioner or an appellate-court clerk. Some may currently be practicing law with a local firm. Because of this background and experience, the instructors have the necessary expertise to evaluate students' writing and provide constructive criticism that is relevant to the context in which it will ultimately be evaluated or used. Evaluating subordinates' writing is a part of an attorney's daily professional life. Similarly, law clerks have the daily experience of reading briefs and deciding whether each brief and its supporting research is persuasive. Both experiences are excellent preparation for evaluating others' writing. Moreover, the instructor will be able to point out some of the nuances of local practice, if doing so is relevant to the assignment. For example, in some jurisdictions, the expected writing style for court documents may be particularly formal; attorneys there may go to great lengths to maintain professionalism towards opposing counsel in their style of writing (a worthy goal for us all, but not necessarily the norm in every jurisdiction). These examples can provide context for the student to understand more fully the concepts the instructor is trying to convey.

Instructors teach legal writing in one of several different ways. One instructor might give only one or two assignments for the semester, but will work closely with the students on drafts of those assignments, monitoring their progress. That instructor may have regular meetings with the students to discuss their progress and provide written feedback on each draft. Another may assign numerous tasks, which may or may not be graded, each of which teaches a specific skill. For example, the assignment for one week might be to draft a business letter to opposing counsel or even a client-engagement letter. Students should defer to the approach chosen by their own instructors. For that reason, this book will not deal specifically with how to write a memo, or even what should be included in it. These are matters best left to the judgment of the instructor, who has himself taken into consideration the goals of his particular school's program and his own preferences for the formatting of such documents. The following are some general, practical suggestions, however, for writing, both in law school and as a new attorney.

The school's legal-writing program likely will include assignments in which students are asked to research specific legal issues and then to prepare a memorandum and/or brief using that research. Some schools have the students prepare an appellate brief for their first piece (or only piece) of formal persuasive writing, while others assign several such projects. Students are generally given ample time to complete the assignments, although some students either procrastinate or use what they may erroneously believe to be this "extra" time to focus on their doctrinal classes. Students are encouraged to start their assignments early, even if they spend that time just looking at some of the resources mentioned earlier in this chapter.

When the assignment is handed out, the student must read it carefully with pen in hand. If the assignment is based upon a fact pattern, some law students find it sometimes helps to circle the most important facts or, alternatively, any facts for which the student cannot immediately see a connection. These assigned problems are generally crafted such that every piece of information is included for a reason. Students should keep in mind, however, that sometimes certain facts are included for the express purpose of distracting them from the real issues; lawyers call these distractions "red herrings." Lawyers use such collateral matters, sometimes effectively, to distract a judge from the core legal issues in a case. Usually, lawyers do this when the central facts and legal issues are not favorable to their client. When writing instructors use red herrings, they often do so to test the student's discernment and to ensure that the student knows how not to get sidetracked from the task at hand. Alternatively, the instructor may include one or more red herrings as a way of introducing facts that opposing counsel might use to evoke an emotional response in the judge reading these papers or the jury hearing the arguments. The lesson from this exercise is as follows: certain facts that may seem extraneous may nevertheless require a considered response from the student. Sometimes, the student (or lawyer) must take the sting out of facts that, while only marginally relevant, are highly prejudicial to his case; other times he simply needs to ignore them.

Students should look up unfamiliar words in the assignment and might consider noting their definitions on the assignment page. Students may also want to make duplicate copies of the assignment, in case one gets marked up beyond recognition or left behind on a library shelf. As the student progresses with her work, she should re-read the assignment from time to time. Although she will, one hopes, already have identified the salient legal issues, facts may later seem more or less important than she originally considered them to be.

After the student has thoroughly read the assignment, she should start with some general reading to become familiar with the issues. This may be an appropriate time to look at a treatise, also called a "hornbook," or a legal encyclopedia such as *Corpus Juris Secundum* to provide some background or general information. Students should avoid becoming locked into a single way of thinking about the legal issues presented by the problem; although the student may be convinced that the problem centers on a contracts issue, for example, it may also include evidentiary or jurisdictional issues that the student has not yet discovered.

Next, the student should make an outline of the issues and the general manner in which they should be addressed. There may, for instance, be an initial question that must be answered before subsequent issues can be addressed. For example, a court cannot address the substance of an arbitrability question unless the court finds that it has the power to hear the dispute in the first place. This type of jurisdictional question is called a threshold matter, and it must be addressed first.

Another helpful approach at this early stage is to set up the framework for the final written product. If the assignment calls for a memorandum to the senior partner of the firm, then the student should go ahead and prepare the To, From, Date, Regarding, and Subject lines for the memorandum. By getting the shell down on paper first, the student may find that the rest will start to come together in an organized fashion. A sample memorandum format is included for the reader's reference in Appendix C. A sample brief is included in Appendix D. Again, in reading these resources, students should be aware that each instructor may have in mind particular information that should be included in the documents that his students prepare, may require students to use different headings from those that were employed in the samples, or may want students to use an entirely different format from that which is presented in this book.

It is generally best for students to save their questions for the instructor until they have made their own attempts to figure out the assigned problem. Once a student has done some initial research, he can ask more focused questions, and may even answer for himself many of the questions that he had when he began his research. Lawyers in practice, similarly, are expected to educate themselves to a significant extent before they begin to ask substantive questions of the assigning attorney. This process saves time for all of the parties involved and prevents an attorney's superiors from thinking that the attorney cannot work independently or that she does not trust her own research and her own instincts. These are examples of the way in which a student or lawyer must take charge, not only of the way that he or she approaches assignments, but also of the perceptions of those for whom the student or lawyer works.

As the student continues her research, she should begin to craft a basic outline of her final work product. Sometimes it may help the student to have the outline handy as she continues to read case law. One advantage of this approach is that it allows the student to stay focused on the issues and the legal elements of those issues. The student may find that one case, for instance, sets forth the law relating to one element of a breach-of-contract claim, and that other cases support other elements of the same cause of action. If the student makes a brief note about where each case fits into the outline, her research will already be organized when she actually sits down to write. Also, by having an outline handy, the student will be better able to recognize whether a court has accurately or wrongly analyzed and decided a legal issue. Crafting a comprehensive analysis of any legal issue takes time and generally is possible only after the student has read many cases and learned the subsequent treatment, if any, of each case by other courts. For example, one case may neatly present the elements of a claim for fraud. Five years later, however, that same case may have been overturned by another court that added an additional requirement for the aggrieved party to prove. Having an outline provides a checklist for the student as he reads cases and reviews each court's analysis, and makes it possible for him to discern how the law changed over time.

Other useful tools include diagrams, flow charts, or decision trees, each of which may assist the student in understanding a cause of action and how a party can prove its claim. For example, Appendix E contains a decision tree for a party claiming to be a victim of pre-contractual fraud. Having this visual picture of a claim for fraud may assist a student or attorney in focusing his research and remaining on track throughout the case. Like savvy law students, attorneys are not above using pictures, diagrams, or flow charts. Indeed, these can be helpful tools to provide to a judge when the attorney is presenting a new perspective on a legal issue in question.

This basic research process will not change substantively when the law student makes the transition to the practice of law. Although the lawyer will work more quickly and more efficiently than she did as a student, she will employ the same kind of discernment and the same analytical tools every single time she writes a brief or prepares a legal document that cites to or relies upon legal research. It is in law school that future lawyers begin to develop these skills, such as the ability to decide which organizational tools will be most helpful to their own research and writing.

As the student's research nears completion, it becomes time to start writing. Sometimes it takes an affirmative decision for the student to commit some words to paper; a student may otherwise never feel "ready" to write. Practicing lawyers sometimes feel this way, too. They wrestle with questions such as "Is the research done?" "Is there something big that I am overlooking?" and "Have I identified all of the issues?" At some point, however, both the student and the lawyer must trust the research that they have done and start writing. All of the research in the world will not help a lawyer's client if it is never turned into a final product.

Many legal writers find it helpful to begin with simple statements. These starting sentences may be as basic as "See Jane run." (No kidding—many a brief has been started with a simple phrase such as "This is a case about corporate greed.") At this early stage, the writer should try not to worry about being concise or even articulate. This polishing will come later, once the student (or lawyer) has gotten her basic thoughts down on paper and starts the process of refining drafts of the document. The student may find that reading court cases will help her to become accustomed to the language of the law. Words often come more easily to students as they review the research they have already done and become comfortable with both the appropriate phrases for this particular case and the language that the courts have employed in similar matters in the past.

Students should be prepared to write and re-write and should try not to become wedded to what they believe to be a particularly clever way of wording any particular portion of the document. If a student feels that he has become stuck, having gotten hung up on some aspect of the writing process, he is encouraged to take advantage of opportunities to consult with teaching assistants, his peers, or the writing instructor, as his law school's policy permits. In a nutshell, this is the learning process involved in legal research and writing: the student is engaging in researching and writing, thinking analytically, and looking at his work with a critical eye.

Once she has created a final draft, the student may wish to step back and take a look at the document as a whole. If time permits, the student should consider leaving the document alone for some period of time and returning to it later with a fresh perspective. When she returns to her writing, she might run through the following checklist:

- ◆ Have I responded appropriately to the assignment? If a client letter is called for, is that what I have written? If a piece of advocacy writing is assigned, have I crafted a persuasive document or have I, instead, drafted a mini-law-review article that presents both sides of an issue?

- ◆ Does my paper answer the specific questions posed? (This may be an appropriate time to re-read the assignment.)

- ◆ Does my work meet my instructor's expectations with regard to grammar, composition, and punctuation?

- ◆ Does my paper make sense?

- ◆ Have I checked the citations to cases and other resources for accuracy?

- ◆ Is each case that I relied upon still good law? Has anything changed since I started this project two months ago?

- ◆ Does my paper look neat?

- ◆ Is my paper formatted correctly?

- ◆ Have I proofread my paper more than three times?

Ultimately, the student should develop his or her own checklist, which will likely grow with experience. After a while, and with practice, these steps become second nature. Law students will want to form excellent writing habits early in law school; no supervising attorney wants to spend time teaching a new lawyer how to write.

The next difficult task for many students and lawyers alike is actually submitting the finished product. It is sometimes hard to let go of a project that has taken up a substantial portion of the writer's time. At this point, the student must trust that the process she followed so carefully was thorough and that every issue has been addressed: Hand in the document!

The student should expect feedback on her work in the form of a grade and/or comments given orally or in writing. If feedback is given solely in the form of a grade, the student should make an appointment with the instructor and get some face-to-face assessment of her writing. As compared to the practice of law, the student's early experience with legal-writing instructors is one of the few times in her legal career in which she will get substantive, constructive comments about her writing in a relatively safe atmosphere. Later, few supervising attorneys will have the time, ability, or patience to teach a junior attorney how to write. Indeed, most of a new lawyer's writing development will occur through the process of actually writing, as well as reading the work of other attorneys. The student should learn how to accept constructive criticism while she is in law school, and should ask *how* to improve the issues that were brought to light by the instructor rather than focus on *why* the instructor made the comments he did. The student should work hard to use this writing and feedback experience to refine her writing and research skills. The ability to take lessons learned through experience and apply them to new and possibly unique situations is a hallmark of maturity and a characteristic of a great lawyer.

HINDSIGHT AND PERSPECTIVE

Students often gain new appreciation for their legal-research-and-writing training after their first summer of employment during law school. Although many students may look forward to having opportunities to attend depositions, or to participate in client conferences, negotiations, or trials, legal research and writing are likely to occupy the lion's share of the student's time during summer employment. Furthermore, students may find that the work product most frequently requested of them consists of a brief or a memorandum of law. Being comfortable with each of these forms of legal communication is extremely important and will give the student an opportunity to distinguish himself or herself quickly. Furthermore, the student is likely to find that even the relatively generous deadlines that are given to students during summer employment require students to work much more quickly on their briefs and memoranda than they did during their legal-research-and-writing classes. For this reason, many students find themselves grateful for the time, care, and attention that they and their professors spent perfecting their legal-research-and-writing skills so that they can now generate these documents much more efficiently.

Another reason for students to give special time and attention to their legal-research-and-writing classes is that, although they cannot generally show a potential employer their fine performance on their torts exam by bringing a copy of the examination paper to an interview, students are very likely to use the memorandum of law or brief that they generated in legal-research-and-writing class as their first writing sample for potential employers. Indeed, although some students will also wish to include a piece of earlier work from before law school of which they are particularly proud, potential employers often will insist on a piece of legal writing as well. Therefore, by honing her legal-research-and-writing skills, a student is also increasing her chances of employment. A further reason for paying attention to the development of these skills is the fact that some schools afford special weight, in the law-review, mock-trial, or moot-court competitions, to strong performance in the first-year legal-research-and-writing program.

CHAPTER 12

Special Considerations for the Second and Third Years of Law School

A New Task

In their first year of law school, many students feel that they are treading water, simply trying to manage all that is required of them and to become accustomed to this new academic environment. During this initial year, many students choose to focus solely on their studies, taking on little in the way of employment or extracurricular activities. Especially during the second and sometimes the third year, students are actually much busier than they were in their first year. Not only are the courses more demanding, but many students also hold jobs and get involved in extracurricular activities during this time. Professors assign more reading to upperclassmen than to first-years, and also might assign papers or other additional tasks throughout the semester.

The significant increase in work occurs, for many students, in the first semester of their second year. It is then that they become involved in moot court, law review, mock trial, and other activities; begin interviewing for summer employment; and sometimes take on part-time jobs. Although students should be able to deal more efficiently with their coursework by their second year, many still find this time to be a period of adjustment. If the student has taken on a challenging schedule that includes several particularly difficult courses, such as Evidence, Constitutional Law, or Federal Income Tax, he may discover that it is very difficult to find sufficient time for his studies, let alone tackle other, new responsibilities. This chapter will help upperclassmen to consider, and make choices among, the many opportunities that are available to them, and to manage their time accordingly.

NEW OPPORTUNITIES: EXTRACURRICULAR ACTIVITIES

It is during the second year of law school that students generally become seriously involved in extracurricular activities that enrich their legal studies. Indeed, many law students find these endeavors, which are described comprehensively in Chapter 9, to be the most enriching part of their legal education. Students who purposefully choose extracurricular activities and courses that complement each other—such as taking Evidence while participating in mock trial, for instance—often find that the combination makes both experiences more enjoyable and more useful. Having a context into which to put their substantive coursework, and being able to put some of the theory conveyed in their doctrinal courses into practice, causes some second- and third-year students to feel like future lawyers for the first time since they began their legal education.

In addition, the second and third years of law school present students with new ways to excel. During the first year of law school, it often seems that every student in every class is focused on a single goal: top grades. Recognition in a variety of areas begins to come to students in their second and third years. Some will be at the top of the class academically; others will excel as advocates, scholars, or student leaders. Because of these additional opportunities, law students often find that the intense competition for grades becomes at least somewhat more amicable once the second year begins.

Each student should consider the extracurricular activities that he or she will enjoy and benefit from most. Some opportunities may be available only to those who have excelled in their doctrinal coursework thus far, but others will be open to the class as a whole, or through a non-grade-based lottery or competition. Those students whose first-year grades were weak may wish to strike a balance between improving their classroom performance and seeking outside experience that may be attractive to potential employers. When hiring, some employers will overlook lackluster grades if a student has demonstrated practical ability.

NEW CHOICES: ELECTIVE COURSES, CERTIFICATION PROGRAMS, AND HONORS PROGRAMS

Elective Courses

In addition to the usual required courses, discussed in Chapter 5, second- and third-year students have the opportunity to take elective courses. Some schools provide, or even require that students participate in, a program in which members of the faculty consult with students about their elective-course choices. Even if there is no such program formally in place, students may wish to speak with members of the faculty about their course selections. This mentoring process can be particularly helpful when the faculty member is well versed in the areas of the law that most appeal to the student.

In choosing courses, students may wish to consider several different approaches, no one of which is better than the others, in and of itself. Some students, for example, take what might be described as a "liberal arts" approach to law school, viewing it as a unique learning opportunity that marks, for most law students, the end of their formal education. These students use their elective courses to explore areas of law that, although they may never use them in their careers, are of personal interest and significance. In the professional world, by contrast, the lawyer continues to learn the law daily, but most of this learning is targeted not to personal enjoyment, but rather to fulfilling the specific needs of a client.

Other students who have already selected an area of practice and are strongly committed to their decision embark on what could be termed the "pre-professional" approach. Such a student selects each course because she believes it will be of assistance to her in her chosen field. Some students find this approach to be very satisfying, especially if they have a strong intellectual interest in their chosen field. For example, students with a strong interest in patent or copyright law may choose to take all of the intellectual property courses and seminars offered. Some gain confidence from the additional training they receive through this focused approach. Others, however, later regret passing up the opportunity to explore different areas of the law. Many students either change their minds about the area of practice that most interests them or find that, because of the realities of the legal market, the area in which they trained is not the area in which they end up practicing. For these students, an approach that is too narrowly pre-professional may ultimately be of disservice.

Another version of the pre-professional approach is to concentrate on those courses that are to be tested on the bar examination. Students who have struggled academically may be encouraged or even required to plan their course of study this way. Students at law schools that are not accredited by the American Bar Association also may be required to take certain courses so as to take the bar in those states that will allow them to do so. Other students simply assume, not without justification, that taking those courses that will be tested on the bar examination is likely to result in a well-balanced legal education.

Students who have already secured post-graduation employment might consider discussing these alternatives with their future employers. Some employers have preferences that might come as a surprise to the student; one major nationwide firm, for instance, actually discourages its new litigators from taking advocacy courses in law school, preferring to train the new lawyers in its own fashion once their employment has begun. At the same time, however, the student should consider her own needs as well as those of an employer; after all, law school is ultimately for her benefit, not solely for that of those who will, during her career, supervise her and work with her.

The following is a list of courses, organized by type, that an upper-level law student may consider in planning his elective curriculum.

Bar Courses. Students who are interested in focusing on those substantive areas of law that are regularly tested on the bar exam should consult the bar association for the jurisdiction in which they expect to practice for a comprehensive list of relevant courses. Those areas of law that are tested on the national multistate portion of the bar exam are listed in Chapter 14.

Foundation Courses. These are courses that will give students at least some exposure to most of the varied areas of law practice that they are likely to encounter throughout their careers. Obviously, there will be significant overlap between the list of "Bar Courses" and the list of "Foundation Courses," because most bar exams attempt to test applicants in a variety of basic subjects. This approach may be particularly helpful to a student who has not yet chosen an area of law in which to specialize or someone who wishes to be a general practitioner and expects to handle a broad variety of matters.

In addition to those courses listed in Chapter 5, which many schools require, students taking this approach may wish to consider some or all of the following courses:

Commercial Paper and *Secured Transactions.* These courses introduce students to the nature and mechanics of negotiable instruments, documents of title, and non-real-estate mortgages that are used to finance the acquisition of personal property.

Criminal Procedure. Although most law schools require that first-year students take civil procedure, criminal procedure is generally not a required course. Students who expect that some or all of their practice may be in the field of criminal law should therefore supplement their procedural education with this course.

Insurance Law. Insurance issues are common to much litigation, regardless of whether the matter involves businesses or individuals. In addition, courts sometimes treat matters involving insurance contracts in substantively different ways from other contract-law cases. Having a basic understanding of how this highly regulated field works is therefore critical to many areas of civil practice.

State Practice and Procedure. Most first-year civil-procedure courses focus on federal law. Those students who expect that some, or most, of their practice will be before state courts, and who are attending law school in the state in which they desire to practice, often benefit from a study of the procedural laws of their own jurisdiction.

Real Estate Transactions. General practitioners often deal with basic real estate transactions. Most lawyers are also likely to deal with real estate law in their personal lives at some time. This course will provide students with a working knowledge of this area of law sufficient to navigate most basic real estate matters.

Family Law. Every general practitioner is likely to be asked to handle some domestic-relations work from time to time. Whether the matter involves adoption, divorce, or the support or custody of children, a basic family-law course will provide an introduction to the relevant material.

Employment Law. Regardless of whether the new lawyer plans to represent individuals, small businesses, or large corporations, she probably will find the material presented in an employment-law course to be useful in practice. This course introduces the law governing the relationship between employee and employer, from employment-at-will to employment pursuant to a contract for a specific period of time. In addition, this course presents the relevant judge-made and regulatory law on compensation, health and safety, privacy, and the ownership of information.

Advocacy Courses. Students who plan to pursue a career in either civil or criminal litigation may wish to take some of the specialized advocacy courses that many schools offer. Once the student has mastered the doctrinal material presented in foundation courses such as civil procedure, criminal procedure, and evidence, she may benefit from the practical material that is presented in courses on civil and criminal trial advocacy skills. In addition, basic trial strategy and the fundamentals of managing a case on appeal are often covered in trial-practice and appellate-advocacy courses.

Lawyering-Skills Courses. Although any attorney is likely to find the practical material presented in the following courses to be helpful, these classes are most likely to be of particular interest to those students who expect to manage their own law firms, either immediately after graduation from law school or later in their careers.

Courses in business ethics, for example, go beyond the material that is covered in a basic professional-responsibility course and provide both practical and philosophical grounding in this important field. Classes that address business problems and business practice attempt to prepare students to navigate stressful everyday business situations. Business-management courses not only provide instruction in trouble-shooting, but also prepare the student to handle other business matters, such as billing, hiring and firing of clients, document management, and staff issues.

Other skills courses focus on the research and writing that will be required of the new lawyer. Some courses on document drafting, for example, attempt to prepare both transactional attorneys and litigators to compose deal documents such as contracts and settlement agreements. Others focus on the drafting of documents used in the pre-trial phases of litigation, such as complaints, answers, discovery requests and responses, motions, and briefs. Many schools also offer courses that provide advanced instruction in legal research, reasoning, and writing.

In addition, there are courses that focus on client counseling and dispute resolution. A class in alternative dispute resolution, for example, introduces students to the fundamentals of extra-judicial dispute-resolution mechanisms such as mediation, arbitration, and conciliation. Other courses introduce students to basic skills such as negotiation, client interviewing, and client counseling.

Seminars. In seminar courses, students usually prepare scholarly papers, rather than take examinations, for their final grade. In some seminars, students have the opportunity to present their papers to the professor or to the rest of the class, and thereby to get feedback before the final product is due. Most seminars involve smaller groups than typical law-school courses, and the classroom atmosphere is often less formal and more collegial.

Seminars frequently address relatively discrete areas of the law that typically represent the professor's current area of personal research. Topics might include Supreme Court First Amendment jurisprudence, feminist legal studies, or advanced problems in partnership taxation. Taking a seminar is therefore a very good way for students to become acquainted with the current developments in areas in which they are particularly interested. In addition, students often have the opportunity to explore interdisciplinary work through seminars, examining connections between the law and other disciplines. Interdisciplinary seminar offerings might include Law and Religion, Law and Psychology, and Law and Literature, for example.

Many law schools require upperclassmen to complete a scholarly paper before graduation. Although some students may satisfy this requirement through participation in a law journal or through independent study, most students choose to complete the required paper in a seminar. Even students who have already satisfied this requirement in some other way might choose to enroll in a seminar for the more informal and comprehensive experience it can provide.

Independent Study. Doing independent study gives the student an opportunity to craft her own coursework, normally under the supervision of a faculty member. Such studies give students a chance to explore areas of law not currently covered by courses offered in the general law-school curriculum.

A student who wishes to engage in independent study may, depending on the requirements of his law school, be required to write a proposal. Even if this is not a formal requirement, the student should be prepared to make a case persuasively to the professor whom he wishes to have as an advisor during his independent study. In seeking an advisor, the student is encouraged to choose carefully, selecting a member of the faculty who is not only knowledgeable in the relevant field, but also personable, generally available, and a good mentor. The student is likely to have a negative experience if he chooses an advisor who makes herself unavailable or who is unduly critical. Sometimes, a student can affirmatively be of assistance to a professor through independent study if the student is pursuing an area that is also of strong interest to the professor in her personal research. Indeed, if the student is close enough to a professor, he might be able to approach her with no specific research idea in mind and ask the professor what areas of the law she would particularly like to see explored. At times, these collaborations between a professor and a student through independent study have resulted in the creation of a new course. A student, having engaged in such study, may then be invited to serve as the teaching assistant for the new course. On occasion, such students have even co-taught the new course.

Clinical Work and Internships. Many students prefer to wait until their third year to participate in clinics. In fact, some states allow only third-year students to work in legal clinics, if the students are actually to practice law, and only under the careful supervision of a senior attorney. Furthermore, because clinics, by definition, involve students working with actual clients and therefore encountering client demands and deadlines, students are likely to find the work extremely time-consuming. Because of these considerations, students often find the experience to be more manageable—and more fulfilling—during their third year, when they have completed most of their core courses and have more flexibility in their scheduling.

Students may find internships, on the other hand, to be manageable during their second year of law school. Many students pursue judicial internships, hoping to be asked to remain as law clerks after graduation, or hoping to use the recommendations of the judges for whom they are interning to get other clerkships.

Regardless of whether the student works in a clinic or as an intern, however, he may gain some experience in any of the following areas: alternative dispute resolution, Legal Aid, elder law, family law, local government, labor-and-employment law, corporate law, immigration law, prosecution, state and federal courts, and criminal defense.

Prerequisites for Elective Courses

Students who know that they are likely to take a number (or all) of the classes offered in a specific area, such as Taxation, should get the foundational courses—such as Federal Income Tax—out of the way as soon as possible. These foundational courses are likely to be prerequisites—or recommended—for the advanced courses the student will take later in law school. Especially if these advanced courses are not offered every semester, are very popular, or both, the student will want to maximize her opportunities to take those courses in which she is interested by making sure she has the background to do so, as soon as possible.

Popular Elective Courses with Limited Enrollments

Some schools have a "point" system that requires students to bid on classes in which they are interested. A class that is very popular and has limited enrollment might require *all* of the student's points in a given semester. Other courses that are less popular or have unlimited enrollment may require very few points or even no points whatsoever. At some schools, the registrar will release information showing how many points were required to get into each course the last time it was offered. The point level for each course will vary by semester, so all the student can do is make an educated guess about how many points a course will require. This does mean, however, that upperclassmen are likely not to be able to enroll in more than one or two highly sought-after courses each semester. Planning, therefore, is critical, and students may wish to ask themselves some or all of the following questions about each course in which they are interested:

Is this course offered every semester?

Does my school give preference to graduating seniors, such that I can be assured of taking this course next semester or next year?

Is there a chance of convincing the professor to increase the enrollment?

Is this course being taught by a professor who is visiting at the school for only a year or who will be on sabbatical next semester or next year?

Students who are unsure about which courses are worth special efforts might consider asking upper-level students, "Is there any course, or any professor whose courses, I should not leave this law school without taking?" Although each student must ultimately decide for herself how she wishes to craft her own legal education, asking well-targeted questions of those whose opinion she trusts may be a good way to become more informed about course selection.

Certification Programs

Schools sometimes allow students to focus on certain areas of the law. Some law schools do this formally, offering Certificates of Concentration in areas such as advocacy, business law, health-care law, or international law. Other schools simply provide students with lists of courses that are recommended for each area of practice. Students who have already chosen a field in which to practice, and who wish to follow the "pre-professional" approach to course selection, as discussed above, may find a certification of concentration in their chosen field to be an attractive option. Students whose grades are below average sometimes pursue a certificate of concentration to demonstrate commitment to a certain field, and also to gain significant knowledge in that field, so as to improve their chances of securing the jobs they desire.

Honors Programs

Some law schools offer special opportunities to students who are at the top of their class academically at the end of the first year. One such opportunity is an honors program. An honors program is often small, thus enhancing its prestige, and admission ordinarily requires outstanding grades. Some programs include certain students automatically because of their grade-point average, and accept others with grades above a certain threshold if a faculty member makes a recommendation on their behalf. Other programs are by invitation- or application-only.

The honors program might simply be a designation, such as Dean's List or Honor Roll, for the student to include on her résumé. Alternatively, the program might include advanced coursework in an area of law such as legal history or jurisprudence, a paper requirement, a merit-based scholarship, or some or all of the above components. At some schools, students chosen to participate in the honors program are also invited to attend faculty-research colloquia and other presentations that are not otherwise open to the student body.

A student who is invited to participate in such a program may, because of her strong academic performance, have other opportunities as well, such as participation in law review, moot court, or mock trial. In addition, she is likely to find herself in great demand during interviewing season. How, then, should the student determine whether she wishes to accept an invitation to join an honors program? In addition to considering the more general factors discussed in Chapter 9, the student should assess her true level of interest in the substance of the program. Many students are delighted at having an opportunity, for instance, to explore the theoretical and historical underpinnings of the law in a small-group setting. Others might decide, with equal justification, that their energies are better spent on other undertakings.

JOINT-DEGREE PROGRAMS

A joint-degree program is one in which a student pursues a J.D. and another master's-level degree concurrently. Joint-degree programs can be very advantageous in terms of the student's marketability after graduation. Although pursuing such an option generally will lengthen the time required to complete the course of law-school study, many students who do joint-degree work find that their study of each discipline is enriched and challenged by the other.

NEW CHALLENGES: PROFESSIONALISM IN THE SECOND AND THIRD YEARS

Certain opportunities are not available to all members of a law-school class. This fact, if not recognized and handled with professionalism, can create tension among the members of the class. This trend is most marked during the second year of law school, when disparities become most apparent. Students who are fortunate enough to be at or near the top of the class, and who find themselves to be very much in demand with regard to both potential employers and on-campus opportunities, should act with appropriate humility and grace. Attitudes of arrogance and entitlement will estrange the student's classmates and will invite hostility. Those students who find themselves without some of the opportunities for which they had hoped may wish to take this time to improve their grades. They should also keep in mind that the second and third years of law school will provide them with other opportunities to excel. Many of these opportunities, which are discussed in detail in Chapter 9, do not require top grades.

Many students are tempted to do everything that is made available to them; others are determined to focus on a single effort—maintaining high grades, participating in law review, or doing advocacy work, for instance—and find the decision to decline other offers to be fairly straightforward. Students who take on too much often find that their performance suffers in at least one area. One student, who was married and had a young child, attempted to work outside of law school while employed as a law-review editor and participating in moot court. She ultimately resigned from both extracurricular activities under unfavorable circumstances, found that her employment relationship had soured due to inattention, and lost her merit-based academic scholarship. Students need not inevitably, however, become victims of their own success. Instead, each student must set her own boundaries and standards for success.

In determining which opportunities are most deserving of time and attention, students are encouraged to resist engaging in résumé building for its own sake. Indeed, choosing activities solely because they provide prestigious credentials often results in an experience that is disappointing, both to the participant and those who are counting on her. In addition, it is simply selfish for a student to take opportunities in which she has no real interest away from others who would value and benefit from them and who would perhaps do a better job with more focused attention. Instead of selecting activities simply for their value as credentials for future employment, students might choose to explore opportunities that remind them of why they came to law school in the first place.

New Horizons: Non-Traditional Paths

Some students complete their first year of law school certain of nothing *but* that they do not wish to practice law. These students might wonder whether they are in the right place or whether, instead, they should drop out of law school, thus minimizing their debt load, and seek to find their true calling. There is no simple answer, and there is no single, correct answer, to this relatively common dilemma. Instead, each student must assess her situation on its own merits. A student whose legal education is being financed by a merit scholarship or by a trust fund, or who has a position waiting for her in a family business after graduation, might be able to afford to attend law school simply for the excellent education it provides. A student with a family and a high debt-load who is attending an expensive, private law school on borrowed money might not, however, find it prudent to continue her legal education if she is certain that she does not wish to practice law.

Students who enjoy law school, but not with an eye toward practicing law, might seek to connect their study of the law with their previous education or career. These students might pursue careers in public-interest law, policy-making, or legal education, instead of the more traditional practice of law. They might find that they benefit from pursuing an additional degree if they are able to do so. This endeavor might include the advanced law degrees discussed in Chapter 15. Alternatively, they might choose to complement their law degree with a master's degree or doctorate in another discipline.

The second and third years of law school are very busy and go by quickly. Students are encouraged to plan ahead so as to maximize their exposure to different professors and areas of the law. They can do this by reading descriptions of upper-level courses, talking with upperclassmen, and thinking about their own interest in the law. This is the student's primary opportunity to personalize her law-school experience.

CHAPTER 13

Maximize the Summer Experience

Deciding how to spend the summer is a common dilemma for many students, particularly those who are preparing for a professional career. Students weigh the relative benefits of working in or working outside of their chosen fields. Often, students get hung up on the financial issues or the potential opportunity underlying each decision. For law students, these issues are debated year in and year out—how should a law student choose between a paid non-legal summer position and an unpaid legal job? What about course credit for a research assistantship versus an opportunity to travel abroad for the summer? For any student without a hefty mortgage, large family, or demanding job, the summer between the first and second years of law school may indeed be an opportune time for extended travel or the pursuit of other interests. For a law student, however, the decision about how to spend the summer should be informed by one important point: the summer experience—whether in the legal field or not— is likely to be the beginning of a lawyer's practical training, allowing the student to experience what lawyers, and those with whom and for whom they work, do on a daily basis. Many summer jobs provide students with the opportunity to forge important personal and business relationships that will shape their growth as lawyers and as people. The student may see how the law affects actual clients and begin to appreciate the enormous financial, emotional, and sometimes physical impact that a brush with the legal system can have on people. In other words, summer experience can provide a context for the formal legal training that law school provides and will challenge the student to broaden his or her perspective on law school.

The heavy emphasis placed by students on securing a summer job, particularly in the legal field, is understandable. After all, many people go to law school to become practicing attorneys. Why else, these students might ask, would they borrow tens of thousands of dollars and, to a large extent, put life on hold for three years? Added pressure comes from the fact that the competition for jobs is fierce and job opportunities are directly affected by the state of the economy and the number of summer positions that are available in the region in which the student wants to live. Moreover, these summer positions are viewed as the best opportunity to obtain useful and relevant experience that will give the student a leg up when looking for a permanent job. Summer positions often shape the direction of a lawyer's career and, at least in the law-firm setting, can be the entree to a permanent job. Although the importance of the summer job is obvious, it should not unreasonably interfere with or overshadow the student's responsibility to put forth her best effort in law school.

DIFFERING CONSIDERATIONS FOR FIRST- AND SECOND-YEAR STUDENTS

For first-year students who entered law school in the fall, the summer job issue surfaces soon after the beginning of the second semester and gains momentum in February and March, when first-year interviews are generally scheduled. Résumé preparation and electronic job searches become regular activities, crowding the time that probably should be spent on learning substantive material. First-year students who enter school in the spring or summer, or students who attend law school part-time, as an increasing number do, sometimes find job-hunting to be even more of a challenge. Many schools require that these students continue their studies through at least half of the summer. In addition, these students may find themselves to be slightly out of kilter with the normal hiring cycle. They may also believe themselves to be at a competitive disadvantage because they will have fewer credit hours behind them, and thus less substantive exposure to the law at that point. For all students, but perhaps especially for those who are off-cycle with the normal hiring process, creativity, flexibility, and energy are critical in seeking employment. One advantage of being in this group is that students who enter school in the spring or summer, or who attend part-time, have *three* summers, rather than two, in which to explore legal employment. Chapter 3, in discussing the process of applying to law school, provides additional guidance on this issue.

The economy drives much of what is available for first-year law students. When the economy is in a downturn, most summer positions in the legal field for first-year students tend to be unpaid or low-paying. Some high-paying summer associate positions with law firms or corporations are available, but there are simply fewer of them. For example, one large law firm typically has a summer class of twenty-six students, and two or three of those positions are reserved for first-year law students. In an economic downturn, the number reserved for first-years may be reduced to one or none at all. A booming economy, however, usually means more and better-paid positions for first-year students. Large firms are generally thinking about their hiring needs two or three or even five years down the road. Getting an early and prolonged look at promising students is simply another way for such firms to recruit top talent. Thus, firms sometimes create additional spots for first-year students when fiscal considerations make it possible for them to do so.

For second-year law students, the summer-job madness coincides with the beginning of the fall semester, and sometimes sooner. Some law schools set aside a week before the semester begins, or even in the midst of the fall semester, for initial and call-back interviews that may require the student to travel out of town. Such a schedule allows second- and third-year law students to interview for summer positions without missing class.[1]

Before a student jumps on the résumé and cover letter bandwagon, it might be useful for her to do some advance planning. The student may want to consider the following: (1) What does she hope to accomplish during the summer—for example, is money the main consideration or is the student looking to strengthen her research-and-writing skills? and (2) what experience, whether in the legal field or not, will best advance those objectives? This type of big-picture planning should lessen the student's agonizing over where to go and what to do. Although no book can (or should) tell a student what he should do during the summer, the focal points set forth in this chapter should at least help the student to narrow down his choices. The chapter begins with a discussion of some possible goals a student might set for the summer experience, and then turns to some specific types of summer jobs that might be available to law students. Finally, this chapter discusses how to make the most of the summer experience no matter what the student chooses to do.

---

[1] A more detailed discussion of the on-campus and subsequent interview process may be found in Chapters 4 through 7 of Carey, *Full Disclosure: The New Lawyer's Must-Read Career Guide* (ALM Publishing 2000).

RELEVANT SUMMER EXPERIENCES TO EXPLORE

As law-firm summer associates, students do legal research, write memoranda, and otherwise assist attorneys in handling litigation and transactional matters. In many law firms (especially larger firms and established "boutique firms," which are firms specializing in a particular area or industry), summer associates are paid a salary, which is sometimes very respectable. A summer associate's weekly salary might be as high as a pro-rata share of a first-year, permanent attorney's salary. The geographical market and the size of the firm will be the most important factors in determining the pay scale. Generally, larger firms bill their clients for a portion of the student's time spent on that client's work, a process that allows firms to pay a comfortable summer salary to the students. Mid-sized and smaller firms also hire summer associates, although the salary they pay may be much lower. Indeed, some firms pay only a few dollars more than minimum wage, figuring that the work experience will be a sufficient incentive for the summer intern or clerk to find the endeavor worthwhile.

Corporations, including banks, insurance companies, and large public or private companies, sometimes hire law students to work in their legal departments. Corporate legal departments may function very much like law firms. Like their colleagues who are working as law-firm summer associates, students working in corporate legal departments may do legal research and writing, and assist corporate lawyers with preparation for litigation or transactional matters. Depending on the company, students may also become involved in assignments or business deals in which legal work goes hand-in-hand with business decisions. Some students find themselves doing market-analysis or even advertising work, with an eye toward evaluating the legal implications of each. For example, a legal intern may be assigned to help a team of employees develop a new product name and package. These corporate positions are as varied as the salaries the students are paid. Students should keep in mind that, even in a bad economy, some corporate jobs are available. Sometimes an economic downturn is actually a terrific time for an intern to seek employment—corporate downsizing often requires that fewer people handle the same workload, and interns can be an efficient way to relieve the strain. Particularly in these situations, interns may find themselves assigned work that is productive and actually relied upon by the employer. The best resources for information about these positions are personal contacts through family members or even a "friend of a friend" at a large corporation or through the career-services office at school. Students may also find it worthwhile to target larger companies in the area where they live, work, or attend school, and ask whether they would consider hiring a legal intern. Such companies do not typically recruit on law-school campuses, nor do they widely advertise these summer positions. Indeed, some students find that their on-campus career-services office is not sufficiently equipped to assist them in seeking internships other than those with law firms and corporations that have previously contacted the office. Thus, taking the initiative may be critical to the student's securing a corporate position for the summer.

Other than law-firm or corporate summer positions, there are not many high-paying legal positions for law students. This is especially true for first-year students. Indeed, many law firms do not have a summer-clerkship program for students who have completed only their first year of law school. Although interested first-year students should pursue such positions, they probably should not be dismayed if no such offers are forthcoming.

Most summer internships pay little or nothing, but can still afford students valuable experience. The office of the local district attorney or public defender, or a crime victim/witness program, can provide some of the best hands-on training a student could want. Such training might include helping investigators by putting together files in preparation for interviews or trial, using a checklist to determine whether files are ready for trial, checking in with witnesses and updating contact information for those witnesses, scanning depositions or listening to transcripts to see whether a witness testified to particular facts in a preliminary hearing, or meeting with victims of crimes and talking to them about what to expect in the upcoming procedures. Some interns work with crime victims to ensure that their medical bills get paid, or may bring to the district attorney's attention a victim's hesitancy to testify. Interns in these positions generally do not do much research and writing, but do get excellent practical exposure to evidentiary issues and hear oral arguments on both procedural and substantive issues. In addition, if the matter is appealed to a higher court, the intern may be involved in the research and writing at that level. These interns may be unpaid, may qualify for a small stipend, or, at an increasing number of law schools, may receive course credit. Student-interns often find this kind of hands-on experience to be invaluable: it frequently follows them back to the law-school classroom the following year and enlivens both their contributions to class discussion and their own understanding of the role of law in society.

Work in the public-interest sector is another important option. Students should understand that public-interest work goes far beyond traditional jobs with a legal-aid clinic or with one of the many well-known advocacy groups that are headquartered in the nation's capitol. Indeed, there is a group or organization advancing almost every public interest that a student could imagine. Although it might take some research to discover these connections, students will find that many areas of public interest, such as the environment, special-needs children, or emerging fields of scientific study, intersect with the law in a way that could involve the student. Students in these types of summer jobs can expect to receive practical experience. For example, they may assist clients in fighting illegal evictions, processing immigration papers, or filing liens for child-support monies that are due them. Students working in legal-aid clinics or other public-interest associations may apply for grants through either their schools or the government, to compensate somewhat for their unpaid or low-paid summer work. In addition, after law school, students accepting offers of permanent employment in the public sector can apply for loan forgiveness or interest deferral. Schools want to encourage students to pursue this kind of work and are therefore finding more and more ways to help bridge the significant pay gap in this field. Many students who participate in such programs return to school reinvigorated about the law, having seen how good and careful advocacy can empower society's most powerless citizens. These students might, for example, as interns, experience the immense satisfaction of having helped a very low-income client to stay in her home, to become a citizen of the United States, or to provide support for her child. Because public-service clients are likely to have been touched by the law in such a personal way, many students find that their caring assistance is rewarded with an enormous outpouring of gratitude on the part of the client.

An internship with a judge or magistrate is also excellent experience, and not just for those students with an interest in litigation. Judicial interns may assist with court filings or simply help with the logistics of moving cases through the system. Sometimes, interns assist with library upkeep or research assignments for particular judges. These experiences are very judge- or court-specific, and the level of responsibility a student should expect is one of the main details on which the student should focus in the interview process for these positions. Often, students concentrate on the federal and state trial-level courts. There are many courts of specific jurisdiction, however, that also provide valuable learning experiences. For example, there may be internships available in admiralty and maritime courts, probate courts, family courts, and bankruptcy courts. Chapter 15 outlines some of the benefits—practical and intangible—of working with the judicial branch.

Many other jobs offer practical experience as well. Like the positions discussed above, these jobs generally pay either minimum wage or just a little more. A student might, for example, work as a runner or file clerk for a law firm, as opposed to being a summer associate. One student worked in a law-firm's recruiting department, where she had an opportunity to get an insider's perspective on the hiring of summer associates and full-time attorneys. Or a student might work with the law-school administration in a particular department, such as in the admissions office as a summer counselor and tour guide for prospective students.

Other types of summer jobs include research assistantships with professors or work-study programs sponsored by the law school or federal government. Students participating in each may be eligible for relatively modest stipends or grants. Research assistants often find that, although their monetary compensation is relatively low, the opportunity to work closely with a favorite professor is well worth the minimal wage. Some professors reserve their most glowing letters of recommendation, as well as their most active job-counseling and job-placement efforts, for students who have worked with them as research assistants. Students wishing to pursue a law-review position may be particularly interested in working as a professor's research assistant, either during the school year or during a summer break. Working in this capacity gives a law student a unique opportunity to view the process of cutting-edge scholarly writing from a professional's perspective. Professors use research assistants in many different ways: some will begin by assigning very specific tasks, such as narrowly tailored research, and will allow research assistants to progress, once they have proven their mettle in this limited capacity, to engaging with them in scholarly debate on the merits of a particular point of view or even, when the research assistant has proven herself to be especially skilled, inviting the student to critique an argument the professor is propounding. The level of formality and interaction between professors and research assistants varies tremendously and often depends on the rapport the two have established. Some former research assistants find that, after graduation, the professor for whom they worked becomes a great ally, confidant, mentor, and friend. In addition, law professors often acknowledge the contribution of student research assistants when the research project ultimately comes to fruition and is printed, and many students enjoy seeing their name in print, often for the first time.

Work-study programs may include work in the law library, in a visitor's center, or in one of the school's administrative offices. These positions are often part-time, which allows a student to get a second, better-paying non-legal job. As discussed above, such jobs may not pay very much, but can provide good experience for a future lawyer.

FINANCIAL GOALS AND SEEKING PERMANENT EMPLOYMENT

In prioritizing the objectives for a summer experience, a student might rank "making money" high on the list. The student may wish to make enough money during the summer to support him through the summer and possibly also to defray some of his tuition and living costs for the following fall, or at least to pay for his textbooks for the year. Any situation that allows a student to borrow less should be high on his list of priorities. Even students who are working as highly paid summer associates are encouraged to live as modestly as possible during the summer, to maximize savings. One student squandered her summer earnings from a large firm on a set of expensive furniture, only to find herself already strapped for cash as the fall term was beginning. Students should try to keep open as many employment options upon graduation as financial concerns will afford. Many students, for example, enter law school intending to become assistant district attorneys but find that they cannot afford to accept this type of job once they factor in loan repayment. This situation is exacerbated if a spouse or partner has a high balance of school debt as well. (Having to work at a large firm, because of the attractive salary, has been referred to as the "golden handcuffs.") In short, the student should strive to create options, even if she believes she already knows what she wants to do with her law degree.

Summer employment also offers students an opportunity to work toward securing a permanent job, or at least getting a foot in the door. A summer position in a law firm may provide excellent exposure that could lead to a permanent position. In addition, some firms actually give former summer associates "credit," in terms of seniority, when it comes to partnership. One student who worked in the same law firm for two years during law school was promoted to partner before his colleagues who had graduated from law school the same year as he had.

The summer program is also a great opportunity to learn detailed information about the employer, particularly about its hiring needs. For example, students may want to investigate the company's or firm's growth plans for the next two or three years. Every company, including a law firm, has a business plan and should know roughly what its hiring needs will be. Often, local legal journals or business newspapers will have articles on these employers that may include discussions about the forecasting done by the firm or corporation. In addition, students may want to use the summer as an opportunity to learn this information through both formal and informal discussions with partners and employees. Students should also attempt to figure out the emerging areas of importance to the corporation or to the firm clients. For example, a student may be interning for a technology client that is developing a niche in the telecommunications field. That student might ask informed people what type of expertise is most useful for this burgeoning area, including what classes might be helpful in preparing for work in this field. Taking advantage of these opportunities can get a student one step closer to a permanent position.

A related, and equally important, goal for the summer job should be using this experience to determine whether the student and this firm, corporation, or other employer are a good fit for each other. The summer will give the student ample opportunity to assess such considerations as quality of life, fiscal health, and intellectual appeal. A student's interests, skills, political goals, financial goals, personal beliefs and values, and work ethic should roughly match up with the organization where the student works. The summer internship provides the best opportunity for her to explore those issues and thereby to avoid making decisions that could have potentially disastrous long-term effects. In other words, this is the time for a conservative student to figure out whether the liberal law firm for which he might be clerking is politically active on the national scene. Students do this by asking thoughtful and detailed questions of anyone and everyone who has the time to answer and also by observing how people work and their expectations with regard to the quality of work put forth. Students are encouraged to focus on questions such as the following: Where is this organization going? Is it financially sound? Are the people in charge committed to its continued existence, or are they ready to retire without ensuring that competent managers are left to run the organization?

Even for a first-year intern, looking toward a permanent position is an important goal. Law firms tend to invite successful first-year summer associates back for a second summer. At the end of the second summer, these law firms will make offers of permanent employment. Thus, strong performance in a summer position, even as a first-year, can be directly related to getting an offer of permanent employment.

In a less direct way, a summer position will provide needed exposure to attorneys and what they do on a day-to-day basis, which will ultimately help the student to obtain a job. Interning for a judge, for example, provides just this type of exposure. Although this experience may not lead to an immediate job with this judge, it will expose the student to attorneys doing things both the right way and the wrong way. Students will see attorneys of every caliber and will observe the effectiveness (or ineffectiveness) of their oral advocacy with the judge and the judge's staff. These observations can be relevant to the student's search for permanent employment because they may help the student to focus his job search by giving him a better idea of what he wants to do or not do, or may prepare the student to ask better and more direct questions when interviewing for subsequent positions. In sum, a student who has clerked for a judge as a summer intern will come from a position of knowledge, which will be apparent in later interviews. Also, in a less direct but important way, summer positions help students to meet people who can help them down the road. These individuals might later write letters of recommendation or make a personal introduction on the student's behalf. Getting the right permanent job should be a top priority for students, and what a student chooses to do each summer during law school does have a direct relationship to getting that job.

BUILDING A SKILL SET AND SEEKING FEEDBACK

The student should also use the summer to cultivate good work habits. These habits will stay with her for some time. Getting to work on time, every day, is a good start. Students also should establish a regular protocol for handling incoming and outgoing mail. In addition, it is good practice to establish a telephone log, even if the student must make one himself, that includes the dates on which a call was received or made and when a call was returned. Getting into the habit of taking notes during all work-related conversations, meetings, or witness interviews, and initiating a reliable process for getting those notes filed, are important skills to cultivate early. To the extent possible, the student should seek to begin and end the day with an orderly desk. Not only will people notice these small efforts, but this will also prevent wasted time when the student is searching for something. Along the same lines, the student should buy or make a calendar on which to record all relevant dates, even if he is not charged with responsibility for keeping a calendar of deadlines for the matters he handles. Even as a summer intern, the student should develop the habit of recording information on, and checking, that calendar every day.

Professionalism is a related concept, which includes discretion, judgment, poise, and maturity. Students are encouraged to avoid dating colleagues or staff, or letting their guard down with staff, younger attorneys, or colleagues. Even the most private or intimate conversations have a way of becoming public knowledge eventually. It is also important for the intern to project the right attitude toward his work and colleagues. A can-do attitude is critical to both short-term and long-term success. An attitude of seriousness about the work, which is not the same as being humorless, will help establish the intern's credibility with colleagues. Along the same lines, seeking to establish one's identity as the office jokester is a risky proposition. Although colleagues and superiors may enjoy the diversion on some level, the student may find that his playful behavior or comments made in fun can prevent him from being seriously considered for a permanent position. A student intern should also take the initiative to introduce herself around the office and to remember the names and faces of everyone with whom she will interact—not just those who the student believes to be "important." Rudeness to support staff has cost more than one student intern an offer of permanent employment.

Students should use the summer experience to hone research, writing, technical, and grammar skills. A good place to start is by reading others' writing. It is not difficult to identify and learn from the strongest writers in the firm or organization. The student may wish to focus on how effective writers communicate with a client or witness. How exactly do they handle difficult or delicate matters? What level of writing do they use for clients who are not lawyers or who are not educated at all? Business correspondence—which includes even the most basic letters to clients, such as a transmittal letter ("I have enclosed. . .")—is an essential part of a lawyer's daily job, as is writing generally. A legal-writing course may not always provide comprehensive training for every kind of legal employment, and the student is responsible for making up for any shortfalls through practical experience. Writing skills can make or break a student's reputation when she is trying to make a good impression. The student should consider asking respected people, both inside and outside of the organization, to review a writing sample and to offer constructive criticism. Students may also learn a great deal from comparing their own writing with that of their peers, if the opportunity to do so is available.

A student must treat every assignment as if it were formally assigned by the head of the group, firm, company, or office, regardless of how it ends up on his desk. In a law firm or corporation, a particular person may be in charge of assigning work. There may be a formal procedure by which assignments are tracked and each student's workload is monitored. Such an elaborate system is not always in place, of course. In addition, even where an established assignment-process exists, there will be times when the student's co-worker pulls her aside and asks her to "take a quick look" at an issue. The student should avoid the temptation to provide an equally informal response. Sometimes, assigned matters are treated even more off-handedly, especially for interns in the public-defender's or district-attorney's offices. There, whatever issues arise in court or whatever witnesses have surfaced may dictate the student's assignment for the day. Regardless of how they receive their assignments, students are well-advised to treat every task with thoroughness and care.

The following is some specific guidance for preparing top-quality work product. Students should come prepared to take notes when they are being given an assignment and should write down the important matters, including the exact final product or action that is required. For example, is the student to draft a letter required for this person's signature or simply to provide an outline? The student should record pertinent dates and names, without scribbling every word that comes from the assigning person's mouth. To ensure that the student gets all of the information she needs, it is often wise that she wait to ask questions until the assigning supervisor has said his piece. The next task is determining the deadline for the project and preparing an estimate of how many hours the project should take. In the law-firm setting at least, students are often told that a general rule of thumb is to multiply any time estimate they receive from a supervisor by at least a factor of two. Attorneys are notorious for underestimating the time it will require for a student to research a matter or prepare a document. The student should find out whether the supervisor wishes to be kept apprised of her progress. The student should consider asking whether there are good written resources to be investigated first; perhaps a knowledgeable person on staff might help the student to get the project underway quickly. Organizations are not necessarily interested in having students duplicate work that has already been done; if there is a way to expedite a project by looking at previously prepared work or talking with an expert within the organization, then the student should do so. This is a good example of how notions of efficiency and value come into play, in practice, in assessing whether an attorney is doing a good job. Law school, on the other hand, does not concern itself with having students complete assignments so as to maximize the value the client receives per dollar; rather, the process of learning is assumed to be of primary importance. It is therefore important for students to realize that a shift in thinking is required as they get out into the business world. These practical considerations are relevant from the very first assignment.

The student should learn to think in terms of client satisfaction, which should come naturally to those with a sales background. The student's supervisor, for each assignment, whether the professor, assistant district attorney, partner, or vice-president of marketing, is the student's primary client. The student may have outside clients as well, such as the institution's client, or the victim or accused, but she should consider those individuals as being in addition to the primary client referenced above. Clients are satisfied when an attorney turns in accurate and error-free work. That means no (yes, zero) avoidable mistakes such as spelling errors, margin abnormalities, incorrect grammar, or missing pages. That also means that the legal analysis is sound (and the law upon which the analysis relies has not been repealed, questioned, or vacated), and that the explanations, decisions, or recommendations given are supportable in both fact and law. The student should proofread her work more than twice and should also ask others to help do a final read-through in the beginning. If the student has a secretary or there are other interns in the program, she might enlist their support as well, especially if the student herself is not yet a good proofreader. (One hint for developing one's own proofreading skills is to read drafts with a ruler to ensure that each line is examined separately.) An attorney's clients (all of them) rely on what he or she does. Along the same lines, the student intern's clients may not stop to consider, in relying on the student's work, that the student has had only had a year or two of law school so far. In fact, often the student will be the only person, or one of a very few, who will have taken an in-depth look at the relevant cases or documents. The student should never assume that anyone will double-check her work to make sure that she has reached the right conclusion. Time does not always permit such an approach, and clients generally refuse to pay for two or three attorneys reviewing the same research in a file.

Client satisfaction also means that an attorney must do what he says he is going to do. The student intern's assignment or project should be done on the day agreed upon, absent (1) special circumstances and (2) the advance approval of the assigning attorney or other supervisor. The student intern must, in addition, ensure that she has examined the issues carefully and performed each of the tasks assigned. Keeping a written record of the assignment—or e-mailing the supervisor to confirm the assignment—is one good way to avoid missing part of the assignment through simple inadvertence. Formalizing the assignment process is another way to avoid this mistake. Attorneys and summer interns often make statements such as "I'll try to look into that" or "I'll ask John about that issue." Those casual comments are relied upon and may make the difference between an issue's receiving thorough analysis or simply being bypassed. The student intern is building credibility, daily, with the assigning attorneys and managers; they generally know very little about the intern other than the work product she turns in and the manner in which she conducts herself in doing it. Intentional and careful communication is part of this package.

A student intern's attitude in handling these assignments or tasks is nearly as important as her work product. Attorneys and managers want to hear that students are interested in the work and will do whatever it takes to get it done (and done well). "We want to know that you will make it happen," many a manager has stated. The same attitude and care should be evidenced even when a student intern is given what she might deem "menial" tasks to complete. One student intern was surprised when her misspelling of client names on the firm nametags she had been asked to complete was raised as part of her end-of-internship review.

Clients are satisfied when attorneys think creatively about problems or issues. Student interns, for example, may have experience that bears on a matter or may have the ability to see an analogy where no one else has. The intern should trust her ideas, and be prepared to support them, when discussing the matter with the client. Thinking creatively or "outside the box" is one way in which an intern or summer associate begins to add real value to an organization. That is also one way in which an intern will begin to stand out from the crowd, in a positive way.

Clients expect a precise and excellent work product, each and every time the attorney performs work on their behalf. To ensure that she is meeting this standard, the student intern must seek feedback from her supervisor once she has handed in an assignment. Similarly, in follow-up discussions, the student should encourage attorneys or managers to critique her writing, ability to convey thoughts clearly, and style of presentation. Not every supervisor is skilled at providing feedback, and sometimes the student may find it difficult to get a supervisor to sit down and focus on her development. Nonetheless, getting this follow-up is part of the student's responsibility and is an essential part of the student's professional growth during the summer.

The flip side of seeking feedback, of course, is responding appropriately when feedback is given. Many managers will say that they expect interns to make some mistakes, but also expect the interns to make each mistake *only once*. In other words, the intern must take the advice to heart and ensure that her future work product demonstrates that she has done so. In addition, supervisors will be watching for interns to have a positive attitude in receiving and responding to criticism. More than one summer intern has been denied permanent employment because she was found to be defensive and argumentative in responding to constructive criticism. Finally, as a worst-case scenario, at least one summer intern has been denied permanent employment because she failed to respond to the supervising attorney's repeated requests that she come by to discuss her work product.

BUILDING AND MAINTAINING PROFESSIONAL RELATIONSHIPS

The development of social and management skills is another important part of an attorney's career and should be a goal for the summer experience. Every lawyer must learn an effective delegation style, proper management of subordinates, and fair and diplomatic assessment of the work of her peers or staff. Furthermore, every attorney must learn to work effectively with supervisors and subordinates alike. Students should use the summer experience to develop or refine these skills. Interns may wish to look for the best managers of people and find specific examples to remember as they observe them dealing with others. Are they supportive when someone introduces a new idea? Do they listen when people talk? Are they fair when reviewing subordinates? The student may wish to talk to these managers about their management style and ask them what lessons they had to learn the hard way. The intern should also take note when she observes ineffective management. Is that person's style too confrontational? Does she challenge colleagues in front of others? Is she inconsistent in setting requirements for those working within the group? Students should practice giving clear deadlines to support staff. It is important that these deadlines are not false ones, which tend to communicate that the student is setting them simply because she can. The student should also provide feedback, both positive and negative, on projects she assigns or reviews. The student should consider whether his reactions are reasonable and whether his co-workers generally know what to expect from him when a problem arises. It is no secret that lawyers are notoriously bad managers of people. Whether this phenomenon results from a lack of time or of training is not clear, but the student intern should take measures to focus on this aspect of her own development.

As part of the summer experience, the intern should invest time in and demonstrate personal commitment to building friendships and establishing professional acquaintanceships. The people she relates to are future friends, potential colleagues, judges, bosses, sources of referral business, and clients. Thinking like a lawyer, even as a summer intern, requires that the intern recognize the value of these relationships and take the time to help them grow, regardless of what happens at the end of the summer. One first-year summer intern had a negative experience with a small law firm in a city that was some distance from her law school. Several lawyers at the firm subsequently tried to keep in contact with the intern. The intern ignored these contacts, and wasted the opportunity for future productive relationships with these established attorneys in a large city. Interestingly, these same attorneys later left the small firm and joined a national law firm, which has a large office in the city where this student attends school. These burned bridges were unnecessary and professionally risky for a fledgling attorney. Another first-year intern ultimately chose to decline an offer of permanent employment from one large firm to take a job at another large firm in the same city. She stayed in contact with the attorneys at the first firm, however, and found their advice to be neutral, confidential, and very helpful when she was considering changing career paths.

The intern should start small when establishing these relationships. It is important that she take the time to say "Hello" and to introduce herself starting on the very first day of her employment. The student should, if necessary, ask others their names two or three times, until she can remember them. Finding out how these people got where they are, what experiences brought them there, what skills were important in that development, and who was influential in guiding their careers are not only excellent topics of conversation, but also valuable sources of information and advice. The student may also wish to ask for advice in handling his own responsibilities. This give-and-take is one way in which relationships deepen. Many students or interns, having grown accustomed to being interviewed, are therefore always ready to talk about their experience or qualifications, but fail to be curious about their employers or colleagues. An intern may even find a person who, either formally or informally, is willing to mentor her throughout the summer. There is no reason why these relationships cannot continue after the summer association ends. Such a relationship takes time and effort; the student should expect to have to take the initiative in staying in contact with these busy people. Letting them know about making law review or being elected president of the student body, sharing the good news upon graduation, and passing along new contact information after a move, are all good and relatively easy ways to stay in touch.

Electronic mail makes staying in contact easy, but a student should also try not to neglect the important face-to-face interaction while he and his mentor are still in the same city. Mentors always appreciate it when a former intern or other student keeps an eye out for significant developments in that person's career. For example, if a manager for whom a student worked at X corporation has been promoted to a vice-president position, she would, undoubtedly, appreciate a quick, congratulatory note or a brief call from the student. Or, the student may see in the newspaper that there has been a conviction in a criminal case on which the manager worked. This occasion provides an excellent opportunity to call the attorneys who are managing the case and congratulate (or console) them for work well done. People appreciate such efforts and remember students who showed interest in matters on which student interns worked.

Cultivating Substantive Knowledge, Professional Ethics, and Business Sense

The summer experience may be used to gain substantive legal knowledge, whether or not the position itself is law-related. This knowledge may be useful for future employment purposes, or it may just round out a student's coursework. For instance, a student may be employed as a non-legal intern for a pharmaceutical company, examining the competitive products that are currently on the market. This student is learning about business practices and the analysis that is involved in product development, but she is also gaining an excellent perspective for learning about the law underlying the Unfair Trade Practices Act. Later, in interviewing for legal employment, this student can give a concrete example of how her non-legal position was useful for putting her coursework into context.

A lawyer-to-be must establish a high bar for his or her own professional reputation and develop a personal code of ethics. As an intern or associate, each student will see many examples of how to conduct herself, and how not to do so. She will learn, early on, which lawyers or managers can be trusted and which cannot. The student must recognize that how she conducts herself, even at this early stage of her own legal career, is absolutely critical. The statement "You only get one good name" is true and worthy of repetition. Just as students will remember the conduct of others in school, so too will colleagues in the workplace. An employer will assume that the student is putting forth her best self; there will, thus, be little tolerance for poor behavior. It is therefore extremely important that both the student intern and, later, the attorney, make ethical decisions even when no one is watching; an attorney's conduct must be beyond reproach as she interviews witnesses, deals with opposing counsel, or simply carries out the judge's instructions for drafting an order. She may have to defend her actions, in each situation, years from now. Along the same lines, attorneys must remember that everything (yes, everything) that is on the record in a court proceeding will bind them forever. More than one young lawyer with political aspirations has found herself nervously combing through transcripts of depositions she took, in an effort to ensure that she said nothing incorrect or untoward. Maintaining a consistent, ethical manner will keep an attorney out of difficulty. Attorneys, as well as student interns, are well served to keep in mind that a negative reputation is established more quickly than a positive one.

Simple exposure to a professional or business environment is another objective to consider. The business or government work setting is entirely different from that of law school. Although students may have experienced a certain amount of cattiness in law school, the work environment sometimes can be rife with politicking of the worst kind. Indeed, in any office of two or more people, office relationships and alliances will affect decisions made by people. A student intern or other newcomer may not always understand that more than the law underlies certain decisions, and she certainly will not always understand why particular things are happening in her career. Students, however, like the attorneys they will soon become, must realize that politicking does occur and that they must give it consideration early in their careers.

Working in a professional environment as an intern can be an immensely interesting and satisfying experience. In addition, the exposure will give the intern confidence as a lawyer, later in her career. She will already know, for instance, how to shake hands, how to learn new telephone systems, and how to figure out who is who in the mailroom. These skills are critical in orienting oneself in a new environment. Interns also get an early glimpse of the importance of figuring out the power structure within an organization and the people who make things happen.

Learning to act like a professional takes experience. Few interns will have someone to pull them aside and lay out the rules. Often, those rules are not even capable of definition. Observing some general guidelines will get the intern started, however. In addition to the earlier exhortations against inter-office dating, especially for interns, the intern should also conduct herself with care both on and off the work site. In smaller communities, but also in larger cities to a surprising degree, an intern's conduct outside the office often will become known and may be important in assessing that intern for permanent employment. Also, students should strive to keep work relationships, at least initially, on professional terms. That means that a student intern, for example, should avoid confiding in her new best work friend that she is having personal difficulties. The intern should participate in events related to the organization; most will have picnics, or other gatherings. It is important that an intern do her best to be part of the organization. Furthermore, these events are excellent opportunities to ask thoughtful and detailed questions about the organization and to observe how others behave in an off-site setting.

FINDING AND KEEPING PERSPECTIVE

In addition to the considerations of employment that have dominated the bulk of this chapter, students should remember that summertime provides a valuable opportunity, and one that will not be available to most of them after law school, for a change of pace. If possible, students should seek to have some fun, as well as to get some good, practical experience, during this time when they are not yet tied to an institution. That means taking time before starting an internship and, if possible, after concluding one, to travel, to relax, or to spend time with loved ones. Even these opportunities provide context for coursework and possibly also for what the student has learned during the summer. One student spent several weeks backpacking in Europe. She was struck by the potentially dangerous conditions she encountered as she climbed through centuries-old stone castles with spikes protruding from archways. In one particularly difficult situation, a group of wheelchair-bound individuals was attempting to board a tourist boat on the Danube River. The dock was sloped and contained no railings. Several individuals began to roll towards the edge of the dock before quick-thinking bystanders intervened. The student thought about the value of litigation and legislation such as the Americans with Disabilities Act to help deter such occurrences, and to provide compensation when they do occur. Travel provides another interesting angle on law school—as people learn that a student is a lawyer-in-training, students will, through observing how these individuals respond to her, get a better understanding of how the public views lawyers. This perspective is especially useful as the student considers that these people are potential jurors, clients, victims, or witnesses in future legal matters. One student found that, after she began law school, a lifelong family friend began to argue with her aggressively at social gatherings. She found it difficult, but valuable, to learn how to manage the way in which her legal education changed the friend's perception of appropriate interaction with her.

In short, regardless of what students actually do during their summers, the most important objective should be to gain a fuller perspective on their legal education. Throughout this book, students are encouraged to be curious. Each student should make a point of examining the events taking place around him, in his job internship, and to relate them to property, contract, torts, or criminal law, for example, where each is relevant. Students also generally enjoy, and benefit from, talking with other students about their summer experiences. What did they learn? What surprised them? What do they wish they had known at the beginning of the summer? Having gotten a glimpse of how law operates in the "real world," students should continue this process during the school year by reading the newspaper and pushing the boundaries in applying knowledge from one area to the next. A student studying pharmaceutical products might look at the potential legal or competitive issues from the point of view of a tort lawyer, a consumer, a competitor, or the federal government considering whether certain advertising is appropriate. Torts, intellectual property, advertising, and regulatory law are all relevant to this matter.

For first-year law students, having formal legal employment during the summer is less important than what the students learn and can apply to their professional development. For second- and third-year law students, decisions about where to work and the type of job to seek are equally important. As each summer approaches, however, one aspect of the planning process should remain constant: Each student should outline his objectives for the summer experience. Whether those objectives include making as much money as possible, securing a job offer, improving writing and technical skills, or simply enjoying some time off before beginning to seek legal employment, the quality and utility of the experiences a student will garner should be the major consideration in deciding among these opportunities. Students may wish to keep in mind that there is not a high correlation between the amount of money a summer law clerk earns and the amount of experience the student will gain. Therefore, a student who can afford to take a non-paying or lower-paying summer position may find that she is amply rewarded with experiences that may outstrip those of her colleagues with more lucrative summer employment.

This chapter outlines a few factors students should consider when deciding how to spend the valuable summer breaks during law school. In addition, this chapter offers some ideas about ways for first-, second-, and third-year students to build upon their summer experience, regardless of whether they work in legal or non-legal positions. Students should remember that, because the law is simply a series of responses to life and to human behavior and experience, there is truly no such thing as an experience that is irrelevant to the student's growth and development as a lawyer.

CHAPTER 14

Preparing for the Bar and Admission to Practice

The next challenge facing law students is one that instills perhaps as much fear as all of the first-year exams combined: the Bar Exam. For some law-school graduates, the bar exam is their personal Jericho—a major obstacle that they must conquer, which at first, second, or even third try may indeed prove daunting. For other graduates, the bar exam is simply another exercise in which hard work and determination will carry the day. Regardless of how the exam is viewed, it is a necessary step in becoming licensed to practice law. This chapter focuses on preparation for taking the bar and admission to practice in the lawyer's jurisdiction of choice. It does not cover actual test-taking strategies or specific admission requirements; those subjects are better addressed in material that is specifically tailored to that purpose and kept current for each state. Instead, this chapter will focus on the bar examination and admission experience in general: the application process, admission criteria, bar-review courses, financial concerns, study time, where to take the bar, useful Web sites, bar failure and re-examination, and some strategies for helping a new lawyer to navigate his employment situation in the weeks leading up to the exam itself.

THE LICENSE TO PRACTICE LAW

Getting a J.D. degree is only the first step in the process of obtaining a license to practice law. Indeed, becoming licensed is much more involved than many law students might realize. A state, commonwealth, or territorial board of bar examiners (sometimes also called the "committee of bar examiners," "office of admissions," "state board of law examiners," or "bar examining committee") normally handles licensing, under the direction of the highest court in the state, commonwealth, or territory. Less commonly, a private board of bar examiners, along with the state bar association, handles the licensure process. The highest court in the jurisdiction generally appoints the board members, and the board may be composed of lawyers and non-lawyers alike. The board members' responsibilities are to evaluate the skills and character of bar applicants; to determine whether each applicant is fit to practice law; and to write, administer, and grade the bar exams. The criteria for admission to a bar differ widely by jurisdiction. In general, however, a jurisdiction will grant a license to practice law only when the applicant has demonstrated his competency in two areas: (1) technical or legal competency, as evidenced by the applicant's having both been awarded a J.D. degree and achieved a passing score on one or more official exams authorized by the board of bar examiners; and (2) the requisite moral and ethical standards, as revealed by an in-depth examination of the applicant's character and fitness to practice law. Some jurisdictions also require that the applicant be over the age of eighteen.

Virtually all jurisdictions require applicants to have been awarded a J.D. degree from a law school accredited by the American Bar Association (ABA). A very few jurisdictions will either allow an applicant from a non-accredited school to seek admission if the school is located within that jurisdiction, or will allow an applicant from a non-accredited school to seek admission if the applicant has practiced law for some minimum number of years in another jurisdiction. On the whole, however, a person holding a J.D. degree from a non-accredited school will not be permitted to seek a license to practice law in most jurisdictions.

The requisite moral and ethical determination regarding each candidate's fitness to practice law is made through an investigation of the applicant's character and fitness. The state board of bar examiners may oversee this investigation itself, assisted by background checking services; alternatively, the applicant may be required to submit a character-and-fitness application to the National Conference of Bar Examiners' (NCBE) committee on character and fitness. In the latter case, a recommendation will then be made to the board of bar examiners in the state to which the applicant has applied.

The main character trait that these bodies are investigating is honesty. The inquiring board, or someone acting on its behalf, may verify that the applicant worked where she says she worked and when. The inquiring board may review the applicant's credit history, looking for discrepancies or serious defaults on student loans and other obligations. The board may also check with medical-care providers, references, colleges, the law school, or police agencies for further information. The character-and-fitness review can take a long time; a six-to-eight-month process is not unprecedented. If, as discussed below, there is a problem with the applicant's review, then the process could take as long as a year or more.

If, during or after this investigation, the board finds a discrepancy or something in the candidate's file that requires further explanation, the board may send the applicant notification that a hearing will be required. Generally, the initial hearing is an informal process in which the applicant meets with members of the board of bar examiners. There may be a fee associated with such a hearing, especially if it is recorded, and the applicant will be required to provide information under oath. In some jurisdictions, a more formal hearing will be the next step, if necessary, followed by a vote on the candidate's admission by the highest court in the state.

In some states, an applicant will be granted a license to practice law once she has demonstrated her worthiness by having achieved a J.D. degree, earned a passing score on the bar exam and the Multistate Professional Responsibility Exam (MPRE) (both of which are discussed below), passed the character-and-fitness review, and met other prerequisites established by the board of bar examiners. In some jurisdictions, however, even after meeting the above criteria, the applicant is granted only a provisional license until she fulfills experience requirements (such as having watched a certain number of hearings or trials, if she wants to be a litigator) or attends a practical-skills course that is given by the state bar association. Failure to complete these requirements within the time allotted will result in revocation of the provisional license. In New Hampshire, for example, a new lawyer is permitted two years within which to complete a skills course offered by the New Hampshire Bar Association. In Virginia, all newly admitted attorneys must complete a professionalism course within their first year of practice. These requirements are just the beginning of the responsibilities a lawyer must fulfill to keep her law license, once it has been granted. But, after these initial requirements are satisfied, the attorney can breathe a sigh of relief and continue with her professional training and development—with her law license in hand.

The process of obtaining admission to the practice of law can be lengthy and begins even before the student graduates from law school. A law student should therefore consider making an initial inquiry into the bar-admission requirements that she will need to satisfy during her *first* year of law school. If the student is intent on practicing in a particular jurisdiction, then she should research the current requirements for practicing there to determine whether she needs to take any preliminary steps during her first or second year of law school. Some states require law students who intend to practice there to register with the state board of bar examiners by, for example, October 1 of the student's second year, or within fourteen months of the student's first day of law school.

Students who fail to register within that time may have to pay a late-registration filing fee. There may also be financial benefits to early registration with, or early application to, a jurisdiction where the student knows he intends to practice: Some jurisdictions reduce either the cost of taking the bar exam or the cost of the admissions application for students who advise them of their interest early. Finally, in jurisdictions like California, law students are required to take the First-Year Law Students' Examination, known colloquially as the Baby Bar, after the first year of law school. Passing this exam, or meeting the requirements for exemption, is one criterion for admission to the bar in California.

PERSONAL CONDUCT AND THE LAW-SCHOOL APPLICATION

The law student should also realize that her conduct during her three years of law school may affect her chances of admission to the bar. For example, a student who defaults on her student loans from college or has serious credit problems such as a recent bankruptcy, may encounter difficulty in obtaining a law license. Also, any incident involving academic dishonesty or inappropriate conduct toward another student, or any negative reference in the student's law-school record, will be reported to the bar in the jurisdiction in which the student seeks admission. These situations are covered in more detail in Chapter 10.

Along those lines, the student should ensure that her law-school application is accurate and complete. The school may share this information, including a student's criminal record, with the board of bar examiners. Any discrepancy between the information contained in the law-school application and that disclosed to the bar could be grounds for a hearing by the board of bar examiners and for possible disciplinary action by the law school. Indeed, in one situation, the board of bar examiners informed a law-school dean that a student at the dean's school had been arrested many years before on minor charges. This information had not been disclosed on the student's law-school application. The school suspended the student's diploma because of this nondisclosure, even though this information was received *after* she had graduated from school. Thus, from the first year of law school, students should be aware of their responsibilities with respect to updating their law-school application and should also be aware of the consequences of any failure to update or disclose information when it comes time for applying for admission to a bar. Students are often surprised to learn that they have a continuing obligation to update their law-school applications by disclosing such information, even once they have matriculated at a school. The fact that bar examiners focus so closely on each candidate's background, particularly his conduct in law school, should serve as a reminder to the student to keep his future in mind in regulating his own behavior when he is away from school as well as when he is on campus.

The board of bar examiners will require the applicant to submit a completed bar application well in advance of the test date. This deadline likely will fall somewhere in the middle to end of the applicant's third year of law school, although some jurisdictions have an earlier deadline. In some jurisdictions, for example, the application must be received five months before the July test date, which means that students must complete the application during the middle of the school year. Applicants should note that boards of bar examiners interpret deadlines differently: some require that the student's application be postmarked on or before the deadline, while others require that the application actually be received in the office of the board of bar examiners at or before the deadline. Some states will process a late application if the applicant pays an additional fee, but other jurisdictions simply will not allow the applicant to sit for the upcoming bar exam. In those jurisdictions, the applicant must wait for the next bar exam, which can have a serious, negative impact on a new graduate's ability to make a living.

DECIDING WHERE TO TAKE THE BAR

Sometimes, students are not sure where they should take the bar and seek admission to practice law. They may not have a job offer in hand or may not even be sure whether they want to practice law. In general, students should consider states with which they have a strong connection, whether because of earlier schooling or ties with family and friends. Job opportunities often come through personal contacts and from the new graduate's ability to demonstrate his commitment to and connection with the local community. A student who is unsure where to take the bar might also consider a jurisdiction with a bar exam that is considered sufficient for admission to another jurisdiction in which the student has an interest as well. This process might make it possible for the new attorney to be eligible to practice in more than one state after taking a single bar exam. For example, a student might want to return eventually to the state where he grew up, but may wish to practice elsewhere for a few years first. In such a situation, this new graduate might consider taking one jurisdiction's exam first and then seeking an examination waiver so as to gain admission to the bar in the second jurisdiction without taking a second bar exam. The waiver process can be complicated, however, and the student is advised to research the requirements imposed by both jurisdictions thoroughly. Jurisdictions that participate in waiver programs generally require that the applicant have received a certain minimum score (above passing) on the first jurisdiction's bar exam. The score will be disclosed to the prospective jurisdiction by the jurisdiction where the exam was taken, upon request of the applicant. In addition, some jurisdictions require that the lawyer have practiced for a minimum number of years before he will be admitted to practice without taking a second bar exam; others require an applicant who has practiced elsewhere to take only the locally written portion of the bar exam. (The major portions of the typical bar examination are discussed below.) Some jurisdictions are more restrictive and will not accept even a multistate exam score from another jurisdiction. Often, the relative willingness of a jurisdiction to admit attorneys who have taken a bar elsewhere depends on the policy of that jurisdiction towards encouraging or discouraging attorneys to practice there. Thus, a jurisdiction with a glut of attorneys is likely to be stricter than one in which few attorneys currently practice. Each jurisdiction has such specific requirements for waiver that an applicant wishing to take advantage of this process simply must make her plans and conduct her research well in advance.

THE PROCESS OF ADMISSION TO THE BAR: APPLICATION AND REGISTRATION

The admission process is initiated either by registration with the state board of bar examiners or by a written application for admission. A few states require separate applications for taking the bar examination and for admission to practice law. During law school or, in the case of a practicing attorney, as soon as she is aware of her need to take another bar exam, the applicant should write to the board of law examiners for the jurisdiction in which she is interested and request an application. Alternatively, the applicant can visit the Web site for the board of bar examiners and download the application, although some jurisdictions charge a hefty fee for doing so. A list of the boards of bar examiners for every state, commonwealth, or territory of the United States can be found at www.barexam.org or by visiting the American Bar Association's Web site at www.abanet.org. The applicant may be required to send a self-addressed, postage-prepaid envelope and remit a handling fee along with her completed application. There will be other fees, as well, including an application fee (which could be more than $900), a background- or character-and-fitness-investigation fee, and any number of other administrative fees. These fees generally cannot be paid by personal check; rather, a cashier's check or bank check is usually required. As is true of the waiver process discussed above, there at least appears to be some correlation between the number and amount of the fees assessed and a jurisdiction's desire either to attract lawyers or to discourage them from attempting to join the state bar.

The admissions application is lengthy and will require information relating to all areas of the applicant's professional and educational life and most areas of the applicant's personal life as well, including the following:

- ♦ basic contact and personal information, such as current and past addresses, telephone numbers, date of birth, and Social Security number;

- ♦ past employment history, including dates of employment and reasons for leaving each position;

- ♦ every lawsuit, administrative hearing, or other legal proceeding to which the applicant was a party;

- ♦ disclosures of any arrest or criminal proceeding involving the applicant;

- ♦ credit and financial information;

- ♦ personal and professional references;

- ♦ comprehensive educational information, including the names and addresses of every school attended, transcripts from each, and information about any disciplinary action or investigations made involving the student;

♦ all prior or concurrent bar applications being submitted or, if relevant, information about every other jurisdiction to which the applicant has applied or been admitted; and

♦ information relating to treatment for mental illness, chemical dependency, and rehabilitation, as well as certain records relating to each such treatment.

In addition to the extensive information that is requested on the application itself, the applicant may be required to submit some or all of the following: a fingerprint card on a form that is deemed to be acceptable by the board of bar examiners; a photograph for identification purposes; letters of recommendation from attorneys or a character reference letter from one or more individuals; test results from any other exams that the jurisdiction requires applicants to take (like California's Baby Bar, as described above, or the Multistate Professional Responsibility Exam, which is discussed below); a statement of intent, addressed to the jurisdiction's board of bar examiners; copies of previous or concurrent bar applications from other jurisdictions; the applicant's law-school application; and a dean's certification from the applicant's law school.

After the applicant submits the necessary documentation to the jurisdiction in which she wishes to practice, an initial determination will be made as to whether she can take the bar exam. Some jurisdictions make a full determination of the applicant's character and fitness to practice law before the bar exam, and grant formal authorization to take the bar when the review is completed. Other jurisdictions complete the character-and-fitness review after the bar exam and provide the candidate with only provisional authorization to take the examination.

From time to time, the applicant may need to update his bar-admissions application. He may get a new job, for example, or may change his address. An intervening brush with the law or an academic issue also may necessitate a modification of information on the application. Applicants must be aware of the deadlines for submitting amendments—some are as short as thirty days after the occurrence of particular events. The applicant's failure to provide such information may be considered a material misrepresentation and could result in the applicant's being denied a license to practice law. Stated more generally, information provided to the board of bar examiners is taken very seriously and may affect the applicant for the rest of his professional life.

THE BAR EXAM

The bar exam assists the board of bar examiners in evaluating an applicant's technical legal competency. Many, but not all, jurisdictions administer an exam two times each year—in February and in July. Some states administer only one bar exam in a given year; thus, early research is vital for the applicant, so as to plan her professional activities properly.

Individual jurisdictions have either a two- or three-day bar examination. The exam will most likely include a full day for the Multistate Bar Examination (MBE), which is a standardized, six-hour, two-hundred-question, multiple-choice examination prepared by the National Conference of Bar Examiners (NCBE). The subjects tested on the MBE are contracts, constitutional law, criminal law, torts, evidence, and real property. An increasing number of jurisdictions are using the Multistate Essay Examination (MEE) as well, which is a three-hour, six-question essay test covering subjects such as agency and partnership, commercial paper, conflict of laws, corporations, decedents' estates, family law, federal civil procedure, sales, secured transactions, trusts, and future interests. In addition, some jurisdictions are using the Multistate Performance Test (MPT), which consists of three ninety-minute questions designed to test an applicant's fundamental lawyering skills, such as factual analysis, problem solving, and legal analysis. The MPT question might include, for example, a file containing documents such as articles, medical records, cases, and police reports, that could be used in answering the question. Finally, many jurisdictions now require that the applicant achieve a designated minimum score on the Multistate Professional Responsibility Examination (MPRE), a multiple-choice examination that is centered on issues of legal professionalism and is usually administered separately from the bar exam. Applicants can take the MPRE on one of three dates each year at many law schools or at other designated locations. The exam is usually given in March, August, and November of each year. Applications for the MPRE are due well in advance of the exam. This exam can be taken while a student is in law school. In fact, some jurisdictions require that the applicant have achieved a passing score on the MPRE *before* she will be allowed to sit for the bar. Applicants can register online for the MPRE at www.ncbex.org. Further information on the MPRE, including an exam study guide, is available at law schools, online at www.ncbex.org, or by mailing a request to the following address:

> National Conference of Bar Examiners
> MPRE Applications Department
> P.O. Box 4001
> Iowa City, IA 52243
> (319) 337-1287

Besides the exams discussed above, each jurisdiction administers a locally written essay exam that may take from one-half day to a full day. Virtually any subject of state or federal law can be tested on the exam, including the state constitution and the United States Constitution. These questions may require that the applicant possess general knowledge of the law relating to bankruptcy, taxation, corporations and partnerships, statutes of limitation, or a host of other subjects. Sometimes, the essay will provide an unfamiliar statute or regulation for the applicant to analyze. In other questions, the applicant will be expected to apply law that she has already learned. In the state-essay portion of the bar exam, the applicant is expected to demonstrate that she can identify legal issues, apply legal principles, and respond to each question posed in a logical and coherent manner. The bar examiners will consider both the content and organization of the answer in grading the examination.

Applicants may want to visit the Web site of the board of bar examiners for the jurisdiction to which they are applying. There, the applicant may find a study guide for the locally drafted portion of the exam. The jurisdiction may also post exams and sample answers from previous bar exams. Increasingly, jurisdictions are providing applicants with helpful information such as exam study tips, frequently asked questions, and charts showing the deadlines for the submission of fees and applications.

As noted above, jurisdictions vary in how the exam is configured. In one New England state, for example, the first day is devoted to the MBE exam, which runs from 9:00 A.M. to 4:30 P.M., with a ninety-minute break for lunch. The state-prepared essay examination resumes the next morning at 9:00 A.M. and follows the same time schedule. Other states follow a three-day exam schedule. Still others set aside one day in advance of a two-day exam for registration and orientation.

Students requiring accommodation for either a physical or learning disability generally must apply with the board of bar examiners well in advance of the test date. The board will most likely require that the applicant fill out a form, which may involve obtaining information from a doctor, psychologist, or other medical-care professional. These forms are generally available online as well as by mail or facsimile. Notably, cigarette breaks will not be considered an accommodation, even for a four-pack-a-day smoker.

The bar examinations generally are graded by examination number, and no applicant may identify her paper by name. The MBE and other objective portions of the exam usually will be machine-scored by American College Testing, a company that has a contract with the NCBE for this purpose. To avoid putting applicants who take a particularly difficult exam at a disadvantage (or giving an advantage to those who have taken a particularly easy exam), each year's MBE exam is equated to a standard exam and the NCBE then assigns a scaled score to each bar-examination paper. The scaled score is reported to the jurisdiction where the applicant took the exam. The bar examiners in the jurisdiction in which the exam was taken grade the essay portions. Usually, that same body of bar examiners will combine the scaled MBE score and the essay scores using a statistical method that has been approved or recommended by the NCBE. Each jurisdiction can, however, determine for itself what constitutes a passing bar-exam grade.

Successful applicants usually are not advised of their score on the bar exam, nor are they given a range or ranking allowing them to approximate their score. Instead, the bar exam measures minimum competency; thus, the number of points by which a successful applicant passed the exam is unimportant. Unsuccessful applicants, however, generally will be provided with their overall scores and may also be provided with their scores for each essay question. The results of the bar exam, which may be published by identifying number or by the name of each successful applicant, will be posted in a manner that has been approved by the highest court in the jurisdiction or other appropriate body. Bar-exam results are sometimes published on courthouse doors, in legal newspapers or other official legal periodicals, online at the state bar association's Web site or the Web site of the state's highest court, or mailed to the applicant. Telephone inquiries about bar-exam results, however, will not be accepted, primarily for reasons of privacy and security.

BAR FAILURE AND APPEALS OF FAILING SCORES

Each year, some percentage of applicants fails the bar exam. For some individuals, the prospect of passing the exam was uncertain all along; they either could not devote sufficient time to studying for the exam, or for some other reason were not able to focus on the endeavor. For others, however, failure will come as a complete shock.

Some jurisdictions automatically review all failing examination papers that received grades close to the passing mark. In addition, after the results are compiled, the board of bar examiners may review a certain number of failing examination papers to determine whether additional points could have been awarded for any essay question. Sometimes, an applicant will receive a passing score upon re-grading; other times, re-grading will result in a lower score. If the applicant has been informed that she failed the bar in a jurisdiction that conducts this kind of automatic review, then it is likely that her exam was already re-graded before the notification was sent. Such jurisdictions, therefore, normally will not allow an applicant to appeal a failing score.

In jurisdictions that do permit appeals or do not automatically re-evaluate close (but failing) exams, the applicant may want to consider challenging a failing score if it is close to the cut-off for passing. Each jurisdiction where such a challenge is permitted will have a procedure for the appeal. Applicants should understand, however, that successful challenges are not common.

Applicants who fail the bar will have to decide whether to take the exam again. Law-school graduates should not allow a failure, or even two or three, to stop them from pursuing a career practicing law, especially given the large amount of money they have already invested in their legal education by this time. Generally, an applicant can re-take a bar exam several times, although some states limit the number of attempts that are permitted. One state, for example, limits the applicant to five or six attempts. Beyond that number, the applicant will need to secure advance permission from the board of bar examiners before taking the examination again.

An unsuccessful applicant may want to consider requesting a conference with a member of the board of bar examiners to go over some of the areas in which she needs to improve before taking the examination again. The board may not honor such a request the first time an applicant fails but, after a second, unsuccessful attempt, a member of the board may be willing to talk with the applicant. These conferences may take place over the telephone or in person. If such a conference is granted, the applicant should understand that this conference is not to dispute the grading on a past exam, nor to focus on specific questions on a past exam, but rather to look for areas of weakness in the applicant's writing style or deficiencies in the structure or organization of the applicant's essay responses.

Applicants who have failed the bar exam may need to inform an employer of this fact. Certainly, no one relishes having such a conversation with an employer, but nonetheless it must be done. The lawyer should carefully consider with whom to discuss this matter first: a supervisor or the office or practice-group leader might be an appropriate choice. The applicant should have this discussion with the employer as soon as possible, and certainly on the same day on which the applicant learns of the bar results. The employer may be able to check online sources or send a courier to the courthouse to see whether certain lawyers have passed, and it would be awkward for the employer to learn of the failure from a source other than the employee himself. Perhaps an overwhelming workload did not permit sufficient study time. Nevertheless, the lawyer bears at least partial responsibility and it is probably not appropriate for him to attempt to excuse the failing grade by stating that work interfered with bar study. Instead, the lawyer may want to focus the conversation on what he is going to do to ensure that he does not fail a second or third time. This may be the appropriate time to discuss having a more formal arrangement (for example, unpaid time off during the weeks before the next exam) for future bar study. The lawyer will most likely find that he is not the first person in the office to have failed the bar and that the employer will be much more supportive than the lawyer has imagined. In general, firms do not automatically regard one failure as a reason for an attorney's dismissal, although this cannot be ruled out in an economy in which qualified lawyers are plentiful or when the lawyer's performance otherwise has been unsatisfactory. In those situations, one bar-exam failure may be a sufficient ground for termination of the employment relationship.

BAR-REVIEW COURSES

Many bar applicants choose to purchase a bar-review course in preparation for taking the exam. These courses may be presented in a classroom by a lecturer, in a classroom with all of the students watching a video tape, through written materials only, or through audio or video tapes personally viewed by the applicant in either her home or with one or two other students. More recently, the Internet has afforded some applicants the opportunity to take bar-review courses online. In evaluating which of these courses to take, students should keep in mind that they are acting as consumers of a rather expensive product. In addition, because each course will offer very specific and comprehensive advice, students are, in many ways, trusting the providers of the product with their chances of passing the bar exam. Students should therefore make careful inquiries before making a decision.

The first question, of course, is whether to take a bar-review course at all. It is strongly recommended that the applicant take some such course, even if he has previously taken a bar exam in another jurisdiction. A bar-review course encapsulates the material that will be tested and presents it in an organized fashion, including a comprehensible, memorizable synopsis of each particular area of the law that is to be examined. Bar-review courses are taught differently from most law-school courses. In law school, students are required to distill the black letter law from a series of cases designed to show the student how the law evolved. Law school is, therefore, often process-oriented and philosophical. Bar-review courses, on the other hand, are very direct and linear. Often, students find the bar-review materials to be exceedingly helpful in bringing entire courses and areas of law into focus, sometimes for the first time. Without taking a review course, the applicant would have to review (or learn for the first time) the black letter law of each area to be tested and decide for herself which parts of that law to study, without knowing which material is traditionally tested on the bar exam. Bar-review courses do this portion of the applicant's work for her, with the assistance of a tremendous institutional bank of historical data showing how often each area of law is tested, and what kinds of questions are typically asked.

A bar-review course will also provide guidance on appropriate pacing and a formal structure for learning the significant volume of material that must be covered. The student can follow recommended schedules that dovetail with the order in which the lectures or tapes are to be presented or viewed. In addition, some applicants find that hearing the tapes or seeing the lecturers present the material makes it easier to remember the information than simply reading it. Many lecturers take pains to ensure that their review of the material is both entertaining and interesting, frequently spicing lectures with mnemonic devices such that some attorneys remember portions of the lectures years after taking the bar exam. Skilled instructors can highlight nuances in the law that might otherwise be lost in the mountain of required reading. Another very important benefit of a bar-review course, and one that is simply not available to an applicant studying on her own, is that these courses teach students how to tackle questions, especially the multistate exam questions. Applicants learn that certain types of answers either are never correct or should be automatically suspect. Applicants also learn to eliminate answers that are obviously false, and to make a reasoned guess, when necessary, among those that remain. Finally, the materials used for bar review will be useful in practice. Many attorneys keep their bar-review materials handy to provide them with an overview, when needed, of areas of law with which they are not readily familiar. This kind of foundational material can be useful to a practicing attorney when beginning her research in an unfamiliar area of law.

Once the applicant has determined that she will take a bar-review course, she should consider whether each course being offered provides a cohesive technique for learning the material. Some bar-review courses, for example, are centered on lengthy black-letter outlines, later distilled to condensed outlines, with timed practice exams interspersed throughout. Applicants should ask the representatives for each course to describe the technique that will be used and why it works.

The applicant may also look at the historical success of each course he is considering. Alternatively, if the course lacks a lengthy corporate history, the applicant might research the background and experience of those who founded the company. For example, the course may have been founded by an experienced bar examiner or an individual who taught for many years for another bar-review course.

The cost of the program is another factor to consider. A higher cost does not necessarily mean that the course is better. Indeed, there is a movement afoot to bring lower-cost bar-review options to students via the Internet. Applicants should not rule out these options simply because they are either free or offered at a low cost. Rather, the applicant should consider the experience of the course designer, the content and quality of the materials if they are available for trial review, and whether the program offers the type of cohesive structure discussed above. Recommendations or personal testimonies might be especially important if the applicant decides to use a lesser-known provider. The applicant should also consider her own level of discipline. Those who tend to be easily distracted may find that they need the greater structure imposed by a classroom-based course.

Before purchasing a bar-review course, an applicant may also want to consider some non-traditional bar-review programs. Private bar-exam tutors are widely available through the Internet. In addition, in the next few years, interactive courses may become available in which a bar-review student can design a course best suited to his learning and listening style. Again, the applicant should act as a wise consumer when considering each service: she should consider, for instance, who is providing the service, what is being provided, and the extent to which supplementary materials or access to a live person will be available.

There are some ways to help defray the cost of a bar-review course or at least to borrow money to pay for the course. Some bar-review-course providers hire law students to market their product at schools. Participating students can earn either a free course or a discount on the course. Some providers offer substantial discounts, along with bar-review-course outlines, to students who sign up for the review course early in their law-school education. Bar-review providers often tout the advantages of having access to their course materials while the student is taking the actual course in law school. These materials should not necessarily be important factors in the student's decision, however; law-school study and bar study are very different, and the student's approach to taking law-school exams will be different from her approach to taking the bar. As a result, bar-review-course materials might not be useful to a student in studying for a law-school exam. The cost differential, though, may be reason enough for a student to purchase a course early. The American Bar Association also may provide bar-review discounts if the student enrolls with the ABA during law school, instead of when the attorney begins her practice.

FINANCING BAR STUDY

Private and federal loans are available for students taking bar-review courses. Students who find that they need to take uncompensated time off from work to study for the bar exam can use these loans for living expenses as well as to finance a bar-review course. The major lenders, including Sallie Mae, the Access Group, and Law Loans, all offer such loans. Each lender imposes its own specific requirements; some require that the student be enrolled at least part time in law school, a fact that may have to be certified by the registrar, or that the student take the exam within a certain time after graduation. To qualify for federal loans, students may also need to demonstrate that they have exhausted other federal aid before applying for a loan specifically to study for the bar. A student can borrow between $500 and $10,000 for bar-exam study, depending on the lender. Most of these loans require that the applicant attend, or have attended, an ABA-accredited law school. These loans all have different repayment options; some, but not all, include a grace period or offer borrowers the option of paying only interest for the first six months. Applicants should begin the loan-application process as early as the loan company will permit them to do so. Once the student begins preparing for graduation, the beginning of bar study, admission to a bar, and employment, she will not want to be distracted by the need to secure money for her bar study at the same time.

Some applicants, in attempting to finance their bar-review course and bar study, will benefit from being offered a signing bonus by the law firm with which they intend to practice. Indeed, some such bonuses are offered with the intention of helping recent graduates to pay expenses like moving and bar study. In addition, practicing attorneys who are moving from one state to another to work at a specific law firm may want to consider asking the new firm to pay for a bar-review course. The recruiter, if one is involved, can handle this matter by talking with the hiring partner directly.

In deciding on a bar-review course, applicants may also consider personal recommendations from lawyers who have already taken the bar. Applicants can inquire at their future place of employment or can even ask recent graduates. Students should be wary, however, of those individuals who, in hindsight, seem to believe that they could have marshaled their own resources and passed the bar on their own. There is so much material to be reviewed, and the stakes are so high, that taking a chance and by-passing any bar review course is simply not a good idea for most applicants.

WORKING DURING BAR STUDY

A special set of challenges awaits those who work during bar study. Some firms expect that lawyers will continue to work full-time, but those firms will make allowances in terms of reducing their billable-hour expectations. New lawyers should keep in mind that, at the end of the year, when associates' billable hours are being circulated and compared, few people will stop to remember that some associates took the bar and were permitted a reduction in their billable hours. Moreover, at many firms, there is an unwritten and unacknowledged expectation that associates will make up the lost billable hours throughout the course of the year. One exception to either rule, however, might exist if a lawyer has made arrangements to receive a reduced salary or to work a formal part-time schedule during the month—or six weeks—before the bar exam.

A new lawyer should gather all of her facts before attempting to discuss the bar exam, and her study requirements, with her new employer. The lawyer should begin by determining whether she will take a bar-review course, and, if so, when the course is scheduled each week. The lawyer should also gather all relevant information with respect to the dates of the exam and her travel requirements, if any. Next, the lawyer should prepare a list of all legal matters in which she is involved, along with a list of important deadlines. For example, if the attorney is the only associate working on a litigation matter, then she should reproduce the calendar of relevant dates for discovery and other deadlines in the case and bring those materials to a conference with the supervising attorney. The lawyer should also consider the nature of her practice and the needs of her employer over the next few months before deciding what to ask of the firm. For example, if the attorney works in the area of securities, and the employer's work for the next few months appears to be scant, then there may not be a problem with her leaving work for bar-review classes and keeping to a regular study schedule. If, on the other hand, the employer is overloaded, then having a more formal bar-study arrangement with fixed, reduced hours and reduced pay might be in order.

Ultimately, it is the lawyer's responsibility to ensure that he is taking all steps necessary to allow him to do his very best on the bar exam. At times, the lawyer may need to inform a supervisor diplomatically that he needs to leave to attend bar-review class, or that the due date for a particular project falls just before or after the bar exam. The lawyer should have a solution in mind when raising these issues with his supervisor. For example, the lawyer may find out whether another lawyer can oversee his work for the three weeks before the exam, or perhaps whether some of his work can be given to another lawyer. Lawyers who are having difficulty juggling bar study with practice need to enlist the help of a formal or informal mentor, or even a supervisor. The supervisor might, if needed, send a memorandum to remind others that the attorney is preparing for the bar; alternatively, the supervisor might be able to steer new matters away from the lawyer for a month or so.

BAR STUDY

Outside of the time she spends in the actual bar-review classes, the applicant should establish a regular schedule of work and study. How she structures this schedule will depend on her work situation, as well as her own study habits. For example, some individuals study better at night and should establish a regular time every night to do this. Family members and friends should be asked to respect this bar-study time. Just as with law-school study, many students find that treating bar study like a job will make the process easier and is a useful way to instill discipline. This mindset may also help the applicant to establish a regular place to study, possibly even leaving books and materials out and set up in her study area. Applicants may wish to minimize change in their personal lives during the two months before the bar exam. This may not be the best time for the applicant to quit smoking, to modify her diet, or to begin or end a relationship. Wholesale changes that could have a detrimental effect on the applicant's life or energy level, however good they might be at any other time, might not be best during this particularly stressful period. The exception to that advice, of course, is exercise. Indeed, exercise is not only a good stress reliever, but it also helps to develop mental and physical stamina for the long days of study ahead.

The type of preparation that is appropriate will change as the exam date approaches. Some applicants find, once they have learned the material sufficiently, that taking practice exams and reviewing the answers is helpful. A bar-review course will provide opportunities and sample bar-exam questions for this purpose. In some courses, the students will take portions of a practice exam under simulated exam conditions so they can start to get a sense of the time pressure they will face. In addition, practice exams are available online at the Web sites of the various boards of bar examiners. Applicants can also find sample bar questions at sites like www.findlaw.com/thebar/samplebar.html.

Some students find it useful to study for the bar exam with a group, particularly if they benefited from a study group in law school. These students may band together with others from their law school who are all taking a particular jurisdiction's bar exam. Study-group members can quiz each other and can go over practice-exam answers together. Sometimes, arguing a position or discussing why an answer falls short helps applicants to remember the material better. The same considerations that apply to study groups in law school apply equally here. See Chapter 7 for an in-depth discussion of working effectively in a study group.

In the weeks before the exam, the applicant should ensure that all logistical arrangements for the bar examination are in order: if the student is traveling to take the bar, he should confirm his plane ticket, hotel reservations, and rental car. In addition, he should triple-check the dates of the exam and should find out when registration begins. The applicant may want to go online to secure directions and maps to the hotel and exam site, even if he is reasonably sure that he can find them on his own. The applicant may find it useful to make a list of the items he will need for the exam, including all forms of required identification, the packet of materials sent by the board of bar examiners to each applicant, and any codes or rules allowed in the testing room by the bar examiners. Some jurisdictions, for example, permit applicants to consult a court-authorized copy of the federal Constitution, the state constitution, and the United States tax code.

JUST BEFORE THE EXAM

In the days before the bar exam, the applicant may want to consider re-reading all of the short outlines she received from the bar-review course, as well as practice exams and answers. (Most bar-review courses will have ended by this time, leaving students free to do their final preparation at home, on their own.) The applicant may wish to gather the items she wants to take with her, including pens and pencils, snacks, a pillow on which to sit, a watch with its alarm function turned *off*, two alarm clocks for the day of the exam, and clothing for any contingency. A student who must travel to take the exam will want to bring these, and possibly all study materials (even the full outlines) with her on the trip. The student should probably not check these items as baggage if she is flying to her destination. Instead, the applicant likely will feel more comfortable just having the full outlines nearby, both on the plane and in the hotel, even if the time for reviewing them has long passed.

In the days before the exam, the applicant should make every effort to get a full night's sleep. Bar exams are also endurance tests, especially if they last for three days instead of two. The applicant needs to be sharp so that she does not make simple, avoidable mistakes—like missing the call of the question—as a result of a lack of sleep.

Applicants may also want to make a trial run to the exam site on the day before the exam. That way, they can figure out parking considerations and avoid unpleasant exam-day surprises like detours due to road construction. On the day of the exam, test-takers should dress in layers. The room temperature will change during the day, given the body heat generated by the crowd taking the exam. Applicants sometimes are not prepared for the physical environment in which the test is administered; the room will be very large, it will be filled with nervous people, and it will have tight security. There will be exam-takers who are sick, those pretending to be unfazed by the whole production, and, of course, those who want to cram in as much learning as possible out in the parking lot before the exam and during the lunch break. Exam-takers are likely to be advised that, if they have not learned the material by this late date, they cannot learn it just before the exam. Some applicants, however, have indeed noticed one small nugget of information that helped them on an exam, even at that late hour. Applicants should stick with what has worked for them in the past: if eleventh-hour studying does not unnerve the test-taker, or if *not* studying will result in unnecessary nervousness, then, by all means, the applicant should continue looking over the material before the exam or at lunch. The applicant has to live with the results of this exam, so he should do what makes him feel comfortable. The same advice goes for the post-exam review: if the student feels comfortable talking about the exam with others who want to talk about it, then he should feel free to do so. Applicants should remember, however, that others might not want to hear any discussion of the exam they have just taken.

The bar exam is a serious business because the practice of law is a serious business. Attorneys, as a profession, interact with the public on a regular basis. Clients, judges, and adversaries all place a great deal of trust and confidence in the conduct and representations of attorneys. People's finances, formal relationships, businesses, and sometimes lives or freedom can be placed in the hands of an attorney. With this great power and responsibility comes the potential for an attorney to do great harm. For this reason, the board of bar examiners considers whether this trust is justified with regard to every new applicant to the bar. The character-and-fitness review and the bar examination itself are the legal profession's attempt to ensure that only qualified individuals are entrusted with the title of attorney.

CHAPTER 15

Continued Development as a Lawyer; Judicial Clerkships, LL.M.s

An attorney's professional training does not end with law school. Throughout her career, the lawyer will increase her knowledge through practice and experience, mandatory continuing-legal-education courses, regular review of legal journals and papers, and in other formal and less formal ways. Some lawyers further their training through clerkships with federal- or state-court judges. Others pursue an LL.M. degree, typically in a relatively focused area of the law. This chapter discusses those avenues of career development.

JUDICIAL CLERKSHIPS

A judicial clerk is a law-school graduate or practicing lawyer who works with a judge in handling tasks determined by the judge. Some responsibilities are fairly universal, such as legal research and preparation of memoranda on legal issues. Beyond these general requirements, a judicial clerk's duties can vary widely. They could include, for example, anything from handling administrative matters such as telephone calls and scheduling to preparing the first draft of a judicial opinion.

A judicial clerkship should not be confused with a judicial internship. A judicial intern is not a practicing lawyer, but rather a law-school or college student who assists a judge with administrative matters and legal research. An internship, unlike a clerkship, is generally a volunteer position. A judicial internship is also excellent preparation for a future lawyer and is discussed in Chapters 3 and 13. Nor should a judicial clerk be confused with a "clerk of court." The clerk of court is a career administrative professional assigned to manage court filings and maintain files. The clerk of court typically manages these matters for an entire court, not simply for a single judge.

WHO SHOULD CONSIDER A JUDICIAL CLERKSHIP?

Certainly, any person who is interested in a career as a private-firm litigator should at least consider a judicial clerkship. The benefits, described in more detail below, are innumerable. Furthermore, many senior attorneys recognize that former clerks are often much better prepared to practice law than their colleagues who did not clerk. Attorneys who enjoy both legal research and writing, and dealing with people, might also consider a clerkship. Clerks interact with all kinds of people, particularly the parties to the litigation, at every level of education and experience—attorneys, *pro se* clients, judges, other clerks, and members of the administrative staff. Judicial clerks experience, sometimes in a visceral way, the disagreements, disappointments, or challenges facing each of these people, particularly the parties to the litigation. It takes a person of maturity and compassion to give the same level of attention to small matters as to high-profile matters, remembering that each small matter is likely to be of major importance to those who are most directly affected by it.

Even those attorneys who are not necessarily contemplating a career in private litigation may want to consider a clerkship. For those who are interested in a career in politics, in working with the U.S. Attorney's office as a prosecutor, or in some other federal position, a federal clerkship is an excellent introduction to the federal judicial system, as well as to some of the influential individuals who are members of the federal judiciary. The clerk will see prosecutors in action and will read and analyze briefs submitted both by the government and by party opponents. In so doing, the clerk will gain insight into how to do the job that she wants, both well and poorly.

Attorneys contemplating an academic career should also consider a clerkship. Clerkships offer a practical view of virtually all of the core courses taught by law professors, from evidence and civil procedure to torts and contracts. This experience, especially at the federal appellate and Supreme Court level, is highly valued by schools when they are considering applicants for teaching positions.

Finally, even for lawyers who may be interested primarily or exclusively in corporate or tax work, a clerkship would not necessarily be a waste of time. Many legal disputes begin with deals put together by corporate lawyers; litigation ensues when the transactions sour. As a clerk, a future corporate lawyer can see the big picture: where the deal went bad, where some of the red flags were, and how these matters are ultimately resolved by the legal system. Even though the future corporate- or tax-lawyer does not plan to litigate, he will benefit greatly from the contacts he will make, as a clerk, in the legal community, as well as from many of the other positive aspects of clerkship, both tangible and intangible, that are described below.

APPLICATION CRITERIA AND OTHER GENERAL INFORMATION

Although the competition for clerkships is extremely fierce, the bare qualifications for serving as a judicial clerk are not onerous. The candidate must either already have a *juris doctor* degree or expect to be awarded one by the time the clerkship starts, and, in most cases, must be a United States citizen. For a position with the United States Supreme Court, the clerk must generally have a year of previous clerking experience. Beyond those minimal qualifications, however, judges are usually free to determine their own, individualized criteria for the law clerks they hire. Generally, the candidate should have a strong academic record, although this does not necessarily mean that top grades are a requirement for all clerkships. For some positions, such as those with the United States Supreme Court or most appellate-level clerkships, grades are likely to be a major consideration. Indeed, these high-level-clerkship candidates generally have stellar academic records, along with strong support from professors or previous judges for whom the candidates have clerked. There are many other opportunities, however, that do not necessarily turn on top grades, but instead may weigh more heavily other factors such as life experience, writing experience, and courses taken in law school. These factors are likely to be of particular importance for clerkships with courts of specialized jurisdiction, such as the United States Court of Federal Claims, a court authorized to hear primarily monetary claims founded upon the Constitution, federal statutes, executive regulations, or contracts with the United States. These other qualifications may also be important for an atypical clerkship, such as for a semi-retired Supreme Court Justice who occasionally hears cases at the federal circuit-court level. This clerk may assist the judge in writing his memoirs or with other writing assignments. Of course, as with all employment opportunities, the student may find that well-placed contacts are of help in gaining a clerkship. The candidate, however, must also have a demonstrated ability to research and write well, which could be evidenced, for example, by participation on a law journal, by a research-and-writing teaching assistantship, or by serving as a professor's research assistant. Some judges, demonstrating the importance they place on applicants' writing skills, will consider only candidates who are members of a law journal.

There are different types of judicial clerkships. Clerks can be hired for a certain term, or for a permanent or temporary position. When a clerk is hired for a certain term it is usually for one to two years, or sometimes eighteen months, and the clerk generally does not remain with the judge past that time. A permanent position has no set time limit. A temporary position might become necessary when a judge is assigned a large class-action case, or when numerous individual plaintiffs are filing lawsuits in a particular jurisdiction. In such situations, so as not to overtax the resources of the court and slow down regular pending matters, a temporary clerk may be hired to assist with the work that the large action has generated.

Judicial clerkships are paid positions. Clerks are paid a decent salary, especially in the federal system or at the appellate levels of state courts. Federal judicial clerks are paid according to the federal pay scale and, in determining their salary, are given credit for previous legal experience. The salary range for state- and federal-court clerks is significant—federal clerks can make anywhere from $40,000 to $100,000 per year, depending on their experience, the court, and the location of the court. The range for state-court clerks can be anywhere from about $28,000 to over $40,000 per year. For clerks who have just graduated from law school, and who therefore might be at the bottom of the pay scale, there may be options for deferral of student loans, including a plan whereby the clerk pays only interest for six months. These programs are helpful, and can often be arranged by a telephone call, but a lawyer may request only a limited number of deferrals throughout the life of a loan and during any given time period. The clerk may want to consider whether the deferral is best left for emergency use, and attempt instead to pay her loans on her clerkship salary. In addition, there is typically a grace period of six months after graduation for law-school loans; some of that time might overlap with a new graduate's clerkship.

Federal clerks who are hired for a defined term are eligible for insurance and certain other employment benefits, although the amount of vacation or sick time they receive is left to the discretion of the judge. Permanent clerks in both state and federal courts are eligible for full benefits. Temporary clerks may or may not have employment benefits.

It is difficult to give a uniform description of a law clerk's job responsibilities. Common duties include research on substantive legal questions, as well as procedural rules; preparation of bench briefs for use by the judge in ruling on issues before the court; and preparation of synopses of the respective parties' claims and the issues to be addressed by the court. In addition to their formal work, clerks often engage in discussions with the judge about what was argued in court that day or what the evidence shows in a particular case. Clerks may research and prepare jury instructions that the court intends to give, or may look up cases that were submitted by the parties in support of jury instructions. Sometimes the clerk then modifies the jury instructions submitted by a party so that they do not appear to favor one party over another. The clerk may also be asked to verify representations made by attorneys, through research or by a telephone call. From time to time, the clerk will be asked to research issues very quickly, for use by the judge in considering a newly emerging issue or while the judge is considering her decision on the bench. Clerks may also prepare *voir dire* questions for the judge to pose to the jury, or review last-minute, pre-hearing submissions by attorneys so as to give the judge an overview of items that the judge does not have time to read. Sometimes the clerk is simply a sounding board for the judge, a confidential and trained ear who is trusted to discuss a case and provide feedback on decisions and opinions. It is in these informal moments that the clerk is likely to realize most clearly how valuable her clerking experience is.

The clerk also may have administrative responsibilities, which can include scheduling hearings, checking the court calendar if the judge does not have a separate calendar clerk, or possibly handling responsibilities in the courthouse library. In some courts, the clerks rotate as librarians, and their library responsibilities may include updating publications, filing supplements and new material, assisting *pro se* parties by directing them to appropriate materials, and helping the attorneys and, sometimes, the judges find what they need in the library. In other courts, the clerks might be responsible for maintaining the library that is located in the judges' chambers. This administrative work is excellent training for a practicing lawyer, who is likely to find herself responsible for at least some of these matters; even in the largest firm, with a professional library staff, the attorney must manage her own calendar and the personal research materials she maintains in her own office.

In addition to more traditional tasks, the clerk may assist the judge by writing speeches or drafting recommendations for committees on which the judge sits. The clerks for a chief judge, especially, may find that they have some responsibilities such as these.

In jurisdictions where the judges are elected, the clerk may have peripheral involvement in the judge's campaign and activities associated with the campaign. The clerk will not be asked to perform volunteer campaign services during the workday, but will likely feel that she should attend political dinners and fundraisers, especially those held for the judge. After all, the clerk has an assured position only so long as the judge has a job, and it therefore may be in the clerk's best interest that the clerk assist the campaign.

The judge's style dictates the nature of the experience for the judicial clerks who work for the judge. Attorneys refer to this as the judge's "judicial temperament." One judge, who was known not to care much for the scholarly aspect of his position, would not have his clerks do much in the way of original research. Instead, he would ask that the parties submit additional briefs if there were a question that required information beyond what the parties had already provided. Other judges rise to the intellectual challenge, personally examining the relevant law in detail and having their clerks conduct comprehensive research on the issues rather than relying on the work done by the attorneys for each side. Some clerks have the benefit of an approachable judge who functions as a mentor to his clerks; such a judge might allow his clerks, after discussing a matter with him, to take a first crack at writing an opinion. Other judges remain aloof and businesslike, conducting themselves with their clerks as formally as they conduct themselves in the courtroom, and maintaining strict distinctions between work that is to be done by the clerks and that done by the judge.

The hours a clerk works are also dictated by the judge's style and temperament. For the most part, clerks work fairly regular hours, perhaps 8:30 A.M. to 5:00 P.M., five days a week, with exceptions to be expected. Some judges, however, require a six-day workweek, with long hours each day. Some, but not all, such judges keep these long hours themselves. Even when the hours are reasonable, though, many clerks find the experience to be demanding. One former clerk described the work as being less physically challenging, but more intellectually challenging, than work in a large law firm where long or irregular hours are the norm.

The manner in which assignments are given to the clerk can vary by judge, as well. For example, if a judge has two clerks and perhaps a staff attorney, the three lawyers may review the work to be handled and divide it up according to their interest or experience. Other judges may handle the assignment process personally, or expect that the clerks will work out a fair system, on their own, for handling the workload. Finally, there may be just one clerk working for the judge, in which case that clerk will handle all of the matters that are assigned to her by the judge.

SELECTING A CLERKSHIP

Potential clerks and the law professors who advise them sometimes engage in lively discussions about whether it is preferable to clerk in a federal or a state court, as well as in a trial court or an appellate court. Law-school advisors may encourage the student to pursue a federal or state appellate clerkship. Such a clerkship clearly benefits the law school, providing high-level recognition to the school, as well as paving the way for future graduates to follow suit. In deciding which kind of clerkship is best, however, much depends on the attorney's ultimate career goals. An appellate clerkship is considered prestigious by firms and law schools alike; it is also a stepping stone to another high-level clerkship, whether for the United States Supreme Court or for the highest court in the student's home state. Thus, an attorney who eventually wants to be in academia or to pursue a higher-level clerkship should focus on the appellate courts initially. Furthermore, if the attorney is truly more interested in the research and writing aspects of a clerkship, and is not necessarily interested in trial practice and motion practice, then the appellate clerkship is a better option. The appellate chambers and work environment are described as a rarefied atmosphere that fully engages the mind. Some law-school graduates know that they want to pursue a career in appellate work and will focus their experience and career in that direction. Certainly, an appellate clerkship will be invaluable experience for an attorney who wishes to specialize in this field. The clerkship will help her to understand how clerks and judges review an appellate record and how judges make decisions given the large volume of material and evidence that may accompany an appeal. The appellate clerk will learn to appreciate the frustration of the parties and the vast financial resources that are expended in seeing a case through the appellate process. Clients will benefit from this first-hand knowledge as the former clerk evaluates appeal options and case strategy with them. An appellate clerk should expect less contact than her trial-level counterpart has with law firms and *pro se* plaintiffs, but she is likely to have a great deal of contact with judges, including, ostensibly, some of the most highly regarded in the jurisdiction. Another interesting aspect of an appellate clerkship is that the clerk will work closely with the judge in writing opinions that will draw support from other judges, perhaps in the form of a vote or a concurrence. Clerks thus find that their writing becomes a diplomatic as well as intellectual exercise, one that therefore prepares them for later practice—where diplomacy is often essential—in a unique way.

On the other hand, trial-court clerkships offer valuable experience that no litigator should lightly pass up. Indeed, the principal benefit of a trial-court clerkship is that it prepares the litigator for court in a way that is nearly impossible to duplicate in private practice. A trial-court clerkship is a compressed course on handling judges and clerks, writing persuasively, arguing effectively, knowing appropriate court conduct, and influencing juries. In addition, the trial-court clerk will deal with many cases, simultaneously, at various stages of preparation, such that she will gain a comprehensive understanding of how the trial system works, from the filing of the complaint, through discovery, to the entry of judgment and beyond. Many new litigators who have not clerked, by contrast, go years without seeing a single case go to trial. It is difficult for a new attorney to understand all of the implications of a statement made in a complaint or answer, for example, if she has never seen how that statement plays out in evidence presented at trial.

There is a similar debate about the merits of a federal clerkship versus a state clerkship, with strong arguments on both sides of the issue. Clerking in federal court has the advantage of exposure to attorneys and law firms throughout the judicial district, and often throughout the nation, as well. This broad exposure affords a perspective that is not as readily available in state court for a variety of reasons. A federal clerk might, for example, gain insight on the strategy favoring hiring a local lawyer in a local court. The clerk might, for instance, have observed the difficulty an out-of-state attorney experienced in being given permission to appear before the court or, once admitted, in navigating the court's procedural rules. The federal clerk, depending on the jurisdiction, might also find the transition to private practice at a larger firm to be easier. Larger firms are particularly receptive to hiring federal clerks and often conduct a good portion of business on behalf of their clients in federal court. In addition, a law firm might be more likely to give full credit, in terms of both salary and promotion toward partnership, for a federal clerkship than for a state clerkship. Sometimes this difference is simply a matter of the difference in perceived prestige between state and federal clerkships. Other times, the differential treatment reflects the value of the practical experience the firm believes a federal clerk would have over a state court clerk.

In reality, many litigators practice almost exclusively in state court, and the rest generally practice in both state and federal court. Often, the citizenship of the parties is the only determining factor as to whether a matter is filed in state or federal court. During the course of representing a single client, the attorney may find herself in both state and federal court. There is, therefore, little question but that a state-court experience will be valuable for any future litigator. On the other hand, the attorney may find that he did less writing as a state-court clerk than his federal counterparts did. Unlike federal court, there are few published opinions at the trial level of most state courts. State-court clerks, with heavy case loads, also generally have less time to spend researching and preparing bench briefs for the use of the court than their federal counterparts do.

Those who are interested in a clerkship should also understand that the distinctions between federal and state clerkships, and between appellate and trial clerkships, are just a few of the ways to categorize clerkships. There are three types of federal trial-court judges, for example, each of which would provide a very different clerkship experience: the regular district trial judge, discussed above, the magistrate judge, and the bankruptcy judge. Magistrate judges are appointed to a term of eight years by the federal judges of a district court. The magistrate is assigned civil cases, which may or may not be heard by a jury, when the parties consent to be heard before a magistrate rather than before a regular federal trial-level judge. A district trial judge may also direct the parties to appear before a magistrate judge for discovery (the pre-trial exchange of information and documents) and other pre-trial issues, as well as for preliminary criminal hearings. A magistrate judge may make findings of fact and conclusions of law for the trial judge to use in a non-jury hearing; alternatively, the magistrate judge may prepare a report and recommendation, with a reasoned opinion appended thereto.

A clerkship with a magistrate judge, although not always considered as prestigious as a clerkship with a regular district-court judge, is excellent experience. Magistrate clerkships are especially valuable in jurisdictions in which magistrates are assigned cases in full, rather than simply handling a preliminary hearing or a matter of fact-finding. If the court's docket is particularly full or the magistrate is highly regarded by the regular trial judges, the magistrate may have wide latitude with the handling of cases from filing to trial. Some magistrates intend to seek appointments as federal district-court judges or to seek appointments as or run for positions as state judges, and thus the clerk might eventually have the opportunity to work with the magistrate judge on another level, as well.

A federal bankruptcy judge is appointed to handle trials involving personal or corporate bankruptcy, as well as to oversee the reorganization or dissolution of a corporation in bankruptcy. A federal bankruptcy clerk will have many or all of the same responsibilities as her counterparts in the federal district court, but will exercise those responsibilities pursuant to bankruptcy law and procedure. Some aspects of the procedural rules and motion practice applicable to bankruptcy matters overlap with those that apply to general litigation. Therefore, a bankruptcy clerkship is good preparation for a career in litigation, as well as excellent preparation for bankruptcy work.

Courts of special jurisdiction, such as tax courts or military courts, also afford valuable clerking experience, especially for someone who has a particular interest in these specialties. Because of the value of such clerkships for attorneys who are likely to practice before these courts, it is becoming increasingly common for an experienced attorney to take a leave of absence from a private firm to work as a clerk in a specialized court.

BENEFITS AND DRAWBACKS OF CLERKSHIPS

A judicial clerk, although often a newcomer to the practice of law, gets a privileged view of the judicial decision-making process. The clerk comes to understand the framework used by the judge in evaluating matters of substantive law such as contracts cases or property disputes. The clerk also learns how the judge weighs public-policy considerations, and comes to recognize the facts that tend to persuade the judge one way or another. Additionally, the clerk has the opportunity to learn how much or how little time a judge can choose to devote to matters before him, depending on both his workload and the merit he ascribes to the matter.

Many law clerks credit their experience with having vastly improved their research, writing, and analytical skills. One of the best ways for an attorney to improve her writing is by reading others' writing, and a judicial clerk reads numerous briefs and court papers of varying quality. Through this experience, the clerk becomes much more familiar with the language of the law; he is able to spot persuasive argument styles and identify solid reasoning that is well supported by the case law. Poor writing is just as instructive. The clerk learns to detect holes in legal analysis, to identify poorly supported arguments, and to spot stylistic affectations that make a document less credible. Sometimes, the clerk learns to identify patterns that operate as red flags; for example, the clerk may recognize that briefs that are the written equivalent of fist-pounding may be attempts to use rhetoric to draw the court's attention away from the fact that few facts support the party's contention. At the end of her clerkship, having been exposed to so many examples of good and bad legal writing, the clerk is likely to find her own reading, writing, and analytical skills to be greatly improved.

Similarly, former clerks know how to write in a way that is helpful to both the judge and the judicial clerk. It is important, however, for former clerks to avoid falling into the trap of writing opinions, in practice, instead of pieces of advocacy. It may take a former clerk a few weeks to break out of the balancing-of-the-law mode and use the writing skills he gained as a clerk to write as an advocate representing a client's interest. That said, many former clerks are able to write persuasively by using the solid fact-and-law analysis that was required of them in drafting opinions. They also know how to draw the clerk's attention to matters that might otherwise be left in the pile for some time, having had the opportunity to observe how their own attention was drawn to certain matters because of the way the parties presented them. An experienced clerk can fine-tune even a basic transmittal letter to be both appropriate and effective. Indeed, a former clerk may have more experience in such matters than an experienced attorney at a private firm and may therefore find herself called upon for advice.

When a judge allows her clerk to prepare a draft opinion, the clerk is likely to learn a great deal from seeing how her first draft is crafted into the final product. By seeing how her own work is edited, shaped and molded, she will learn the language, style, and format that this judge, an experienced legal writer, believes to be most effective and appropriate. These skills are directly transferable to writing briefs, a task in which litigators regularly engage. A clerk who has participated in preparing an opinion that is subsequently published may also, if the opinion is cited by others, have the opportunity to see how other judges and legal scholars comment on or criticize the reasoning that is contained in the opinion. For example, if a matter on which the clerk worked is appealed, the appellate court could write a scathing (or glowing) opinion that mentions the flawed (or thorough) district-court analysis. Even when the feedback is negative, the experience is instructive.

Judicial clerks also learn to translate the judge's spoken words into a written product. To do this effectively, the clerk must know how to listen to the judge and must get a sense for how the judge roots the decision in the law. To get a sense for matters of style and individual judgment, such as how strongly worded the draft opinion should be, the clerk must pay attention to subtle clues.

During her clerkship, the clerk should expect to gain broad exposure to the law, including areas of law that she might not otherwise have considered. In the space of a single week, a trial judge might hear a Social Security case, a sexual-harassment lawsuit, a probation-violation matter, and several property disputes. At no time in law school does the student receive such a comprehensive overview of the law. Moreover, by the end of her clerkship, she is likely to have definite ideas about the types of work that are most—and least—attractive to her, having seen these matters progress from filing to final disposition before her judge. Because of this early and in-depth view, many clerks find that they encounter relatively few negative surprises throughout their careers.

Judicial clerks also benefit from frequent exposure to other judges in the jurisdiction. A judge might loan out his law clerk temporarily to help an especially busy judge or to assist another judge with discrete legal issues. In smaller counties or jurisdictions, two clerks may be assigned to rotate among three judges, such that each clerk ultimately has an opportunity to work with each judge. Through these experiences, the attorney gets an excellent understanding of what each judge believes is important and how that judge evaluates the evidence. In other clerkships, the primary interaction with different judges may occur in social gatherings, giving the clerks an opportunity to get to know the judges in a relatively relaxed atmosphere.

Clerks develop inside knowledge about which legal resources the judge regards as authoritative or uses in deciding evidentiary or procedural questions. If the clerk plans to be a litigator, and especially if she may appear before this court in the future, this information is incredibly useful. If, for instance, a judge looks to the McCormick hornbook in considering difficult matters of evidence, the clerk will know that it may be a good idea to cite this source in making an evidentiary argument. Stated more generally, attorneys can make more persuasive arguments that are less susceptible to attack by opposing counsel when they are relying on the same resources that the judge will use to decide these matters.

The judicial-clerkship experience demystifies the process of filing a lawsuit and seeing it through to completion. The clerk will learn the local rules, as well as the applicable state or federal evidentiary and procedural rules, inside out. In addition, having day-to-day experience scheduling deadlines, filing pleadings, and knowing both who will consider these pleadings, and when and how they will be used, is simply invaluable to a future litigator. The clerk will develop a comprehensive knowledge of how the hearing calendar works in a particular jurisdiction, how many copies of each pleading should be filed, when documents should be separately delivered to the judge's chambers, and how long it is likely to be before the judge rules on various types of motions. The clerk will also get to know other court personnel, such as the clerk of court, who can be of great assistance to a beginning attorney who is navigating the litigation process for the first time. Having this experience, which would otherwise take years to acquire, will be a confidence booster for the new attorney as he begins his practice.

Law firms recognize the value of this kind of knowledge. It is not unusual for an attorney who was a former clerk to be regularly consulted when her firm has a case pending in the jurisdiction in which the clerk worked. Some supervising attorneys will request that a former clerk, even if he is not assigned to the case, view a particularly important brief simply for the purpose of making suggestions about style and tone.

Judicial clerks have an excellent opportunity to see attorneys practice their craft, both orally and in written form. The clerks may see some of the best attorneys in the jurisdiction, possibly in the country, at work, and also some of the worst. Many clerks derive comfort from the fact that, even as recent graduates, they can do a better job than many practicing lawyers.

Furthermore, clerks observe how both the attorneys and the judge handle discovery disputes, and will develop a feel for when it is appropriate for attorneys to contact a judge to mediate a discovery dispute. For a litigator in private practice, handling discovery, and the inevitable discovery disputes that arise, is a regular part of the job. For example, an attorney who is defending a deposition might instruct his client not to answer certain questions posed by opposing counsel. The lawyer who is asking the questions might believe that the refusal to answer questions is incorrect and, during the deposition, may therefore call the judge to request a ruling. Attorneys all know that calling a federal district or magistrate judge for assistance in resolving a discovery dispute is a last resort, to be used only when the attorneys have exhausted all other means of working out the matter. Attorneys may be of different opinions, however, with regard to whether a particular dispute has progressed to the point at which it merits the judge's intervention. There are appropriate boundaries to be respected vis-à-vis the judge, and a former law clerk will understand these boundaries well. As a clerk, she will have seen the judge's reactions (both positive and negative) to inquiries and requests of this nature and will carry these lessons through to her own practice.

A judicial clerkship provides an excellent introduction to the members of the local legal community as well as an orientation to the practice of law in that community. After her clerkship, the law clerk will have a well-grounded understanding of how the members of the court where she clerked view the reputations of many of the firms within that judicial district, as well as those of many individual attorneys. Because a firm (or an attorney) may have a different reputation with the bench than with other members of the bar, this inside information is of particular value to the clerk as she considers future job prospects. Many judges will refrain from making overt comments about attorneys and their integrity or lack thereof; nevertheless, an observant law clerk will learn how the judge feels about certain attorneys and their behavior, both in and out of the courtroom. In making these observations, the clerk will get a good sense of what it means to act with integrity as a professional, as well as how a reputation for integrity can be destroyed even by a single incident.

Because clerks are required to view cases objectively when making recommendations to the judge, they learn to detect situations in which an attorney inappropriately minimizes facts that strongly favor the other side. There indeed may be a compelling other side to the story, and the advocate for the other position may simply be too immersed in his client's viewpoint to see this counterargument. Sometimes, however, lawyers skew the facts in a deliberate attempt to mislead. The clerk is likely to have observed both situations. The ability to approach matters in an even-handed manner is learned most often through experience. The clerk can learn from attorneys who failed to view their cases objectively, and can therefore strive to maintain a more balanced perspective in his own post-clerkship practice.

Sometimes the clerkship experience has a very direct impact on an attorney's legal career. One clerk had the benefit of clerking for a judge who was assigned to what was, at that time, the largest multi-district-litigation (MDL) case ever filed. During her first one-year appointment, this clerk handled her regular duties as a federal-court clerk, plus some matters associated with the MDL. For example, she fielded telephone calls from potential class-action members. This clerk was then asked to spend a second year as the clerk for the MDL case. Because the case, and the administration of its settlement terms, would involve the work of several law firms for many years, this clerk made a natural progression from the clerkship to working with a law firm that handled the administration of the MDL settlement. She eventually earned partnership with the firm; thus, her entire professional career centered on a particular area of litigation that she almost certainly would not have chosen had she not clerked.

Perhaps most important, the clerk often finds a lifelong friend and mentor in the judge and may develop long-term friendships with fellow clerks, as well. These are benefits that many clerks do not fully appreciate until after the clerkship experience is over. Many judges are personally invested in the careers of their clerks, such that hearing about their progress and career direction is always of interest to the judge. Former clerks should make a special point of keeping "their judge" (as they are likely to come to call him or her) apprised of career moves, promotions, or even significant personal events such as the birth of a child. Many judges have reunions at which former clerks dine and visit with the judge and other current and former clerks. These are wonderful networking opportunities, as well as opportunities to cultivate friendships further. In fact, the attorney should consider whether his current law firm would pay for, or at least be supportive of, trips to reunions as part of a marketing venture. It is often hard for a clerk to imagine that the judge, an authority figure whom he holds in high esteem, will ever be a personal friend but, as the attorney and judge correspond about professional and family matters over time, a friendship may develop. As part of the reciprocity that any real friendship requires, former clerks should make a point of keeping tabs on their judges' professional lives as well. The clerk might let her judge know that she knows, and cares, that her judge has been appointed to a different bench or that the judge's name has been mentioned in connection with a confirmation proceeding as the judge advances up the judicial ladder.

A judge invests in the careers of his or her clerks for other reasons, too. A judge's name will be on a clerk's résumé for the clerk's entire professional life. Subsequent employers know that that particular judge is the one who played an initial and important role in training this lawyer, and perhaps shaped much of the way the lawyer thinks about the law. In many ways, the lawyer's legal competency and professional ethics reflect on the judge with whom she clerked. Judges recognize the responsibility that goes along with having such an influential role in a lawyer's professional life and, for that reason, many judges take the time to mentor their clerks.

There are few real drawbacks to a judicial clerkship. Although the pay is certainly less than a large law-firm salary, the clerk may find that this disparity is reduced when a firm gives her credit for the year she spent as a judicial clerk, such that she joins the law firm as a second-year attorney who is paid a second-year salary. Judicial clerks are paid a livable wage, and the clerk is likely to be eligible for deferment of student loans, which should ease some immediate money concerns. Some law students might hesitate to take clerkships because they do not wish to delay doing what they believe to be "real" legal work. This temptation is often particularly great if the student plans to join a firm that will not give her, as a new attorney, credit toward partnership for her year or two of experience as a judicial clerk. In evaluating their options, students should keep in mind that the year and pay level at which they are hired is not necessarily where they will remain for the duration of the partnership track. Therefore, a law student might consider accepting an offer with a firm that does not give credit for judicial clerkships, and taking the clerkship anyway. Then, upon joining the firm, the new lawyer should do her best to demonstrate superior experience and knowledge that is worthy of an additional year of pay or credit. She can revisit the issue during the firm review period and, if the facts warrant it, request to be elevated to the next year level for either pay or partnership purposes.

Many students who would not hesitate to take a one-year clerkship will wonder whether a two-year clerkship is worth the additional investment of time at the lower salary. These doubts may be compounded if the student is planning to join a firm that will give her credit only for the first year, or perhaps will not give clerkship credit at all. During the first year of any clerkship, the clerk is likely to learn a tremendous amount of both substantive and procedural law. By the second year, however, the clerk may feel that she has stagnated and is ready to begin practicing law. Some judges, sensitive to this issue, give additional responsibilities and make particular, enriching opportunities available only to second-year clerks. In other situations, the concern that the second year might be less fruitful than the first may be a valid one; the student must understand that each clerkship, and each judge, is different and must gather facts accordingly.

Another potential downside of a clerkship is that the student may accept a job with a difficult judge. This possibility, although certainly not limited to the clerkship context, is perhaps particularly risky in circumstances in which the employer and employee are likely to be working very closely together. The judge will set the tone for the clerk's experience, and not all judges are clear communicators or competent at being judges, let alone mentors. Some are simply disagreeable on a personal level. These factors, probably more than anything else, are likely to determine the clerk's level of satisfaction. Finally, the clerk's job security may be wholly or partially tied to the success of one, single individual: the judge. During the student's clerkship, the judge may resign (or be forced to resign) from the bench or may get promoted. The clerk's options in each of these situations are discussed towards the end of this chapter.

PROCESS AND APPLICATION

Law schools vary in terms of the importance they attach to clerkships and the support they give to students who are interested in pursuing clerkships. Some schools barely mention to first- or second-year students that clerking opportunities exist and may be worth considering. These schools recognize that few students will be given the opportunity to clerk and thus decide that it is not worth the time or effort to maintain a formal program in the school. Instead, they may rely on professors to encourage top students or others whom the school believes have a chance at a clerkship. Other schools, however, encourage the active pursuit of clerkships. At such schools, in any given year, many, or even most, upperclassmen actively pursue clerkship positions. At these schools, students are made aware early in their legal education of the benefits of clerkships, are given helpful materials such as a checklist for the application, and also receive direct guidance from faculty members and students who are assigned to advise clerkship candidates.

A student or recent law-school graduate who is interested in clerking should begin by consulting the judicial-clerkship resources available at her law school. These resources may include a committee consisting of faculty and students, or an employee who was hired solely to assist students with judicial clerkships. At schools at which judicial clerkships are not actively promoted, helpful resources may nevertheless be available in the career-services office or law-school library. The following section describes the clerkship resources that these various people or entities are likely to maintain.

Students should keep in mind that some schools have formalized the process such that interested students must register with the person or persons in charge of clerkships. This registry may not be available to those who have already graduated from the law school, however. This formal approach makes it possible for schools to track who is applying for clerkships and where, as well as to be aware of the students who are interested in clerkships, in the event that a judge approaches the school for a recommendation or a new judge is appointed or elected. Regardless of whether the school has a formal clerkship-support program, schools almost always appreciate clerkship candidates' efforts to apprise them of their continuing interest, employment status, pending interviews, and, of course, acceptance of clerkship positions.

Some schools maintain a database of information about federal judges, and possibly state judges as well. The information collected may include newspaper articles about these judges or particularly interesting cases handled or managed by them. Some databases also include information about living in the city where the court is located or where the judge hears cases, which may be two different places. In addition, law schools may maintain files on individual judges that include a statement or detailed description of the experiences that previous students from the school had with them. Law firms often maintain such dossiers as well, although lawyers are circumspect about the information that they are willing to share, and may be reluctant to allow themselves to be attributed as sources of such opinions. Former clerks may be especially cautious in giving negative information about their former employer; thus, an interested candidate may find it difficult to build a full picture of what her daily professional life would be like, working for an individual judge. Nevertheless, students still benefit from having access to information about individual judges; reviewing this information gives an interested student a glimpse of the daily workings of a particular court and perhaps even a description of a given judge's judicial temperament. The information contained in these databases also often makes it possible for interested students to contact former clerks and speak with them directly about their experiences, thus getting a better understanding of the skills that the judge values.

Some law schools maintain a Web site or other source listing the judges who have previously hired clerks from that school. These sites generally include the name of the clerk and the year in which the clerk worked for the judge. This information allows students to locate judges who have a solid connection with the school, and it gives candidates an opportunity to speak with former clerks about the nature of their experience with each particular judge. The student may also be able to identify judges who have other connections with the school—perhaps the judge taught at the law school at one time, currently teaches there as an adjunct professor, or even attended law school there. These, too, are valuable connections; even if the candidate does not directly take advantage of these ties, she should be aware of them. These judges are not only likely to hire their clerks from the law school with which they are affiliated, but may also be willing to provide guidance to students who are seeking clerkships with other judges in the jurisdiction.

In addition to databases and other information that is specific to each school, the school may make available some standard resources that are valuable as a student begins his research. The *Almanac of the Federal Judiciary* is an excellent tool. It not only provides biographical information on every federal judge, but also includes commentary on the judges by lawyers who have appeared before them. The commentary is not composed wholly of thoughtless flattery and empty compliments; rather, many attorneys provide honest, sometimes negative, impressions about their personal experiences before each judge. The *Almanac* also includes selected portions of important or interesting opinions authored by the judges. Westlaw provides an online version of the *Almanac*.

Both Westlaw and LEXIS have databases from which students can access information about federal and state judges. On LEXIS, students may want to check out the NALP Judicial Clerkship Directory, which contains responses to questionnaires submitted to judges. Candidates should know that not all judges respond to these questionnaires, but this is nonetheless a valuable resource. Westlaw, similarly, includes databases relating to judges and judicial clerkships, including an online version of the *Almanac of the Federal Judiciary*, referenced above. In addition, students can use both LEXIS and Westlaw to search legal and general-interest periodicals for articles mentioning particular judges. These resources may be helpful in providing the student with an outsider's view of the judge, including the general public's perception of some of the opinions the judge has authored.

Most schools have some faculty members who have amassed particular knowledge about judges and the clerkship process. Many professors are themselves former clerks and may continue to keep up with their judges, as well as with others in the judiciary. These professors are often interested in supplying the judges with whom they are acquainted with highly talented clerks, a process that works to the benefit of all parties and, at the same time, enhances the prestige of the law school. Professors also sometimes have more generalized connections with the legal community that include knowledge or awareness of individual judges and their reputations. Alternatively, a professor might have law-firm connections in a particular city through which an interested student may be able to gather some basic information about local judges.

Often, schools provide students direct assistance with the logistics of the clerkship-application process itself. Some law schools assist their students in preparing and disseminating videotaped applications. Others provide clerkship-specific guidance on résumé-drafting and interviewing. Some schools will even pay the postage and actually mail letters of recommendation and transcripts for students. It may be important for a student with limited financial resources to know about this assistance in advance, as the school's assistance may permit the student to apply for more clerkship positions than would be possible if the student were fully funding the endeavor herself.

The Internet also affords students a free and relatively quick way to research judicial clerkships and, at some Web sites, even to read personal testimonials from former clerks. One especially helpful site, which is maintained by the federal government, can be found at http://www.uscourts.gov/vacancies/judgevacancy.htm. This site includes up-to-the-day information on judicial vacancies or nominations and may be of particular assistance to a student who decides at the last minute to apply for a clerkship, or whose judge has left the bench for whatever reason, such that the would-be clerk is now out of a job.

In addition to clerkship Web sites created and maintained for the general public, many law schools have posted clerkship information online. There are also law-student Web sites, not affiliated with a specific school, that may provide information relating to clerkships. As with all advice received over the Internet and through any school resource, students should keep in mind that individuals will always be of varied opinions, especially regarding experiences as personal and intensive as clerkships.

Potential clerks should never rely on secondary sources for information relating to application deadlines or the proper spelling of an unusual name. Instead, the student should seek this critical information from an official judiciary Web site, or from the judge's secretary. Some sites of interest include:

https://lawclerks.ao.uscourts.gov (an excellent site that provides a description of the duties of a federal clerk, as well as detailed information about all federal-court clerkship opportunities);

http://judiciary.senate.gov/nominations.cfm (furnishes information relating to federal judicial nominations and recent openings); and

www.uscourts.gov/judbususc/jud.bus.html (provides interesting insight into the business of the federal courts, including the number of cases pending in each jurisdiction, by age of case).

Even the student who does not receive the wholehearted support of her school in seeking a clerkship may find at least one professor or dean who is interested in steering motivated students in that direction. One former clerk indicated that she applied for the position due solely to one professor's encouragement, even taking his advice on where to apply and with whom. Other students in her class, lacking this personal mentoring relationship, were unaware that clerking was a viable opportunity.

Once the student decides that she is interested in a clerkship, she should begin to narrow her search. Some of the factors discussed at the beginning of this chapter will be important in that process; the student should consider her own ultimate goals in deciding where she might wish to clerk. Does she want to litigate, eventually to pursue a clerkship with the highest court in a state or with the Supreme Court, or ultimately to teach? The candidate may also want to consider the areas of the country where she would like to practice. A judicial clerkship provides such excellent exposure to the local legal community that the clerk may well ultimately choose to practice in the jurisdiction where she has clerked. Therefore, having some previous connection with or interest in an area should help the clerk to make a decision among cities, employers, and areas of practice, when his clerkship ends. Another consideration might be salary; a candidate who is supporting a family may find that some state-court clerkships are not a viable option, for financial reasons. The most important general consideration is the following: No candidate should apply to a court where he would not accept a clerkship if it were offered. In other words, students should not apply for any clerkships simply as "safe" bets, even though they may have chosen to take this approach in applying to law schools. It is bad form for a candidate to turn down an offer for any reason other than having accepted an offer with another judge. Even so, as discussed below, a student who has accepted a clerkship with one judge should withdraw his name from consideration for other clerkships as soon as possible. A candidate who declines an offer for any other reason is likely to find that his decision reflects badly on the school and especially on the those professors and attorneys who have chosen to recommend him. Indeed, many professors regard the recommendations they make to judges as a reflection on their own credibility, which becomes damaged when the candidate turns down an offer.

Students might also wish to consider, in evaluating potential clerkship opportunities, the reputation of an individual judge or the bench as a whole in a particular area. In addition, the student might research the likelihood that the judge offering the clerkship will be promoted or, instead, might resign, leaving the clerk without a position. For example, the student might be aware of confirmation proceedings for a more prestigious judgeship (or rumors of an inquiry into allegations of judicial misconduct). Potential clerks might also try to learn whether a judge is balanced in her decision-making, not showing favoritism to plaintiffs or defendants. Clerks who work for judges with a strong bias favoring either side may find that they have difficulty leaving behind their judge's views, both during and after the clerkship. Trial lawyers practicing in a jurisdiction for a significant period of time will have a sense of which judges are heavily biased one way or another and should be able to provide some guidance to interested students.

Many candidates are concerned about the political affiliation of the judges with whom they are interviewing. This should not be a primary consideration; indeed, few judges make decisions on overtly political grounds and even fewer, if any, would instruct a clerk to do the same. Political affiliation is not something that a candidate should bring to the judge's attention, nor should it be a reason to rule out an otherwise excellent clerkship opportunity. Indeed, many judges particularly enjoy working with clerks who provide a different political perspective from their own and these differences sometimes spark productive debate. In sum, there are myriad other factors for a candidate to consider in evaluating those clerkships that may be of interest, but the level and type of court, the candidate's eventual career plans, the judge's reputation, and family considerations should be paramount for most candidates.

After the candidate has identified those clerkships in which she is most interested, she should determine the dates for collecting and sending out her application materials and mark them on a calendar. She should prepare a system for storing information on the courts to which she has applied, as well as the individual judges contacted. The calendar deadlines may differ according to the level of the court, and may also vary between federal and state judges. Thus, the student should begin with a general understanding of application deadlines, and should then fill in more specific dates as she narrows in on particular courts and judges. Federal appellate judges have adopted a more formal plan for hiring law clerks, a move that is supported by many district-court judges. Information about the plan can be found at the following Web sites:

http://www.cadc.uscourts.gov/lawclerk (presents the guidelines as adopted, and lists frequently asked questions about applying for judicial clerkships); and

http://nalp.org/schools/judgefaq.htm (lists the guidelines, and includes endorsements and commentary on the guidelines from law-school deans and others).

The essential provisions of this plan are as follows: Previously, federal judges hired clerks throughout the year, sometimes as early as September or October of the candidates' second year of law school. The new guidelines encourage judges to focus exclusively on students who are in their third year of law school or who are recent graduates. These guidelines are supported not only by the courts, but also by various law-school associations and by the law schools themselves. In fact, schools are promulgating their own internal policies as to when a professor can make a call on behalf of a student or prepare a written recommendation. These guidelines are taken seriously; a judge may notify a law school when a student or professor has acted outside of these directives.

Once the student has identified those clerkships in which she is most interested and has determined the deadlines that will apply to her application process, she should start gathering her application materials and approaching potential references. The student will need an up-to-date résumé, a cover letter, two or three letters of recommendation, a law-school transcript and possibly a college transcript, and a writing sample. Many of the general guidelines for law-student cover letters and résumés, some of which are found in Chapter 3,[1] are equally applicable to the clerkship process. In addition, however, there are some specific considerations that the candidate should keep in mind when applying for judicial clerkships.

As a general matter, timing is very important. For federal clerkships, the application time is governed by the guidelines adopted by the federal appellate judges. For state courts, the timing may be entirely different. Applicants are encouraged to apply early, perhaps a year to a year-and-a-half before the start date for the clerkship, unless the judge has specified other dates after which a student may apply. Applicants who decide, late in the process, to pursue a clerkship should not be discouraged, however. Circumstances change, and these changes sometimes mean that judges of all levels may be looking for qualified law clerks to hire immediately.

It is very important that the student's cover letter include the appropriate salutation. The recipient of the letter should be identified as "The Honorable _____." The body of the letter should begin "Dear Judge _____," unless the judge is a member of the United States Supreme Court or, possibly, a state supreme court justice. In those cases, the first line of the letter should read "Dear Justice _____." Because the appropriate salutation may vary, this information should always be double-checked beforehand, either by calling the court, viewing the court's Web site, or looking up the

---

[1] A more detailed discussion of law-student cover letters and résumés may be found in Carey, *Full Disclosure: The New Lawyer's Must-Read Career Guide* (ALM Publishing 2000).

appropriate form of address in library resources that provide advice on how dignitaries of all types should be addressed. The law-school librarian should be able to help candidates in this regard.

The cover letter should clearly state why the candidate is writing and for what time period he seeks a position. The letter should also state the nature of the materials included and should specify which materials will arrive under separate cover. The candidate's law school, for example, may send sealed letters of recommendation or the student's transcript in a separate mailing. The student may wish to highlight any particular ties to the area in which the judge sits or a close professional connection with the judge. For example, if the candidate is a former student of the judge, that information, which would not be immediately evident from the student's résumé, should be noted in the cover letter. The cover letter should not, however, be used to drop important names or to note political connections that the candidate and judge may have in common. Indeed, doing so is unseemly and may negatively affect the candidate's chances of securing an interview with the judge.

The student may choose to include, as his writing sample, a portion of a law-review note, or the entirety of a shorter document such as a comment. Indeed, many judges view a law-review note or comment as an ideal writing sample. The writing sample should be from seven to twenty pages. If the student either has not participated in a law journal or feels that his law-review work is not the best example of his writing, then the candidate may want to consider using a research memorandum or other scholarly writing that he has prepared. Under no circumstances should the candidate use an opinion drafted by him when he was an intern or clerk for another court, even though the judge in that case may have left that opinion virtually unchanged. Alternatively, the candidate may want to consider submitting a moot-court brief as his writing sample. Many judges will insist that the portion submitted have been drafted solely by the student, rather than as a collaborative effort with the student's moot-court partner. Finally, the candidate may want to use material he prepared while clerking at a law firm. If he chooses to do so, the candidate should select material that was left virtually unchanged by the supervising attorney. The student should redact any references to specific clients or companies. If the law firm will give the candidate permission to use this work product, the candidate may want to consider including a cover page that indicates that the sample was used with the express permission of the firm. The candidate should be sensitive to other concerns, as well, when using client materials as a writing sample. Most important, if this case could ever come before this particular judge on an appeal or transfer, then work product relating to that matter should not be used as a writing sample, at all. The judge's review of such material could compromise the judge's objectivity; furthermore, such conduct would create the appearance of impropriety, which ultimately would reflect badly on the candidate. Indeed, how the candidate prepares his application speaks volumes about his ability to maintain confidentiality and integrity, two qualities that are essential in working with a judge.

The candidate should solicit recommendations from two or three people, at least one of whom should be a law professor or dean. The other one or two recommendations may be from an employer. It would be particularly helpful if at least one person making a recommendation on the candidate's behalf were herself a former clerk. In addition, the student might ask an undergraduate or graduate professor with whom the student had an especially close working relationship for a recommendation. If the candidate worked as an intern with a judge or has another professional relationship with a judge, the student should consider asking that judge for a recommendation, as well. Chapters 3 and 7 include some guidelines for approaching professors about a written recommendation. Many of these suggestions are appropriate when seeking recommendations from other sources, too.

A candidate may consider giving the professor from whom she seeks a recommendation copies of her writing sample, transcript, and résumé, and a list of all judges to whom she is applying. The professor may want to tailor a letter to a particular judge if that professor has a prior relationship with that judge or jurisdiction. Occasionally a judge will make a telephone call to follow up on a letter of recommendation; in such cases, the professor or employer should have some idea of which judges may be calling her.

The student should try to submit all application materials as early in the process as is permissible. The student may also consider continuing to update his application by letter, as appropriate, once the materials are sent. For example, after applying for a clerkship, the candidate may earn excellent grades, may be notified that his law-review comment or note has been selected for publication, or may receive a prestigious award. That information may be useful for the judge and is certainly worthy of being passed along.

The candidate will most likely have an idea, both from his school and from the judge herself, of when the process for interviewing and hiring clerks will begin. The candidate may get a telephone call from either the judge or her secretary to schedule a personal interview. Candidates pay for these in-person interviews out of their own pockets. Students should keep this in mind when deciding where to apply for clerkships and therefore perhaps attempt to schedule interviews for their top clerkship choices as early as possible, and schedule less desirable choices toward the end of the available period. That way, the candidate can maximize the chances of hearing from his top choice without (1) having to withdraw his name from consideration because he has accepted an offer that ranked lower on his list of preferences, or (2) turning down a lower-ranked choice and hoping that another offer is forthcoming. The candidate may, however, ultimately have little or no discretion in scheduling interviews for these highly competitive positions.

Candidates who are chosen for in-person interviews should prepare for them well in advance. The candidate should first research all published facts about the clerkship, many of which can be found at the Web sites referenced above. The candidate should know, for example, whether this clerkship has a specified term and, if so, the duration of that term. He should be familiar with the judge's major opinions. He should also know whether the judge was appointed or elected, and, if elected, when the judge's term ends. The candidate may want to examine newspaper articles that mention the judge, especially those that note any interesting issues surrounding the judge's appointment or election. The candidate should also thoroughly review his own writing sample and résumé, as well as any other writing and research mentioned on his résumé. Some judges like to engage candidates in a semi-substantive legal discussion; if so, any legal matter listed on the candidate's résumé could provide a potential subject for discussion.

The candidate should consider in advance the questions he wishes to ask the judge. He should avoid asking questions that he could have found answers to by doing some basic research. He should also avoid putting the judge on the defensive by discussing the judge's previous hiring practices or penchant for lawyers from particular schools. After reading newspaper articles about the judge, the candidate may have questions about what really occurred behind the scenes in a particularly interesting case; the candidate, however, should not ask these questions. Nor should he ask about a controversial reversal of one of the judge's opinions, or the judge's political leanings or ambitions. In sum, the candidate should exercise good judgment in discussing the subjects raised. For example, he may want to ask the judge about the level of responsibility given to clerks in her court or may wish to inquire about whether clerks have opportunities to hear oral argument in the courtroom from time to time. The questions can certainly be in-depth and substantive, so long as they are kept within the bounds of appropriate subjects.

There is no standard judicial-clerkship interview, so the potential clerk should be prepared for just about anything. The applicant should keep in mind that, if he has been granted an interview, then the judge has probably already determined that he is qualified as far as grades and the other criteria described on his résumé are concerned. Therefore, during the interview, the judge may be interested in more subjective information, particularly because the clerk will work so closely with the judge, the judge's secretary, and other clerks. One clerk recalls interviewing with a judge who asked questions to find out about the candidate's psychological make-up, rather than his legal acumen. The judge wanted to know about the applicant personally, including his ethical standards. The clerk attributed this to the judge's practice of actively trying to surround himself with clerks who had different life experiences from his own, so as to broaden his perspective on the matters before him. Other applicants report being questioned about law-school classes that they particularly liked or disliked and why, about their law-review notes or comments, or about their participation in extracurricular activities. A judge might ask an applicant to describe himself or to assess his own strengths and weaknesses. A judge may also ask where else a candidate has applied for a clerkship, and why the candidate chose particular judges and jurisdictions rather than others. Alternatively, the judge may focus on general matters of law, particularly those with which the judge knows or expects, from the candidate's résumé, the candidate to be familiar. Although the candidate is not expected to know the law in great detail or to predict how motions should be decided, he should be able to discuss the legal issues in his law-review note intelligently and to talk with specificity about the classes he has taken. The interviewing judge may also want to know the areas of law that are of most interest to the candidate and where he plans to live after the clerkship. Many judges seek this information because they prefer clerks who have a strong interest in litigation, such that their clerkship experience will prepare them nicely for their chosen career.

The judge may, in addition to interviewing the candidate, have him communicate or meet with her current staff and law clerks. Some judges do not consider their clerks' opinions in the hiring process, unless the applicant has made a very strong negative impression on one or more of them. Other judges do consider the input of current clerks, and the applicant should certainly assume that his conversation with the judge's current clerks or staff is very much "on the record." To be safe, the applicant should therefore ask only questions that he is certain are appropriate, even if he is invited to "ask anything."

Although it would be impossible to state accurately and in detail what judges look for in clerkship candidates, it is possible to identify some general qualities and skills that any successful clerk should possess. The ability to organize and to manage many different tasks simultaneously is critical. Good time-management skills are very important, and some judges or court administrators will help clerks in this area. In addition, judges will expect their clerks to pay great attention to detail. Furthermore, the ability to communicate clearly and well is extremely important. The clerk deals on a day-to-day basis with court staff, attorneys of all levels of skill and experience, *pro se* parties, court reporters, and even other judges, and must communicate effectively with all of them. Moreover, the clerk must have common sense and must be able to make rational decisions on her own, sometimes on the spot, in handling the matters in her care. Attorneys of both high and low ethical standards will call the clerk and will attempt, either innocently or by design, to get information that is either confidential or requires the clerk to dispense legal advice. The clerk must be able to handle these questions confidently and firmly, and let the attorneys know that she cannot discuss the matter or that the opinion sought involves legal research that the attorney must do himself. To the outside world, the clerk *is* the court; therefore, the clerk must ensure that her communications are both limited and clear.

The applicant should also be skilled at research and writing, because this is what the clerk will spend much of her time doing. It is important to have an adaptable writing style; the opinions drafted by the clerk must reflect the judge's style, not the clerk's. Some clerks spend significant amounts of time in the courtroom listening to matters both exciting and dull. Sometimes, the judge will solicit the clerk's opinion on testimony or evidence that was introduced at court that day. To respond in a way that is helpful to the judge, the clerk will need to pay attention for extended periods of time, even to a matter as unexciting as the fifth motion in a row for entry of default judgment.

After an interview, the student must send a thank-you note to the judge immediately. Just as other employers do, judges sometimes make their decisions quickly. Although the thank-you note is unlikely, on its own, to convince a judge to hire or reject a candidate, sending the note certainly cannot harm his chances of selection. Furthermore, an applicant should regard sending a thank-you note as a matter of simple courtesy and an expression of his appreciation for the time the judge spent talking with him.

When the judge chooses to make an offer, she may ask her secretary to make the call. Some, however, prefer to do this themselves. Many judges expect an immediate response to a clerkship offer. Some will expect the candidate to respond that same day, or even during the telephone call communicating the offer. Judges are generally free to determine both the manner in which an offer is communicated to the candidate and the terms for its acceptance. The reason many judges expect a quick response is not entirely arbitrary, although some of it may stem from the level of respect that is due to the judge as a jurist. Rather, the competition for top students, even from the judge's standpoint, is tough. Often, the judge hires from a list of schools known to her personally, whether from working with graduates of those law schools in the past or from being a graduate of or teacher at those schools. Sometimes, in an effort to secure the best candidates, judges move quickly so that they can make offers to especially promising candidates before other judges hire them.

If the offer comes from a judge who is not at the top of the candidate's list of preferences, then the candidate may think about politely asking the judge whether he might have one business day to consider the offer. During that period, the student should contact other judges with whom he has interviewed, inform them of the offer, and inquire about whether they expect to make decisions soon. This may prod the other, higher-priority judges to extend an offer; alternatively, the candidate may be advised that he should strongly consider the initial offer, indicating that he is unlikely to be offered the higher-priority clerkship.

In making this final determination, what should the potential clerk consider? Before submitting his applications, the candidate should already have ruled out those that he knows he will not accept. Therefore, once he has applied for a clerkship, matters such as location should not be a basis for declining an offer. In making his decision, the candidate might consider judicial temperament and the overall reputation of the judge. Again, however, these are matters that he should already have considered. Thus, after the application and the interview process, the most important remaining consideration may be whether the applicant seemed to get along well with the judge, such that he can imagine himself in a close working relationship with this person. In making this decision, the applicant should consider his impression of the judge and her clerks from meeting with them.

If the candidate accepts a position with a judge, he should immediately send a withdrawal letter to every other judge with whom he has interviewed. The letter should be polite and appreciative. The candidate may want to consider telling the judge where he has accepted a clerkship. In addition to these letters, which should be considered obligatory, the candidate may want to send withdrawal letters to other judges who are perhaps actively considering him for an interview, thereby avoiding the embarrassing situation of having a judge call to schedule an interview and having to inform the judge that the candidate has already accepted a position. A withdrawal letter is not necessary in the situation in which the candidate is not under active consideration or when a significant amount of time has passed between the time the materials were submitted and the candidate last heard from the court, and no interview has been scheduled.

Once the candidate has accepted a position, there are still outside circumstances that could affect his clerkship. The judge may, for example, resign her judicial appointment due to poor health, a promotion, or scandal. If this occurs, the clerk should look first to the judge for direction; the judge may plan to bring the clerk along to the appellate level, if a promotion is the reason for the departure, or may recommend that her successor interview the candidate. Alternatively, the judge may offer advice or help in interviewing for other vacancies.

A judicial clerkship can be a valuable and enriching experience. It is one of the few times in a lawyer's career when a lawyer can review the facts and balance the law without having to advocate for a position in which she might not believe. The overall benefits of such an experience cannot easily be achieved in practice, which makes the experience one that most law students should at least consider.

ADVANCED LAW-DEGREE PROGRAMS

Another option for a recent law-school graduate or a practicing attorney is an LL.M., a masters degree in the law. The terminology is somewhat confusing; although the student has already received a J.D., or *juris doctor,* the post-graduate degree is called a master's degree. There is also a third law degree: the J.S.D. or S.J.D., depending on the institution conferring it. The J.S.D. or S.J.D. is the academic doctorate in law, as compared to the J.D., which is the professional degree required for the practice of law.

While the S.J.D. or J.S.D. is almost always a scholarly degree and the J.D. is a professional degree, the LL.M. may be either or both. Some law-school graduates choose to pursue an LL.M. so as to develop expertise in a specialized area, such as tax law. Many top-level tax departments expect or even require this degree, and some will be willing to pay the student's tuition for an LL.M. if the student has already accepted a position with the firm. The LL.M., thus, is an additional credential for the practice of law. In this case, the student will spend the period of the LL.M. program, typically a year, fine-tuning very specific skills and knowledge in preparation for practice.

For others, the LL.M. is the gateway to a career as an academician. Indeed, some law-school graduates seek to get an LL.M. from a particularly prestigious school so as to supplement their existing academic credentials when looking for employment as professors. Again, the LL.M. program is normally a one-year degree, and the student should expect to spend the year honing skills she needs to be a competitive candidate for teaching positions. In addition to coursework that may consist of both required and elective courses, some law schools will require that LL.M. students complete a thesis prior to graduation. A student who is interested in a teaching career should use the thesis requirement to prepare a scholarly article that she can then try to have published.

In sum, there are several ways in which a lawyer can continue her formal professional training after law school. Some of these opportunities, such as a clerkship, afford the graduate many benefits beyond those that could be garnered from classroom learning. Others, such as advanced legal studies, provide the graduate with an opportunity to fine-tune her substantive knowledge and practical skills through specialized coursework.

CHAPTER 16

Ready, Counselor?

This book has covered a lot of law-school ground. It has discussed everything from a prospective student's early preparation at the pre-law stage to the specific concerns of students in their final year of law school. At each stage, and in virtually every chapter, the themes of active learning, personal responsibility, and practical application have been emphasized. Students have been encouraged to think prospectively about their legal careers and to work purposefully towards developing skills, gaining knowledge, and seeking experiences that will round out their professional development. In other words, this book tries to teach the law student how to make law school *relevant* to law practice.

Earning the J.D. degree, and securing and starting a job as an attorney, are simply stages in the professional development of a lawyer. The same comprehensive approach that helps a student to get through law school is also an effective way to conduct one's practice as a lawyer. The difference is that, in actual law practice, the consequences of a lawyer's actions (or inactions) can be more significant—clients can lose money, face jail time, or simply lose faith in the legal system because a matter is badly handled. There can be significant positive results too—a company can be cleared of a charge of unfair or deceptive trade practices, a client accused of a crime can get a fair hearing, or a foreigner can become an American citizen. As a new lawyer contemplates the extraordinary trust that is placed in him by clients, whether individuals or corporations or both, he might easily become overwhelmed. Some new lawyers doubt whether they know enough substantive law, and do not see an easy way to acquire the additional knowledge, training, and experience they need to become comfortable with the practice of law. Many, not for the first or last time, question whether they should even be practicing law. Before these thoughts take root and threaten to derail what can be a wonderfully exciting time in a lawyer's career, it is important for the new law-school graduate to focus on the same comprehensive and practical approach that carried her through law school.

Here are some parting thoughts on how to stay focused.

The concept of active learning is not simply an academic exercise, but, rather, is a valuable lifetime habit. This book has discussed at length how to approach law school comprehensively and why it is important to do so. Active learning provides context and a perspective for learning the law, and brings courses to life. Coursework is more memorable when it is tied to real-life situations that the prospective lawyer has encountered or will encounter. This active approach to learning the law becomes even more important when the student begins the practice of law. Lawyers become better lawyers when they understand the business or economic climate in which their clients operate. Lawyers are better lawyers when they focus on *owning* their field and keeping up with the latest case law or trends in that area and related areas. Such lawyers are better able to strategize with clients about events that may come to fruition years down the road. But acquiring this knowledge takes work. Obtaining this level of expertise involves educating oneself and finding the time to keep on top of the field, even when that broad perspective is not absolutely required in day-to-day practice. An active approach to practice also requires that the lawyer seek to understand the various roles he plays for a client, which change not only with the client's different legal needs, but also for the same client, in the same matter, in perhaps the same meeting. These are just a few examples of what it means to take an active approach to learning, even as a lawyer. Legal education does not end with law school—instead, it is a lifelong exercise, and an intentional endeavor that should be part of a new lawyer's mindset from the very first day of practice.

The concept of taking personal responsibility for one's career is somewhat easier to implement as a law student, but it is much more important once that student becomes a lawyer. In practice, much more than in law school, lawyers face situations that test their commitment to professionalism on a daily basis. Attorneys encounter ethical or moral dilemmas, social situations that throw together their private and professional selves, and supervising attorneys who may or may not care about the lawyer's training and development. The bottom line is this: the lawyer, and only the lawyer, is in charge of her career. It does not matter whether she works for a large firm that purports to train new lawyers or a public or private institution with five layers of supervisors above her. She (and only she) is ultimately responsible for the actions she takes, the papers she signs, and the reputation she develops. This responsibility requires that the lawyer seek certain experiences, find mentors, whether on a formal or informal basis, and adopt a learning mindset. It also requires a healthy dose of appropriate self-confidence.

A sense of personal responsibility is relevant to the attorney's professionalism and his maturity as a lawyer. To the extent that he can exercise control over matters, he must exercise it. Many of the factors that affect the lawyer's reputation, reflect on his judgment, or demonstrate his integrity or a lack thereof, are matters that are within his control. Personal responsibility means acknowledging one's mistakes, learning from them, and not repeating them.

Finally, this book discussed the practical application of law school to lawyering. It suggested some strategies for learning the substantive law and advocating an issue or position. If those strategies worked in law school, then they can be used in practice to prepare for client meetings or discussions with a supervising partner. For example, the student may have found briefing a case or preparing a short information sheet to be useful in law school to distill the essential elements of a matter. Lawyers use those learning strategies too. A lawyer should not feel constrained by handling matters in a certain way or differently from the way she approached them in law school simply because then she was a student and now she is in practice. By the time she graduates from law school, she should have a good sense of her learning style and the devices and strategies that help her to remember important information or concepts. She should rely on these same techniques in practice. Also, just as she did in law school, she should use every situation and experience as a learning tool for her development as a lawyer and a human being. Many attorneys, for example, work with difficult or volatile supervisors. In such a case, the junior attorney might focus on observing management strategies that work or do not work for such a person, and why. Each new attorney ultimately must develop her own management style and sense of ethics, and taking active notice of how others handle these matters is an excellent way for her to develop her own approach.

In short, just as approaching law school comprehensively yields many benefits, so too does approaching the practice of law in the same manner. Having the ability to carry forward those skills and perspectives that the student developed in law school will go a long way toward ensuring her success as a lawyer, no matter how she defines that goal for herself. Successful lawyers know that their connection to and knowledge of their community and of current events and their compassion are at least as important as their technical and analytical proficiency. Such lawyers are skilled, but also satisfied and fulfilled by what they do. Finally, these individuals recognize that the practice of law is a privilege, not a right. They treat the profession, and conduct themselves, in a way that is consistent with the dignity required of the role.

This book began with the question "Does law school matter?" The answer is an unqualified "Yes," so long as each student approaches law school in a deliberate manner and attempts to personalize the experience. Law school will be as relevant to each lawyer's practice as that lawyer seeks to make the endeavor. Law school presents the student with practical learning opportunities from the moment she begins to consider applying, throughout the experience, to graduation and beyond. This process continually presents opportunities to develop the technical skills, the communication skills, and the substantive knowledge and analytical skills that will be required of each lawyer on a daily basis. The experience also provides opportunities to develop appropriate professional discretion, and professional and personal relationships with others who may become future colleagues, clients, judges, business partners, and sources of business. More generally, law school provides the student with the opportunity and the responsibility to begin her practice of law now, in many respects, in law school. In other words, what happens during those three or more years in law school is directly relevant to the practice of law.

Does law school matter? It does, absolutely. Thus, this book closes with a chapter entitled "Ready, Counselor?" This is the question that, traditionally, the judge or bailiff asks of each attorney when a hearing or trial begins. In answering "Ready for the Plaintiff (or Prosecution), Your Honor," or "Ready for the Defense, Your Honor," each lawyer signals that she is fully prepared to present her client's case. This phrase sums up the professionalism, confidence, and readiness that we wish for each student as he or she leaves behind the practice of law school for his or her *own* practice of law.

Contracts Exam

Reproduced here is a Contracts Exam that was designed to be given at the end of the first semester of a two-semester, six-credit Contracts course. Along with the exam itself is a copy of the grading grid that was used to score the exam. In addition, the Appendix includes six "prescriptions," written for individual students, that are intended to explain the students' strengths and weaknesses, both in their understanding of the law and in their test-taking skills, as demonstrated by their performance on this exam. Included are prescriptions for two students who received relatively low scores, two who were near the class average, one in the top 25% of the class, and one who received the highest grade in the course.

CONTRACTS EXAM

Honor Code Pledge: "I HAVE NEITHER GIVEN NOR RECEIVED AID ON THIS EXAMINATION NOR WITNESSED ANY VIOLATION OF THE HONOR CODE." _____ (Exam Number)

(1) This is a three-hour, closed-book examination.

(2) This examination consists of eight pages, including the cover memorandum and all instructions. Please make sure you have the correct number of pages before you begin.

(3) The examination contains three questions. The questions are equally weighted, so you should spend exactly one hour on each. The first two are traditional, complex hypothetical fact patterns, and the last is slightly different.

(4) You have been given an envelope containing a copy of the examination, a packet of statutes for your reference as

needed, and eight pieces of legal-sized paper. Each student must turn *everything* back in (including the examination, the statute packet, your blue books or other materials containing your answers, and all scratch paper) in the envelope I have provided, at the end of the examination. BEFORE YOU DO ANYTHING ELSE, WRITE YOUR EXAMINATION NUMBER ON EVERYTHING—EACH PAGE OF THE EXAMINATION, THE ENVELOPE, YOUR BLUE BOOKS, AND THE SCRATCH PAPER.

(5) Legibility is crucial. Skipping lines and writing on one side of the page will help me read your work if you are writing the exam by hand.

(6) I will read your scratch paper and exam packet in addition to the exam paper or blue books that contain your formal answer to each question. If you jot down something brilliant on the exam packet or your scratch paper that does not make it into your formal answer, I will find it and give you credit.

QUESTION ONE:

Analyze the contract-law issues raised by the following fact pattern:

Mild-mannered Contracts professor Katherine Cason had decided to change her image. Tired of wearing suits—and the occasional cowboy hat—she decided to purchase a Harley-Davidson V-Rod motorcycle for driving around the small college town of Rome, where she worked. She had been to view "her" bike several times already. It was two-toned black, a special, limited edition that was hard to find. During each visit, she sat on the bike, admired her reflection in the mirror, and even tried on all of the necessary accoutrements, such as a helmet. Each time, sales manager Frank Alexander would attempt to put the hard sell on her, mentioning the favorable interest rates that were then available and the fact that no payment would be required of her for the next six months, if she were to purchase the bike now. One time, he even went so far as to run a credit check, with her permission; to give her an exact quote on the motorcycle as she wished to have it accessorized; and to let her know how much her monthly payments would be, if she paid 10% of the purchase price down. Each time they had this exchange, Cason neither expressly agreed to nor disagreed with the terms that were quoted to her, but simply smiled and said, "Those sound like very favorable terms." The sales manager responded by saying, "And this is definitely *your* bike." Whenever he would say this, she would reply, "I'm counting on that. Don't you dare sell this bike to anyone else."

The last time this exchange occurred, Cason decided that she really ought to get some of the sales manager's statements in writing. Therefore, before she got to the dealership that day, she wrote down the terms as she remembered them—well, almost as she remembered them. She changed the 10% down payment to a 5% down payment and left the monthly payments the same. She handed the piece of paper to the sales manager without mentioning this change, and he signed it, "F.A. Live Fast, Die Young." He did not read the piece of paper before he signed it, but said, "I trust you. You're a lawyer, after all." She responded by saying, "And this is just a quote. We can work out any details— like the warranty—later."

The next morning, Cason decided to purchase the motorcycle. On her way to the dealership, she stopped at Leon's Leather Shop and purchased an entire black leather outfit to go with her new bike. The clothes were not returnable, but the price was excellent. Besides, she could afford to make this purchase because she knew that the first payment on her bike would not be due for six months. When she arrived at the dealership, to her dismay, she found that her bike had been sold. Although another V-Rod was available, it was electric blue and did not look good with her new clothes. In addition, the sales manager indicated that he was not willing to sell her this other bike on the terms that they had discussed before. Instead, he was now requiring a 15% deposit, and the six-month deferred-payment option was no longer available to her.

QUESTION TWO:

Analyze the contract-law issues raised by the following fact pattern:

Ichabod Crane, the local eccentric, never had any friends. He was, quite frankly, not an unpleasant person, but he had never put much effort into attempting to be sociable. Therefore, when he won the lottery one day, he decided to buy some friends. To accomplish this feat, he walked through the streets of the city where he lived and promised to pay $10,000 to each person who would be his friend. Because he had never had any friends before and wanted to make sure that his new friendships were lasting ones, he said to each person, "Don't promise that you will be my friend. Instead, be my friend, and I will pay you $10,000." A large crowd of people who indicated that they were interested in being his friends soon surrounded Ichabod.

After Ichabod had assembled a sufficient number of friends (he thought a dozen was plenty), he realized that this endeavor would leave him with a great deal of money left over. Therefore, he continued walking through the city and looking for ways to dispose of the rest of his money. He saw a poor woman with her child, both of whom were hungry and cold, and he decided that he wanted to give them some of his money. When he told them that he would like to give them $10,000, the woman shook her head sadly and said, "We do not accept charity from anyone." He then responded, "If you will consider doing the same for someone else some day when you are able to do so, that will be sufficient compensation as far as I am concerned." She agreed, and he was very pleased, thinking of the reputation he was building for himself as a philanthropist with this generous act. More friendships—and recognition—would soon be his, he believed. Perhaps these two individuals would want to be his friends, too.

After this conversation, Ichabod realized that he still had one piece of unfinished business to take care of in order to set his conscience at rest. He remembered that his high-school English teacher had always treated him kindly, and he decided that he wanted the rest of his money to be hers at his death. He wrote her a letter on his personal stationery, stating as follows:

Dear Mrs. Anderson:

I have come into a significant sum of money. I have not forgotten that you were always so kind to me, spent a great deal of time with me during study hall making sure that I understood Chaucer, and loaned me $10,000 for my medical bills when I was fifteen, which I never repaid. I would like to repay you now. Therefore, I would like you to have whatever remains in my estate when I die, after my bills are paid. My estate should be approximately $1 million. Please let me know, within the next week, whether this will be acceptable.

Best regards,
Ichabod

Mrs. Anderson responded on the seventh day by sending an e-mail to the address printed on his stationery, reading as follows:

Dear Ichabod:

You are too kind. You really shouldn't have. I accept your offer.

Best regards,
Mrs. Anderson

Ichabod never checked that e-mail address, and the electronic-mail system ultimately deleted her reply.

Ichabod died without paying any of the promised sums, and his estate, which totals $4 million and is being administered by greedy distant relatives, refuses to pay either his new "friends," the poor woman, or Mrs.Anderson.

QUESTION THREE:

At its July 2002 meeting, the National Conference of Commissioners on Uniform State Laws approved the following changes to

UCC § 2-206 and § 2-207. These changes are intended to address what we have referred to in class as "the battle of the forms." At this time, the legislatures of the various states are expected to begin considering whether they wish to adopt these amendments to the version of Article 2 that each has codified.

Imagine that you are working as an intern for your state's General Assembly during its 20__ legislative session and have been asked to review and comment upon these proposed changes. First, exactly what is the effect of each change, in terms of the contract-law analysis that is to be applied to a battle-of-the-forms problem? Second, if you were asked to make a recommendation to the legislature as to whether it should keep the current versions of § 2-206 and § 2-207 intact or adopt the new versions, what advice would you give and why? You can ignore the reference in § 2-207 to § 2-202.

SECTION 2-206. OFFER AND ACCEPTANCE IN FORMATION OF CONTRACT.

(1) Unless otherwise unambiguously indicated by the language or circumstances

    (a) an offer to make a contract shall be construed as inviting acceptance in any manner and by any medium reasonable in the circumstances;

    (b) an order or other offer to buy goods for prompt or current shipment shall be construed as inviting acceptance either by a prompt promise to ship or by the prompt or current shipment of conforming or non-conforming goods, but ~~such a~~ the shipment of non-conforming goods does not constitute an acceptance if the seller seasonably notifies the buyer that the shipment is offered only as an accommodation to the buyer.

(2) Where the beginning of a requested performance is a reasonable mode of acceptance an offeror ~~who~~ that is not notified of acceptance within a reasonable time may treat the offer as having lapsed before acceptance.

(3) A definite and seasonable expression of acceptance in a record operates as an acceptance even if it contains terms additional to or different from the offer.

SECTION 2-207. ~~ADDITIONAL TERMS IN ACCEPTANCE OR~~ TERMS OF CONTRACT; EFFECT OF CONFIRMATION.

~~(1) A definite and seasonable expression of acceptance or a written confirmation which is sent within a reasonable time operates as an acceptance even though it states terms additional to or different from those offered or agreed upon, unless acceptance is expressly made conditional on assent to the additional or different terms.~~

(2) The additional terms are to be construed as proposals for addition to the contract. Between merchants such terms become part of the contract unless:
    (a) the offer expressly limits acceptance to the terms of the offer;
    (b) they materially alter it; or
    (c) notification of objection to them has already been given or is given within a reasonable time after notice of them is received.

(3) Conduct by both parties which recognizes the existence of a contract is sufficient to establish a contract for sale although the writings of the parties do not otherwise establish a contract. In such case the terms of the particular contract consist of those terms on which the writings of the parties agree, together with any supplementary terms incorporated under any other provisions of this Act.

If (i) conduct by both parties recognizes the existence of a contract although their records do not otherwise establish a contract, (ii) a contract is formed by an offer and acceptance, or (iii) a contract formed in any manner is confirmed by a record that contains terms additional to or different from those in the contract being confirmed, the terms of the contract, subject to Section 2-202, are:

(a) terms that appear in the records of both parties;

(b) terms, whether in a record or not, to which both parties agree; and

(c) terms supplied or incorporated under any provision of this Act.

CONTRACTS GRADING GRID

Exam No. _____

Total Raw Score: _____

QUESTION ONE:

◊ Trips to view the bike
  ◊ Were the parties simply engaging in preliminary negotiations?
  ◊ Did the parties enter into an oral contract?
    ◊ Offer
    ◊ Acceptance
    ◊ Consideration
  ◊ This transaction probably implicated the UCC Statute of Frauds because it involved a sale of goods for $500 or more

◊ The writing and the Statute of Frauds
  ◊ Was the writing sufficient to satisfy the SoF?
    ◊ The writing was informal, but this is not generally problematic
    ◊ The sales manager's initials would suffice as his signature
    ◊ The writing was, as the law requires, signed by the person who is now being sued
  ◊ Even if the writing were not sufficient to satisfy the Statute of Frauds, there is a promissory estoppel exception for the Statute of Frauds, if Cason engaged in reasonably foreseeable detrimental reliance.

◊ Could the writing serve other functions?

◊ Could it be construed as a letter of intent?

◊ Could it be construed as an agreement to agree?

◊ Because Cason is a contracts professor, perhaps she should be held to a higher standard of conduct or level of knowledge.

  ◊ When Cason changed the terms of the contract, did her behavior amount to fraud in the factum or fraudulent inducement?

  ◊ How is this question affected by Alexander's duty to read the contract for himself and his duty not to rely on an adversary for explanation?

◊ Was there an option contract between the parties?

  ◊ Note that separate consideration is lacking, even if we find an express promise to keep this offer open for a period of time.

  ◊ Under certain circumstances, promissory estoppel can substitute for the separate consideration that is normally required in an option contract, if the plaintiff engaged in reasonably foreseeable detrimental reliance.

Raw Score:

Any Extra Issues Mentioned?

QUESTION TWO:

◊ Ichabod's attempts to make friends

  ◊ Ichabod made several offers to enter into unilateral contracts with others—he requested performance (friendship) for his promise (payment of money).

  ◊ Under classical theory, acceptance would not occur until performance of the promised friendship was complete.

    ◊ This creates difficulties here because what it means to perform "friendship" is so hard to define.

    ◊ Thus, arguably this offer is too ambiguous to be enforced.

  ◊ Under modern theory, assuming that the offer is valid, an option contract will be created, pursuant to Restatement 45, when part performance of the promised friendship is made.

◊ When this occurs, Ichabod is estopped from revoking his offer, and must allow the offerees a reasonable time to complete performance.

◊ The consideration promised here was unusual because it seems to be a bad business decision—an exchange of a great deal of money for something relatively small (friendship).

◊ However, unless this promise is sham, illusory, or a condition for a gift, the law will enforce a bad business decision. Economic adequacy is not required for the consideration to be deemed legally sufficient.

◊ Ichabod's transaction with the woman and child

◊ This may simply be an attempt to confer a gift disguised as a contract—he wanted to make a gift, she would not accept it, and now he is trying to couch the gift in the language of contract to make it more palatable to her.

◊ Alternatively, his request may call for illusory consideration because she does not really have to perform in exchange for his promise—instead, she can choose to perform or not to do so, and he has promised to pay in either event.

◊ This may also be, like Professor Williston's overcoat hypothetical, a mere condition for a gift, if we find that her return promise is not really the price of the gift, but is incidental performance that is requested so that he can confer a gift.

◊ Even if Ichabod desires a reputation as a philanthropist, this secret wish cannot constitute consideration for the parties' contract—instead, this merely lets us know Ichabod's motive in making the offer.

◊ The transaction with the English teacher

◊ When he promises to pay her for something that she did in the past for him, this promise is unenforceable because it is supported only by past consideration—there is nothing new that she must do to receive the promised performance on his part.

◊ This promise may, however, be enforceable under a theory of promissory restitution
  ◊ One could argue that Ichabod is making an after-the-fact promise in exchange for material benefit that he received from his English teacher many years ago. This, generally, will be enforceable in courts that recognize promissory restitution.
  ◊ To the extent, however, that the court deems the value now promised to be disproportionate to the value that was given many years ago, the court may decline to enforce the promise.
  ◊ Promissory restitution is one way to enforce promises that otherwise are supported only by moral consideration.
  ◊ To the extent that Mrs. Anderson was merely fulfilling a pre-existing duty, however, this promise should not be enforced under promissory restitution.
◊ An argument could be made that Ichabod made a promise to enter into an option contract with his English teacher.
  ◊ There is, however, no separate consideration for any such option contract.
◊ If we can show that Ichabod was unjustly enriched by accepting the benefits his English teacher conveyed to him, in that he accepted and kept the benefits she conferred on him, knowing that they were not intended as a gift, then we might argue that he should be required to reimburse her under a theory of restitution even if he made no enforceable promise to pay her.
◊ When he makes this offer to his teacher, one could argue that, because the offer is so clearly beneficial to her, her acceptance could be implied by silence, because no reasonable person would reject the offer.
  ◊ This argument is weakened somewhat by the fact that he expressly requests acceptance, however.
◊ When she sent her acceptance, whether it is valid may depend on whether it is protected by the mailbox rule.

◊ Courts are split on whether the mailbox rule applies to e-mail.

◊ In addition, courts are split on whether the mailbox rule applies to option contracts.

◊ If the mailbox rule does apply, then Mrs. Anderson should be able to show that it was reasonable for her to respond by e-mail to an offer sent by mail because (1) it was faster than the mail and (2) Ichabod's stationery included the e-mail address, thus making it reasonable that she would use it.

◊ If the mailbox rule does not apply, then like all other elements of contract formation, the acceptance was to be valid on receipt.

◊ Arguably, this acceptance was never received. This depends on whether receipt into an in-box is deemed to constitute receipt.

◊ When Mrs. Anderson paid for Ichabod's medical services when he was in school, this was a contract of a minor, and contractual promises of minors generally are voidable.

◊ The minor can seek to disaffirm the promise within a reasonable time after obtaining majority.

◊ If he does not do so, the promise is deemed to be affirmed.

◊ He affirmed this promise, but much later.

◊ In addition, these medical services may be the kind of "necessities" for which minors will be required to pay (along with shelter and food) even if they do not affirm their agreement to do so.

Raw Score:

Any Extra Issues Mentioned?

QUESTION THREE:

◊ Effect of Changes

◊ Changes to § 2-206

◊ Changes to § 2-207

◊ Recommendations

◊ Changes to § 2-206

◊ Changes to § 2-207

Raw Score:

Any Extra Issues Mentioned?

PRESCRIPTIONS

This student received a relatively low score. Her legal analysis was quite good, but she identified and analyzed fewer issues than most of her colleagues.

Exam No. 1639 (Cynthia Y.)

There were several items that you noticed in the fact pattern and outlined on your exam scratch paper, but that were not included in your formal answer. As I promised the class I would, I gave you credit for these items. This tells me a couple of things: (1) "active reading," which is the process of making informal notes while you read, before crafting a formal answer, seems to work well for you, so I would tend to recommend that you continue doing this; and (2) something (time, perhaps) is keeping you from getting these good thoughts into your formal answer.

To the extent that time is of concern, we need to find a way to free up some time for you during the exam to handle the additional issues that you clearly noted, but did not have time to cover in your formal answer. In addition, there were a number of other issues on the exam that were not covered. We should figure out how to bring those in, as well.

Considering the question of time, I have one specific suggestion. Although your outlining on the exam scratch paper is comprehensive and is substantively quite good, it may have taken too much time away from crafting the final answer and including some additional issues that you might otherwise have had time to cover. If it feels natural to you to mark up the exam paper instead of making notes on the scratch paper, you might be able to do so more quickly.

Here is what I noticed, looking at your exam paper: Everything you handled in your answer, you handled beautifully. Your analytical skills are simply excellent, and each issue you mentioned, you covered comprehensively and insightfully. In short, your answers demonstrated extensive knowledge of contract law and a strong ability to engage in exactly the kind of legal analysis that is required of you. In addition, your answers are particularly well-crafted and well-organized, and both of these qualities make them extremely easy to follow.

Therefore, the only tasks before us this semester, in getting your exam performance more in line with your level of knowledge and ability, involve exam-taking strategy and perhaps time management during the exam.

You have all of the fundamentals well in order for success in Contracts II, and the exam-taking-strategy skills just require some practice.

This student received a relatively low score. Although he did a good job with basic contract-formation issues, his answer did not address some of the more advanced points the class had studied.

Exam No. 1539 (Kip M.)

I like your mnemonic outline very well, and I think that something like this could be very helpful in jogging your memory during the exam to help you make sure not to forget to cover any of the main issues. I wonder, though, whether writing such a comprehensive outline took too much of your time away from reading the fact patterns and outlining your answers. Perhaps a shorter outline would work just as well for next time.

You have a very methodical approach, and that is a good way to navigate through the problems. Your analysis of certain issues is quite good, but you did not cover all of the issues. Along the same lines, your answers are a bit brief, and this seems to be keeping you from covering more of the issues that are raised in the fact pattern. If time constraints were a major factor for you, we should work on freeing up enough time to allow you to cover more of these additional issues. You are doing a very comprehensive job on the foundational contract-formation issues, and I like to see that solid analysis up front, so that is very good. We simply need to make sure that you end up with enough time to get into some of the advanced issues, as well (on this exam, those included fraudulent inducement, option contract, contracts of minors, and some of the finer points of the mailbox rule, for example).

In addition, if it feels natural for you to do so, you might consider marking up the exam paper a bit more while you are reading. This might remind you to cover some of those very detail-oriented points that I mentioned above.

Your answers are very well-organized and easy to follow. In addition, your application of UCC sections and the elements of each cause of action is precise and well-done. Your analytical skills are quite strong. In short, you are in very good shape as far as all of the foundational skills that you will need for success in Contracts II. Therefore, this semester, let us focus on test-taking strategies and issue-spotting practice.

This student's grade was close to the class average.

Exam No. 1916 (Heather N.)

Your issue-spotting in the first question is stronger than in the second question.

Marking up the exam paper and noting issues seems to work well for you—everything you noted was correct, and everything you noted made its way into your exam answer. Therefore, if this process feels natural to you, I would be inclined to recommend that you do even more of this in the future. This is particularly useful in helping you make sure that you do not miss some of the smaller issues—things you might notice when you are reading, but that you might quickly forget if you do not make a note of them. In addition, a mnemonic device might be helpful to make sure that you do not miss any of the larger issues—that way, if you get to the end of the exam and have not covered a major topic, you can go back and look for it.

In the first question, you did get somewhat off-track by mentioning the Battle of the Forms, which was not relevant to this question. Two strategies might help you avoid something like this in the future. First, a practical consideration: As I told the class, I am likely to test each major issue only once on the exam. Therefore, if you had browsed through the exam and noted that Section 2-207 would be the subject of Question Three, you might have known to steer clear of it in Question One. In addition, asking the threshold questions, "Is this a battle of the forms?" and "If so, how do I know this?" might have reminded you that this situation, because it involved only one writing, was not likely to implicate Section 2-207. Sometimes, these strategy tips and threshold questions can keep you from expending resources in going down the wrong path.

Remembering case names and *Restatement*[1] section numbers seems to come naturally to you, and you used them well in your answer. You were able to incorporate both as a form of shorthand that was very effective in allowing you to communicate information efficiently and concisely. I would counsel you to keep up the good work on this front.

Your answers are very well-organized and easy to follow. Although I do not grade on writing style, I do think that good organization generally assists students by reminding them to include everything of importance that they noticed in the fact pattern. In addition, this suggests to me that you did not feel too much time-pressure or stress when taking the exam, which is a good sign.

Your analytical skills are very strong. You clearly have all of the foundational skills you need to do even better on your Contracts II exam. Most of our work should center on test-taking strategies and issue-spotting practice, both of which are relatively easy to refine. You should be in very good stead for Contracts II.

This student's grade was close to the class average.

Exam No. 3617 (Nancy T.)

Marking up the exam paper seems to come naturally to you. Everything you marked on the exam paper was substantively correct (with the exception of your reference to a Battle of the Forms in Question 2). In

---

[1] *Restatement (Second) of Contracts* (1981). The *Restatements* are a product of the American Law Institute, a prestigious private organization that is composed of law professors, practitioners, and judges. The Institute's *Restatements* of the law are heavily relied upon by many courts in stating and interpreting the law.

addition, almost everything you noted on the exam paper made its way into your answer. Therefore, I would tend to recommend that you continue this practice, as it seems to work for you. You may find that, because you have marked up the exam paper itself so thoroughly, it is unnecessary to also make an outline on the scratch paper.

I like your mnemonic outline very well, and I think that something like this could be very helpful in jogging your memory during the exam so that you do not forget to cover any of the main issues. I wonder, though, whether writing such a comprehensive outline took too much of your time away from reading the fact patterns and outlining your answers. Perhaps a shorter outline would work just as well for next time.

Your issue-spotting in the first question is stronger than in the second question. In the first question, you missed only relatively discrete points, such as the promissory-estoppel exception for the statute of frauds and the law professor's greater level of knowledge. In the second question, you spotted all of the major issues except option contract, but you sometimes did not carry your analysis all the way through each issue, once you had spotted it. You will note this when you look at the grading grid and see where you handled contract formation, promissory restitution, and contracts involving juveniles.

Remembering *Restatement* and UCC section numbers seems to come naturally to you, and you used them well in your answer. You were able to incorporate both as a form of shorthand that was very effective in allowing you to communicate information efficiently and concisely. I would counsel you to keep up the good work on this front.

Your answers are very well-organized, well-written, and easy to follow. In addition, you have demonstrated excellent analytical skills. Indeed, everything you wrote was of very high quality—we simply need to find a way to ensure that you handle *all* of the issues in the same strong manner that you have employed for the issues you covered on this exam. Your answers are relatively short and, to the extent that you need to free up some time to allow you to examine additional issues, some of the suggestions I made above regarding shortening your mnemonic process and perhaps cutting out the outlining on scratch paper, in favor of simply marking up the exam paper, may be of assistance for next time.

Your foundational skills are very, very good, and you are in a strong position, both in terms of your substantive knowledge and your analytical skills, as you begin Contracts II.

This student's grade was in the top 25% of the class.

Exam No. 9163 (Caroline J.)

While your answers to Question One and Question Three were quite good (you received 100% of the available points for Question Three), your answer to Question Two was exceptional. Indeed, you garnered the highest number of points in the class for your answer to the second question.

Your issue-spotting skills are very strong. In addition, once you spotted an issue, you were invariably comprehensive in your analysis of it. As you will notice at the bottom of each page of the grading grid, you garnered a number of additional points for your particularly comprehensive treatment of the elements of contract formation in both Question One and Question Two, as well as your analysis of sophisticated, discrete issues in Question Two such as reverse unilateral contract, true unilateral contract, the comparison between Ichabod's offer and an advertisement, and the ambiguity of the meaning of friendship. Indeed, you earned a whopping 9 "bonus" points (out of your total raw score of 26) on the second question.

Those few issues you missed, with the exception of option contract in the second question, generally involved relatively minor matters, such as the level of sophistication of the law professor in Question One and the "necessary item" argument regarding the provision of medical services to a minor in Question Two.

In the first question, you did get somewhat off-track on the Battle of the Forms. Although you quickly noted, near the beginning of that analysis, that there was no real battle of the forms here, you then went on to do a fairly comprehensive analysis of the issue. This may have taken some time away from other issues that you would otherwise have chosen to address in Question One. Two strategies might help you avoid something like this in the future. First, a practical consideration: As I told the class, I am likely to test each major issue only once on the exam.

Therefore, if you had browsed through the exam and noted that § 2-207 would be the subject of Question Three, you might have known to steer clear of it in Question One. In addition, asking the threshold questions, "Is this a battle of the forms?" and "If so, how do I know this?" might have reminded you that this situation, because it involved only one writing, was not likely to implicate § 2-207. Sometimes, these strategy tips and threshold questions can keep you from expending resources in going down the wrong path.

Marking up the exam paper seems to come naturally to you. Everything you marked on the exam paper was substantively correct. In addition, everything you noted on the exam paper made its way into your answer. Therefore, I would tend to recommend that you continue this practice, as it seems to work for you. You may even find that, because you have marked up the exam paper itself so thoroughly, it is unnecessary for you also to make an outline on the scratch paper. If you discover that this second step is unnecessary, then eliminating it will free up some additional time that may allow you to capture the few remaining issues that you did not address this time.

Your answer reads as though you were working hard, but were fairly relaxed—there was even some humor in there, which suggests that you were not experiencing too much stress. Being very well prepared (as you obviously were), yet not too anxious is often the best way to approach an exam.

You are in excellent shape as you begin Contracts II, both in terms of your demonstrated knowledge of the course material and your analytical and writing skills. From here, improvement is simply a matter of refinement and fine-tuning, both of which are likely to come with time and practice. Keep up the good work.

This student received the highest grade in the class.

Exam No. 5791 (Rebecca A.)

Beautiful!

Not only did you spot every single issue on the exam, save one, and earn a large number of bonus points, as well, but you also analyzed the issues comprehensively and very clearly.

Because your writing style is concise, you were able to get a tremendous amount of information down in a very efficient fashion.

Your use of legal terms of art is excellent and very precise.

The outline style seems to work very well for you: your use of shorthand expressions does not get in the way of a complete development of the relevant issues and an appropriate application of the facts.

You have a knack for thinking on paper, and your conversational style makes it possible for me to tell what you are thinking.

You did not miss anything in translation from your notes on the exam paper to the answer you typed. That is rare and impressive and shows careful attention and a methodical approach. It does not appear that you felt overly rushed while you were taking my exam. In addition, I believe your logical organization was of help to you—it appears that you handled the issues, on your exam paper, in the order that you spotted them in the fact pattern. That seems to work very well for you.

You used a lot of *Restatement* sections and UCC sections, and it appears that you have a very good memory for them. This, too, seems to work very well for you. You will find this to be a great advantage in Contracts II, where the UCC and *Restatements* figure much more prominently. In addition, your use of case names seems natural and efficient, and you rattle off elements of each cause of action easily. This, too, helps you keep your answer concise, yet comprehensive.

Prescription for next time—keep up the excellent work, and let us figure out how best to take your obvious strengths—precise use of language, efficient, concise writing, and a very methodical approach—and make them work for you in all of your exams just as well as they did here.

Your answer reads as though you were working hard, but fairly relaxed—there was even some humor in there, which suggests that you were not experiencing too much stress. Being very well prepared (as you obviously were), yet not too anxious is often the best way to approach an exam.

Evidence Exam

Included here is an Evidence exam that was designed to be given at the end of a four-credit Evidence class to be taken by students in their second or third year of law school. Along with the exam itself is a copy of the grading grid that was used to score the exams.

EVIDENCE EXAM

Honor Code Pledge: "I HAVE NEITHER GIVEN NOR RECEIVED AID ON THIS EXAMINATION NOR WITNESSED ANY VIOLATION OF THE HONOR CODE." _____ (Exam Number)

(1)   This is a four-hour, "modified" open-book examination. Students may use required texts, the Federal Rules of Evidence, their class notes and handouts, and any student-created outline or other student work product on the exam. Commercial materials, even those heavily annotated by the student, are not permitted.

(2)   This examination consists of thirteen pages, including the cover memorandum and all instructions. Please make sure you have the correct number of pages before you begin.

(3)   The examination contains four questions. The questions are equally weighted, so you should spend exactly one hour on each. The first three are traditional, complex hypothetical fact patterns, and the last is slightly different.

(4)   You have been given an envelope containing a copy of the examination and eight pieces of legal-sized paper. Each student must turn back in *everything* (including the

examination, the blue books or other materials containing your answers, and all scratch paper) in the envelope I have provided, at the end of the examination. BEFORE YOU DO ANYTHING ELSE, WRITE YOUR EXAMINATION NUMBER ON EVERYTHING—EACH PAGE OF THE EXAMINATION, THE ENVELOPE, YOUR BLUE BOOKS, AND THE SCRATCH PAPER.

(5)   Legibility is crucial. Skipping lines and writing on one side of the page will help me read your work if you are writing the exam by hand.

(6)   I will read your scratch paper and exam packet in addition to the exam paper or blue books that contain your formal answer to each question. If you jot down something brilliant on the exam packet or your scratch paper that does not make it into your formal answer, I will find it and give you credit.

(7)   I will not grade you on spelling, grammar, or style. Feel free to write in outline format. Incomplete sentences are fine so long as they express complete thoughts. Abbreviations are fine so long as I can understand them.

(8)   You are likely to feel time-pressured on this exam. Please do not spend time re-stating the facts. The only facts that should appear in your answer are the ones you use in your analysis.

(9)   I do not deduct points for incorrect answers—I will simply ignore that part of your response.

(10) Show your work. I give a lot of partial credit.

(11) Citing specific rule numbers and case names is optional— just make sure I can understand what you are talking about.

(12) For each question, I recommend that you spend at least ten minutes reading and thinking and outlining your answer before you begin to write.

(13) If you know that you are about to run out of time, do your best to outline the rest of your answer so I can, at least, see

where you were planning to go with the part you were unable to complete.

Good luck and stay in touch.

QUESTION ONE:

Imagine that you are preparing for trial. Analyze the evidentiary issues presented by the following scenario:

There was a collision in an intersection between an automobile and a school bus carrying elementary-school children. Although the drivers of both vehicles were seriously injured, the children were unharmed except for minor cuts and bruises. The automobile had a magnetized sign affixed, reading, "Fred's Fast Pizza Delivery," and twenty steaming pizzas in the back seat. Dennis, the driver, had been en route to the local law school to deliver pizzas to hungry students studying for exams when the accident occurred. He had stopped, however, to pick up his friend Elaine, who lived about five miles out of his way and who had called asking him to give her a ride to the library if he passed through her neighborhood. The accident was less than a mile from where Dennis had picked up Elaine. She was not injured.

When Officer Addison arrived on the scene of the accident about two minutes later, the view from a distance was one of pure carnage. As she approached, however, she realized that what she was seeing was simply that the pizzas were scattered across the road, creating a mess of oregano and tomato sauce. There were only two children remaining on the bus at the time of the collision, and she asked both to describe what occurred. The two children, Blake and Caroline, were both six years old. Blake was visibly shaken and sobbed as he told Officer Addison, "This bus driver never pays attention! The light was red, and she went through anyway." Caroline seemed much calmer, although Officer Addison noted that Caroline's relatively thick glasses had broken in the impact of the crash. Caroline said, "I didn't see whether the light was red or green, but our driver is very careful. I don't think she would ever run a red light."

Officer Addison was also able to take a statement from Dennis while he was bleeding from the head, before he lost consciousness. He said, "I am so sorry. I guess I just wasn't paying attention. I knew if I made another late delivery to the law school that the students would call the store and complain. I have been warned that I would lose my job if the store received one more complaint about me. It didn't help that Elaine was screaming at me to watch out for the bus. I know she meant well, but I probably would have seen the bus if not for her. Please tell my parents I love them."

Dennis recovered, miraculously, and has now joined a monastery in Tibet to escape the stresses of his past life.

The bus driver, Frances, recovered completely—well, almost completely. Because of the incident, she now has panic attacks whenever she smells pizza. Her husband George and two small children have suffered immensely from this injury. They felt vindicated by a recent study citing the deep psychological harm that can be caused by long-term pizza deprivation. (Had they examined the study more closely, however, they would have found that it was financed by the American Pepperoni Council.) Frances also has amnesia regarding the details of the accident. Because Dennis is absent, Frances and her family are suing Fred's Fast Pizza Delivery and Elaine. During his deposition, George made the surprising statement that Frances told him, right after they filed suit on the one-year anniversary of the accident, that she had no idea whether the light was red or green when she went through the intersection. Six months earlier, however, at her lawyer's direction, she had written a three-page, single-spaced account of the accident and her resulting injuries. In that writing, she had clearly stated that the light was green in her favor when she went through the intersection.

Dennis had a prior history of speeding tickets—at least four per year for the ten years since he had begun to drive at age sixteen. It appears that this information may have been known to Fred's Fast when the store hired him. In addition, when he was fifteen, he was arrested for forgery. Finally, last year the store itself had him arrested for taking money from the cash register. After he was convicted and sentenced to three years' probation, and while his conviction was on appeal, Fred prevailed upon the prosecutor to dismiss the action, indicating that it had all been a simple misunderstanding.

QUESTION TWO:

You have recently tried a nailbiter—and lost. The matter involved an educational malpractice suit by a disgruntled student—your client Ms. Natalie Davis—against Mr. Chips, the teacher who taught her to write in cursive. Due to the student's particularly fine penmanship, the student was rejected from every medical school to which she applied. She has now become a lawyer with a practice consisting almost entirely of writing the contracts to be enclosed with new credit cards. Because she speaks almost entirely in "whereas" clauses, she has no friends and few close acquaintances. Her suit focused on the emotional distress to which this way of life had subjected her. In examining the record for appeal, analyze the evidentiary issues raised by the following:

During your opponent's opening statement, his attorney repeatedly referred to your client as "that whining lawyer." This characterization appeared to resonate strongly with the jury, which consisted of twelve retired schoolteachers, three of whom rapped their rulers, which they carried with them at all times to correct unsuspecting youngsters wherever they might be, against the jury box in sympathy every time this phrase was repeated. You had become stuck with this jury because, during *voir dire*, you had not been permitted to ask a single question regarding the attitudes of potential jurors about lawyers and teachers.

The direct examination of Mr. Chips began right after lunch on the second day of trial. Opposing counsel got his client to introduce himself to the jury by describing his teaching awards and his extensive involvement in the community, particularly with the Humane Society and with his church. The attorney elicited these remarks by inviting his client to "tell the jury about [his] marvelous teaching awards" and so forth. After this introduction, opposing counsel asked only one more question—"So, what's this case about?"—before falling soundly asleep. In response to that one question, Mr. Chips rambled on for the rest of the afternoon. He described his childhood in the plains of West Texas, his calling to become a teacher, his education and training, and what little he remembered of having the plaintiff in his class. Because he could not remember having taught penmanship to her, he described, in great detail, his general method of teaching the material. He was careful to emphasize the fact that he tries never to cramp students' natural handwriting style. Indeed, he claimed that he often actively encouraged students with poor penmanship to maintain their individuality. As this testimony wound on interminably, you objected several times, although Mr. Chips' attorney did not notice. He had his head on his trial notebook and was snoring softly. Each time you objected, the judge responded, "For crying out loud, let the man finish his story." Then, she would turn to the witness and say, "I apologize for that very rude interruption. Please do continue, Mr. Chips."

When you were finally able to cross-examine Mr. Chips, you sought to confront him with a portion of his deposition testimony in which he had stated, "Good handwriting is essential for all young men and women. I know what good handwriting is, and I will stand for nothing less from my students. Even if they can't write when they enter my class, they will be able to write when they leave." During this dramatic moment in the trial, just before you handed Mr. Chips the relevant portion of the transcript, your opposing counsel began to snore much louder than before. Misinterpreting one of his louder snores as an objection, the judge responded, "Sustained." She then turned to you and said, "You are badgering the witness. Please move on to something else." Before complying with the judge's request, you requested a sidebar conference to explain the critical—and highly relevant—nature of your line of questioning. She responded with a yawn: "I really don't want to hear about it. You whine as much as your client does. Just move on."

During his case in chief, Mr. Chips presented a handwriting expert who testified that whether a person's handwriting is neat or messy is entirely genetic and has nothing to do with the way in which she is taught. The expert closed his testimony by turning to the jury and saying earnestly, "You know the right thing to do here." In addition, Mr. Chips called your client's mother to the stand, and she testified that your client's handwriting really wasn't that neat anyway. In fact, she indicated that she thought your client had been rejected from medical school because she didn't apply herself, unlike her brother Herman, who is now a successful podiatrist. Your efforts to exclude the testimony of both witnesses as not being helpful to the trier of fact were fruitless.

Opposing counsel finished his closing argument by stating, "Ladies and Gentleman, you have now heard it from every witness that

Ms. Davis is a whiner. Even her own mother said so." When you objected that your opponent was arguing facts not in evidence, the judge responded, "He's sleepy. Give him a break."

Finally, you have heard that, during deliberations, the jury itself called several medical schools to ask about their applications requirements. Specifically, the jury wished to know whether a handwriting sample was requested from each applicant. Each school indicated that it was not.

QUESTION THREE:

Jerrie Carpenter, a very spoiled and tuna-loving housecat, has been arrested for the theft of a can of organic albacore tuna from the kitchen of his owner and is currently awaiting trial. Assuming that both criminal law and the law of evidence apply to housecats in the same way that they do to humans in this jurisdiction, analyze the evidentiary issues raised by the following:

Shortly after his arrest, Jerrie was read his *Miranda* rights and called his lawyer. As he awaited the arrival of his attorney, the arresting officer attempted to ply him with catnip to get him to talk. The catnip got him to purr, but not to talk—at least not until later, when he apparently confessed the crime to his cellmate Max, a giant schnauzer who had the ear of the prosecutor. Jerrie now claims that the confession was obtained in violation of his Fifth Amendment rights. In addition, Jerrie wishes to show that Max was trying to obtain extra Milkbones through his cooperation with the prosecutor.

At trial, Jerrie's lawyer wishes to introduce evidence that the crime actually bears the hallmarks of the work of Jerrie's brother Teazer. Indeed, the defense lawyer wishes to show, such a snatch-and-grab could only be the work of the relatively nimble, twelve-pound Teazer, not his twenty-something-pound big brother. In fact, she has created a trial exhibit comparing the leaping abilities of both cats. Although it is not to scale, it is intended to convince the jury that Teazer can get almost twice the height of Jerrie. Only Teazer, the defense wishes to show, could have reached the kitchen counter in question. In fact, the defense believes this fact will be abundantly clear to any person who has seen Jerrie and wishes to ask the court to take judicial notice of this information.

Unfortunately for the prosecution, there are some problems with the evidence. Specifically, there has been significant difficulty in showing that the tuna can that is in police custody is the very tuna can that was purloined and is now the subject of the criminal case against Jerrie. Although the can shows clearly that the tuna is of the same brand and type that Jerrie's owner purchased regularly, the pawprints have now been wiped clean. When the can was first brought into police headquarters, it was to be processed and tagged. Unfortunately, the lead forensic investigator in the animal crimes section left the door open when she left the lab that night, and several of the sheepdogs who patrolled the halls had access to the can and its contents. When the investigator returned the following morning, she found several marks that looked like nose-smudges, but nothing that resembled a pawprint. The can was otherwise licked clean.

In addition, the surveillance photograph that captured the culprit shows nothing but a blur of white fur. As both cats in the household are white and of the same breed, it is not possible for unskilled laypersons to tell which cat took the tuna, despite the significant size differential in the animals. Although the cats' owner has the requisite skill to identify the pictured animal, she refuses to cooperate with the prosecution. If the jurors were to look closely at the photograph, however, they would be able to see a flash of blue. The testimony will establish that Teazer always wears a blue collar, while Jerrie's collar is always red.

Finally, there is Max's account of the confession itself. Although Max immediately wrote down everything he allegedly heard from Jerrie, the original document became so soiled with Milkbones and schnauzer drool that it became totally illegible. The document then disappeared. The prosecution believes Max may have eaten the writing but also embraces the possibility that Jerrie's owner absconded with the document to protect her cat. Therefore, the prosecution wishes to have Max testify as to his memory of the confession, which is extremely poor. The defense wishes to have Max's testimony excluded as unduly prejudicial. Specifically, the defense is concerned that, due to Max's superior skills in making puppy-dog eyes at the jury, the jury will simply believe anything Max says.

QUESTION FOUR:

Thirty-eight states have adopted the Uniform Rules of Evidence, a body of evidence law prepared by the National Conference of Commissioners on Uniform State Laws, the same body that promulgated the Uniform Commercial Code and that collaborates with the American Law Institute in preparing the *Restatements*. In most respects, the Uniform Rules of Evidence closely track the Federal Rules of Evidence. Indeed, in many cases, the two are identical. Rules 104 and 702, however, divert from this pattern, as each Uniform Rule is different, in at least one significant way, from the Federal Rule on point. Both versions of each rule are reproduced below. First, identify the material differences between each Uniform and Federal Rule. Second, analyze the practical effect of each difference. Third, express a considered opinion as to which rule, in each case, represents a more appropriate expression of public policy.

UNIFORM RULES OF EVIDENCE, RULE 104. PRELIMINARY QUESTIONS.

(a) *Questions of admissibility generally.* Preliminary questions concerning the qualification of an individual to be a witness, the existence of a privilege, or the admissibility of evidence must be determined by the court, subject to subdivision (b). In making its determination, the court is not bound by the rules of evidence except the rules with respect to privileges.

(b) *Determination of privilege.* A person claiming a privilege must prove that the conditions prerequisite to the existence of the privilege are more probably true than not. A person claiming an exception to a privilege must prove that the conditions prerequisite to the applicability of the exception are more probably true than not. If there is a factual basis to support a good faith belief that a review of the allegedly privileged material is necessary, the court, in making its determination, may review the material outside the presence of any other person.

(c) *Relevancy conditioned on fact.* If the relevancy of evidence depends upon the fulfillment of a condition of fact, the court shall admit it upon, in the court's discretion, or subject to, the introduction of evidence sufficient to support a finding of the fulfillment of the condition.

(d) *Hearing of jury.* A hearing on the admissibility of a confession in a criminal case must be conducted out of the hearing of the jury. A hearing on any other preliminary matter must be so conducted if the interests of justice require or, in a criminal case, an accused is a witness and so requests.

(e) *Testimony by accused.* An accused, by testifying upon a preliminary matter, does not become subject to cross-examination as to other issues in the case.

(f) *Weight and credibility.* This rule does not limit the right of a party to introduce before the jury evidence relevant to weight or credibility.

FEDERAL RULES OF EVIDENCE, RULE 104. PRELIMINARY QUESTIONS.

(a) *Questions of admissibility generally.* Preliminary questions concerning the qualification of a person to be a witness, the existence of a privilege, or the admissibility of evidence shall be determined by the court, subject to the provisions of subdivision (b). In making its determination it is not bound by the rules of evidence except those with respect to privileges.

(b) *Relevancy conditioned on fact.* When the relevancy of evidence depends upon the fulfillment of a condition of fact, the court shall admit it upon, or subject to, the introduction of evidence sufficient to support a finding of the fulfillment of the condition.

(c) *Hearing of jury.* Hearings on the admissibility of confessions shall in all cases be conducted out of the hearing of the jury. Hearings on other preliminary matters shall be so conducted when the interests of justice require, or when an accused is a witness and so requests.

(d) *Testimony by accused.* The accused does not, by testifying upon a preliminary matter, become subject to cross-examination as to other issues in the case.

(e) *Weight and credibility.* This rule does not limit the right of a party to introduce before the jury evidence relevant to weight or credibility.

UNIFORM RULES OF EVIDENCE, RULE 702. TESTIMONY BY EXPERTS.

(a) *General rule.* If a witness's testimony is based on scientific, technical, or other specialized knowledge, the witness may testify in the form of opinion or otherwise if the court determines the following are satisfied:

(1) the testimony will assist the trier of fact to understand evidence or determine a fact in issue;

(2) the witness is qualified by knowledge, skill, experience, training, or education as an expert in the scientific, technical, or other specialized field;

(3) the testimony is based upon principles or methods that are reasonably reliable, as established under subdivision (b), (c), (d), or (e);

(4) the testimony is based upon sufficient and reliable facts or data; and

(5) the witness has applied the principles or methods reliably to the facts of the case.

(b) *Reliability deemed to exist.* A principle or method is reasonably reliable if its reliability has been established by controlling legislation or judicial decision.

(c) *Presumption of reliability.* A principle or method is presumed to be reasonably reliable if it has substantial acceptance within the relevant scientific, technical, or specialized community. A party may rebut the presumption by proving that it is more probable than not that the principle or method is not reasonably reliable.

(d) *Presumption of unreliability.* A principle or method is presumed not to be reasonably reliable if it does not have substantial acceptance within the relevant scientific, technical, or specialized community. A party may rebut the presumption by proving that it is more probable than not that the principle or method is reasonably reliable.

(e) *Other reliability factors.* In determining the reliability of a principle or method, the court shall consider all relevant additional factors, which may include:

(1) the extent to which the principle or method has been tested;

(2) the adequacy of research methods employed in testing the principle or method;

(3) the extent to which the principle or method has been published and subjected to peer review;

(4) the rate of error in the application of the principle or method;

(5) the experience of the witness in the application of the principle or method;

(6) the extent to which the principle or method has gained acceptance within the relevant scientific, technical, or specialized community; and

(7) the extent to which the witness's specialized field of knowledge has gained acceptance within the general scientific, technical, or specialized community.

FEDERAL RULES OF EVIDENCE, RULE 702. TESTIMONY BY EXPERTS.

If scientific, technical, or other specialized knowledge will assist the trier of fact to understand the evidence or to determine a fact in issue, a witness qualified as an expert by knowledge, skill, experience, training, or education may testify thereto in the form of an opinion or otherwise, if (1) the testimony is based upon sufficient facts or data, (2) the testimony is the product of reliable principles and methods, and (3) the witness has applied the principles and methods reliably to the facts of the case.

EVIDENCE GRADING GRID

Exam No. _____

Total Raw Score: _____

QUESTION ONE:

◊ There are issues as to the capacity of both drivers involved.
  ◊ Dennis suffered a head injury at the time of the accident.
  ◊ Frances now suffers from amnesia.

◊ There are issues as to the capacity of both children on the bus.

◊ Blake was crying and may therefore have been too emotional to form an accurate impression of the scene.
◊ Blake's statements to Officer Addison might qualify as an excited utterance or a present sense impression.
◊ Caroline wore thick glasses, which were shattered in the collision. She may therefore have been unable to form an accurate impression of the scene, insofar as her testimony rests on her ability to observe.
  ◊ Caroline's statements to Officer Addison might qualify as an excited utterance or a present sense impression.
  ◊ She is somewhat less likely to qualify for excited utterance than Blake is, because she did not appear to be shaken.
◊ Because both children were six years old at the time of the accident, there may be issues as to whether they should be deemed competent as witnesses.
  ◊ The modern trend is to allow this testimony and to let the jury determine the weight to be afforded to it.
  ◊ When an excited utterance is involved, the event is deemed to speak through the witness, so as to increase the reliability of the statement. For these reasons, as well, child witnesses are likely to be accepted.
◊ It is unclear whether Dennis was acting as an agent for Fred's at the time of the collision.
  ◊ Dennis had signs for Fred's on his car.
  ◊ In addition, there were hot pizzas in his car.
  ◊ Finally, he was hurrying as if trying to deliver the pizzas on time.
◊ Dennis, in speaking with Officer Addison, may have made statements against his pecuniary, civil, and possibly penal interest.
  ◊ Some portions of his statement, however, tend to inculpate Elaine rather than Dennis and therefore should be segmented out for purposes of this hearsay exception.

◊ Dennis's statements may be considered a vicarious admission of Fred's, if he was acting within the scope of his agency for Fred's when the statements were made.

◊ If so, his statements would fall within a hearsay exemption.

◊ Dennis's statements to Officer Addison may qualify as a dying declaration, which is an exception to the hearsay rule that requires unavailability on the part of the declarant.

◊ Because Dennis is in Tibet and likely beyond the reach of civil process, most courts will find him to be unavailable.

◊ It is sometimes necessary, however, that counsel demonstrate that it tried everything within reason to secure the attendance of the witness.

◊ Officer Addison's report is likely to generate its own hearsay issues.

◊ It is probable, however, that his report would qualify as an official record, so as to fall within an exception to the hearsay rule.

◊ To the extent that Officer Addison reports the statements of Blake, Caroline, and Dennis, her report may implicate double hearsay issues.

◊ To get around such issues, it is necessary to find a hearsay exception for each layer of hearsay—the Officer's report and the statement of another person that is being reported.

◊ Caroline has made a statement regarding Frances's habit or routine, insofar as her driving is concerned.

◊ Alternatively, this may also be seen as a statement of Frances's character.

◊ Normally, these statements will not be permitted in civil actions such as this one, so as to show action in conformity with this character.

◊ Blake has made a statement regarding Frances's habit or routine, insofar as her driving is concerned.

◊ Alternatively, this may also be seen as a statement of Frances's character.

◊ Normally, these statements will not be permitted in civil actions such as this one, so as to show action in conformity with this character.

◊ To introduce the pizza study, Frances's family will probably try to qualify the document as a learned treatise.
  ◊ This will be difficult, given the obvious bias involved in its creation by the Pepperoni Council.
  ◊ Alternatively, Frances's family might seek to bring this in as the report of an expert witness.
    ◊ If so, the standards of *Daubert* and *Frye* will come into play.

◊ Frances's earlier statement regarding the accident is likely to come in as a past recollection recorded.
  ◊ The problem with this approach is that it may have been created too long after the accident, rather than when the accident was fresh in her memory.
  ◊ In addition, it may be possible to argue that, because the recollection was recorded in anticipation of litigation, there is reason to question its reliability.
  ◊ Because of her amnesia, it is probably not possible to use this document to refresh her present recollection, so as to avoid the hearsay question altogether.

◊ George's statement during his deposition might be used as a prior inconsistent statement for purposes of impeachment.

◊ Dennis's prior character is likely to be relevant for purposes of showing his propensity to engage in bad conduct.
  ◊ Courts are, however, very reluctant to allow this evidence to be used this way in civil cases.
  ◊ If, however, it is possible to establish alternative grounds for the logical relevance of this information, other than propensity, it may be admissible.
  ◊ The following elements of Dennis's record may be considered:
    ◊ Because the store knew of Dennis's speeding tickets, these might be raised against the store if the store is accused of negligent hiring.

◊ Because the forgery is a crime of dishonesty, courts will tend to find it admissible.
  ◊ However, this conviction occurred when Dennis was a juvenile, and this factor militates against its admissibility.
  ◊ Because, however, Dennis is not the defendant in this action, it is possible that the juvenile conviction will be admissible.
  ◊ The theft conviction, which was dismissed on appeal after Dennis was sentenced to probation, will not be brought in if the dismissal is found to be on the grounds of innocence rather than mere procedural issues.

Raw Score:

Any Extra Issues Mentioned?

QUESTION TWO:

◊ During his opening statement, your opponent engaged in argumentative behavior by characterizing the plaintiff in a negative fashion.
  ◊ The response of the jury suggests that there was sufficient prejudice generated by this misconduct that perhaps a mistrial would be appropriate.
◊ During jury selection, some judges permit attorneys to ask questions of the jurors, while others require that questions be submitted through the judge.
  ◊ Attorneys generally may exercise a limited number of peremptory challenges without citing a reason for doing so.
    ◊ The only limitation on this practice is that the peremptory challenges may not be exercised for reasons due to discrimination based upon race or other protected classifications.
  ◊ In this case, the attorney might, for example, have chosen to use peremptory challenges to excuse some of the schoolteachers, even if grounds for challenge for cause were not demonstrated.

◊ In addition, attorneys typically may exercise an unlimited number of challenges for cause.
  ◊ Bias—such as the bias that a schoolteacher might have in favor of other schoolteachers—is a classic ground for the exercise of a challenge for cause.
  ◊ Judges are often hesitant, however, to excuse jurors, and might try to rehabilitate the juror by getting her to state that she can, despite the apparent bias, nevertheless consider the matter neutrally.

◊ In addition, because the jury consisted entirely of schoolteachers, a demographic that probably does not correspond with the pool from which the jury was drawn, it is appropriate to consider a challenge to the array, the process by which the jury pool was selected.

◊ A number of errors were made during the direct examination of Mr. Chips.
  ◊ By getting his client to speak about his teaching awards, his church involvement, and his work with the Humane Society, the attorney engaged in impermissible bolstering.
    ◊ Introducing the defendant is allowed up to a point, but this line of questioning almost certainly crossed that line.
  ◊ In addition, in asking the defendant to "tell the jury about [his] marvelous teaching awards" and so forth, the attorney engaged in improper leading of his own witness on direct.
    ◊ Limited exceptions are available for introductory matters (to save time) and for hostile witnesses. Only the first consideration may come into play here.
    ◊ Although this is not a traditional leading question in the sense of calling for a "yes" or "no" answer, it is nonetheless leading because it suggests the answer by the way in which the question is phrased.
  ◊ In addition, in asking the single, open-ended question, "What's this case about?" the attorney improperly calls for a narrative response.

◊ Much of the material given in response to this question is logically irrelevant and a waste of court time, two problems that the rule against narrative questions is meant to avoid.

◊ In addition, the question improperly calls for legal speculation on the part of the witness.

◊ Because Mr. Chips cannot remember Ms. Davis, his testimony regarding his habit or routine in teaching handwriting is appropriate and permissible to establish his conduct in conformity therewith, when he taught Ms. Davis.

◊ The behavior of the judge, throughout, suggests severe partiality in a way that may have seriously interfered with the conduct of the trial.

◊ The conduct is sufficiently egregious that this matter is likely to be preserved for appeal even if counsel chose, as a strategic matter, not to object at trial for fear of angering the judge.

◊ Evidentiary issues are also raised by your cross-examination of Mr. Chips.

◊ In seeking to confront Mr. Chips with his deposition statement, you were seeking to impeach him with a prior inconsistent statement

◊ Assuming that you laid the proper foundation (giving him a chance to respond) and got him to authenticate the document, this is entirely proper.

◊ Whether the previous testimony was inconsistent with what is now being said in court is judged by a functional test, rather than by a literal test.

◊ The judge's having sustained a non-existent objection that you were badgering the witness was thus improper, because you were doing no such thing.

◊ In addition, having the judge make an objection on behalf of a party goes against the usual adversary process that is followed in American jury trials.

◊ Once you were denied the opportunity to introduce the deposition testimony, you attempted to make an offer of proof.
  ◊ The judge refused to hear the offer of proof, which is improper.
  ◊ To preserve the matter for appeal, the attorney should have the court reporter note, in the record, where the offer of proof was attempted.

◊ Whether the testimony of the handwriting expert should be admitted is to be determined according to the *Frye* or *Daubert* standard, depending on which this jurisdiction follows.
  ◊ It is not necessary, to be admissible, that the expert testify on matters that are totally beyond the understanding of laypersons. Thus, having lay and expert testimony on the handwriting is not problematic.
  ◊ In modern evidence law, there is no prohibition against having an expert give his opinion as to the ultimate facts in a case. It is not, however, appropriate for the expert, as this one did, to instruct the jury on how it is to rule.

◊ The mother's opinion testimony is probably admissible as a lay opinion, insofar as it is helpful to the jury.
  ◊ That portion of the mother's opinion that speaks to the superior qualities of the brother, however, is logically irrelevant.
  ◊ In addition, Rule 403 might be brought in to keep out this evidence as highly prejudicial. (This is a mother testifying against her own daughter, after all.)

◊ During closing argument, your opponent improperly argued facts that are not in evidence.
  ◊ Although it is generally poor form to object during another party's opening or, especially, closing, arguing outside the evidence is the one good reason for doing so.

◊ The jury engaged in misconduct by calling medical schools on its own.

◊ The jury might properly have asked the judge to call a witness for this purpose, had it known that it had the right to do so.

◊ The jury may not, however, seek outside information along these lines.

◊ The extent to which the jury's misconduct can be discoverable through having a juror testify depends on which of three rules the jurisdiction follows in considering the issue.

Raw Score:

Any Extra Issues Mentioned?

QUESTION THREE:

◊ The post-*Miranda* efforts to get Jerrie to talk must be considered in light of whether he was improperly pressured to do so.

  ◊ In addition, his post-*Miranda* silence is generally considered to be insolubly ambiguous.

    ◊ It cannot, for example, be used as a tacit admission of guilt, by showing that a reasonable cat (is there such a thing?) would have spoken out and asserted his innocence.

◊ The fact that Max is a private citizen rather than a police officer, however, may make the confession discoverable.

  ◊ One could argue that the catnip functioned as a drug, making it impossible for Jerrie to refuse to speak.

  ◊ In addition, one could argue that, given the significant size differential between the animals (even this big cat was smaller than a giant schnauzer), Jerrie was intimidated into speaking.

◊ Max's bias in being "on the take" for Milkbones will be considered highly relevant, however.

  ◊ In addition, if Max is in jail for a crime of dishonesty, this information may be brought in to impeach his character for truthfulness.

  ◊ Bias is a preferred means of character testimony. Thus, testimony regarding bias will not be barred by the collateral fact rule.

◊ The defense may also wish to implicate Teazer instead of Jerrie.
  ◊ To do this, the defense might wish to show that the way in which the crime was committed more closely fits the modus operandus of Teazer rather than Jerrie.
  ◊ Some courts will require that, to exculpate Jerrie and inculpate Teazer, the evidence be corroborated to prevent collusion by Jerrie's friends.

◊ The trial exhibit comparing the jumping abilities of Jerrie and Teazer is demonstrative evidence, rather than real evidence in this case.
  ◊ To be admissible, demonstrative evidence must be shown to bear a substantial similarity to the physical evidence that it is meant to represent.
  ◊ The fact that the demonstrative evidence is not to scale normally will not keep it from being admitted.
    ◊ Normally, demonstrative evidence is more easily admitted if it is not drawn to scale because a less elaborate foundation is required.
    ◊ In this case, however, the opponent of the evidence might argue that it is misleading because it is not drawn to scale.
  ◊ Demonstrative evidence is sometimes admitted into evidence for purposes of making the record clear, but is not sent into the jury room during deliberations.

◊ The defense attorney would like the court to take judicial notice of the fact that Jerrie cannot jump as high as the kitchen counter.
  ◊ As a preliminary matter, taking judicial notice of this fact takes the fact away from the jury, which is the normal fact-finder, and establishes it conclusively. Given the centrality of this fact—if it is true, then Jerrie cannot be guilty—a court is unlikely to take judicial notice of this information because that would dispose of the case.
  ◊ In addition, whether a fact is ripe for judicial notice depends on whether it is a matter of common knowledge, a matter of verifiable certainty, or just a highly probable fact.

◊ Especially because Jerrie could feign a poorer leaping ability than he has, this matter is likely not to satisfy even the most liberal of these tests.

◊ The tuna can is physical evidence that is historically connected to this case. Its logical relevance depends on its being *the* tuna can that was stolen from the kitchen counter, so authentication issues are very important here.

  ◊ There are significant breaks here in the chain of custody. Although not all jurisdictions will require that every link in the chain be established, here the conduct of the sheepdogs makes it seem probable that the evidence was tampered with, such that a looser chain of custody should not be permitted.

   ◊ Here, the chain of custody is particularly important because the evidence that is of central importance—the pawprints—is very fragile.

  ◊ In addition, this can is not readily identifiable—there are many such cans of organic albacore tuna in the world—although it might have been readily identifiable if a police officer at the scene of the crime had scratched his initials into it.

◊ The surveillance photo is real evidence in this case, as well.

  ◊ Because the photo is blurred, image enhancement or restoration may be appropriate, especially so long as the process merely removes "static" from the picture, rather than adding to the image.

  ◊ Because the cat's owner will not cooperate with the prosecution, it may be possible to hold her in contempt until she expresses willingness to identify the cat in question.

  ◊ Because an unskilled layperson cannot identify the cat in the photo, so as to authenticate it for purposes of admissibility, whether the photo is allowed will depend on the theory of admissibility that the court uses for surveillance photos.

◊ Some courts treat these automated "regiscope" photos just like regular photographs, requiring a fairly minimal foundation.

◊ Others require significant testimony regarding the machine, the way in which it was operated, and perhaps even the chain of custody for the film.

◊ To the extent that the surveillance photo is treated as a normal photograph, there are two major ways that the photo may be treated.

◊ Under the silent witness theory, the picture speaks for itself, such that the jury would be allowed to see, on its own, the flash of blue and to deduce, from other testimony regarding the habit of Teazer in wearing a blue collar, that Teazer was the real culprit.

◊ Under this theory, the photo is real evidence.

◊ Under the pictorial testimony theory, the picture is allowed only insofar as a witness has testified to everything that is depicted. Thus, unless a witness spoke about the blue flash and the blue collar, the jury would be expected not to discern this information for itself.

◊ Under this theory, the photo is demonstrative evidence.

◊ The best evidence rule may govern whether Max is permitted to testify as to his memory of Jerrie's confession.

◊ In this case, the written document has disappeared, and it is unclear who is to blame.

◊ Parties are not permitted to profit by destroying documents so as to prevent the best evidence from being introduced.

◊ There is no second-best evidence rule. Thus, if the document is unavailable through no fault that can be attributed to the prosecutor, then bringing in Max's testimony is fine.

◊ Max's memory is poor, and he can be impeached on this fact.

◊ Although the defense attorney may wish to challenge Max's fundamental competency to testify, the modern trend is to allow witnesses to testify, and merely to have this information elicited on cross-examination.

◊ Even if Max's testimony is logically relevant, it may be excluded as legally irrelevant under Rule 403 if its probative value is substantially outweighed by the danger of unfair prejudice.
  ◊ Here, Max's persuasive mien is unlikely to keep him from testifying. Instead, jurors are normally expected to assess the credibility of each witness.

Raw Score:

Any Extra Issues Mentioned?

QUESTION FOUR:

◊ Material Differences between Rules
  ◊ URE 104 and FRE 104
  ◊ URE 702 and FRE 702

◊ Practical Effect of Each Difference
  ◊ URE 104 and FRE 104
  ◊ URE 702 and FRE 702

◊ Opinion as to Which Is Better
  ◊ URE 104 and FRE 104
  ◊ URE 702 and FRE 702

Raw Score:

Any Extra Issues Mentioned?

Sample Memorandum

MEMORANDUM

TO: Litigation File
FROM: Associate
DATE: July 17, 2___
RE: Georgia Law Regarding Conspiracy to Breach a Contract

QUESTION PRESENTED

Does Georgia law recognize a cause of action for conspiracy to breach a contract? If so, what are the applicable standing requirements?

SHORT ANSWER

Georgia law recognizes a cause of action for conspiracy to breach a contract. This tort is similar, in application, to the cause of action for tortious inference with business relations. Although no Georgia case has addressed the standing requirements for conspiracy to breach a contract, cases decided under the laws of other jurisdictions have indicated that only those persons or entities with a contractual interest in the contract that allegedly was breached have standing to sue on this basis.

DISCUSSION AND CITATION OF AUTHORITY

I. THE CAUSE OF ACTION

Under Georgia law, a cause of action exists for conspiracy to breach a contract. *See, e.g., Gaines v. Crompton & Knowles Corp.*, 190 Ga. App. 863, 380 S.E.2d 498 (1989). *See also Baker v. American Oil Co.*, 90 Ga. App. 662, 83 S.E.2d 826 (1954). The *Gaines* court, in justifying the existence of such a cause of action, cited the case of *Luke v. DuPree*, 158 Ga. 590, 124 S.E.13 (1924). The *Luke* court had held, in the context of a real estate sales transaction, that:

> The breach of a contract is unlawful. It is unlawful for others, without lawful excuse, to induce the maker of a contract to break it, or to aid him in its breach; and for the maker and others to combine to break it is a conspiracy, which entitles the other party to the contract to his action against the conspirators for any damage which he may sustain.

Id. at 596, 124 S.E. at 19. The *Luke* court noted that the plaintiffs had not contended that the *conspiracy* of the defendants to break the contracts involved furnishes a cause of action; but that they had contended that the *breaches* of these contracts were unlawful, and that, when the defendants conspired to commit these breaches and the contracts were broken in pursuance of such conspiracy, a cause of action accrued to them. *Id.* at 598, 124 S.E. at 21 (emphasis added).

A. *The Basis of Liability*

The center of liability under this tort is the underlying breach of contract, not the conspiracy to do the same.

> The averment of a conspiracy in the declaration does not ordinarily change the nature of the action nor add to its legal force or effect. The gist of the action is not the conspiracy alleged, but the tort committed against the plaintiff and the damage thereby done wrongfully. Therefore, where there has

been no breach of contract, no cause of action can exist for conspiracy to breach the contract.

Wells v. L.W.A., Inc., 221 Ga. App. 116, 117, 470 S.E.2d 510, 512 (1996). Where damage results from an act which, if done by one alone, would not afford a ground of action, the same act would not be rendered actionable if it were done by several in pursuance of a conspiracy. *Kem Manufacturing Corp. v. Sant,* 182 Ga. App. 135, 143, 355 S.E.2d 437, 445 (1987) (affirming the lower court's granting of summary judgment to the plaintiff on the defendant's counterclaim for civil conspiracy to destroy defendant's business). Thus, a conspiracy to effect what one has a legal right to accomplish is not actionable. *Id. See also U.S. Anchor Manufacturing, Inc. v. Rule Industries, Inc.,* 264 Ga. 295, 297, 443 S.E.2d 833, 835 (1994).

B.   *Formal Defects in the Underlying Contract*

The case of *Studdard v. Evans,* 108 Ga. App. 819, 135 S.E.2d 60 (1964), clarified somewhat the relationship between the enforceability of a contract and the existence of a cause of action for procuring its breach.

While liability for procuring the breach of a contract or interfering with the performance of a contract is based upon property rights in the contract, . . . the existence of a valid contract is necessary to create liability. . . . However, formal defects affecting the enforceability of the contract between the parties, or the fact that employment is at the will of the employer, do not give immunity to a third person who without justification interferes with the relation between the parties to the contract.

108 Ga. App. 819, 822-823, 135 S.E.2d 60, 63-64 (1964) (internal citations omitted). Along these same lines, in the case of *Skyway Cycle Sales, Inc. v. Gordon,* 148 Ga. App. 150, 251 S.E.2d 118 (1978), the court of appeals found a cause of action for the conspiracy to breach an oral contract. No cause of action, however, exists for conspiracy to breach an illegal contract. *Mathews v. Greiner,* 130 Ga. App. 817, 818, 204 S.E.2d 749, 751 (1974).

C. **The Relationship Between Conspiracy to Breach a Contract and Tortious Interference with Business Relations**

Later cases have clarified the relationship between conspiracy to breach a contract and tortious interference with business relations. In *Original Appalachian Artworks, Inc. v. Schlaifer Nance & Co.*, 679 F. Supp. 1564 (N.D. Ga. 1987), the district court considered the relationship between these two tort claims. The court held that:

> While Georgia courts have recognized that a conspiracy to breach a contract is actionable, the courts have tacitly acknowledged that such an action in conspiracy is essentially the same as an action for tortious interference with business relations. In *Georgia Power Co. v. Busbin,* . . . the court approved a jury instruction delivered by a trial court regarding the appropriateness of a conspiracy action against the defendant. In finding no error in the charge, the court cited with approval *Luke v. Dupree,* . . . which is commonly recognized as the leading Georgia case on tortious interference with business relations.

Id. at 1573 (internal citations omitted). Similarly, in the case of *Rome Industries, Inc. v. Jonsson*, 202 Ga. App. 682, 683, 415 S.E.2d 651, 652 (1992), the court held that "the conspiracy count set forth in the tortious interference count [was] merely a restatement of the claim set forth in the tortious interference count." Having granted summary judgment on the latter claim, the court granted summary judgment on the former claim, as well. *Id.* at 684, 415 S.E.2d at 653.

II. EVIDENCE

Several Georgia courts, applying the law set forth above, have considered whether the evidence presented to each supported a cause of action for conspiracy to breach a contract.

A. *Insufficient Evidence*

1. *Green v. Sams*

In the case of *Green v. Sams*, 209 Ga. App. 491, 433 S.E.2d 678 (1993), a landowner sued the prospective purchaser of his land, as well as the lending institution and its officer, alleging that the three had participated in a conspiracy to breach the land sale contract. The bank officer, who had supervisory authority over the Athens, Georgia branch of Citizens and Southern Bank, lived directly across the street from the two lots the prospective purchaser had planned to use to build an access road to a new subdivision he was planning to build. The officer wrote to the landowner and communicated not only his objection to this proposed use of the two lots, but also his opinion that a restrictive covenant would prevent the building of the road. *Id.* at 491, 433 S.E.2d at 479.

The prospective purchaser had contacted the Athens branch of C&S Bank to obtain a loan for the closing, and had received a verbal commitment for the loan. Before this loan was confirmed in writing, the officer told the loan officer handling the transaction that his objections needed to be communicated to the parties before the closing proceeded. The officer also threatened legal action in his individual capacity. The day of the closing, the bank withdrew its verbal commitment to fund the loan. The title insurance company also withdrew its authorization to issue a policy without exception as to access. *Id.* at 494, 433 S.E.2d at 681.

After the parties had met and extended the closing date by agreement, the prospective purchaser's attorney informed the landowner that his client would not close on the property because of title problems that had rendered the title unmarketable. These title objections were, specifically, the threat of litigation and the previously discussed potential access problems due to the restrictive covenant. *Id.* at 495, 433 S.E.2d at 681.

The court found no basis to conclude that any conspiracy existed to interfere with and breach the contract. *Id.* at 498, 433 S.E.2d at 684. Specifically, the court found no *direct* evidence of a conspiracy. *Id.* Rather, the court noted, the plaintiff had relied on circumstances, claiming that the bank officer used his position and influence to cause the bank to withdraw its verbal loan commitment. *Id.* In addition, the plaintiff had alleged, the prospective purchaser cooperated by refusing to close because he feared the bank and its officer would retaliate against him by withdrawing further credit. *Id.* In considering these allegations, the court held that, even assuming that evidence existed that the bank officer used his position and influence to cause the bank to withdraw its verbal loan commitment, the evidence shows the sale failed to close because of access problems and the threat of litigation resulting in withdrawal of title insurance and failure of marketable title. *Id.* The evidence showed that the failure of closing was not due to the withdrawal of the loan commitment, which, in any event, had been made subject to the securing of title insurance. *Id.* In addition, the court noted, the officer was legally entitled to voice his private objections to the development, and to threaten suit in his individual capacity. *Id.* The court found that there was nothing wrongful in the officer's disclosure of this information to the bank and the closing parties. *Id.* The court found no evidence that the prospective purchaser colluded with or succumbed to pressure from the bank or from its officer in refusing to close the sale. *Id.*

In reversing the lower court's denial of summary judgment to the defendants, the court held as follows:

The gravamen of any civil conspiracy claim is not that the defendants acted in concert to damage the plaintiff, but that such action was tortious conduct which proximately caused injury to the plaintiff. Here, the actions taken by the defendants were either legal, or not the proximate cause of the damage alleged by the plaintiff. The circumstantial evidence pointed to by [the plaintiff] from which he claims a conspiracy may be inferred is purely speculative. An inference cannot be based upon evidence which is too uncertain or speculative or which raises merely a conjecture or possibility.

Id. at 498, 433 S.E.2d at 684 (citations omitted).

2. *Walton v. Avant Development Corp.*

In the case of *Walton v. Avant Development Corp.*, 1983 WL 516 (M.D. Ga. 1983),[1] the court considered the defendant's motion for summary judgment on the issue of conspiracy to breach a contract. In that case, the court further explored the issue of how to establish the existence of a conspiracy. The issue arose in the context of an employment dispute involving a television station. After the station was sold, the new management became increasingly dissatisfied with the general manager, who had been an employee of the station for twenty years. The evidence showed that, in the opinion of the new management, the general manager was abnormally slow in filing reports, resistant to their direction of the station, and very slow in accomplishing the tasks assigned to him. After approximately eighteen months, the general manager resigned, having been given the option to do so to avoid termination. He was replaced by a much younger man from a station in Indiana. *Id.* at *1.

Initially, the plaintiff had alleged that the sole stockholder of the corporation owning the station, the director of operations, and the man who replaced him had conspired to terminate him. However, by the time the defendants had moved for summary judgment, the plaintiff had narrowed his claims to include only the man who replaced him. *Id.* at *4.

---

[1] This unreported case is included for illustrative purposes, despite its limited precedential value.

In finding that the evidence presented was insufficient to establish conspiracy, the court held that "[t]he law is well settled that because a corporation can only act through its agents, acts of agents are considered to be acts of a single business entity, and therefore do not constitute a conspiracy." *Id.* The court further held, "[I]t takes at least two persons to conspire." *Id.* In other words, the corporation and one of its employees could not conspire, together, to effectuate some wrong. The court rejected as untenable the plaintiff's argument that the plaintiff's replacement had no employment contract and therefore would not be considered an agent or employee of the corporation. *Id.* The court noted, in dismissing this argument, that this individual was not only named in the lawsuit as an employee of the corporation, but also admitted this association in his deposition. *Id.*

3. *Carusos v. Briarcliff*

Similarly, in the case of *Carusos v. Briarcliff, Inc.*, 76 Ga. App. 346, 45 S.E.2d 802 (1947), the court found insufficient evidence of a conspiracy to breach a contract. That case revolved around a contract involving a shopping center called Briarcliff Plaza. The plaintiffs had leased a space for fifteen years and had established a lucrative dry cleaning business. One portion of the lease contract provided that no other dry cleaner would be allowed to lease space in the center. After fifteen years, the shopping center was sold to a newly formed corporation, which entered into a lease agreement with a second dry cleaner. As a result of this direct competition, the plaintiffs suffered a significant loss of profits. *Id.*

The petition alleged that, approximately two months after the corporation contracted with the second dry cleaner, a new corporation was formed. The deed to the shopping center was conveyed to the new corporation. The plaintiff alleged that the old and new corporations had conspired in breaching the plaintiff's lease contract. The lower court had granted the general demurrer of the new corporation, and the plaintiff appealed. *Id.* at 348, 45 S.E.2d at 804.

The court of appeals noted, in affirming the lower court decision, that the corporation in question had not been chartered until almost two months after the plaintiff's cause of action had accrued. *Id.* at 350, 45 S.E.2d at 806. In addition, the court noted, "[t]he petition did not allege that [the new corporation] . . . had any connection with the making of the alleged contract or induced [the other corporate defendant] to break the contract." *Id.* at 350, 45 S.E.2d at 806. The court therefore held that the plaintiffs' claim for conspiracy to breach their lease contract was insufficient. *Id.* at 350-351, 45 S.E.2d at 806.

B. *Sufficient Evidence*

1. *Nottingham v. Wrigley*

In the case of *Nottingham v. Wrigley*, 221 Ga. 386, 144 S.E.2d 749 (1965), the Georgia Supreme Court addressed a claim for conspiracy to breach a contract arising in the context of a closely held family corporation. After the plaintiff had worked for the corporation for approximately three months and had made a number of loans to the corporation, he was dismissed by action of the three defendants, directors of the corporation, at a directors' meeting. The plaintiff alleged that the three directors had conspired maliciously to procure a breach of the plaintiff's employment contract. *Id.* at 387, 144 S.E.2d at 750.

The evidence was sharply contested, with the defendants maintaining that the plaintiff's dismissal was occasioned by his own mismanagement of the corporation. In addition, the defendants claimed that certain shifting of corporate assets that occurred after his dismissal was done, not to prevent him from recovering the money he had loaned the corporation, as the plaintiff had alleged, but rather to repay loans and keep the business operational. After a jury found against two of the defendants,[2] the court of appeals reversed in part. *Id.* at 386-387, 144 S.E.2d at 750-751.

In reversing the court of appeals, the Georgia Supreme Court held that:

> The law recognizes the intrinsic difficulty in proving a conspiracy. The conspiracy may sometimes be inferred from the nature of the acts done, the relation of the parties, the interests of the alleged conspirators, and other circumstances. To show conspiracy, it is not necessary to prove an express compact or agreement of the parties thereto. The essential element of the charge is the common design; but it need not appear that the parties met together either formally or informally, or entered into any explicit or formal agreement; nor is it essential that it should appear that either by words or by writings they formulated their unlawful objects. It is sufficient that two or more persons in any manner either positively or tacitly come to a mutual understanding that they will accomplish the unlawful design. Also, where transactions between relatives are under review, slight circumstances are often sufficient to induce belief on the part of the jury that there was fraud or collusion for a conspiracy . . . .

Id. at 388, 144 S.E.2d at 751 (citations omitted). Applying this law to the case at bar, the court found evidence sufficient to send the question of conspiracy to breach a contract to the jury, and reversed the court of appeals's decision to the contrary. *Id.* at 389, 144 S.E.2d at 751-752.

The court held, in reversing the lower court decision, that: "[a]t the outset, it is significant that the business here was a closely held family corporation." *Id.* at 389, 144 S.E.2d at 752. In addition, the court found evidence that the plaintiff had a definite contract of employment with the corporation.

---

[2] The lower court directed a verdict in favor of the third defendant. This portion of the decision was left undisturbed on appeal.

Id. To controvert the defendants' assertions to the contrary regarding this issue, the court found that the defendants' own testimony showed that the plaintiff was continually present at the place of business and performed executive duties on its behalf until he was discharged. *Id.* Furthermore, the court noted, it was the manner of his performance of these very duties that the directors had recited as the reason for his discharge. *Id.*

In addition, although the defendants claimed the plaintiff was dismissed due to mismanagement, the testimony showed that the company's business during the plaintiff's tenure was "much better than ever" and declined after he was dismissed. *Id.* at 389, 144 S.E.2d at 752. Furthermore, the court found no indication whatsoever that the defendants had complained of any mismanagement by the plaintiff prior to the directors' meeting at which he was discharged. *Id.* at 390, 144 S.E.2d at 752.

In addition, the court found, "there was no discussion whatever at the [directors'] meeting." *Id.* at 390, 144 S.E.2d at 752. The evidence showed that Mr. Wrigley, one of the defendants, had simply announced that he was going to dismiss the plaintiff "on account of his mismanagement." *Id.* Another defendant testified, "If Wrigley said it was time to get rid of the man, I thought it was, too." *Id.*

The court also was persuaded by evidence confirming the plaintiff's allegations of shifting of the corporation's assets after the plaintiff's discharge. *Id.* at 390, 144 S.E.2d at 752. One of the defendants, a Mr. Cox, even admitted to having a part in the corporation's attempt to conceal its money from the plaintiff. *Id.* at 390, 144 S.E.2d at 753. In addition, the evidence showed that, shortly after the plaintiff's discharge, Mr. Wrigley opened additional corporate bank accounts, some of which were in other cities. *Id.* The court found that Mr. Cox's admitted involvement in the shifting of corporate assets, which prevented the plaintiff from recouping the loss he had sustained due to the defendants' breach of his contract, was a telling circumstance inferring that Mr. Cox had acted in connection with Mr. Wrigley to maliciously injure the plaintiff. *Id.* at 391, 144 S.E.2d at 753.

Finally, the court noted the testimony of Mr. Cox, after seeing and hearing Mr. Wrigley testify as to these various transactions, that he "knew about every one of them." *Id.* Weighing all of this evidence, the court held that the lower court had properly sent to the jury the issue of conspiracy to breach a contract. *Id.*

2. *Sheppard v. Post*

Similarly, in the case of *Sheppard v. Post*, 142 Ga. App. 646, 236 S.E.2d 680 (1977), the court of appeals held that sufficient evidence of conspiracy to breach a contract existed to withstand the defendants' motion to dismiss. In that case, the plaintiff alleged that three individuals, Ms. Post, Mr. Wilson, and Ms. Bernal, acting in conspiracy, had maliciously induced North Fulton Realty Company to breach a contract it had with Mr. Sheppard and Ms. Post. North Fulton Realty Company had entered into a fifteen-year contract with Mr. Sheppard and Ms. Post whereby the two of them were to be co-managers of a Dekalb County office of the realty company. *Id.* at 646-647, 236 S.E.2d at 680-681.

The month after this agreement was signed, Sheppard and Post entered into a partnership agreement with Ms. Bernal to help finance the new business. Approximately eighteen months later, Mr. Sheppard gave notice of termination of the partnership. He alleged, at that time, that prior acts of Ms. Bernal, Ms. Post, and a Mr. Wilson, the owner of North Fulton Realty Company, had induced the realty company to put Ms. Post in sole control of the Dekalb branch in breach of the contractual provision that stated that the two were to be co-managers. *Id.* at 646-647, 236 S.E.2d at 680-681.

The court of appeals held, in reversing the lower court's granting of Defendant Post's motion to dismiss, that "Post presented no evidence conclusively establishing that North

Fulton did not breach the contract it had with appellant and herself." *Id.* at 648, 236 S.E.2d at 682. In addition, the court held, "Post did not conclusively negate that she and the other appellees had maliciously and successfully conspired to cause a breach." *Id.* at 649, 236 S.E.2d at 683. The court took note of the evidence showing that (1) Ms. Post and Mr. Sheppard disagreed about the branch management, (2) branch files were locked away from Mr. Sheppard's access, (3) the mailbox lock was changed so that Mr. Sheppard's key would no longer fit, (4) Sheppard's papers were taken from his desk, (5) Ms. Post had meetings alone with Ms. Bernal and Mr. Wilson, and (6) Ms. Post eventually acquired complete control of the branch. *Id.* The court further held, in reaching its decision, that "the matter of conspiracy has long been recognized to be solely a question for the jury." *Id.*

III. Standing

No Georgia case has addressed the standing requirements for a cause of action for conspiracy to breach a contract. However, several cases from around the country may prove instructive. In the case of *Welch v. Metro-Goldwyn-Mayer Film Co.,* 254 Cal. Rptr. 645 (Cal. Ct. App. 1989),[3] the court held that standing to bring suit under this cause of action is predicated upon the plaintiff's rights under whatever contract the plaintiff is alleging has been breached. In that case, MGM had argued that Raquel Welch lacked standing to sue for MGM's alleged conspiracy to breach its contract with her, because MGM technically had contracted with Ms. Welch's "loan-out" company, rather than with Ms. Welch as an individual. In rejecting this argument, the court held that "Welch signed the employment contract, and it detailed the mutual obligations which she and MGM owed to each other. We therefore conclude that a contractual relationship existed between MGM and Welch which gave Welch standing to sue to enforce her contractual rights." *Id.* at 654.

---

[3] California law limits the precedential value of this case.

Similarly, in the case of *Koehler v. Cummings*, 380 F. Supp. 1294, 1314 (M.D. Tenn. 1974), the court held that a corporation's principal shareholder and a creditor lacked standing to bring suit for conspiracy to breach a contract with the corporation, called S.O.S. The corporation was a plaintiff in the action, as well. The court held that the right to bring suit on this basis belonged solely to S.O.S. *Id.* The court held that, "[w]here the cause of action is being prosecuted on behalf of plaintiff S.O.S. as a legal entity, . . . the principal shareholder and creditor of S.O.S., does not have standing to bring suit as an individual or shareholder." *Id.*

The court further held that "a mere creditor" lacks standing to assert a claim for inducement to breach a contract. *Id. See also Luisoni v. Barth*, 137 N.Y.S.2d 169, 2 Misc.2d 315 (1954) (holding that a plaintiff may not maintain an action for illegal interference with a contract unless he can show that the contract gave him specific rights for a definite period of time). *But see: Cedar Point Apartments, Ltd. v. Cedar Point Investment Corp.*, 693 F.2d 748, 754 (8th Cir. 1982) (finding that a plaintiff to whom a partnership interest had been assigned had established proper standing to enforce the contractual rights of the partnership); *Canton Lumber Co. v. L. H. Burton Lumber Co., Inc.*, 121 A. 834, 837 (Md. 1923) (holding that a corporation which, absent others' tortious acts in preventing consummation of a certain contract, would have had a contractual interest in the transaction in question, could maintain an action for the tortious conduct depriving it of this interest).

Georgia law appears to be in accord with these out-of-state decisions, although no Georgia case exists that is precisely on point. O.C.G.A. § 51-1-11 (2002) provides that no privity is required to establish an action in tort. However, if the tort results from a violation of a duty, itself created by contract, the right of action is generally confined to the parties and privies of that contract, except in those cases in which the party would have the right of action for the injury, even independent of the contract. *Id. cited in: Shell v. Watts*, 125 Ga. App. 542, 188 S.E.2d 269 (1972); *University Apartments v. Uhler*, 84 Ga. App. 720, 67 S.E.2d 201 (1951).

In addition, in the similar context of an action for malicious procurement of breach of contract, the court of appeals has denied a right of action to a party it found to be a stranger to the contract. *Kenimer v. Ward Wight Realty Co.*, 109 Ga. App. 130, 135 S.E.2d 501 (1964). The court cited, in reaching its opinion, "the general and well established proposition that parties to a contract have a property right therein and the malicious interference in this right by third parties constitutes a tort." *Id.* at 134, 135 S.E.2d at 503. The court held that the plaintiff had failed to establish that the cancellation of the contract in question, which was done by mutual consent of the parties thereto, could have any effect whatsoever on the rights of the plaintiff. *Id.* at 134, 135 S.E.2d at 504. The court of appeals therefore affirmed the lower court's granting of summary judgment to the defendant. *Id.*

Sample Brief

IN THE STATE COURT OF FULTON COUNTY STATE OF GEORGIA

	*
Plaintiff	*
	Civil Action File No. 00VS004422H
	*
v.	*
	*
Defendant	*

PLAINTIFF'S SUPPLEMENTAL RESPONSE TO DEFENDANT'S MOTION TO DISMISS

Plaintiff hereby files her supplemental response in opposition to Defendant's Motion to Dismiss. Plaintiff previously addressed the impropriety of the Motion to Dismiss in her earlier-filed Motion for Entry of a Default Judgment, or, in the Alternative, Motion for Summary Judgment ("Motion for Entry of Default"). Plaintiff hereby submits additional and expanded grounds that mandate denial of Defendant's Motion to Dismiss. First, the Motion to Dismiss is moot, and thus should be denied, because Defendant failed to file an answer in this matter and is in default. Defendant failed to move this Court within the appropriate time to open the default, and neglected to pay Court costs. Second, the Motion to Dismiss, which was premised upon a misnomer argument, is moot because Defendant has already admitted *in judicio* that it is the proper party in this action. Third, even if the Motion to Dismiss is not deemed moot by this Court, it should be denied because Georgia statutory law plainly states that Defendant's grounds are not properly the subject of a motion to dismiss.

I.   FACTUAL BACKGROUND

This case stems from an incident that occurred on _____ when raw sewage backed up into the mobile home owned by Plaintiff, destroying both her home and much of her belongings. Complaint, ¶ 7. Her home is uninhabitable. Complaint, ¶ 8. Among other things, Defendant admits that it owned, operated and/or managed the mobile home park in which Plaintiff lived at the time of the incident described above. Complaint, ¶ 7.

Plaintiff filed this action against the Defendants on April 27, 2000. On May 22, 2000, service of process was effected on Defendant by serving its registered agent, Agent, as well as by filing with the Georgia Secretary of State on May 23, 2000. Along with the Complaint, Plaintiff served upon Defendant written discovery, including Requests for Admission (First Set) ("Requests for Admission"). A true and correct copy of the Requests for Admission is attached to Plaintiff's Motion for Entry of Default as Exhibit B.

Defendant should have filed its Answer by June 21, 2000. It failed to do so. Defendant failed to move this Court to open its default and neglected to pay its Court costs within fifteen days of that date, which would have been July 6, 2000. Finally, Defendant has failed to respond to the discovery served upon it, including the Requests for Admission. The responses would have been due on or before July 6, 2000.

The Requests for Admission cover every factual issue in this case, including those relating to jurisdiction, venue, proper naming of the Defendant, liability, causation, and entitlement to punitive damages. Requests for Admission, ¶¶ 1-12. Specifically, Defendant admits that it has been correctly named as Defendant in the present cause insofar as the legal designation of name is concerned. Requests For Admission, ¶ 1.

With respect to Defendant, the Complaint similarly sets forth detailed allegations pertaining to jurisdiction, venue, proper parties, liability, causation, entitlement to punitive damages and attorneys' fees, as well as an allegation relating to the minimum property loss suffered by Defendant. Complaint, ¶¶ 1, 3, 4-19, 29-39.

II. ARGUMENT AND CITATION OF AUTHORITY

A. *The Motion to Dismiss Is Moot, and Thus Should Be Denied, Because Defendant Failed to File an Answer in This Matter and Is in Default.*

Defendant's Motion to Dismiss is moot, and should therefore be denied. Defendant was automatically in default at the time the Motion to Dismiss was filed. Not only did Defendant fail to file a timely answer or even move the Court within fifteen days of the expiration of its time for answer, but Defendant also failed to pay Court costs. O.C.G.A. § 9-11-55(a) and (b); see also *Hazzard v. Phillips*, 249 Ga. 24, 287 S.E.2d 191 (1982) (full payment of costs within the fifteen-day grace period being a condition precedent to opening a default). Simply put, Defendant was in default *before* the Motion to Dismiss and *remains* in default to this day. The Motion to Dismiss is therefore moot.

The Motion to Dismiss, which was filed after the expiration of thirty days from the time of service of process, does not constitute an answer. Georgia law requires that each and every defendant file an answer within thirty days of service of a summons and complaint. O.C.G.A. § 9-11-12(a) ("A defendant shall serve his answer within 30 days after the service of the summons and complaint against him . . ."). Defendant failed to file an answer or response of any kind within thirty days of service. Thus, even if the Motion to Dismiss could somehow constitute an answer, which it does not in this case, it is untimely. See *Bosworth v. Cooney*, 156 Ga. App. 274, 277, 274 S.E.2d 604,

607 (1980) (in the unusual circumstance where a motion to dismiss could be considered an answer, the motion to dismiss "*must* be within the time for responding").

There is no "three day additional time rule" as Defendant has represented to the Court in pleadings filed today. O.C.G.A. § 9-11-6(e) ("Whenever a party has the right or is required to do some act or take some proceedings within a prescribed period after the service of a notice or other paper, *other than process,* upon him, and the notice or paper is served upon him by mail, three days shall be added to the prescribed period.") (emphasis added). Incredibly, in its Response Brief to the Motion for Entry of Default, filed today, Defendant omits the "other than process" language and contends that its Motion to Dismiss, which was filed thirty-two days after service of process, was a timely answer. This argument is disingenuous and should be rejected.

In very limited and unusual circumstances, Georgia courts may deem a *timely* motion to dismiss as sufficient to constitute an answer. See *Bosworth*, 156 Ga. App. at 278, 274 at 607; see also *Perrin v. Kilgore*, 158 Ga. App. 300, 279 S.E.2d 714 (1981) (plaintiff entitled to default judgment where no answer filed and defendant estopped from contesting merits of her case via her motion to dismiss). Those rare cases, however, involve a party that has filed a motion to dismiss on certain O.C.G.A. § 9-11-12(b)(6) grounds, and which set forth general and specific denials of the allegations contained within the complaint. None of those circumstances is present here. Defendant's Motion to Dismiss was filed *after* the expiration of the time for responding and thus cannot be considered a response as contemplated by the Georgia law. Furthermore, the Motion to Dismiss is premised upon misnomer grounds, not the appropriate 12(b)(6) grounds. Finally, the Motion to Dismiss does not contain specific denials of any of the allegations in the Complaint, and thus those allegations are admitted. Simply put, the Motion to Dismiss does not and cannot constitute an answer in this case.

B. *The Motion to Dismiss, Which Is Premised Upon a Misnomer Argument, Is Moot Because Defendant Has Already Admitted in Judicio That It Is the Proper Party in This Action and That Venue Is Proper.*

The Motion to Dismiss is premised on the ground that Defendant was misnamed in the Complaint. Defendant, however, has admitted that it owned, operated and/or managed the mobile home park in which Plaintiff lived at the time of the incident described above. Complaint, ¶ 1; Request for Admission, ¶ 1. Further, Defendant has admitted that venue is proper. Complaint, ¶ 1; see O.C.G.A. § 9-11-15(a) ("... If the case is still in default after the expiration of the period of 15 days, the plaintiff at any time thereafter shall be entitled to verdict and judgment by default, ... as if every item and paragraph of the complaint or other original pleading were supported by proper evidence . . . ."); see also *Shankweiler v. McCall Procter/Densham, Ltd.*, 183 Ga. App. 257, 358 S.E.2d 657 (1987) (a failure to respond to requests for admission means that those matters stand conclusively admitted). The Motion to Dismiss is therefore moot and should be denied.

C. *The Motion to Dismiss Should Be Denied Because It Does Not Present Proper Grounds Under Georgia Law for Dismissal.*

Defendant contends that it was wrongly named or mis-named in the lawsuit because it is not the owner of the mobile home park where Plaintiff lived at the time of the incident, but rather Agent, individually, is the owner. Assuming, arguendo, that this is a valid contention, which Plaintiff denies because Defendant has admitted *in judicio* that it is a proper party, this contention is not a proper ground for a motion to dismiss. O.C.G.A. § 9-11-21 ("Misjoinder of parties is not grounds for dismissal of an action"). Instead, the party bringing the action should amend his or her pleadings, or seek leave of court, if necessary, to join a party. *See* O.C.G.A. § 9-11-21. Defendant, however, is a proper party to this case because it has specifically admitted that fact.

Plaintiff will be adding as an additional defendant Agent, individually.

III. CONCLUSION

There is no dispute that Defendant is in default and was in default at the time it filed a motion to dismiss. Moreover, Defendant has admitted facts that render its Motion to Dismiss moot. On those grounds alone, denial is mandated. Further, if this Court does consider the basis for the Motion to Dismiss, it should be denied because misnomer is not a proper ground for dismissal and should therefore be denied. Plaintiff respectfully requests that Defendant's Motion to Dismiss be denied and that entry of a default judgment as to liability is made against Defendant.

Respectfully submitted, this ___ day of _____, 2_____.

_____

Georgia Bar No.

Attorney For Plaintiff

_____

_____

_____

CERTIFICATE OF SERVICE

This is to certify that I have this day served all parties in the foregoing matter with the foregoing Plaintiff's Supplemental Response to Defendant's Motion to Dismiss by depositing a copy of same in the United States mail, with adequate postage thereon, properly addressed as follows:

_____

_____

_____

_____

This _____ day of _____, 2___.

Decision Tree

The following is a visual study aid used by a trial lawyer in thinking about a case. In the case, one party contends that another party has defrauded him. The relevant state law provides a victim of pre-contract fraud two options for redress.

DECISION TREE:
FRAUD IN THE INDUCEMENT

Victim of pre-contract (K) fraud:

- Affirm the K, and sue for damages, but bound by terms of K, including waivers
  - If waiver by conduct or merger clause, then no grounds for suit
  - If no waiver, then proceed
- Disaffirm the K, rescind and tender benefits
  - Did victim tender benefits and rescind timely?
    - Yes, then possible to proceed
    - No, then expect challenges

Index

A

I

J

K

L

M

R

S

ALSO FROM **ALM PUBLISHING:**

Game, Set, Match: Winning the Negotiations Game
by Henry S. Kramer

The Essential Guide to the Best (and Worst) Legal Sites on the Web
by Robert J. Ambrogi, Esq.

Full Disclosure: The New Lawyer's Must-Read Career Guide
by Christen Civiletto Carey, Esq.

On Trial: Lessons from a Lifetime in the Courtroom
by Henry G. Miller, Esq.

Going Public in Good Times and Bad: A Legal and Business Guide
by Robert G. Heim

Inside/Outside: How Businesses Buy Legal Services
by Larry Smith

Arbitration: Essential Concepts
by Steven C. Bennett, Esq.

Courtroom Psychology and Trial Advocacy
by Richard C. Waites, J.D., Ph.D

Negotiating and Drafting Contract Boilerplate
by Tina L. Stark

Other publications available from AMERICAN LAWYER MEDIA:

LAW JOURNAL PRESS professional legal treatises—over 100 titles available

Legal newspapers and magazines—over 20 national and regional titles available, including:

The American Lawyer
The National Law Journal
New York Law Journal

Visit us at our websites:
www.lawcatalog.com
and
www.americanlawyermedia.com